BEST LITTLE STORIES
from
VIRGINIA

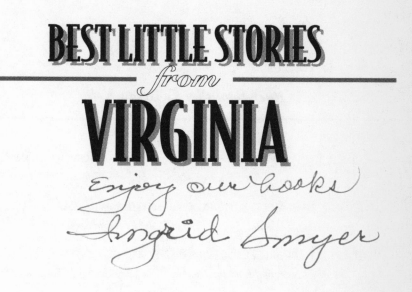

Enjoy our books

Ingrid Smyer

Other Books by C. Brian Kelly

BEST LITTLE STORIES FROM THE AMERICAN REVOLUTION
with "Select Founding Mothers" by Ingrid Smyer

BEST LITTLE STORIES FROM THE CIVIL WAR
with "Varina: Forgotten First Lady" by Ingrid Smyer

BEST LITTLE IRONIES, ODDITIES & MYSTERIES OF THE CIVIL WAR
with "Mary Todd Lincoln: Troubled First Lady" by Ingrid Smyer

BEST LITTLE STORIES FROM THE WHITE HOUSE
with "First Ladies in Review" by Ingrid Smyer

BEST LITTLE STORIES FROM THE WILD WEST
with "Fascinating Women of the West" by Ingrid Smyer

BEST LITTLE STORIES FROM WORLD WAR II

BEST LITTLE STORIES OF THE BLUE AND THE GRAY
with "Generals' Wives" by Ingrid Smyer

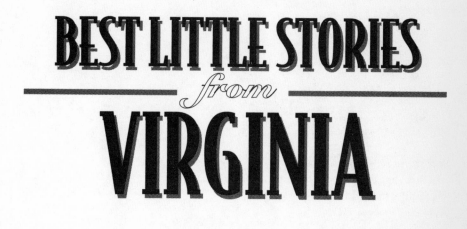

BEST LITTLE STORIES
from
VIRGINIA

C. Brian Kelly

with "The Women Who Counted" by Ingrid Smyer

CUMBERLAND HOUSE
NASHVILLE, TENNESSEE

BEST LITTLE STORIES FROM VIRGINIA
PUBLISHED BY CUMBERLAND HOUSE PUBLISHING, INC.
431 Harding Industrial Drive
Nashville, Tennessee 37211

Cover design by Gore Studio, Inc., Nashville, Tennessee

Library of Congress Cataloging-in-Publication Data

Kelly, C. Brian.
  Best little stories from Virginia / C. Brian Kelly ; with The women who counted by Ingrid Smyer.
       p.   cm.
  Includes bibliographical references (p.   ) and index.
  ISBN-13 978-1-58182-358-5 (pbk. : alk. paper)
  ISBN-10 1-58182-358-4 (pbk. : alk. paper)
  1. Virginia—History—Anecdotes. 2. Virginia—Biography—Anecdotes. I. Smyer-Kelly, Ingrid, 1927– Women who counted. II. Title.
F226.6.K45 2003
975.5—dc22

                                                                    2003018203

Printed in Canada

3 4 5 6 7 8 9 10—10 09 08 07

For Aven, Blake, and Mabry

Contents

Part 4: Twentieth Century

Part 5: Twenty-First Century

The Women Who Counted *367*

Introduction and Acknowledgments

Virginia, you say? Why write yet another history of Virginia, albeit an anecdotal one that attempts to tell the Commonwealth's four-hundred-year story in the form of many *little* stories, all true, but each one a self-contained tale of place, event, person or persons all by itself?

Why indeed, except that the year 2007 marks the four-hundredth anniversary of Jamestown, first permanent English settlement in North America . . . and thus four centuries of Virginia history, American history, too.

Except that Jamestown, first capital of the Virginia Colony, in 1619 would become home to the first legislative body in America. That, less proudly, Jamestown in the same year would see the colony's first importation of African Americans, as precursor to the institution of slavery in America. That the English settlers and the original residents of Jamestown and environs, the American Indian, would begin here the alternating saga of war and peace between the races due to mark the engulfing white settlement of all America until the passing of the nineteenth century.

Except that Virginia and Jamestown would be the double font of the first widespread revolution in America: Bacon's Rebellion of 1676.

Why write about Virginia, except that one hundred years later Virginians would be in the forefront of those urging, leading, fighting, and justifying the Revolutionary War against imperial Great Britain? That Virginia alone would field George Washington, Thomas Jefferson, Patrick Henry, George Mason, and so many others of the small band we today call the Founding Fathers. That the victory at Yorktown just about would end the British appetite for more warfare against the rebellious colonies.

That starting with George Washington, Thomas Jefferson, James Madison, and James Monroe, and later including William Henry Harrison, John Tyler, Zachary Taylor, and Woodrow Wilson, Virginia would provide the new nation eight presidents, a total rivaled only by Ohio's seven.

That Virginia once, in theory, stretched all the way to the Mississippi River and the Great Lakes. That its storied geographic features include the James, Potomac, York, New, and Rappahannock Rivers; the famed Blue Ridge Mountains; the beaches along the Atlantic shelf; a vast section of the even more vast Chesapeake Bay; the Eastern Shore; the scenic Shenandoah Valley, and, of course, the Tidewater counties and the Hampton Roads cities to the east; the bustling Washington, D.C., suburbs of northern Virginia; the "Mountain Empire" of the coal-laden southwest; the flat tobacco fields of the southside, and the lush Piedmont at center of it all.

Except that it gave birth to explorers Meriwether Lewis and William Clark, that it gave more western locales great leaders, explorers, and founders such as Stephen Austin and Sam Houston. That among its more recent "exports" was Earl Hamner, author and creator of the Virginia-based Waltons television series.

Why write about Virginia? Except that it played such a crucial role in the Civil War, not only by providing its own capital city of Richmond as capital of the Confederacy, but also as a more frequent battleground for the armies of North and South than any other single state. That it provided the icon of all icons to emerge from that fratricidal conflict: Robert E. Lee.

That from the settlement of this affair came another state altogether, West Virginia.

That in the twentieth century, a restored Virginia, its Norfolk naval base soon growing into the world's largest, fully would share in the triumphs and sorrows of America's wars—World War I, World War II, Korea, Vietnam, Gulf War I, and, in the early twenty-first century, Iraq.

That tiny Bedford would lose more men per capita in the Normandy invasion of World War II than any city, town, or village in America. And so would become home to the National D-day Memorial.

Why write about Virginia? Except that its doctors in the twentieth century were pioneers in the field of organ transplants, that its NASA engineers and scientists were crucial to developing the nation's space program, that it became a battleground in the great twentieth-century struggle for civil rights and public school integration.

That women all through its history would make their own mark, from the Indian maiden Pocahontas, to Martha Washington, to Dolley Madison, to the women who saved Mount Vernon, to Lady Nancy Astor (MP), to black educational and business leader,s to literary giant Ellen Glasgow and more.

That its political leaders of the modern era would range from the late Harry F. Byrd Sr., a conservative Democrat whose "Byrd Organization" ruled Virginia politics for many decades, to L. Douglas Wilder, the first black elected governor of any state of the Union.

Why Virginia? Except that it became a home for schools, parks, roadways, and physical plants known nation- and worldwide: the University of Virginia, Virginia Tech, the Medical College of Virginia, and the College of William and Mary among the schools; the Skyline Drive and Blue Ridge Parkway, both running along the spine of the Blue Ridge, among the roadways; the Shenandoah National Park among the parks; the Pentagon among the physical plants of renown. That it became home also to the unique replica of the early capital town of Williamsburg, now known worldwide as Colonial Williamsburg.

That from its, and America's, start of just a hundred or so settlers at Jamestown in 1607, Virginia has seen its population swell to more than seven million at last count.

That among those seven million are the two persons, transplants— settlers from afar, if you will—who came to love Virginia and to write this book. Please enjoy!

While we have cited our sources all along in the corresponding text, we nonetheless would like to emphasize our thanks to the many authors and researchers who went before us in digging up the historical facts that make up this book. As in all our previous historical books, we urge any readers especially interested in a specific topic to go to the source material we mention for more on the subject.

Beyond that, we do owe a few special thanks. The stories herein titled "Major Washington's Steadfastness," "That Other Famous Clark," "An Avoidable Death?" "First Glimpses of Cadet Jackson," "Final Days for Virginia's 'White House,'" "Meeting 'Bobby' Lee," "A Dinner Party for 'Such a Rebel,'" and "The Reunion to End Reunions" were previously published in the same or similar form in *Military History* magazine as Best Little Stories columns by C. Brian Kelly, and we thank the editors and Primedia, Inc., publisher of *Military History,* for permission to reprint them here.

Further, the stories titled "Turmoil in Jamestown," "'Soldier, Statesman Saint,'" "Boomtown Days for Hopewell," "Pulled Out of the Fishbowl," "'Watch Out, She's a-Coming In!'" "Life with a New Heart," "Night the Mountains Fell In," "Day on the Job at Dulles," "New 'Byrd Machine,'" and "Father on Lee's Staff" originally were written for and published in largely the same form by the *Washington Star,* C. Brian Kelly's employer during the 1960s and 1970s. Unfortunately, the late, lamented *Star* no longer is in existence.

In addition, the story "Medical Marvel Kept Secret" is reprinted with permission of Yankee Publishing, Inc., which first published the story in the *Old Farmer's Almanac* (www.almanac.com) in the *Almanac's* 1985 issue under the title "A Sharp Knife and Some Stout Thread."

Other materials appearing herein by either one of the authors that first appeared elsewhere in somewhat altered form have been acknowledged in the text.

Friends and colleagues also have been most helpful. In this regard, we wish especially to thank professional historian John Sayle Watterson for his wise counsel, his review of some of our stories, and suggestions leading to their inclusion in the first place. In like vein, for her helpful suggestions, review of our text, and for furnishing related materials, we owe multiple thanks to Mary Lou Werner Forbes, who won the Pulitzer Prize for her coverage for the *Washington Star* of Virginia's desegregation crisis of the late 1950s. Both of the foregoing have been wonderful friends and working colleagues for quite some time as well. Another friend, stockbroker William Moore, called our attention to the Thomas Jefferson correspondence cited on pages 126–27, and so we thank him also.

Finally, let's hear it for our readers! Rest assured, without your wonderful reception of our first six Best Little Stories historical books, we wouldn't be here before you with Number Seven today.

And, yes, we do have others in the same series and format in mind. Hope to be seeing you again soon!

C. Brian Kelly
Ingrid Smyer-Kelly
Charlottesville, Virginia
May 2003

BEST LITTLE STORIES
from
VIRGINIA

Prologue

1526
Came, Saw . . . and Left

Like the English eighty-one years later, they came in three ships steadily moving up the vast bay and then into the first broad-mouthed river to their left and on up to a beckoning island-isthmus to their right, on the north shore. In some future day, their landing site would be called Jamestown* . . . but not just now, since these pioneers of the New World were Spanish rather than English, and it was early in the sixteenth century, not the seventeenth. All told, the new arrivals numbered about six hundred, both men and women. They were led by Lucas Vasques de Ayllon, a judge from the Caribbean island of Santo Domingo. They brought horses and seemingly ample supplies. They erected small buildings, and in one of them the Dominican priest Antonio de Montesinos, an early opponent of enslaving the New World's Indians, celebrated only the second Mass to be offered in the land destined to be known as the United States of America.

Their settlement, begun in the early summer of 1526, would not last even a year . . . perhaps because Ayllon succumbed to a fever in October. With their leader gone, the settlers mounted a rebellion even while contending with the hostile natives inhabiting the new land. A second in command, Francisco Gomez, decided to give up the attempt at settlement and took his remaining people back to sea in two of their vessels in the spring of 1527. One of the ships sank on the return voyage to San Domingo. Of the original 600, apparently only 150 survived the attempt to settle on the James River of future Virginia.

And now, with the Spanish busy far to the south in their "Florida" territory, *nothing*. Nothing but quiet, and no more intrusions for a full

---

*The Spaniard Ecija, pilot in chief of Spanish Florida, placed the landfall as that of future Jamestown.

generation of the native peoples living along the James, along the parallel York River, on the heavily wooded peninsula in between, and generally in the region of the great bay. And then came part of a second generation. All told, nearly forty years now passed . . .

1 5 6 1
His Name Was Don Luis

Like aliens from another planet, their clothing totally outlandish, their language incomprehensible, their skin pale and nearly white, *they* again appeared off the Virginia shoreline, this time in a pair of towering war canoes of many levels, with great cloths attached above to catch the wind. These strangers, showing no sign of staying, proceeded to walk among the natives, then took aboard one of their *ships* a native boy and sailed off with him until the ships no longer could be seen. And then nothing again. For eight, nine, nearly ten years, *nothing!*

And so, a second reminder that the modern history of Virginia begins in the Chesapeake Bay area, on the banks of the James and York Rivers, but the new arrivals, the aliens, once again were the Spanish, rather than the English.

The Indian youth carried away in one of the great ships by the Spanish would become a young man named Don Luis de Velasco. He crossed the vast ocean to the east aboard the flagship of Pedro Menendez de Aviles, who *may* have obtained permission from the youth's father, a chief, by pledging to return him one day with many valuable gifts.

The great ships now traveled all the way to Cadiz, Spain. And here Don Luis was introduced at the court of King Philip II as an Indian "lord" from the New World region the Spanish called Florida. He was given garments of the finest cloth and placed with the Dominicans at Seville for education in the Spanish language and instruction in the Catholic faith.

He remained in Spain for two years or so, during which time he proved to be an excellent student. "All observers testified to his powerful intellect and also to the fact that he was 'wily' and 'crafty,'" according to early American historian Carl Bridenbaugh. "In after years, it became abundantly clear that during his stay in Spain he also accumulated, through observation and inquiry, a formidable body of information about the great number of Spaniards, their social life and ways, military strength and technology."

His next stop in the alien galaxy would be Mexico, a giant step toward his return home to the Virginia Peninsula lying between the York and James Rivers, to his people there, the Powhatan. In Mexico, however, a local bishop decided the sincerity of the Indian youth's conversion to Christianity was suspect. He forbade Menendez from returning the young man to his homeland. As a result, Menendez had to abandon his ward for the time being.

Three years now passed, with the Virginia-born Indian living among the Dominican friars in Mexico. And there, Governor Don Luis de Velasco was so taken with the young man that he acted as his Christian godfather and even gave the Indian youth his own name. "Thus," explained early Jesuit chronicler Juan Rogel, "the son of a petty chief of Florida was called Don Luis."

In 1565, there was good news for Don Luis! His Spanish mentor, Menendez, was appointed *adelantado,* or conqueror and governor, of the region the Spanish called Florida. Even better, King Philip issued an order to his authorities in Mexico remanding the newly named youth to Menendez's custody, "upon demand." The *adelantado* quickly followed up with instructions to send Don Luis to him in Spanish Florida. He had not forgotten the pledge to return him home someday. Still, it would be a long leap from the *adelantado's* Florida base at San Mateo to the Chesapeake Bay region—Menendez must find some way to send Don Luis northward.

This, in fact, was done in mid-1566, five years after the youth's leave-taking from Virginia. As *adelantado,* Menendez was able to order two Dominican friars to accompany Don Luis north to the *Bahia de Santa Maria,* today's Chesapeake Bay, as part of a colonizing expedition accompanied by a troop of thirty soldiers. Menendez's orders included the statement: "[It] is in the service of God, our Lord, and of his Majesty that I send Don Luis, the Indian, to his country, which according to him is between the 36th and 39th degrees [north latitude] along the shore, and all the people of that territory are his friends and the vassals of his three brothers."

One of those three brothers may have been Chief Powhatan, so well known later to the English settlers of Jamestown. And Don Luis? "Don Luis" may have been Powhatan's brother, the dreaded Opechancanough (O-pa-CHAN-ca-no), later the scourge of the English in Virginia.

But that's getting ahead of the Don Luis story, the first really compelling story in the modern history of Virginia.

The fact is, Don Luis was not destined to rejoin his own people in 1566 . . . nor for another three or four years.

The expedition to the still-virginal Chesapeake Bay region had set sail from today's Parris Island, South Carolina, with its special passenger himself expected to find the right landing along the Virginia shoreline. Unfortunately, notes historian Bridenbaugh, neither the Spanish nor Don Luis himself recognized the entrance to the Chesapeake Bay—their wooden sailing ship, *La Trinidad,* sailed right past, then took up anchorage nearby, perhaps in Chincoteague Bay. At this point, a storm blew the ship southward. "After coasting along the Carolina Outer Banks and making a brief landing," added Bridenbaugh in his book *Early Americans,* "the Portuguese pilot, Domingo Fernandez, retraced his course northward . . . but again a gale, four days in duration, drove *La Trinidad* far out to sea."

Giving up on the notion of landing in Virginia, the Spanish decided to sail on, back to Spain. They did not consult their special Indian passenger.

As a result, Don Luis now—in October 1566—found himself back at Cadiz. Soon after, for reasons unknown today, the two Dominican friars dropped him off at Seville. He turned up two years later in a Franciscan historian's reference to the Indian Don Luis living with the Jesuits in Seville and "advancing in the Spanish language, both in reading and writing, together with the branches of knowledge which they surely taught him."

Surely, too, the primitive native of North America long since would have become *his* world's leading expert on the "aliens" of the Old World. He would have witnessed the good and bad in Spanish society and practice, including, in the latter case, the forced enlistment of New World Indians as slave laborers. By now also, the young man had been confirmed in the Catholic faith and was partaking in the sacrament of Communion. But he still hoped to see his native land again. And, indeed, late in 1567, the Jesuits decided to include Don Luis in a missionary group settling among his own Powhatan tribe in future Virginia—he would be an invaluable ally and exhibit in the effort to convert his fellow Native Americans.

His old mentor, Governor Menendez, back in the picture again, was delighted and offered a ship that would carry the missionary party into the Chesapeake.

Another year passed, but by the autumn of 1568, both Menendez and his protégé, Don Luis, were in Havana, Cuba, where they would meet with the Jesuit priest Juan Bautista de Segura, who would be leading a group of eight missionaries in all.

It appears that the pious Father Segura was more trusting of the supposedly converted young Indian than the other Jesuits, who were not all pleased at the idea of his traveling with them into the unknown. "Despite the objections of nearly all of the other missionaries," wrote Bridenbaugh, "Father Segura believed the American and accepted his offer to join the expedition . . . in the capacity of both guide and interpreter." And so, "after a delay of many months, the ships, commanded by Vincent Gonzales, left Santa Elena and arrived 'in the land of Don Luis' on September 20, 1570."

The young man now disembarking with the aliens from their strange ships likely was in his mid-twenties. He had been gone for nearly ten years. No surprise, then, that the Virginia natives, his own people, at first thought he had risen from the dead and come down from heaven.

As a surprise in earnest, however, Don Luis and his Spanish companions "were disconcerted to find that for several years both famine and disease had plagued the natives and that food was very scarce," wrote historian Bridenbaugh. Still, the area's Indians appeared kind and helpful.

Don Luis himself was especially stunned by more personal news that awaited him, a scenario that fits neatly with the accepted historical knowledge of the Virginia Indian chief Powhatan of later fame among the English at Jamestown, nearly a half century in the future. The "long-lost" wanderer learned that an older brother of his had died and a younger brother now was ruling as chief. "The latter was almost certainly the chieftain known to history as Powhatan," surmised Bridenbaugh.

Reportedly turning aside his younger brother's offer to relinquish the chieftaincy to him, Don Luis at first appeared to embrace his role of a missionary convert to Christianity. One of the Jesuits in the newly landed party wrote: "Don Luis turned out as well as was hoped; he is obedient to the wishes of Father [Segura] and shows respect to him, as also to the rest of us here."

But not for long. Don Luis soon shocked his Jesuit patrons by taking on more than one wife, an "entitlement" by tribal custom for one of his high family standing. Then came reprimands by the Spaniards, "sanctimoniously administered before the entire religious company, as well as delivered privately by Father Segura and others," noted Bridenbaugh.

Furious and humiliated, Don Luis renounced all his Christian teaching "and went to live with his brothers in their village on the Pamunkey River."

As a final prelude to disaster, three of the Jesuits searched him out about four months later. They entreated him to return to the mission down by the mouth of the York River . . . and to their joy, he seemed to agree and, with Indian companions, followed them on their return journey to the mission huts.

But the Indians and the Spanish missionaries had different purposes in mind. Don Luis and his party killed all in the Jesuit mission group, except for a boy who was able to escape into the woods and elude the Indians for a time. Thus would end the Spanish presence in the Chesapeake Bay region of the New World . . . and the affiliation of Don Luis with the Spanish.

At first, of course, neither the other Jesuits nor their Spanish patrons were aware of the events in the isolated Virginia wilderness. They didn't know until Gonzales returned in the spring of 1571 to visit and resupply the Jesuits—only to see Indians walking around on the shore in priestly cassocks, a chilling clue to the fate of the missionaries.

Gonzales and company took two Indians as captives before sailing away, and from one of them discovered that the missing boy, Alonso de Olmos, remained in the area under the care of local Indians.

The news of the "converted" Indian's treachery, quite naturally, was a shock to the Spanish, whose King Philip II himself once had been concerned with Don Luis's clothing, education, and return home as part of a missionary group. Even the pope, Pius V, had consented to the mission's formation in his role as general of the Society of Jesus (the Jesuits). Governor Menendez, previously so faithful to his pledge to return the youth, was furious . . . so much so that in September 1572, he reappeared in the bay region with a punitive force that landed on shore, killed more than twenty Indians, seized another eight to thirteen

as captives, and rescued the boy Alonso. The captives were hanged—
after supposedly first converting to the Christian faith.

Menendez did *not* find his one-time protégé in the unspoiled wilds
lying beyond the shoreline of the Chesapeake Bay or along its rivers
running into the very heart of the future Virginia.

And so who was left behind when the great alien ships once more
departed from the Virginia shores? A Don Luis who, despite his unique
travels among the Europeans of the sixteenth century, merely finished
out his life in the forests of the New World as an older brother of the
great Chief Powhatan? Or, as Bridenbaugh suggests, a Don Luis whose
next historical appearance would be as the scourge of the English?
"Hatred of all Spaniards and Christians took the place of submission
and respect," wrote Bridenbaugh. "To signalize the transformation he
discarded the name Don Luis and took a new one, Opechancanough,
which in Algonquin meant, 'He whose soul is white.'"

As history records, it was Opechancanough who succeeded younger
brother Powhatan as chief of their Indian confederation and then mas-
terminded the horrifying massacres of 1622 and 1644 in which hundreds of English settlers—men, women and children—were killed.

☆ ☆ ☆

Additional note: In the meantime, quite unwittingly to be sure, Don
Luis may have set in motion a chain of events leading to the eventual
canonization of eight new saints by the Roman Catholic Church, "Virginia" saints at that.

To explain: The early years of Spanish missionary efforts among the
Indians of the southeastern quarter of the future United States, in lands
running west of the Mississippi, produced one priestly martyr after
another. From 1527 to 1542 alone, just fifteen years, fifteen or more
priests died trying to bring Christianity to the native Indians of the
region. Then came conversion attempts farther to the east. In one such
case, a priest and two companions who had landed in 1749 at Tampa
Bay, home to the Calusa Indians, "had hardly touched the shore when
they were killed by the assembled savages in sight of the[ir] ship, being
thus the first missionary martyrs of the eastern United States," reports
the online *New Advent Catholic Encyclopedia* (www.newadvent.org). In
1566, a priest landing on Cumberland Island off Georgia with a small

party also was slain by Indians. Soon after, "Father Juan Bautista Segura, as Jesuit vice-provincial, took over missionary work among the Calusa, Tegesta, and Tocobaga tribes in the vast region the Spanish called Florida."

Then came his ill-fated assignment to future Virginia, where he and his companion Jesuits—another priest, three Jesuit brothers, and three Jesuit novices—also died as martyrs to their faith. And now, in more recent years, the Diocese of Richmond, Virginia, has begun the official investigations needed to declare the eight eligible for sainthood status.

As the *Catholic Virginian* reported in June 2002, "Father Segura came unaccompanied by the customary contingent of Spanish troops." Father Russell Smith, appointed as postulator of the sainthood process, explained that lead priest Segura felt he and his companions "had the best chance of bringing the Word of God to Native Americans by not bringing troops, because the soldiers generally set a bad example and acted scandalously." That fact, added Father Smith, "proves the mission was entirely evangelical. The Spanish missionaries were not interested in political advantage or territorial expansion."

Accordingly, they (and, for part of the time, Don Luis) left their ship at a James River landing site, then proceeded only after the ship sailed off. "They [the missionary group] came up College Creek to present-day Williamsburg and took what is now Queens Creek to near what is now Yorktown," Father Smith also explained. There, they established their St. Mary's Mission.

The youth with them, fondly called "Aloncito," had accompanied the missionary group as an altar boy. When the Indians struck, added Father Smith, "Aloncito alone remained alive and begged to be killed with the Jesuits. But they spared the life of the young altar boy." Ironically, it was the brother of Don Luis, "a chief of the tribe," who now became the boy's protector and guardian . . . until the avenging Spanish rescued him in August 1572.

"Aloncito is the key," Father Smith told the *Catholic Virginian*. "He is the one by whom we know all things."

☆ ☆ ☆

Also worth noting: To the south, meanwhile, the English in the 1580s established a settlement on Roanoke Island in the Albemarle Sound of today's North Carolina, only to discover all its settlers gone, with hardly a tangible trace, four years later. The disappearance of the Lost Colony remains a mystery unexplained to this day.

✯

1570 - 1600
Hidden Empire Developing

✯

Behind the shoreline walls of foliage hiding the Virginia interior from the outside world, a Native American named Wahunsonacock was busy creating a minor empire. Chief Powhatan, as the English later would call him, originally had inherited six chiefdoms, but now, by a combination of diplomacy, threat, or naked force, he was busy expanding that original base into alliances with thirty or more tribes based in two hundred or more villages, thus to become head of an estimated fourteen thousand Algonkian (or Algonquin) Indians living in eastern Virginia.

Within the Powhatan society awaiting the first English settlers of today's Virginia, the men did the hunting, fishing, and fighting, while the women not only were the homemakers, they were the home-*builders*. The women also tilled the vegetable plots that provided corn and other staples of the Indian diet. And, most of the time, neither group was very busy, by English standards.

As historian Edmund S. Morgan explained in his book *American Slavery, American Freedom: The Ordeal of Colonial Virginia*, Powhatan was a strong leader who exacted tribute from the other tribes in his confederation, but he and his fellow Indians nonetheless lived a life marked by "a minimum of worldly goods and a maximum of leisure time."

They spent most of their lives in established towns or villages in which the primitive "houses" consisted of strips of bark, hides, or mats thrown over a framework of saplings anchored in postholes. A hole at the top allowed the venting of smoke from an internal fire, and a ground-level hole on one side served as a door. "There were no chairs or tables. And platforms raised from the ground on forked sticks served as beds. House and furniture alike could be put together without heavy labor. Building them was women's work."

Clothing came from skins procured "in the hunt" by the menfolk. "But Indians, like well-to-do Englishmen, apparently regarded hunting as sport. Hunting grounds might be some distance from the village; and when hunting season came around, the whole tribe picked up and moved, the women preceding the men in order to build temporary housing."

The men tended to hunt as a group, driving herds of deer into enclosures or bodies of water and then killing them wholesale. The men also fished in this watery area later known as Tidewater Virginia. "But the Virginia Indians did not rely on hunting or fishing for most of their food. They relied principally on the nuts and fruits they gathered and on the corn, beans, and squashes or melons that they grew."

Tending the crops also was women's work, Morgan wrote. "Indeed, nearly any activity that could be designated as work at all was left to the women."

Even so, the men occasionally did bestir themselves, it also seems. They made the tribe's canoes, its weapons and weirs, or traps, to catch fish. And they did clear the fields for planting—but by an easy-come, easy-go method that created parklike vistas of forest in place of a tangled, untrammeled wilderness. "Clearing consisted merely of girdling the trees and burning brush around them to hasten their death. The next year the women worked the ground between the trees, using a crooked stick as a hoe and planting corn, beans, squash, and melons together in little hills."

It was a system that required little work "other than clearing, planting, and harvesting." It also was a system that resulted in vistas of trees "too large or thick-barked to be affected by fire" and with little undergrowth beneath them. "The repeated burnings prevented the forest from renewing itself, so that the large trees became widely spaced, with room for light to penetrate between them. The English noted that you could see for more than a mile through the woods, that you could ride a horse through them at a gallop, or that you could drive a coach through them."

And so, instead of unmanaged wilds, parklike forestlands, interspersed with gaily flowered meadows, would be just one of the many surprises that awaited the first English settlers of Virginia.

★ Part 1 ★
Seventeenth Century

1 6 0 6
Supplies Eaten Up

The history of *English* Virginia was delayed for six weeks by stormy seas that held up three wooden sailing ships beyond the mouth of the Thames River, downstream from London, their departure point. Seasick, crowded—nay, *jammed*—together for these forty-plus days, was an assortment of untrained "gentlemen," key artisans, a single clergyman, and a bantam-sized adventurer-soldier full of braggadocio. Tossed about in violent seas from December 1606 to February 1607 were the one-hundred-ton *Susan Constant;* the *Godspeed,* forty tons; and the *Discovery,* only twenty tons. The lead ship, the flagship of the tiny fleet, was the *Susan Constant,* captained by the one-armed Christopher Newport, a seasoned naval officer. Aside from their crews, the ships held a complement of more than a hundred would-be settlers, all men, bound for the unknown shores already called Virginia in honor of the late "virgin queen," Elizabeth I, who died in 1603.

The artisans ranged in vocational skills from bricklayers and carpenters to a blacksmith and a mason. Also on hand were a doctor, a barber, and a tailor (but no shoemaker!), plus a few soldiers. The fifty-nine or so "gentlemen" also sailing to the New World were strictly nonprofessionals, most of them totally unprepared for the rigors lying ahead.

As the first English settlers of Virginia waited for calm seas, they didn't dare break into a sealed box to be opened only upon arrival in Virginia and containing secret instruction from the King's Council appointing those seven men who would form the new colony's first governing body.

The Reverend Robert Hunt of the Church of England would not be among the seven . . . but then he was a clergyman and already known as the group's chaplain. One of the most seasick of the travelers during the six weeks spent standing off the Thames in wait for good weather, the Reverend Hunt vomited violently and frequently but made no move to return to his All Saints parish in Old Heathfield, East Sussex, just twelve miles by seagull's flight from the flotilla's anchorage. And, if he would not give up his own commitment to sail across the Atlantic, he also would not hear of weakened resolve on the part of his compatriots. He, in fact, would be noted for his unflagging determination and religious zeal, both on board ship and at the Jamestown landfall in distant Virginia . . . before he died an early death in the New World.

By then, his fellow pioneers would have realized how crucial to the colony's very survival were the rations they had consumed, seasick or not, during their six-week sojourn awaiting clear weather. But rampant disease also would stalk the settlers in their first months at Jamestown, and nobody, not even the unfortunate Robert Hunt himself, had any idea that he was a typhoid carrier, a seventeenth-century "Typhoid Mary" who would be at the center of the original Jamestown settlement—and, it so happens, would be helping with the daily food preparations.

1 6 0 7
Already a Formidable Résumé

By the spring of 1605, the adventuresome young Englishman John Smith already had developed a résumé that would have taken many another man a lifetime to achieve. Returning to London in the winter of 1604, he came fresh from travels through Europe and northern Africa, through Russia and Poland . . . and relatively fresh from slavery in Turkey as well.

The slavery episode was only the tail end of his story, which began peacefully enough with his birth in Willoughby, Lincolnshire, England, in 1580. But he left home and hearth as a youth of sixteen after his father died to begin a now-historic career of travel, adventure, soldiering—and heroics. Small in stature, still a teenager but fierce in demeanor, he jumped right into the soldier's life by joining the volunteer forces in France fighting for Dutch independence from the Spanish.

Then, just before the turn of the century, he was to be found having a turn at the seafaring life, aboard a merchant ship plying the Mediterranean Sea. Next, in 1600, would come more soldiering, this time on behalf of the Austrians fighting the Turks in Hungary. Promoted to captain in recognition of his bravery and prowess in battle, he soon, by 1602, was on the frontlines in nearby Transylvania.

But here, the year before the death of Queen Elizabeth I, came a severe trial for the adventurous Capt. John Smith—he was wounded, captured by the Turks, and sold as a slave. Fortunately for him, however, his owner gave the new slave to a young woman in Istanbul . . . and she promptly fell in love with the young Englishman, Smith himself later recounted in possibly embellished terms. She arranged with her brother to have Smith placed in training for the Turkish military forces, but Smith killed the brother and escaped from the Turks. He returned to Transylvania by way of Russia and Poland, gathered in a nice reward for his services, and began his travels in Europe and North Africa.

In London during the winter of 1604–5, he heard of the Virginia Company's plans to establish a colony in distant Virginia and eagerly signed up for this latest adventure.

As the three wooden ships carrying the colonists crossed the Atlantic by way of the Canary Islands, fleet commander Christopher Newport, already a veteran of several visits to the American coastline, had the support of an additional two veteran voyagers, Bartholomew Gosnold and Gabriel Archer. All told, 108 settlers (some accounts say 104 or 105) had set sail for Virginia in the *Susan Constant*, the *Discovery*, and the *Godspeed*. Finally bidding farewell to English waters in mid-February 1607, they reached the West Indies in March, stopped for three weeks, then sailed on northward to their first sighting of Virginia shores on April 26. By now, it had been an eighteen-week crossing.

With their ships cautiously moving up the Chesapeake Bay and then the Powhatan River (later the James), the settlers obtained the first sightings of their prospective Indian neighbors—bold, athletic men with ornamented bodies, feathers stuck in their hair, and colored animal skins as clothing. As an accurate portent of the settlement's future relationship with the Powhatan confederation, however, some Indians offered food while others attacked.

The flotilla passed a shoreline point, which the leaders named Archer's Hope, in search of a safe anchorage—not so much from the Indians, but from the Spanish who might seek to oust the English interlopers. Finally, sixty miles above the mouth of the bay, the crowded little vessels nosed into the waters of an island-shaped peninsula set among marshes but offering deep water so close to the shore that the ships could be moored to the trees.

This, then, would be James Fort—Jamestown.

This, too, would be the setting for resumption of the rough-hewn Capt. John Smith's historic story, much of it an unlikely development since he had spent the last half of the Atlantic crossing as a prisoner charged with insubordination, dissension, or even mutinous behavior. Now, he would be the source of considerable consternation when the prospective settlers opened the sealed box containing the names of the settlement's first ruling council members—and discovered the bold and brassy Smith was one of them.

As the colonists of the first permanent English settlement in North America stepped ashore at Jamestown in May 1607, none had any inkling that the same soldier of fortune one day would be their shaky colony's firm-handed leader . . . indeed, perhaps its not too much to say, its savior.

1 6 0 9
"Bowling in the Streets"

The history of the English in Virginia, and therefore of America as it is known today, begins with the ordeal and near-destruction of the first permanent English settlement in America. But why? What a set of questions the pioneers at Jamestown left behind! Questions more puzzling, really, than speculation on the fate of the Lost Colony on Roanoke Island in North Carolina in the 1580s.

The English who set up shop at Jamestown in 1607 were so lacking in food their third winter there, some turned to cannibalism. Many died not only of disease but of outright starvation during the colony's so-called "starving time." But why? Why didn't they make the effort to take care of themselves? Why hadn't they made an effort to grow or obtain the foods they needed?

What were they thinking during the many idle man-hours that could have been spent working for the good of the settlement?

As historian Edmund Morgan noted in *American Slavery, American Freedom: The Ordeal of Colonial Virginia,* the "starving time" came during the winter of 1609–10, a period when the Jamestown Colony was five hundred strong and surrounded by woods teeming with game and by waterways rife with fish and dotted with edible ducks and geese. Three planting seasons had passed since the colony began, Morgan noted. During that time, too, the settlers had "fallen into an uneasy truce with the Indians, punctuated by guerrilla raids by both sides, but they . . . had plenty of time in which they could have grown crops."

In fact, the settlers occasionally obtained corn from the Indians, to say nothing of supplies arriving from England. And they had the firearms needed for hunting.

Five hundred people, and yet they were starving. Five hundred armed settlers, and there they were, scouring the woods "listlessly for nuts, roots, and berries."

Worst of all, they resorted to cannibalism, the only such instance known in Virginia. "One provident man chops up his wife and salts down the pieces," added Morgan. "Others dig up graves to eat the corpses. By spring only sixty are left alive."

Nor did the survivors and subsequent settlers seem to learn by experience. Newcomers arriving in the spring of 1611, a full year later, found the colony "still . . . not growing its own corn." When "all hands could have been used in planting," the only planting was done in a private garden or two. Morgan cited Ralph Hamor's remark in his 1615 work, *A True Discourse on the Present Estate of Virginia,* that the settlers were busy with "their daily and usual workes, bowling in the streets."

By this time, it seems clear, the colony that once had been quick to erect a triangular-shaped fort as protection against Indian attack now had come to rely upon the same local Indians for food . . . and yet it still suffered occasional Indian attacks. Suggested Morgan: "The Indians can finish them off at any time simply by leaving the area." One Indian, according to Capt. John Smith, told the English, "[W]e can plant any where . . . and we know that you cannot live if you want our harvest, and that reliefe we bring you."

That being the case, the settlers dared not upset their symbiotic relationship by taking any overly aggressive actions against the Indians . . . one would think.

But no, just consider the summer between the starving time (1609–10) and the spring of 1611. What had the still-surviving colonists done to provide for the intervening winter of 1610–11? Well, they had grown *some* corn, true, but they also launched attacks on local Indians thought to be "harboring" runaway members of the Jamestown Colony. The Englishmen killed a number of Indians in their villages, burned down their corn crops, and captured a tribal queen and her children. Traveling back to Jamestown by boat with the prisoners, one group of Englishmen threw the children into the James River and commenced "shoteinge owtt thewir Braynes in the water." Later, at Jamestown itself, the English put the queen to death by the sword—stabbed her to death.

Aside from such atrocities (and, true, the Indians had committed a few of their own before this), it is fair to again ask, Why . . . why a course of action certain to infuriate the Indians all around the small colony while also destroying their helpful corn crops? Or, as Morgan stated the madness: "Thus the English, unable or unwilling to feed themselves, continually demanding corn from the Indians, take pains to destroy both the Indians and their corn."

The same English, by the way, in the spring of 1612 concocted extreme punishments for those of their number running away to live with the Indians. According to George Percy, the man who had thrown the queen's children into the river to be shot in the head, Governor Thomas Dale's proposed punishments for such runaways ranged from hangings, to burnings, to shootings, to being "broken upon wheles."

Historians in general have blamed many of the colony's early problems on its weak form of self-government by a council composed of men appointed by the king, their identities kept secret in a locked box until their arrival in Virginia. At that point, they had to choose a president from among themselves. But there was the heart of the matter. As historian Morgan stated the case: "The president had virtually no authority of his own; and while the council lasted, the members spent most of their time bickering and intriguing against one another and especially against the one man who had the experience and assurance to take command."

That one man, of course, was John Smith, whose rough, cocky manners had antagonized his fellow council members all along, but who in the end likely saved the fragile settlement from going under altogether. Ironically, he dealt more effectively with the Indians than with his fellow Englishmen, even though he himself had been held captive by the Indians for some weeks while three companions were killed by the Indians, at least one of them by torture. Everybody is familiar with the famous story that resulted: When Smith was taken before Chief Powhatan for possible execution, the fair Pocahontas, Powhatan's daughter, twelve or thirteen years old, intervened, and Smith lived to tell the tale in his own way.

Remaining in Virginia until the fall of 1609, added Morgan, John Smith wound up conducting "most of the colony's relations both with Powhatan and with the tribes under Powhatan's dominion."

Then, too, gradually taking more power in the council as weaker members died off or returned to England, Smith eventually was able to drive a stake into the heart of the colony's poorly conceived commune system. Taking control of Jamestown as council president in October 1608, he dispensed with the notion of common fruits for common labor by saying, "[H]e that will not worke, shall not eate (except by sickness he be disabled)."

To be sure, Smith also felt the English should treat the Indians with an absolutely firm hand. "He bullied and threatened and browbeat them, but we do not read of any atrocities committed upon them under his direction, nor did he feel obliged to hang, break, or burn any Englishmen who went off to live with them."

Back in London, meanwhile, the Virginia Company saw the need for change but balked at giving the rough-hewn Captain Smith lasting authority. Henceforth, the word came in due time, the colony would be ruled by a governor given "absolute powers" and only assisted by a council. It wasn't the perfect solution, but for the next "eight or nine years, whatever evils befell the colony were not the result of any diffusion of authority," declared Morgan.

But what about the horrific "starving time" of 1609–10? The fact is, it came right after John Smith left for England and before the first new governor arrived; it came during a hiatus created when the first Jamestown governor, Lord De la Warr (or Ware), was delayed leaving England, an unfortunate circumstance compounded when his deputy, Sir Thomas Gates, was shipwrecked at Bermuda. "The starving winter of 1609-1610 occurred during this interval; but Gates arrived in May, 1610, followed by De la Warr himself in June. Thereafter, Virginia was firmly governed under a clear set of laws, drafted by Gates and by De la Warr's subsequent deputy, Sir Thomas Dale."

Actually, conditions in the colony were so bad, Gates discovered that May, he agreed with the survivors it was time to pack up and leave. They all were setting off, downriver, for England when they more or less bumped into the incoming De la Warr aboard a ship full of new settlers and fresh supplies. All then proceeded back upstream to the Jamestown site.

The new governing system with an authoritative governor at the lead was an often rigid, even harsh change from the early laissez-faire approach to daily life in Jamestown. The new system, noted Morgan, "set the colonists to work with military discipline and no pretense of gentle government." Meanwhile, the complexion of the settlers by now had changed—no longer were their ranks half filled with gentlemen totally unfamiliar with hard, physical labor. Now, too, both on Jamestown Island and in the lands beyond, private ownership of real estate would have an impact as the Jamestown settlement moved away from collectivism toward private enterprise. Satellite colonies and individually owned plantations would appear more and more frequently.

John Smith probably would have approved of all these changes, but, suffering severe burns from accidentally ignited gunpowder, he had returned to England in October 1609, just weeks before "starving time."

☆ ☆ ☆

Additional note: John Smith never would return to Virginia, but he did return to America—sailing to Maine and Massachusetts in 1614, he in fact gave New England its name. Back in *old* England, he wrote a series of books about his adventures, many of them raising questions as to their exact veracity due to his penchant for exaggeration, but most of them were judged to be true at their core. By any man's measure, in Smith's own or any other time, his indeed had been quite a life. As Dennis Montgomery wrote in the spring 1994 issue of the *Colonial Williamsburg Journal,* "Smith was a compiler and writer of exuberant travelers' tales, an explorer, a mapmaker, a geographer, an ethnographer, a soldier, a governor, a trader, a sailor, an admiral, and the editor of a seaman's handbook." The extraordinary man who was all of these things, and probably more, died in 1631 at the age of fifty-one.

★

1623
A Plea for Help

★

Soon after Jamestown, there would be the settlement less than ten miles away called Martin's Hundred, a plantation and home at one time to more than two hundred settlers. From there, soon after nearly eighty of them were murdered by rampaging Powhatans in the Massacre of 1622, would come an indentured servant's pitiful plea for help. He wrote in March 1623, just a year after the Indians killed an estimated three to four hundred settlers up and down the James River corridor. At Martin's Hundred alone, it is estimated, seventy-eight were killed and sixty-two more either were captured by the Indians or fled to nearby Jamestown. Now, a year later, with disease and other natural causes taking their customary toll among the white settlers, only about fifty persons remained at the once-thriving farm on the north banks of the James.

One of them was Richard Frethorne, who had arrived in Virginia only three months before taking up pen to plead with his father to buy out his term of servitude.

Complaining of near starvation and a lack of decent clothing, he said those still working the plantation could be overrun again at any time by the Indians who lurked in the surrounding wilderness. "We are but 32 to fight against 3,000 if they should come," he wrote. More generally, he added, "I have nothing to comfort me, nor is there nothing to be gotten here but sickness and death."

Just five years before, prospects had looked so much brighter for the 220 men and women who set sail from England, bound for Virginia, in their wooden sailing vessel called the *Gift of God*. Their New World settlement, named for Richard Martin, recorder for the city of London, would become one of the "subsidiary 'particular plantations' of the joint-stock Virginia Company of London," explains a Colonial Williamsburg online history. It would be owned by investors calling themselves the Society of Martin's Hundred. (*Hundred* in those days meant a subdivision of a county.)

Located downriver from Jamestown, the new plantation of twenty-one thousand acres included ten miles of river frontage. At its center, as home to forty of the settlers, was the fortified Wolstenholme Towne, named for major investor Sir John Wolstenholme.

Just like Jamestown and its growing number of satellites, of course, the plantation was on land once belonging to Chief Powhatan's federation of thirty or more Indian tribes. And, as the same Colonial Williamsburg source notes, "For seven years after the first English settlers arrived at Jamestown in 1607, the English and the Indians often fought for control of the Tidewater lands and resources." In the years since Powhatan's daughter Pocahontas married the Englishman John Rolfe in 1614, however, "the two peoples had been at peace."

All well and good . . . except that Chief Powhatan had died by the time the good ship *Gift of God* arrived in Virginia. And now in charge of the great Powhatan confederation was his brother, Opechancanough. Whether Opechancanough really was the Indian youth known to the Spanish in the late sixteenth century as Don Luis (see pages 6–13) didn't really matter—he, in any case, bore the new English settlers no goodwill.

It was at his direction, apparently, that the Indians struck at the white intruders—in their homes, on their plantations and farms, up and down the James from the future site of Richmond upriver to the lands below Jamestown—140 miles in all. It was March 22, 1622, Good Friday of that year, and by some prearrangement known only to the Indians, they rose up exactly at eight o'clock.

"With tomahawk, club, and scalping knife, they slaughtered men, women and children wherever they could be found—as they sat at breakfast, walked about their farms, hoed their crops or fed their cattle, or as they lay in their beds," wrote Virginius Dabney in his history, *Virginia: The New Dominion.* "Many bodies were mangled, and portions were carried off by the rampaging redskins. More than 350 persons of all ages and both sexes perished."

Thanks to Chanco, a Christianized Indian youth who had been befriended, even treated as a son, by settler Richard Pace, Jamestown and its immediate environs escaped the horrors that befell others. Chanco was one of two brothers who were in on the plot. Both spent the night before the planned strike at Pace's Paines homestead, but Chanco arose while his brother slept and warned Pace of the great conspiracy. "The latter rowed three miles across the James before dawn and alerted Jamestown," added Dabney's account. As a result, Jamestown "escaped destruction," but the highly coordinated Indian attacks elsewhere were devastating, especially at Martin's Hundred and its nucleus of Wolstenholme Towne.

Whether named massacre or outright revolt, the Indian attack "nearly accomplished its purpose," says the Colonial Williamsburg website. "The English withdrew from their scattered settlements to the safety of Jamestown."

But not for good. A relative handful of settlers returned to Wolstenholme Towne "a year or more later." And it was at Martin's Hundred that young Richard Frethorne found himself in truly dire straits, it seems, just a year after the Indian attack. "But I have nothing at all, no, not a shirt to my back but two rags, nor clothes but one poor suit, nor but one pair of shoes, but one pair of stockings, but one cap, but two bands [collars]," he wrote to his "Loving and Kind Father and Mother." His only cloak, he also wrote in his letter home, "is stolen by one of my fellows, and to his dying hour [he] would not tell me what he did with it; but some of my fellows saw him have butter and beef out of a ship, which my cloak, I doubt [not] paid for."

Frethorne complained that he and his fellow indentured servants had to "work hard both early and late for a mess of water gruel and a mouthful of bread and beef." They "never saw" a plate of venison, and they were not allowed to hunt local fowl such as ducks.

All around, people were sick or dying—"for our plantation is very weak by reason of the death and sickness of our company." They had taken two Indians captives and "made slaves of them," but he and his companions lived in fear of a renewed attack. "They may easily take us," he wrote, "but that God is merciful and can save with few as well as with many, as he showed to [the people of the biblical region of] Gilead."

Young Frethorne had been fortunate, he also reported, to have been helped out from time to time by a kindly Jamestown gunsmith named Goodman Jackson. "And he much marvelled that you would send me [as] a servant to the Company; he saith I had been better knocked on the head."

In sum, the miserable Richard Frethorne wrote, "[I]f you love me you will redeem me suddenly, for which I do entreat and beg." And . . . send food! "For God's sake," send beef, cheese, and butter, he begged.

Nor was he necessarily a complainer or malingerer. According to historical sources, two-thirds of his own shipmates had died in the new Virginia Colony since their arrival three months before he took pen to hand on March 20, 1623. Conditions were difficult, to say the least—

so difficult, says the Association for the Preservation of Virginia Antiquities (APVA), that nearly half of the fifty settlers returning to Martin's Hundred *after* the Indian massacre of 1622 were dead and gone by 1625. Still surviving life on the "particular plantation" were nineteen men, five women, and three children, twenty-seven total . . . and all, in 1625, apparently "well-provisioned." Not only that, but prepared to defend themselves as well. "Perhaps in anticipation of another attack from the locals, the little community at Martin's Hundred in 1625 was well armed, with a full set of armor for just about each man, 26 matchlocks, 27 fixed pieces, 29 swords, a cannon, 91 pounds of powder, and 361 pounds of shot," according to the APVA website (at www.apva.org) titled *Jamestown 2007.* "The ordnance and most of the other weaponry were under the control of William Harwood, the 'governor' of the settlement."

In a short time, however, the "focal point of the hundred" moved from Wolstenholme Towne near the river to a site on a bluff where the Carter's Grove mansion would be built in the mid-eighteenth century by Carter Burwell, grandson of the fabled Robert "King" Carter. Indeed, Wolstenholme Towne had pretty much been abandoned by the year 1645, says the Colonial Williamsburg account. And then, "what remained of Wolstenholme Towne and its dead lay forgotten beneath the plantation's fields and woodlands until 1976."

That's when the archaeologists examining historic Carter's Grove got to work and began uncovering more of the Martin's Hundred–Wolstenholme Towne story. According to Colonial Williamsburg, owner of the 720-acre Carter's Grove property today: "Before they were finished in 1981, the archaeologists had discovered six sites of habitation dating from about 1620 to after 1645. Half or more of the village site had been lost to riverbank erosion, but much remained."

After three centuries, it's fair to ask, What possibly *could* have remained? The fact is, the good earth covering the old settlement had preserved "shadows of the seventeenth-century postholes, which formed outlines of buildings." Thus, emerging from those shadows "as the loamy topsoil was scraped away," was "the trapezoidal shape of a fort with a watchtower, a gun platform, [and] musketeer platforms," among other exciting finds.

Then, too, inside the outlines of the fort, the excavations revealed an old well, settlement commander Harwood's home, even a cattle pond. Safe to say also: "An outlying pen protected livestock at night."

A logical conclusion from all this: "Less than one-fourth the size of the 42,800 square foot Jamestown Fort, Wolstenholme Towne was built as a place for villagers to flee during attack."

Still to emerge from all the diggings were the remains of a barn, a "company" compound, "and a palisaded dwelling near the river."

Also found were a number of archaeological treasures, vital clues as to how the early settlers lived and protected themselves. Unearthed was "the first American find of a hinged-faced [closed] helmet from a suit of armor," albeit "reduced to a thin shell of rust." A second helmet was found in the remains of a potter's pond. So were "plates from an armor shirt, examples of seventeenth-century earthenware, and a spectacular piece of a colonial still called an alembic." Additional artifacts ranged from broken crockery to tools, firelock muskets, even frying pans, with many now displayed at the adjacent Winthrop Rockefeller Archaeology Museum. According to the APVA, artifacts such as woven gold and strands of silver or a Dutch delft tile reflected "high social status."

Significant also, two ancient graves gave up a mystery woman and a man "whose skull had been holed by a blow (perhaps from a spade) between the eyes." Possibly the man was a victim of the Indian attack of 1622, but the remains of the woman showed no signs of a violent death. Found in an ancient trash pit, she was "curled on her right side as if asleep." The conjecture is, "she may have hidden there after escaping an attempt to scalp her, but bled to death or died of exposure in the night." Whatever the cause of her death, "she had rested in the same position for almost 320 years when the archaeologists found her."

Other graves were found during the excavations, but, so far as is known, none was that of Richard Frethorne, who, along with twenty-two others at Martin's Hundred, did *not* survive the winter of 1623–24.

1 6 2 4
Nailed by the Ears

Going to court in the early days of Jamestown was no laughing matter for those convicted of wrongdoing. Ever had your ears pinned back, figuratively speaking? In Jamestown during the 1620s and 1630s, it was more like having your ears *nailed* back . . . to a pillory post. And that's literally, rather than figuratively. Or perhaps one or both ears simply would be cut off.

In short, the justice meted out at Jamestown's Quarter Court was swift, harsh, and, by our standards of today, unmerciful. A youthful male servant accused of raping two young girls? Execution was the sentence—*perhaps* understandable today, when Virginia's death penalty still applies in the most heinous of criminal cases. But in Jamestown, they whipped the two girls, the victims, as well. Not quite so understandable.

In addition, one girl's mother was flogged for failing to report the assault on her daughter right away.

Another time, in March 1624, sea captain Richard Quaile wrote a document that didn't sit well with the authorities. He not only was "stripped of his command and fined," wrote Martha W. McCartney in her book *Jamestown: An American Legacy*, he was nailed to the pillory in the marketplace by both ears. Just to add insult to injury, his sword was broken and he was given an ax, "the symbol of a carpenter."

The Quarter Court, like a circuit court of today, dealt with both civil and criminal matters. It really was the blue-blooded Governors Council convening as a court to keep law and order in the tight little world that was Jamestown in the first years of its existence. A fairly commonplace case going before the court could involve perjury, and conviction could involve the loss of one's ears. Other cases might involve capital offenses such as murder and treason, McCartney noted. Or violation of the colony's religious laws—that is to say, infractions such as failure to pay church dues, or hunting hogs on Sundays.

Name-calling was not taken lightly either. "In a society that prized reputation and status," wrote McCartney, "insults were serious. One Jamestown Island resident ran afoul of the law when he made disparaging remarks about a local minister. Another was summoned to court for calling a neighbor a 'Virginia whore.' Slanderers usually had to apologize publicly or post a bond guaranteeing good behavior."

Ranking officials who disparaged one another often would go to church and take Communion side by side to show their "willingness to put the matter behind them." No Quarter Court for them; but woe to the man, like sea captain Quaile, who might offend a public official! And others were known to have suffered even worse fates for a similar misstep or two. Edward Sharples, clerk to the Quarter Court itself, apparently sent "unauthorized writings" to the king. For that, his ears first were nailed to the pillory, then cut off. He then was banished from Jamestown Island, unarmed, and forced to become an indentured servant for seven years.

Still worse was the treatment suffered by Richard Barnes, who was critical of a Jamestown Colony governor. "He had both arms broken and his tongue bored through with a sharp instrument. A gauntlet of forty men butted and kicked him out of the fort at Jamestown."

Slightly different was the case of indentured servant Peter Martin, who dared to say another man was innocent of the accusation against him. For this, Peter Martin was whipped, deprived of an ear, and sentenced to another seven years as an indentured servant, even though he had just finished his original seven years of servitude.

In fact, with the colony's labor shortage worsening, McCartney wrote, "sentences involving servitude became increasingly common." Not too surprisingly, a cynic might say, the wrongdoers often "ended up serving the governor or a member of his council, the same men who handed down the sentence." Once, too, a prominent clergyman, David Sandys, was rumored to be planning to kidnap a "slow-witted" orphaned girl of twelve or thirteen. But the Quarter Court dismissed the allegations against the minister, "whose brother, incidentally, sat as a justice." In another case, Jamestown physician John Pott, immediate past governor, was convicted of cattle-rustling, a violation carrying a possible death penalty. The sitting governor, John Harvey, then recommended leniency for Pott, whom Harvey described as "the only physician in the colony skilled in epidemical diseases." In the end, Pott won a king's pardon. (But historians still recall the added allegation that he poisoned "a number of Indians in the course of the running fight between the colonists and the Indians," said Virginius Dabney in his history, *Virginia: the New Dominion.*)

As the Pott case might suggest, and as McCartney noted, many a dispute coming before the Quarter Court did relate to livestock problems of one kind or another, especially those posed by *wandering* livestock. "Cases, on occasion, revolved around the ownership of cattle, which generally roamed at large and bore earmarks." Typically also, two Jamestown settlers were unhappy with a neighbor whose pigs rooted through their vegetable gardens. In another case, a laborer and a gunsmith were accused of stealing and butchering a calf—a calf owned by Deputy Governor George Yeardley. Not a great choice. The gunsmith admitted helping in the butchering of the calf but said the other man, the laborer, actually killed it. It turned out the laborer also had stolen items from the colony's provost marshal (similar to a police chief; again a bad choice). In the end, both defendants were sentenced to death, but the gunsmith was offered a reprieve, said McCartney, "perhaps because of his occupation."

Meanwhile, "Severe punishment awaited unmarried people who had sexual relations or indulged in inter-racial liaisons," wrote McCartney. "Men and boys usually were whipped. Women and girls were shamed publicly, sometimes made to stand up in church, draped in a white sheet, and hold a wand, a symbol of lost innocence."

Among the earliest laws imposed in Jamestown, by the way, was the rule ("upon paine of death") against running away to join the nearby Indians. Only appointed agents could even trade with the Indians (again, "upon paine of death").

The earliest Jamestown settlers saw the dangers of befouling their immediate environment inside the triangular-shaped fort that protected them against Indian attack. Thus, no laundering of dirty clothes and no washing of pots and pans could take place in the open street within the wooden palisade—or even close by on the outside of the high fence. The same activities could not take place near the "olde well," for that matter. Then, too, "Every man," said one early rule, "shall have an especiall and due care, to keepe his house sweete and clean, as also so much of the streete, as lieth before his door." Also forbidden near the dwelling places: doing "the necessities of nature, since by these unmanly, slothfull and loathsome immodesties, the whole Fort may bee choaked, and poisoned with ill aires."

More generally, noted Kathleen M. Brown in the essay "Women in Jamestown" on the Virtual Jamestown Internet site (www.iath.virginia.edu/vcdh/jamestown/essays/brown_essay.html), "chronic shortages of food, fabric, clothing, bedding, household equipment, and tools are reflected in the details of other laws outlining stringent punishments for theft and illicit trade."

Furthermore, the colony's rules to live by were firm as applied to the few women of the colony's early days as well as the men. "Although men were the vast majority of victims who suffered painful and disfiguring corporal punishments, disobedient women were also punished," she wrote. "When several women ordered to make shirts under the regime of [Deputy] Governor [Sir Thomas] Dale dealt with the shortage of cotton thread by unraveling some of the shirting, they were whipped for failing to produce garments of the requisite length."

Meanwhile, the case of the "dull-witted" girl and the clergyman allegedly planning to "steale" her away created a real mare's nest for the Quarter Court to unravel, and not only because of the minister's rumored interest. As explained by author Brown, the girl was Mara Bucke, the twelve- or thirteen-year-old orphaned daughter of the deceased Richard Bucke, himself a minister. She was "at the center of a struggle in 1624 that pitted her guardians, brother-in-law John Burrows and sister Bridget Burrows, against the overseers of her deceased father's estate," wrote Brown. "Several" neighbors then heard rumors that "a prominent" Jamestown resident—they suspected the Reverend David Sandys—planned to "steale Away" Bucke from the Burrows plantation on the south side of the James River. Apparently to head off that potential problem, the girl's sister and brother-in-law did their best to "arrange a marriage with a man they preferred."

Not so fast, however. Now, at the demand of the estate overseers, the court intervened, telling the Burrows couple it would not permit "any motione of marriage be made" by the girl. As a result, the teenager, "described as 'dull' witted by two witnesses," remained with her sister and husband at least until reaching the age of fifteen. At that point, "she disappears from the records."

But not the Reverend Sandys, who, it seems, "successfully sued the parties who suspected him of planning to kidnap Bucke."

Next case?

1 6 7 6
Turmoil in Jamestown

The pervading quiet beneath the tall trees and across the greensward of Jamestown will never tell. It provides little clue to the tumult that a rebellious young English squire brought to the Virginia Colony hardly three generations after its start. And who knows what the ghosts of the past may think of the firebrand Nathaniel Bacon Jr., whose visits here in the year 1676 rocked the earliest permanent English settlement in America to its foundations?

The trail he followed to Jamestown on three critical occasions began at his Longfield plantation set on a curl in the northern shoreline of the James River just below future Richmond, in what is today's Henrico County. That was where young Bacon, twenty-nine, and his wife, Elizabeth, established residence after their arrival—at Jamestown—from England in 1674. They had been heartily greeted by the elderly Royal Governor Sir William Berkeley and his own much younger wife, so heartily they briefly stayed with the Berkeleys, and the governor accorded Bacon, an English squire's son, a seat on the blue-ribbon colony council.

Two years later, though, in the summer of 1676, a full century before the American Revolution, the same Nathaniel Bacon emerged as an unlikely rebel ruling mainland Virginia, population just short of forty thousand. Calling himself "General, by consent of the people," he drove Royal Governor Berkeley onto the Eastern Shore. He publicly defied the governor to his face. He burned Jamestown to the ground. He even talked of defying the distant king of England if he sent troops to quell the Virginia rebellion—"Bacon's Rebellion."

Variously described in the years since as a cursing rabble-rouser whose favorite oath was "Dammne my blood," or as a democratic prototype for better-known revolutionary leaders such as George Washington, Bacon left a trail with no real end.

To this day his burial site remains unknown. His place in history is disputed by those aware of his revolt against an autocratic royal governor. His motives, his ultimate goal, his personal appearance and character are all shrouded in argument and mystery.

Yet, had he not died, apparently of a malarialike fever, at a crucial point, there is no telling what course American history might have followed for the next four centuries. And historians still debate the extent of Bacon's influence upon the independence movement of 1776.

In Bacon's day, of course, there was no town in the Virginia Colony but Jamestown. There were few roads, and the highways were the rivers, and high up the rivers were the outflung, small planters of the new colony—its frontiersmen reaching out for new lands, seeding tobacco fields, courting Indian trade, but sometimes meeting "Indian trouble" instead. And it was "Indian trouble" that set off Bacon's cometlike ride across the Virginia firmament—that, and a gathering of Bacon's fellow frontiersmen at Jordan's Point, roughly across the James River from his own homestead.

They were angry and fearful over economic issues and recent Indian raids. They were especially upset because Governor Berkeley, thought to have a lucrative Indian trade of his own, appeared unable or unwilling to take steps to stop the Indian depredations. This was in the spring of 1676, and the agitated frontiersmen who gathered at Jordan's Point were a restless volunteer force only looking for a leader.

On the north side of the river and some miles upstream, near the falls destined to become the site of Richmond, four more planters were gathered round, drinking, talking, deploring the Indian situation: William Byrd I, father of the founder of Richmond; James Crewes, Henry Isham, and their friendly new neighbor, Nathaniel Bacon Jr.

According to a report compiled for King Charles II the very next year, the four were "making the Sadness of their times their discourse, and the Fear they all lived in, because of the Susquehannocks who had settled a little above the Falls of the James River, and committed many murders upon them, among whom Bacon's overseer happened to be one."

And now, on this spring day, Bacon's drinking companions may have talked him into visiting the volunteers at Jordan's Point with a supply of rum. According to the report prepared for the king by three commissioners sent over from England, Crewes and his companions already had laid the groundwork for Bacon's visit. "(As Crewes etc. had before laid the plot with the soldiers) they all at once in field shouted and cry'd out, a Bacon! A Bacon!, which taking fire with his ambition and Spirit of Faction and popularity, easily prevailed upon him to resolve to head them."

So began America's first widespread rebellion. Offering to cover the costs himself, the English squire's son declared he indeed would lead the volunteers against the Indians. But . . . which ones? Tangling briefly with the normally friendly Pamunkey Indians, he then set out on an unauthorized expedition against an Occaneechee Indian trading center on a Roanoke River island near today's Clarksville, Virginia, seventy miles to the south and close to the North Carolina border. There, by his own and other accounts, he achieved a major victory—but still others said he surprised and killed essentially friendly tribesmen. In either case, his destruction of the trading center may have been aimed at Governor Berkeley's trading ties. As another possibility, some Bacon critics have suggested he or his men only wanted the valuable beaver pelts gathered by the local Occaneechees.

In any case, by the time Bacon returned home in May 1676, Royal Governor Berkeley had branded him a rebel and outlaw, allegedly even visiting Bacon's homestead on the James River and telling Bacon's wife that he would be hanged. Plaintively, she wrote his sister back in England: "If you had been here, it would have grieved your heart to hear the pitiful complaints of the people, the Indians killing people daily and the governor not taking any notice of it for to hinder them. The poor people came to your brother."

And now came Bacon's three critical visits to Jamestown of 1676 that set the English colony on its collective ear.

☆ ☆ ☆

Jamestown Visit I: First, Bacon, even though freshly branded as an outlaw, would go to Jamestown, the bustling capital of the Virginia Colony, with a fresh triumph in his favor—dismissed from the blue-ribbon council for his rash conduct, Bacon had capitalized on the wave of popularity generated by his unauthorized "Indian expedition" to win election to the House of Burgesses.

Overly optimistic as to his likely reception, or just plain foolhardy, Bacon now traveled to Jamestown by boat, accompanied by about forty friends and supporters. And he promptly was taken into custody. With the town soon aswarm with up to two thousand of his fellow frontiersmen and others agitating for his release, a strangely subdued Bacon went along with a humiliating public scenario conceived by Governor Berkeley. It began with Berkeley announcing: "If there be joy in the presence of angels over one sinner that repenteth, there is joy now, for we have a penitent sinner come before us. Call Mr. Bacon."

Bacon then submitted a written confession and promise to remain a dutiful subject in the future. He apparently then knelt as Berkeley, in priestlike manner, three times intoned: "God forgive you; I forgive you."

☆ ☆ ☆

Jamestown Visit II: But that wasn't the end of the affair. Two weeks later, by now totally unrepentant and backed by a force of five hundred men, Bacon burst into Jamestown again, this time for a stormy, very public confrontation with the seventy-year-old royal governor that set onlookers agog. When Bacon appeared with his following, described by some historians as no more than a rabble, Berkeley emerged from the statehouse to meet him.

As their confrontation unfolded, Bacon supposedly taunted Berkeley with a customary "dammne my blood" oath and demanded a commission to fight the Indians. "I came for a commission, and a commission I will have," Bacon apparently declared.

And at some point in their angry exchange, Berkeley tore open his blouse to bare his chest and shouted, "Here! Shoot me, 'fore God, fair Mark, shoot!" To which Bacon replied, "No, may it please Your Honor, we will not hurt a hair of your head nor of any man's."

Berkeley turned on his heel and stalked off, with members of the council straggling behind in confusion while delegates from the House of Burgesses stared from the statehouse windows at Bacon and the armed men ranged behind him. They no doubt were shocked to see the young rebel following the governor, posturing contemptuously behind his back and often tossing his hands from his sword to his hat and back. According to twentieth-century historian Wilcomb E. Washburn, the elderly Berkeley courageously offered to duel Bacon, saying, "For prevention of the efusion of Christian blood, let you and I decide this controversye by our swords."

But Bacon refused, saying he came not on personal grievances, but upon the grievance of the people. Moments later, as the shocked Burgesses took in the fact that the angry men with Bacon were aiming their guns at the delegates themselves, Bacon declared, "Dammne my blood. I'll kill Governor, Council, Assembly, and all."

Waving a white handkerchief from his window, one of the Colonial legislators shouted back, "You shall have it [the commission], you shall have it."

With the legislators in retreat, Berkeley then agreed to give Bacon his commission. In effect, Bacon had taken command. In short order, too, the Burgesses enacted legislation setting out the surprising measures known today as "Bacon's Laws." Considered by some historians to be the first glimmers of democracy in America, these measures strengthened local government powers, voter rights, and churchmen's rights, and were a blow to the aristocratic cabal gathered around Berkeley at Jamestown.

As an indication of the controversy still surrounding Bacon, one twentieth-century scholar compared the reforms of 1676 with adoption of the Magna Carta, while a dissenting Washburn asserted that Berkeley was a fair-minded governor, that he did *not* oppose the reforms, and that Bacon himself had *no* hand in their passage.

Meanwhile, hearing of an Indian presence not forty miles from Jamestown, Bacon had rushed off to begin organizing his Indian fighters.

☆ ☆ ☆

Jamestown Visit III: The confrontation with Governor Berkeley had taken place in June. Bacon's next critical visit to the Jamestown of 1676 didn't come until mid-September. In the interim, a civil war had swept through the Virginia Colony, the wealthiest, most populous English settlement in America. It had been a struggle between the forces loyal to Berkeley and Bacon's own following, and, amazingly, it had been the upstart English squire's son, just two years in America, who virtually had ruled the colony while Berkeley was forced to regroup aboard ships or across the Chesapeake Bay on the Eastern Shore. As Berkeley himself once complained, not five hundred of every fifteen hundred persons remained "untainted" by the rebellion bug.

Typical of the rebellion's back-and-forth movements, Berkeley had abandoned Jamestown, then retaken it from Bacon's men on September 1 without a fight—after defeating a small rebel "navy." Now, in mid-September, Bacon himself was leading a force intent on recapturing the Colonial capital. As his men approached, they built barricades for their own protection, but they hardly needed them. In an act that even Bacon's staunchest advocates find difficult to defend today, he forced captured wives of the Loyalists to line up in front of his men as a living shield of "white aprons." Berkeley attempted an attack once the women were withdrawn but was repulsed. The governor then fled again to his ships in the James River for a second respite on Virginia's Eastern Shore. Bacon took over Jamestown once more.

That very night he burned it down, with his two chief lieutenants, men of wealth, prestige, and political power—Richard Lawrence and former North Carolina Governor William Drummond—setting the torch to their own Jamestown homes. "The rogues will harbour here no more," said one.

Thus, at the hands of an Englishman rather than hostile Indians or more traditional enemies of the English such as the Spanish or the Dutch, the statehouse, the local church, and other Jamestown structures, among them two of its grandest homes, were destroyed or significantly damaged.

1 6 7 6
"Soldier, Statesman Saint"

The comma may be missing from the flowery language hand-chiseled into an undated marble tablet on a wall of the Gloucester County Courthouse, but the message remains clear enough.

Somebody remembered.

"Nathaniel Bacon," it says, "originator of his so-called rebellion, whose influence in the formation of the spirit of Americanism is immeasurable, the Washington of his day, popular patriot, whose magnanimity strongly contrasts with [Royal Governor Sir William] Berkeley's malignancy, a soldier, a statesman a saint."

One of several memorials on view in the old, single-story courthouse of brick (built in 1766), the marble tablet says it was erected "through the generosity" of unnamed friends and by authority of the circuit court. "Gloucester, who honors the noble dead, and cherishes the memory of kingly men, and in whose soil the body of Bacon is said to sleep, erects this monument to the great patriot."

Soldier, statesman, saint, and great patriot, somebody really did like the rebellious young Englishman who crisscrossed Gloucester in the turbulent year of 1676 and even died there, presumably at Gloucester's Thomas Pate house, with his final resting place a mystery that spawned rumor and speculation in Gloucester for many years—and still is unknown. By most old accounts, Bacon's followers buried a casket full of rocks in a Gloucester churchyard or plantation field to mislead a vengeful Governor Berkeley, then disposed of their hero's body elsewhere. Many historians think the rebel's body was weighted down with more rocks and consigned to the depths of the nearby York River.

Early in the twentieth century, however, the town of Gloucester removed an ancient "honeypod" tree that stood in the middle of the main street. Some say the tree once was a local gallows and later the location of a slave auction block; some say not. According to local historians, workmen found human bones beneath the tree—briefly reviving legends that Bacon secretly had been buried beneath the tree.

But the skeleton was of a man more than six feet tall. And with his remains was a Revolutionary period sword. For some, those two facts suggested he was a Hessian mercenary fighting for the British about the time of the Cornwallis surrender at Yorktown, across the York River from the county of Gloucester.

Some years ago, local historian Joseph J. Nicolson, a retired soil conservationist and former host at Colonial Williamsburg, recalled the honeypod story a bit differently. "They bulldozed the road," he said. "They did find a skeleton, but it was an Indian, a great tall man. He'd be a basketball player today. We took it up to the high school up there and put it together with pins. It was about 6-foot-7. The Indians were tall people, you know. That was 1926, I believe—'26 or '27. I graduated from high school in '27."

Nicolson and other county historians also confirmed that Bacon was thought to have met his end in the home of Major (and Doctor) Thomas Pate, located on a knoll next to today's U.S. Route 17, the "Historyland Trail," near Adner in the northern part of the county. "Up on that hilltop, he [Bacon] could watch," said Nicolson. "It covered two roads. He was very sick, probably of dysentery, and he died there, and nobody knows where he's buried."

The house in which he died apparently survived until the 1920s, but then was torn down.

Commenting on the disposal of Bacon's remains, the local historian added, "They [his followers] figured Governor Berkeley would dig him up and hang his body and hang it with chains, as was the custom."

Asserting that Berkeley did order the false grave opened, Nicolson also recalled, "They used to hang pirates at Gloucester Point and after they were dead, they hung a chain on their neck and left them there." The royal governor, he added, was vindictive . . . but, then, Bacon himself could be "absolutely ruthless" as well.

"The Gloucester people didn't think much of Bacon," said Nicolson, who prized an antique washstand thought to have come from the Governor Berkeley Room in an old Gloucester house where Berkeley once stayed during the rebellion. "I don't know why they called him [Bacon] a saint on that thing [the tablet in the courthouse]," Nicolson added. To him, Bacon simply burned to fight the Indians after they killed his overseer. To historian Wilcomb E. Washburn, for that matter, Bacon lost all claim to truly democratic impulses with his vows to "exterminate" Indians in general.

Also according to Nicolson, his fellow Gloucester residents "used to consider him [Bacon] the torchbearer of the Revolution," but by the 1970s they tended to share his own view that Bacon was "a reckless young man." Said history buff Nicolson: "He set things back right much."

Three centuries earlier, it also seems, the citizens of *Colonial* Gloucester wanted no part of the fighting on either side during Bacon's Rebellion—and they certainly resented the local plundering by his followers. The late Princeton historian Thomas Jefferson Wertenbaker, the leading twentieth-century advocate of Bacon's cause, related in his book *Torchbearer of the Revolution* that some of the rebel's lieutenants ran roughshod over Gloucester's local leadership during the summer of 1676. During that period, too, Berkeley sallied forth from Jamestown in an effort to put a stop to the raging civil war in his colony. He picked Gloucester as his battleground on the pretext of a phony petition "from the people of Gloucester" saying they needed the governor's protection from Bacon and his men.

Traveling to Gloucester on the north side of the York River, the royal governor attempted to rally local support for *his* cause. But when the Gloucester men realized they were being asked to fight their own countrymen, their fellow Colonials, they reportedly turned their backs and walked off muttering, "Bacon! Bacon! Bacon!" At that point, the aging Berkeley is said to have "fainted away on horseback in the field."

When Bacon heard of Berkeley's attempt to raise forces against him, the rebel also descended upon Gloucester, his Indian fighters in tow, only to find that Berkeley had fled to the safety of the Eastern Shore—giving Bacon undisputed control of the colony's mainland. But Bacon, too, was rebuffed when he assembled a militialike force at the Gloucester courthouse and asked the men to take an oath, not only against Berkeley as a "traitor and enemy of the public," but also to fight the king's own troops if need be. The Gloucestermen initially balked, but in a second meeting with Bacon they did subscribe to the pledge calling for defiance of the British Crown itself.

Meanwhile, Bacon and his men would rush to Gloucester on another occasion—this time in response to Indian attacks. As Wertenbaker began this story:

> The Indians [he doesn't say what tribe] were on the warpath again, this time not on the frontier, but in the very heart of Gloucester, one of the older counties. . . .
>
> Seven [whites] were killed within four miles of Tindal [now Gloucester] Point, across the York River from the present Yorktown, and eight near the county courthouse.
>
> The savages slowly roasted their wretched captives alive, cutting off pieces of flash and offering it to other victims to eat, pulling off their fingers and toenails, slitting them open and running their intestines around the trunks of trees.

The Indians responsible apparently struck from a lair in the depths of Dragon Swamp to the north. And Bacon, with no proof of their complicity, set out in pursuit of a Pamunkey band led by an Indian queen and thought to be hiding in the same swampland. When some of his own men tired of the days-long chase, Bacon was frank to tell them that if he failed in his Pamunkey expedition, his enemies would "insult and reflect on me; that my defence of the country is but pretended . . . and (as they already say) I have other Designs and make this but my Pretense and cloke."

As events turned out, Bacon's force did find the Pamunkeys, attacked, killed some, and took forty-five prisoners, while the Pamunkey queen escaped farther into the marshlands with a little boy. Members of the royal commission sent by King Charles II to investigate the Virginia rebellion reported that the queen had ordered her people *not* to fight the pursuing Englishmen. Therefore, the Indians "did not at all oppose, but fled, being followed by Bacon and his forces killing and taking them prisoners and looking for Plunder of the field."

The commissioners also cited an assertion by the Pamunkey queen that only eight of her followers were killed in the Dragon Swamp engagement, "though Bacon brag'd of many more to please and deceive the People, with a mighty conquest."

In any case, however one views Bacon's image as an Indian fighter, his Pamunkey "campaign" apparently ended Tidewater Virginia's "Indian troubles," quite aside from the probability that the real source of those "troubles" in 1676 had been a wandering war party of Susquehannocks. "Bacon's solid contribution was to clear the Tidewater of Indian menaces," wrote Southern historian Clifford Dowdey of Richmond. In Tidewater Virginia, Dowdey also said, "the age of the Frontier ended, for all practical purposes, with Bacon's rebellion and the aftermath."

Historian Washburn, on the other hand, thought there was no need for Bacon to fight the normally peaceable Pamunkey. The Indian raids ended not with Bacon's campaign against them, he argued, but with the departure of the more warlike Susquehannocks from the area. Either way, Indians of any stripe soon would hear no more of Nathaniel Bacon, who died of "the bloody flux" on October 26.

☆ ☆ ☆

Additional note: With Bacon gone, the insurrection he had led collapsed like a house of cards, but it still can be argued, however brief his moment in the sun, that Bacon had led the first American revolution. Not only did his movement display widespread appeal, but (a) he had shown elements of democratic leanings by pronouncing himself general "by consent of the people"; (b) he had talked of defying the king's own forces; and (c) he allegedly had discussed the possibility of an autonomous union of the several colonies—in effect, an independent state of *united* colonies.

On the other hand, few if any leaders of the *real* American Revolution held up Bacon as an example for their own contemporaries to follow. Then, too, not only Washburn but other modern historians have tended to dismiss Bacon's impact, among them Edmund S. Morgan, who wrote (in his book *American Slavery, American Freedom: The Ordeal of Colonial Virginia*): "It was a rebellion with abundant causes but without a cause: it produced no real program of reform, no revolutionary manifesto, not even any revolutionary slogans. Bacon had probably never intended it to turn into a rebellion."

In the aftermath, Royal Governor Berkeley temporarily resumed power in Jamestown and promptly executed about two dozen of Bacon's followers, most by hanging, but former North Carolina Governor William Drummond may have been drawn and quartered—torn apart by horses set off in different directions. Richard Lawrence, who like Drummond had fired his own Jamestown home when Bacon burned down the town, apparently set off into the wilds of the Virginia Colony and disappeared, his fate unknown.

Berkeley soon was recalled to England, presumably to explain himself to King Charles II, but he died soon after his return.

★

Jamestown Highlights

★

Many were the growth spurts, transformations, and other evolvements in the lifetime of Jamestown, where the continuous, uninterrupted history of modern Virginia—and thus America—began nearly four centuries ago. A few of the highlights* seen along the way:

1606

June: King James I of England grants London entrepreneurs operating as the Virginia Company a charter to establish an English settlement in the Chesapeake Bay region of North America.

December 20: On a Saturday, the *Susan Constant, Discovery,* and *Godspeed* embark from London with 104 to 108 settlers bound for the unknown in the New World.

1607

April 26: The English flotilla of three ships, commanded by veteran sailor Christopher Newport, enters Chesapeake Bay.

May 13: The ships tie up to the trees on Jamestown Island; the James River channel here, sixty miles from the mouth of Chesapeake Bay, is six fathoms deep.

May 14: "We landed all our men, which were set to worke about the fortification," wrote colonist George Percy later.

May 26: The colonists at Jamestown are attacked by two hundred Indians while John Smith, Percy, Christopher Newport, and others are away exploring the upper James River. One settler killed, eleven wounded.

---

*Based upon online timelines offered by the Association for the Preservation of Virginia Antiquities (APVA) (www.apva.org/history/timeline.html) and the Jamestowne Society (www.jamestowne.org/chronology.htm) as well as the book *Jamestown: An American Legacy* by Martha W. McCartney.

June 10: John Smith gives oath to serve on the council after being released from arrest by his fellow settlers.

June 25: Triangular fort made "sufficiently strong for these Savages" and "most of our Corne" sown, said Percy.

June 22: Newport sails back to England.

September 10: First council president is replaced after a brief, fractious tenure.

December: John Smith is captured by Powhatan's brother, Opechancanough; three men with Smith are killed.

1608

January: Only thirty-eight of the original settlers who landed at Jamestown the previous May 14 survive to greet Newport on his return with the "First Supply" and 120 new settlers. Powhatan, after intervention by his daughter Pocahontas, releases Capt. John Smith. Meanwhile, fire burns down "all the houses in the fort."

April 10: Newport sails again for England.

April 20: Francis Nelson arrives with another forty settlers.

September 10: John Smith is elected president of the council for a one-year term.

October: Newport is back with the Second Supply and more settlers, two of them women, Mrs. Thomas Forrest and her maid, Ann Burras, who by year's end will marry laborer John Laydon in the first wedding to take place in the Virginia Colony.

December: Newport's shuttle service resumes . . . back to England again.

1609

May 23: Virginia Company replaces the weak president-and-council system with a strong governor only *assisted* by a council.

August: Seven ships carrying settlers and supplies reach Jamestown after being scattered by a hurricane at sea; two hundred to three hundred men, women, and even children step ashore.

September 10: John Smith steps down as president, is replaced by Percy.

October: Badly burned by accidentally ignited gunpowder, John Smith returns to England for treatment and recuperation. He will visit and even name New England but never see Virginia's shores again.

Winter of 1609–10: the horrific "Starving Time."

1610

May 23: Deputy Governor Sir Thomas Gates finally arrives after being shipwrecked at Bermuda by the 1609 hurricane, finds only sixty survivors are left after the past winter's "Starving Time." Wrote newcomer William Strachey: "We found the palisades torn down, the ports open, the gates from off the hinges, and the empty houses . . . rent up and burnt, rather than the dwellers would step into the woods a stone's cast off from them to fetch other firewood [due to fear of Indian attack]." Another newly landed settler is John Rolfe.

June 7: Totally discouraged, Gates and the remaining settlers have decided to abandon Jamestown.

June 8: Proceeding downriver, they bump into Lord De la Warr's three incoming ships, and all proceed upriver to Jamestown after all.

August 9: English attack on Paspahegh Indian village, destruction of the Indian cornfields, capture of the Indian queen and her children—all then brutally killed.

1611

March 28: Lord De la Warr sets off for England, never to return; Percy left as deputy governor for the 150 settlers still on hand.

May: New deputy governor Sir Thomas Dale arrives with supplies and three hundred new pioneers; appalled by conditions at the settlement, he imposes martial law.

August: Gates returns from a voyage to England with another 280 souls, resumes governor's chair. He "happily arrived about the second of August, with six good Shippes, men, provisions and cattle," wrote Jamestown colonist Ralph Hamor.

This year also, colonist John Rolfe experiments with domestic and imported tobacco strains, the imported coming from Trinidad.

1612

John Rolfe harvests and begins to export improved tobacco.

1613

Spanish spy Diego de Molina reports the Jamestown fortifications are "so weak that a kick would break them down," while the men "are poorly drilled and not prepared for military action." Fortunately, the Spanish, busy in Florida and the Southwest, keep their distance and make no attempt to attack.

April: Capture of Pocahontas, who will be held at Jamestown.

June: John Rolfe sends first shipment of West Indian tobacco grown in Virginia.

Lord De la Warr (Thomas West) remains governor in name despite his long absence.

1614

February: Gates departs Virginia, leaving Dale as acting governor.

April 5: John Rolfe's historically celebrated marriage to the Indian maiden Pocahontas ushers in a period of better relations with Powhatan's Indian federation.

1616

Outflung settlements established; only fifty persons actually live on Jamestown Island, most as farmers.

May: Rolfe, Pocahontas, and son, Thomas, depart for London with Dale, leaving George Yeardley in charge of the Virginia Colony.

1617

Just before returning to Virginia, Pocahontas dies in England, where she had been introduced to royalty and visited with John Smith. Rolfe leaves their son with relatives and returns to Virginia alone.

1618

Lord De la Warr dies en route back to Virginia, and now newly knighted Sir George Yeardley returns from a London visit with the so-called "Great Charter," bringing English common law to the colony and allowing the election of local legislators called Burgesses, as well as private land ownership.

1619

A historic year: The first legislative assembly in America (and of the future nation) meets in a Jamestown church on behalf of Virginia's eleven settlements. Also, about twenty captive blacks are taken ashore from a visiting Dutch slave trader in exchange for provisions—not exactly slaves, they become indentured servants. "The popular conception of a race-based slave system did not fully develop until the 1680s," notes the APVA at www.apva.org/history/index.html.

1622

With Chief Powhatan now dead, his brother, Opechancanough, directs a concerted Indian attack against the white settlements up and down the James River—350 or more settlers are killed in the massacre—men, women, and children. Jamestown, home to nearly 120 colonists, is spared, thanks to an Indian boy's warning to an English planter.

Unrelated: John Rolfe, who had married Jane Peirce after losing Pocahontas, dies. Also, former Governor Yeardley, his wife, and three children live in a section of Jamestown Island called New Towne with their twenty-four servants, eight of them Africans.

1624

King's charter for the Virginia Company is revoked as Virginia becomes a Crown colony.

1632
War with Indians, and corn is scarce due to a major drought.

1633
Assembly establishes Middle Plantation, later the location of Williamsburg. A palisade is erected across the peninsula between the York and James Rivers to keep out the Indians.

1634
Virginia is administratively divided into eight shires, or counties—Henrico, James City, and Charles City among the familiar names still in use today. Jamestown is still the Colonial capital but also the seat of James City County.

1636
Virginia sends off twenty-one tobacco-loaded ships to London.

1641
Royal Governor Sir William Berkeley, former playwright, arrives to take up a long stewardship of the Virginia Colony.

1644
Second great massacre of the English settlers by Opechancanough's Indians, with their chief so elderly and infirm he allegedly was carried into battle on a litter with sticks propping his eyes open. Four hundred to five hundred settlers killed. Opechancanough is then captured, jailed at Jamestown, and subsequently murdered.

1648
Virginia population is now about "15,000 English and 300 Negroes," says the Jamestowne Society. An estimated two dozen or more ships a year put in at Jamestown.

1653
Berkeley is in hiatus, and Virginia governs itself during the rule of Oliver Cromwell and his Parliamentarians in England.

1656
Friendly Pamunkey and Chickahominy Indians join with the colonists in the battle of Bloody Run against six hundred to seven hundred other Indians who are blamed for raids against frontier planters in the area of today's Richmond. Pamunkey leader Totopotomy killed.

1660
Monarchy in the form of Charles II is restored in England, and Berkeley is reaffirmed as Virginia governor by the House of Burgesses.

1667
Dutch warships sailing up the James River burn six ships.

1672

By Berkeley's estimate, Virginia's population is now forty-eight thousand, "with 6,000 indent[ured] servants and 2,000 Negroes," reports the Jamestowne Society.

1676

In response to unchecked Indian raids on frontier planters, English squire's son Nathaniel Bacon Jr. leads unauthorized foray against basically friendly Indians. Branded a rebel and outlaw after only two years in the colony, Bacon leads "Bacon's Rebellion" against elderly Royal Governor Berkeley, controls mainland Virginia for a time, and burns the capital Jamestown to the ground before his death from a raging fever in October, followed by collapse of his rebellion.

1677

While a royal commission investigates causes of the rebellion, Governor Berkeley hangs Bacon's confederates and sails home to England, never to return because he dies soon after.

1695

Foundation stone is laid for the future College of William and Mary at Middle Plantation, soon to become Williamsburg.

1698

Statehouse at Jamestown burns down; capital shifts to Williamsburg.

1700

Assembly meets at the College of William and Mary.

1750s

Jamestown is slowly crumbling and disappearing into the ground, while two families, the Travises and the Amblers, turn the historic islandlike peninsula into farmland.

1780s

American and British prisoners are exchanged here during the American Revolution.

1781

French Admiral de Grasse lands three thousand troops here to join in the pending siege of Yorktown on the York River side of the peninsula.

1861

Confederates occupy the island, build an earthen fort near the old church site to stop Union ships sailing up the James toward Richmond.

1893

Jamestown owners Mr. and Mrs. Edward Barney donate 22.5 acres, including the site of the 1639 church tower, to the APVA. "By this time James River erosion had eaten away the island's western shore," the APVA says at its Internet site. "Visitors began to conclude that the site of the James Fort lay completely underwater." Not so, it turns out—recent archaeological digs have uncovered remains of the fort and associated artifacts on dry land after all.

1900

A seawall is built with federal assistance to prevent further erosion.

1907

Jamestown Exposition is held at Norfolk to celebrate the three-hundredth anniversary of Jamestown.

1934

The rest of Jamestown is acquired by the National Park Service (NPS); Jamestown is to become part of the Colonial National Historical Park and to be jointly operated by the APVA and the NPS.

⭐ Part 2 ⭐
Eighteenth Century

Major Washington's Steadfastness

Short and deep was the trench dug into the rough wagon road on a July morning. When all was ready, the slain British general's body was lowered down. Selecting the spot and conducting the abbreviated service was a tall young officer, a Colonial, still shaken by the ravages of fever and battle.

The officer being laid to rest, said the same "Colonial" many years later, "was generous and disinterested, but plain and blunt in his manner, even to rudeness."

Was it not also rude, then, to form up the retreating column and march it forward—all infantry, all wagons—right over the slain man's hastily filled-in grave?

Not if the purpose was to keep his body well hidden from an advancing enemy. And what a prize he would have been, even dead, for the French and their Indian allies, still exultant over their incredible victory of five days before.

Nor did they ever find him. The road remained; it became known as the National Road (and in more recent days as U.S. Route 40), and in time it would carry thousands upon thousands of emigrants to St. Louis and environs, their jumping-off place for the trek westward, beyond established civilization.

He remained there, in the road he and his troops had labored so mightily to widen, that it might accommodate heavy, unwieldy cannon and wagon upon wagon of supplies for his brightly uniformed army as it inched slowly westward toward the forks of the Ohio back in 1755.

He remained only until the early years of the nineteenth century, actually. At that point, workmen making repairs in the road one day came across a buried skeleton. Tattered bits, insignia of rank, seemed to identify the remains of the British major general.

"We shall better know how to deal with them another time," he had muttered hours, or perhaps just minutes, before his death the evening of July 13, 1755, a mile or two west of Fort Necessity at Great Meadows in western Pennsylvania.

Plain and blunt he, indeed, had been, even brave to the very end. But stubborn and blind to wise advice as well.

Hurry on to Fort Duquesne at the site of today's Pittsburgh, the Colonials had urged him, hurry before the French can reinforce it.

Use packhorses rather than get bogged down trying to take wagons across this rough country, urged one Colonial in particular, the general's volunteer aide-de-camp, George Washington.

But no, Maj. Gen. Edward Braddock, commander of all British forces in North America, had been brought up to fight in the European style. Surely his regulars could hack out a twelve-foot-wide road for the wagons he must have. They could, and they did, but only at the cost of moving at a snail's pace toward the awaiting French and their Indian allies. Then, on that last day, while twice fording the twisting Mononga-hela River near the French fort, what possibly could be wrong with openly marching the men in rank, full uniform, parade-ground style?

Why, it might even scare off the French and their Indian allies to see his advance guard of nearly fourteen hundred men . . . to see, and then to hear the mighty tramp of their feet.

Ironically, with a much smaller force at their disposal, the French holding the fort were quite ready to pass up a pitched battle with Braddock's armada of the wilderness. They would settle for a bit of harassment from the flanks. Unexpectedly, however, the "harassment" from hidden positions behind trees, rocks, and even clumps of grass, accompanied by the banshee war whoops of the Indians, threw Brad-dock's marching troops into complete panic.

Some were so undone they formed in clumps, ignored the orders of their officers, and fired blindly through the smoke of battle, often strik-ing their own men instead of the foe. Others simply ran, after flinging down weapons, even pieces of clothing that might slow them up. "They broke and ran as sheep pursued by dogs," said Washington later.

The officers responded bravely, by all accounts, but they were prime targets from the start, and sixty or more soon were gunned down. Braddock himself, before his fatal wound that July 9, had three to four horses shot out from under him, by various accounts. Young George Washington came home with four bullet holes in his own clothing and hat . . . but none in himself.

An onlooking hostile Indian, according to one story, was amazed to see how long and actively the tall Virginian rode back and forth on one mount after another, exhorting his men, all the while a prominent target . . . and yet sailing through the firestorm unscathed.

The British regulars and their officers clearly looked down upon the Colonial militiamen contributing to Braddock's army . . . but by virtually all accounts, it was the "regulars," the professional soldiers, who ran first, and the provincials who held the best. Most accounts also credit Washington, a former lieutenant colonel of the Virginia militia, with helping to restore *some* order among the demoralized troops. Indeed, he was a whirlwind of activity. Said an onlooker named Paulding: "I saw him take hold of a brass field-piece as if it had been a stick. He looked like a fury; he tore the sheet-lead from the touch-hole; he placed one hand on the muzzle, the other on the breach; he pulled with this, and he pushed with that, and wheeled it around as if it had been nothing."

And all this after Washington had been sick for a good ten days with a raging fever! Still weak and unsteady, he had ridden a supply wagon to rejoin Braddock's column only the day before the battle . . . and yet, with two horses shot out from under him, he apparently proved the most outstanding (albeit, unwounded) officer on the battle scene. As one further service, he found the cart and team that would carry the fatally wounded Braddock from the battleground.

Not quite so well known is the ordeal Washington faced that same night. For it was young George whom the dying Braddock sent flying to the rear, where Col. Thomas Dunbar had been following Braddock's vanguard with a slow supply train and more soldiers. Dunbar's nearby presence, of course, offered hope of safety in case of enemy pursuit.

Sent first to rally scattered troops in the immediate area, Washington hadn't gone far before he overtook another historical figure of some note—Lt. Col. Thomas Gage, who twenty years later would achieve lasting notoriety as the British commanding general in Boston who sent troops into Lexington and Concord, Massachusetts . . . with revolution and American independence resulting. Oddly, at Monongahela, Gage had commanded the most forward element of Braddock's column, and now he was somewhat to the rear . . . but reorganizing about eighty men.

Soon it was dark. Washington and two guides were moving to the rear . . . to Dunbar. "Now the blackness was so overwhelming that if the movement of the horses or the snapping of bushes under their hoofs indicated the animals had gone off the trail, the guides had to stop, dismount, and feel long stretches of the ground until they reached the powdered earth, the ruts and the tree stumps of the road," wrote Douglas Southall Freeman in his biography, *George Washington*.

Eerily, the woods on either side "were vocal with the misery of men"—men who had fled the battle scene hours before. "It was amazing how far into the woods some of the soldiers wounded early in the battle had made their way."

But George Washington couldn't stop to help any one of them. "To stop to succor one man was to be false to hundreds," noted biographer Freeman. George Washington never did forget that night's terrible ride, its heart-piercing groans and cries, he himself said years later.

While the two sections of Braddock's ill-fated army safely did rejoin that next day, July 10, Washington caught up on his sleep after his twenty-four hours of nonstop action. The eleventh and twelfth were occupied with organizing full-scale retreat, destroying supplies, gathering in the stragglers, tending the wounded. It had been a setback, a disaster, but the British were destined to win the French and Indian War.

Steadily slipping away from life, meanwhile, Braddock turned over official command to Dunbar. But it was to Colonial Colonel Washington that he reportedly bestowed a favorite horse, along with a manservant named Bishop. And after Braddock died the evening of July 13, it was Washington who said the parting words and buried his British general in the middle of the road the morning of the fourteenth. Such are the ironies of life . . . of history as well.

1755
The Gang's All Here

Trivia question for the American or Virginia history buff: Where and when were the incomparable George Washington, pioneer *extraordi-*

naire Daniel Boone, Washington's backwoods guide Christopher Gist, Revolutionary War hero Daniel Morgan, future American Gens. Horatio Gates and Charles Lee, and future British Gen. Thomas Gage, plus many others of slightly less historical import, all gathered at one time, at one spot, for one very dramatic moment in American history?

And every one of them lucky to have survived their historically spectacular joint encounter.

At least twenty truly historical figures all told, and, as time passed, what further history they did make! As just one for-instance, suppose British Lieutenant Colonel Gage (please see previous story) had been killed on this dark day in 1755. Who, then, would have commanded the British forces in North America from a base in Boston twenty years later, in 1775? Who, then, would have sent the British troops into Lexington and Concord, Massachusetts, thus setting off a powder keg of Colonial resentments that quickly escalated into a full-blown revolution? Would another British general serving in his place have done the same? And if not, the effect upon American history? Or, for that matter, upon George Washington's future résumé?

Or take Daniel Boone, future member of the Virginia General Assembly, who would be captured by the British in Charlottesville during that same Revolution, but, more important of course, the pioneer who created the Wilderness Road into Kentucky, future county of Virginia, as pathfinder for thousands of settlers headed west. Yes, present with G. W., Gage, et al., as a twenty-one-year-old wagoner, he also could have died at this extraordinary gathering of historical figures.

Gens. Horatio Gates and Charles Lee (he of Virginia but British-born), of course, were destined to fight under Washington in the Revolutionary War . . . but not without considerable friction between them and the commander in chief. Gates, best known as the victor at Saratoga, New York, over "Gentleman Johnny" Burgoyne in 1777, was the apparently willing choice of those in the so-called Conway cabal hoping to replace Washington as commander of the Continental army. Lee, another resentful general with a head full of pretensions, was sacked at the battle of Monmouth, New Jersey, for countermanding Washington's specific orders. And just as well, too, since he all too willingly discussed anti-American strategies with his British captors during a short stay with them as a prisoner of war.

Virginia's own Daniel Morgan, on the other hand, was true and blue all the way as a minor but highly effective Revolutionary War leader. A young teamster in 1755, just like Daniel Boone, but only nineteen years of age, Morgan two decades later was picked by Washington to lead a regiment of the Continental army's best rifle shots. In that role, he took part in Benedict Arnold's foray against Quebec and in the battle of Saratoga—where he no doubt frequently rubbed shoulders with his old acquaintance Gates from 1755, now, in 1777, a fellow *American.*

Morgan's crowning achievement, historically, came the day he humiliated the marauding British raider Banastre Tarleton and his dreaded dragoons in the battle of Cowpens, South Carolina.

Still another to survive the gathering of 1755, two decades before the Revolution, was a little-known soldier with an odd connection, later, to George Washington. This, as recalled by Robert C. Alberts in a sprightly article for the February 1961 issue of *American Heritage* magazine, was Capt. Roger Morris, "who was wounded and carried back to Virginia on a litter." Three years later, and presumably recovered, Morris married "the celebrated Mary Eliza ('Polly') Philipse of New York—the great heiress whom Washington also courted." Unfortunately all around, however, Washington's comrade-in-arms from 1755, along with his in-laws, remained loyal to the British cause in the Revolution—"and their lands were confiscated."

Also unfortunate would be the later adventures of young Capt. Adam Stephens, who had been with Washington at the surrender of Fort Necessity just the year before the gathering of 1755. A Continental army major general under Washington in the Revolutionary War, Stephens would be "dismissed from the service" for being drunk during the battle of Germantown on the outskirts of Philadelphia.

Yet another now widely forgotten "alumnus" of the 1755 entourage was Washington's future land agent William Crawford, destined to serve in six major Revolutionary War engagements, survive those, and achieve the rank of colonel—but destined also to be captured in a 1782 foray against Indian allies of the British in Ohio and die horribly at their hands . . . burned at the stake.

Also somewhat obscure today is John Neville, a twenty-four-year-old militia private from Virginia at the time of the fateful encounter of 1755. Twenty years later, he would be a militia colonel commanding Fort Pitt—close to the very spot where all these historical gentlemen shared their traumatic experience in 1755. A brigadier general by the end of the Revolution, Neville later became a member of the Pennsylvania Council, "which ratified the Federal Constitution." As a natural outgrowth of that work, he also served in the Pennsylvania state constitutional convention.

His son Presley, it might also be mentioned, married one-time teamster Daniel Morgan's daughter Nancy.

Also, on a personal rather than a strictly military level, a busy participant in the debacle of 1755—for that it was, a debacle, with sixty-two of the ninety-six British and American officers present killed or wounded—was a doctor, George Washington's longtime friend and personal physician in later years, James Craik. For that matter, he would be at Washington's bedside when the great man died forty-four years later. Then, too, on hand as commissary general for the Virginia militia was another doctor, Thomas Walker, close neighbor in Albemarle County to Peter Jefferson, father to future Founding Father and President Thomas Jefferson. Walker, in fact, became the guardian of young Thomas after Peter Jefferson died in 1757. Not only that, two decades later it was at Walker's Castle Hill estate that Banastre Tarleton and his dragoons briefly stopped on their way to Charlottesville one Revolutionary War morning in hopes of seizing outgoing *Governor* Thomas Jefferson and the retreating Virginia General Assembly. The delay at Dr. Walker's may have been all that was needed for Jefferson and most assembly members to escape Tarleton's snare—*most* except for assembly member Daniel Boone (and six fellow legislators).

Also personal, in a way, was the relationship between Washington and George Croghan, later to be known as the frontier's "King of the Indian Traders." The two Georges came out of the great defeat of 1755 publicly feuding over Croghan's role in the affair as captain of the friendly Indian scouts.

In addition to the British and Colonial American personnel in attendance for the same battle in 1755 were, of course, their enemies, the French and assorted Indian allies, with Chief Pontiac possibly among the latter. One of the British survivors, by the way, would be Lt. Henry Gladwin, who eight years later commanded a small garrison that withstood a six-month siege against Detroit by Pontiac and his fierce Indian warriors.

Still others went on from the engagement of 1755 to other things, of course, but in the main those named here were the real history makers and their subalterns. And what was the single, searing experience they all had shared in the deep woods of western Pennsylvania close to the site of today's city of Pittsburgh? It was the terrible defeat of British Gen. Edward Braddock and his twelve-hundred-man force by a relative handful of French and Indians.

Interestingly enough, the Virginia militia's George Washington and British officer Thomas Gage, later to be adversaries at Boston, shared another distinction of some dubiousness. Gage, it can be argued, set off the American Revolution by his now rash-looking dispatch of troops to Lexington and Concord . . . even though he was only following orders from England to use force, if deemed necessary, to discourage the more troublesome Colonials confronting their British masters. And George Washington, quite arguably, kicked off the worldwide French and Indian War (also known as the Seven Years' War) by ambushing a small French contingent in 1854, also in the western Pennsylvania woods. As a result of Gage's action, the British lost their American colonies, and the United States of America came into being; whereas Washington's clash with the French, declared author Alberts, "started the Seven Years' War, involved England, Prussia, Germany, Austria, and Sweden, devastated Germany, swept across India, and cost a million lives."

☆ ☆ ☆

Additional note: As for George Washington's faithful guide Christopher Gist, here was a progenitor of historic figures reaching down through the ages, even unto Horace Greeley's ill-fated presidential campaign of 1882 against U. S. Grant. How so? Well, Gist, forty-nine at the time of Braddock's defeat in 1755, soon was appointed Indian agent for the South, but died of smallpox in 1759 while "returning from a mission to win support of the Cherokee Indians for the British." Still, his direct descendants, wrote Alberts in his *Braddock's Alumni* article, included "the builder of Blair House in Washington and the Postmaster General in Lincoln's Cabinet." On the opposite side of the Civil War divide was Confederate Brig. Gen. States Rights Gist of South Carolina, who "was killed at the Battle of Franklin, Tennessee." And then, too, as yet another direct descendant, there was U.S. Sen. Benjamin Gratz Brown, the now obscure Liberal Republican from Kansas who was the vice-presidential candidate on the Horace Greeley ticket of 1872.

✯

1755

Incredible Wilderness Trek

✯

In a manuscript preserved at the University of Virginia, the son of Mary Draper Ingles begins the story of her capture by Indians with the observation that few, "if any," white families had settled on the New River west of the Allegheny Mountains before his parents established a homestead at Draper's Meadows about 1750.

All was well for several years, although parties of Shawnee frequently passed by, en route to "depredations" committed against the Cawtaba to the south. "However, this happy state of things did not last long."

The Indians, adds the John Ingles manuscript in eighteenth-century language, "at length commenced a warfair on the fronteer settlements & at a time it was little expected a partey of Shawnees fell in upon my fathers family and an uncles familey [that of John Draper] . . . which lived at the same place and killed several and took the balance prisoners, to wit, my mother and her 2 children Thos. 4 years & George 2 & Aunt Draper [John's wife, Bettie] & others."

Killed in the Draper's Meadows Massacre of 1755 were two male settlers, an infant child, and an older woman—narrator John's maternal grandmother Draper.

Today, the site of the Indian attack is a piece of the Virginia Tech campus at Blacksburg. In 1755, the same year as British General Braddock's defeat at the hands of the French and their Indian allies near future Pittsburgh, Draper's Meadows was a barely cleared settlement on the edge of a vast wilderness stretching westward seemingly forever.

When the Indians struck that grim day, the men of the multifamily settlement were busy harvesting crops in a nearby field and "new [knew] nothing of the attack untill it was intirely out of Their power to render any survice to the familey."

By then, the Indian party had plunged back into the deep forest together with the four family members they had seized—John's mother, Mary, age twenty-three; his brothers Thomas, age four, and George, age two, and his aunt Bettie Draper, who was nursing an agonizing gunshot wound in one arm.

While young Mary, apparently pregnant at the time, was destined to make frontier history in relatively short time, her sister-in-law Bettie remained with her captors for six years before her husband, John, would find her and pay a ransom for her freedom. Mary's child Thomas also would be freed by ransom . . . but not for thirteen long years. Young George, soon separated from his mother, disappeared from sight. A man named Henry Lenard (or Leonard), also taken prisoner by the Shawnees, was another who would vanish from the historical record.

Mary Draper Ingles would prove to be another story altogether.

But first, was she pregnant at the moment of her capture? According to West Virginia's nineteenth-century historian John P. Hale (her own great-grandson), she gave birth to a daughter on the third night of travel west with her Indian captors. And yet, the manuscript account composed by her son John many years after her capture makes no mention of her pregnancy or the birth of a sibling.

In his comprehensive frontier history *Trans-Allegheny Pioneers*, however, historian Hale treats the child's birth in captivity as fact. He notes that the two young frontier wives, sisters-in-law, were fortunate to be traveling together, since each could render the other services "as nurses, as occasion required."

The Shawnee party did not halt or even slow up in deference to the women—or the newborn child—but continued west at a fast pace. Still, the women and small children were allowed to ride horses, some of them stolen from the Draper's Meadows settlement itself.

While the exact route taken by the Indians is not known today, it is presumed that they followed the New River westward into today's West Virginia, then crossed into Kentucky Territory to reach the mighty Ohio River. Still pressing westward, they would have crossed both the Big and Little Sandy Rivers, plus the Licking and Big Miami Rivers, before at last coming to a stop at a major Shawnee village southwest of Cincinnati, Ohio, but still in the Kentucky of today.

Along the way, the war party and its captives had stopped to make salt at a spring above the mouth of Campbells Creek in West Virginia's Kanawha Valley. "After several days of resting, feasting, and salt-making," wrote historian Hale, "the party again loaded up their pack-horses and resumed their onward march down the Kanawha and down the Ohio to the capital town of the Shawnees, at the mouth of the Son-hioto, or Scioto River, which they reached just one month after leaving the scene of the massacre and capture at Draper's Meadows."

Here, Bettie Draper and Henry Lenard were forced to run a gauntlet of Indians striking at them, but Mary and her children, for reasons unknown, were spared that punishment. Worse in the long run for Mary, however, she was separated from her two boys and her sister-in-law. Only her infant child stayed with Mary, according to Hale's account. Young Thomas, it seems, was carried to territory near future Detroit, Bettie Draper to future Chillicothe, Ohio, and young George to "somewhere in the interior, not . . . now known," wrote Hale.

Two or three weeks after the war party's arrival at the Shawnee village, a party of Indians took Mary and other prisoners—among them an elderly "duch" woman—on a salt-making visit to Big Bone Lick, about 150 miles west of the Scioto and a short distance up Big Bone Creek from the Ohio River in future Boone County, Kentucky. This was a spot to become famous in early America for its mastodon bones, samples of which Lewis and Clark sent to President Thomas Jefferson before setting off on their expedition into the American West in 1804. The county, of course, was named for early pioneer and woodsman Daniel Boone.

Here, wrote Hale, Mary Ingles, through no desire of her own, became the first white woman known to have traveled "within the bounds of [future] Ohio, Indiana, or Kentucky, all then still parts of Virginia." (The same would apply to the old Dutch woman.)

And it was here, at Big Bone Lick, that Mary Ingles laid her plans for escape—together with her elderly companion, who had been captured somewhere in western Pennsylvania. Fortunately for Mary Ingles, she was both wilderness-wise and in excellent physical shape, thanks to an upbringing largely on the frontier. According to her descendant Hale, the young mother "could stand on the ground, beside her horse, and leap into the saddle unaided," or "stand on the floor and jump over a chair-back." Born of Irish parents in Philadelphia in 1732, the year of George Washington's birth, she had accompanied her father and mother in a move to Irishman James Patton's Pattonsville settlement at the headwaters of the James River on the Virginia frontier. Her restless father, George Draper, bent upon a move into the wilderness itself, one day entered the nearby forest . . . and never came back, his fate unknown.

At that point, wrote Luther F. Addington in the Southwest Virginia Historical Society's *Historical Sketches of Southwest Virginia* of 1967, Mary's mother, Eleanor, "not wanting to be left alone at Pattonsville, followed some of her neighbors to a new homeplace on the New River, later to be called Draper's Meadows." There, she raised her two children, Mary and John. And there also, in 1750, eighteen-year-old Mary Draper married William Ingles, son of another pioneering family, "their wedding being the first one on this frontier."

The day of Mary's capture five years later had begun normally enough for the settlers of Draper's Meadows. James Patton, the same of Pattonsville and commander of the area militia, happened to be visiting to deliver gunpowder and lead. He was sitting at a table writing, his broadsword right beside him. William Ingles, Mary's husband, "was in the fields some distance from the house, looking over his grain field, which was to be harvested on the morrow." William Preston, a nephew of Patton's, would have been present but had been sent to Sinking Creek to ask settler Philip Laycock to join in the harvesting work the next day.

From a vantage point outside the house, John Draper's wife, Bettie, was the first to spot the approaching Shawnees. Rushing inside, she shouted an alarm and swooped up her sleeping baby, then dashed out the opposite side in hopes of escaping. But the Indians saw her, and one fired a shot that broke her right arm. She ran on, still clutching her baby, but in seconds, the raiders were upon her. "The child was brutally brained against the end of a house log and left lying on the ground," said Addington.

Inside, meanwhile, Colonel Patton had leaped up, sword in hand, and chopped down two of the attackers before succumbing to a ball fired by a third.

It was all over in minutes. Killed on the spot were Patton, Mary's mother, Eleanor, a man named Casper Barrier, and Bettie's baby. In addition, a James Cull was left wounded, and the Indians made off with Mary, the wounded Bettie Draper, Henry Lenard, and Mary's two little boys as captives. First, though, they "gathered up all the guns and ammunition and all the household goods they could get." They also set the settlement's few houses ablaze.

That's when William Ingles realized what was happening. "Seeing the flames and smoke, he started running toward home, hoping he could be of assistance in protecting his family." But when he drew close enough, he saw that the raiding Indians "were loading plunder on the horses, were well armed; and he stopped." He could see that his wife and others were prisoners, and all the settlement's horses were being taken as well.

Before he could react, he was spotted by the Indians. Immediately, two tomahawk-wielding Shawnees set out after him. Dashing into the nearby woods, he fell while jumping over a log—"and there he lay while the pursuers ran around the roots of the upturned tree instead of jumping over it as he had." As a result, "when the Indians passed on, still looking for him, he eluded them by running in the opposite direction."

Mary, though, would not learn his fate for many months, since the last she saw of her husband, he was entering the woods with the two Indians hard on his heels.

For the next few hours, all she would know would be even more horror and cruelty, since the Indian raiding party was not yet through with the area's white settlers. "Some distance out on their trail," added the Addington account, "the Indians stopped at the home of Philip Barger, an old white-haired man, attacked him, and cut off his head. They put the head into a bag and carried it to the house of Philip Laybrook on Sinking Creek, where they gave it to Mrs. Laybrook, telling her to look into the bag and she'd see one of her acquaintances."

Fortunately for Philip Laybrook, he and Colonel Patton's nephew William (Preston) already were on their way back to Draper's Meadows to help with the harvesting—they missed the Indian war party altogether. Once organized, the male settlers set off in pursuit of the raiders, but too late to catch up.

Three days into the Indian party's flight westward, according to West Virginia historian Hale's account, nature caught up with Mary Draper Ingles. She gave birth to a baby girl—"far from habitation, in the wild forest, unbounded by walls, with only the bosom of mother earth for a couch." Ordinarily, Hale surmised, the Indians would have killed the baby rather than risk any delay, but in this case they might have wanted to keep the young mother relatively happy in order to demand a ransom for her safe return later. Perhaps they also figured the infant would keep her too preoccupied even to *think* of escape.

Still, they did insist upon resuming their travel the very next day, with Mary holding her newborn as she rode horseback. At the salt-making stop on the banks of Campbells Creek, noted Addington, "Mary proved very adept at salt-making, and her skill, the Indians knew, would prove of value to them after they reached their Ohio River homes." As the party then resumed the trek west, Mary's heart sank, for every step covered was a step farther from home . . . and possible rescue.

Then came her unhappy sojourn at the Shawnee war party's home village at the mouth of the Scioto on the north side of the Ohio. Soon after the gauntlet run for all the captive adults except Mary, the prisoners were divided up—Bettie to go with "a hunter who said he'd take her farther north"; little George, screaming and trying to twist away as he was given to a group going elsewhere; four-year-old Tom, carried off by a third group, "and away they all went, leaving Mary sitting on a log, the baby in her lap." This had to be her worst moment yet.

Her situation hadn't improved much when French traders passed through, with bright, checkered fabric as the most prized of the bartering items they offered the Indians. Mary, "who had long been adept with a needle and thread," saw a chance to ingratiate herself by making shirts for her captors—"as she turned them out, the Indians would hoist them atop sticks and run through the town proudly showing them."

It was a few weeks after her start on the shirts that the Indians announced the foray 150 miles down the Ohio by canoe to make salt, with Mary, her baby girl, and the old Dutch woman all included. The journey took the Indians and their captives down the river to Big Bone Creek, "which flows into the Ohio from the south," then up the creek for three and a half miles to the salt lick itself. Once established in Boone County, they were just a few miles downriver from the Cincinnati of today . . . but probably five hundred miles from Mary's home at Draper's Meadows.

And it was autumn. The fall leaves were coming down; the nights were chilly.

More and more frequently, Mary's thoughts turned to escape. After all, she and her older companion often were left alone in camp, boiling their salt for hours at a time while the Indians went out to hunt.

Still, what would they do for food? How would they travel such a long distance? "There'd be streams to cross and gorges to climb through up where the Great Kanawha [River] roared through the narrows of the Alleghenies," Addington noted. And if they failed and were caught, warned the older woman, it would mean burning at the stake.

Worst of all, Mary couldn't carry a weeks-old infant on such a perilous journey—she would have to leave her baby behind . . . leave the tiny girl and just hope one of the Shawnee women would adopt her. On the other hand, Mary reasoned, if she stayed and made no attempt to escape, she and the child faced a totally uncertain future as captives in an alien world. Wrote Addington: "They both might die."

The same applied to the "duch" woman, who finally was persuaded to join Mary in the ploy of leaving camp for a longer period every day to gather grapes and nuts . . . but always returning unbidden, albeit a bit later each time. Then came the day when, hoping for the best, Mary carefully wrapped up her baby one last time and, together with the older woman, casually walked into the forest . . . this time never to return, never to see her child again, her ultimate fate to be unknown.

The two women, each carrying a tomahawk and a single blanket, made their way down Big Bone Creek toward its confluence with the Ohio, then turned eastward.

They spent that first night sleeping in piles of leaves and wrapped in their blankets. Back in the Indian camp, meanwhile, the Indians thought they merely had strayed off, become lost, or run afoul of dangerous wild animals, Mary's husband, William, would learn years later at an Indian treaty conference. The Indians did search the path the women were thought to have taken and fired their guns to give the "lost" women a rallying point. "They gave up the search that night, however, and did not renew it the next day," wrote historian Hale. "They did not at all suspect that the women had attempted to escape."

Resuming their trek the next day, the two fugitives first had to retrace the 150 miles of their captors' route from the main Shawnee village at the mouth of the Scioto. They trudged along the Ohio River for days simply to get that far, but of course with no intention of revisiting the village itself. They ate nuts, grapes, and papaws, wrote Addington, "and occasionally they found a small corn patch and they chewed raw kernels and swallowed them."

They eventually came across an abandoned cabin next to a corn patch and stopped to nibble and rest. "And while lying there," wrote Addington, "Mary let her mind survey the rugged mountains between this point and her home. She knew she must cross the Big Sandy before reaching the mouth of the Kanawha; besides, there were smaller rivers to cross. There'd be no canoes, and the rivers would be so deep that neither she nor the old woman could wade them. When rested and strong, Mary could have swum the Big Sandy; but now, in her weakened condition, she knew an attempt would mean suicide. Yes, she was a month from home in time and already they were weak; besides, winter was coming on and there would be danger in sleeping out because of the likelihood of contracting pneumonia. Food would be more difficult to find, for edible plants already were dying from frostbite. Had Mary known the trails over the mountains, many miles would have been subtracted from the long way home; but she didn't know them and her only hope was to follow the streams."

If she felt a bit bleak at the thought of the grim odds stacked against them, the very next morning produced a surprise that improved their prospects tenfold. It was a horse, an old but usable horse, grazing near their corn patch.

Stuffing ears of corn into sacks fashioned from their blankets, they loaded up their gallant steed and marched on east, each woman alternately riding or walking. "There were times when both women would have to walk and one lead the horse, for the terrain was too rough for a person to be safe on horseback."

After a time they passed the future sites of Ashland and Catlettsburg, Kentucky, near the western border of today's West Virginia. They wasted time and energy searching for a fordable crossing on the Big Sandy, but at last did find one. Fortunately, it had been a dry autumn and the rivers were low. Not so fortunately, this was where they had to abandon their horse.

The two women crossed the river on "a big drift of wood," but when they returned and tried to lead the horse across, his legs broke through the wood, leaving him with "his feet in the rushing water below and his belly resting on top of the drift." The frightened animal tried to extricate himself, but couldn't—"and there he lay, helpless."

Unable to help, and still fearful for their own safety, the two women trudged on and on, always to the east. Their feet bare, their clothing torn to tatters, they continued to subsist on nuts, edible roots, and remnants of their corn.

And they fought. Discouraged, the older woman "vilified Mary for having persuaded her to leave the Indians." Mary usually was able to calm her companion with encouragement to keep going—certainly a far better choice now than returning to the Indians or just giving up in the middle of the wilderness—but this was only the first sign of a smoldering resentment that in the end would force the two women to go their separate ways.

They spent some of the ever-chillier nights in hollow logs, under cliffs whenever possible . . . or in the open when there was no other choice. "Their slow, plodding steps brought them to the mouth of the Kanawha." That meant perhaps two hundred more miles to go.

Already past future Huntington, West Virginia, they now passed the site of Charleston, the state's future capital.

Doggedly placing one foot in front of the other, they plodded on along the Kanawha River. They inched along, but not in any companionable way. Far from it. The older woman was so desperate, in such a black mood, that she threatened to kill Mary and eat her. Finally, despite Mary's efforts to humor and cajole her, she attacked Mary outright. They struggled, feebly to be sure . . . Mary managed to twist away and hide under a riverbank until her crazed companion gave up looking for her and stumbled on alone.

Relieved for the moment, Mary had the good luck to find an abandoned canoe filled with debris. She scooped it out and pushed her way across the river with a fallen tree branch, thus separating herself from the other woman. That evening, another stroke of luck: an empty cabin to sleep in . . . but no leftover foodstuffs.

"Though so hungry she thought she would collapse," wrote Addington, she trudged on the next day. "Farther upstream she sighted the old woman on the opposite bank. They stopped and shouted across to each other. The old woman was persistent. She begged forgiveness and asked Mary to cross the stream and continue the journey with her. But Mary refused, thinking it would be wiser to keep the river between them. So, they continued their journey, each on her own side of the river."

So far, Mary had met—and overcome—one challenge after another. In her perilously weak condition, however, every mile, every day, would be still another new challenge. Still, she struggled on . . . and on. Day after day. And finally the day came when, instead of hundreds of miles from home, she suddenly was just thirty miles from her goal.

But now, just ahead, loomed a huge, physical challenge. It was a great cliff, past which the river rushed in a deep gorge replete with racing waters. With snow falling all around, she waded into a shallow eddy to test the current, but was quickly staggered by a surge of the icy water. Clearly, the river would be far too dangerous, especially in her weakened condition.

That left no choice but the cliff itself.

After a fitful night's sleep on the ground and nothing to eat, she awoke to face the towering cliffside again. She had to try it.

"Setting her face to the slope, she began to climb, a few inches at a step. As she ascended, she caught onto bushes and let her arms help her legs propel her higher and a little higher. She would climb a few yards and rest, then climb and rest again. By sheer willpower she reached the summit just before sundown."

Briefly pausing to catch her breath, hardly believing her good fortune, Mary then half slid, half fell down the opposite side of the high ridge in the winter's twilight.

As she again regained the banks of the river at the bottom, she dared to think, to hope. Positive that she was nearing the line of scattered frontier settlements left behind so many months before, she ignored the darkness to push ahead with fresh energy . . . and, lo! Sure enough, she stumbled into a recognizable corn patch. "Here [near Eggleston's Springs, Virginia]," wrote Addington , "she hallowed as loudly as she could and dropped to the ground. Night was on her again, and she knew she couldn't go farther on her own."

But she could shout again. And when she did, she was heard! "Then, there came through the corn patch two men, rifles raised for shooting." They were Adam Harman and a son. She knew them both. She was safe. She was home . . . almost.

After a delicious night spent wrapped in blankets and lying on a pallet by the roaring fire in their cabin, Mary would be taken the last twelve miles to Draper's Meadows by horseback, her ordeal over after an incredible escape saga of probably eight hundred miles in all, what with the need to follow curving streams, skirt difficult obstacles, and avoid Indian towns and trails.

☆ ☆ ☆

Additional notes: In the aftermath of Mary's homecoming forty-two days after escaping the Shawnee saltworks on Big Bone Creek, her friends the Harmans located the "duch" woman and brought her to safety as well. She was sent on to her home in Pennsylvania, but no record was kept of her name and ultimate fate. Bettie Draper was found and recovered six years after her seizure. She reported hearing that little George Ingles died in captivity soon after he was wrenched away from Mary at the Shawnee home village.

Young Tom, Mary's oldest son, was recovered after another seven years—a captive for thirteen years in all, he no longer was the child that Mary and her husband, William, once had known. More Indian than white in attitude, he needed considerable persuasion to return to home and family. Once his location was known, an intermediary, himself a former captive, went to bring back the youth, but Tom escaped and returned to his Shawnee "family." A year later, in 1768, Tom's white father, William Ingles, and the former captive traveled across the wilderness to the Ohio country together and finally did succeed in bringing Tom home to Virginia.

At first, he didn't speak English, dressed as an Indian, and spent long hours in the woods with his bow and arrow. After a time, though, he began to relearn the mother tongue, dress more normally, and show greater interest in the ways of his original white family. He was sent off to study under the tutelage of the family's good friend, Dr. Thomas Walker of Castle Hill in Albemarle County, who not only was a doctor and one-time guardian of Thomas Jefferson but also an early explorer of Kentucky credited with discovering the Cumberland Gap. "Here," wrote Luther Addington, "young Thomas got acquainted with Madison, Monroe, Jefferson, Patrick Henry, and many other distinguished people who were constantly in the neighborhood. In later years, Thomas Jefferson made him a colonel of militia."

Thomas Ingles married Eleanor Grills and took up frontier homesteading himself in the upper Clinch River Valley . . . only to have his own home attacked by marauding Indians, with his wife suffering a disfiguring tomahawk wound to her head and two of his children killed.

His mother and father had produced four more children after Mary's return. Living for a time in Bedford County, they moved to the banks of the New River and operated a ferry there. William Ingles died in 1782 at the age of fifty-three, while his widow, Mary, lived to age eighty-three before she died in 1815.

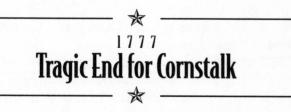

1777

Tragic End for Cornstalk

In the pantheon of great American Indian leaders and warriors was Sitting Bull. Among many others, Crazy Horse, Red Cloud, and Geronimo also come to mind. Even Virginia's own Chief Powhatan and his murderous brother, Opechancanough. And then there was . . . Cornstalk.

There was who? And no, not a vegetable, but rather the great Shawnee chief and warrior who, like many another legendary Native American, also met a tragic and unnecessary end . . . no longer as an enemy but as a friend to Virginia.

"There was a time when the name of Cornstalk thrilled every heart in West Virginia," wrote William Henry Foote in the *Southern Literary Messenger* before there really was a West Virginia. And yet, even then, at the time of his writing in 1850, Cornstalk was fading from the collective memory. "Here and there among the mountains may be found an aged one, who remembers the terrors of Indian warfare as they raged on the rivers, and in the retired glens, west of the Blue Ridge, under that noted savage," added the Reverend Foote (also author of the book *Sketches of Virginia*). "Cornstalk was to the Indians of West Virginia what Powhatan was to the tribes on the Sea Coast."

Little is known of the great chief's boyhood, but of his later life it certainly is known that he lived west of the Ohio River, and he repeatedly led murderous Shawnee raiding parties against the Virginia frontier settlements in the years before the American Revolution. In one such escapade, "he led an expedition in 1763 against the inhabitants of Greenbrier, and exterminated the infant Settlements." The Indians had appeared at one stop posing as friends, but "after being feasted murdered all the males but one."

That one, "being a little distance from the house when the carnage began," managed to flee and warn other settlers, who then fled to Augusta County while Cornstalk "passed on to Carr's Creek in Rockbridge, and massacred or took [as] prisoners many families." Over the next year, "the depredations were extended to the neighborhood of Staunton, with great ferocity."

It would be awhile, quite awhile, clearly, before Cornstalk could be called a friend of Virginia, true.

First, there would be the battle of Point Pleasant, considered by many as the first real battle of the American Revolution . . . a significant prelude at the very least. After years of back-and-forth fighting as more and more Virginia settlers moved beyond the Shenandoah into Kentucky and the Ohio River basin, often vying with Pennsylvania settlers for traditionally Shawnee lands to the west, Chief Cornstalk's Shawnee were determined to stop the white tide threatening to engulf their hunting grounds. The frontiersmen, meanwhile, fed up with years of "Indian troubles," eagerly joined a punitive force of Virginia militia being gathered by Irish-born Brig. Gen. Andrew Lewis of Botetourt County (originally a part of Augusta County). Eleven hundred strong, his force set out in early October 1774 from Fort Union, today's Lewisburg, West Virginia, for the Shawnee country.

The frontiersmen covered the 160 miles to their destination in nineteen days, traveling by packhorse with a train of cattle behind.

Also taking part in the expedition would be Virginia's Royal Governor John Murray, fourth earl of Dunmore, at the head of another column that would proceed north of the Lewis column to Fort Pitt, with plans to come down the Ohio River, meet the frontiersmen, and catch the Indians in a classic pincer movement. But Lord Dunmore, who had called out the frontier militiamen in the first place, eventually sent word he had been delayed. When he didn't show up at the right time and place, a suspicious Lewis and his men had to face Cornstalk and his fierce warriors alone at the point where the Kanawha River empties into the Ohio River, today's Point Pleasant, West Virginia.

Expecting Dunmore's support and spoiling for a fight against the longtime Shawnee enemy anyway, Lewis and company nearly were taken by surprise the morning of October 10, 1774, by a Shawnee force variously estimated at five hundred to a thousand strong. Well aware of the oncoming column's exact whereabouts ever since it left Fort Union, the Shawnee surreptitiously had crossed over the Ohio on rafts, west side to east side, the evening before. They were encamped not two miles away and preparing to attack the white militiamen when two of the Virginians, out deer hunting before dawn, stumbled upon the huge Shawnee assembly.

One of them was killed on the spot, but the other managed to run back to the Lewis encampment and give the alarm. "He stopped just before my tent," said militia Capt. John Stuart later, "and I discovered a number of men collecting around him as I lay in my bed. I jumped [up] and approached him to know what was the alarm, when I heard him declare that he had seen about five acres of land covered with Indians, as thick as they could stand behind [one] another."

Coolly lighting his pipe (by the Reverend Foote's account), Andrew Lewis immediately ordered out two detachments to confront the Indians, one of them led by his brother, Col. Charles Lewis. But the Indians already had advanced to within four hundred yards of the militia's camp, and both sides began firing. Charles Lewis and future Virginia Governor William Fleming, leader of the other detachment, were wounded right away, Lewis fatally so.

The fighting continued all day, with the Indians often melting into the woods only to reappear and attack all over again. Above the fray, said Captain Stuart later, the voice of Cornstalk could be heard urging his braves in Shawnee dialect, "Be strong, be strong." The Indians tried to intimidate the frontiersmen by shouting they were eleven hundred strong and had two thousand more warriors coming as reinforcements. Since Lewis, in fact, originally did march with eleven hundred men and was expecting his rear guard of more than two hundred men at any time, the Virginians wondered how the Indians seemed to know their exact number. Could such knowledge have come from only the observations of scouts spying on the nineteen-day march?

In the meantime, the Indians had succeeded in pinning the militia-men against the point between the two rivers by forming a line from one river to the other.

With nightfall threatening after many hours of on-again, off-again fighting, General Lewis was not anxious to carry the battle into the hours of darkness—he sent a detachment upstream on the Kanawha, and then up its tributary Crooked Creek, with instructions to descend upon the Shawnee flank as a surprise attack of his own. And that did do the trick, it seems. "The unlooked-for appearance of this company in their rear alarmed the Indians," wrote Foote. "They supposed the detachment to be the expected reinforcement . . . and gave way. Before sundown they crossed the Ohio, leaving many of their dead."

The real reinforcements arrived by midnight, and all in the Virginia camp were expecting another Shawnee onslaught . . . but the battle already concluded had been, wrote Foote, "decisive" so far as the Indians were concerned. None too pleased with the outcome, they faded back to their villages, but not before Cornstalk gathered his warriors in a final council and laid down a desperate challenge: "Let us kill our women and children, and go fight until we die."

When no one spoke up in agreement, he took his tomahawk and, in a dramatic gesture, slammed its blade into the center of a wooden post. "I'll go and make peace," he declared.

True to his word, Cornstalk met with Lord Dunmore near future Chillicothe, Ohio, and over a period of several days negotiated a peace for his own Shawnee, although other tribes, such as the Mingoes, would not join with him. His eloquence and oratory while addressing Dunmore and his retinue were so impressive, onlooker Col. Benjamin Wilson would say years later, "I have heard the first orators in Virginia, Patrick Henry, Richard Henry Lee, but never have I heard one whose powers of delivery surpassed those of Cornstalk on that occasion."

With this conclusion to "Dunmore's War," the royal governor returned to the Virginia capital of Williamsburg an immensely popular figure among some Virginians, especially speculators who viewed the apparent victory over the Indians to the west as an invitation to proceed with their plans for land acquisition.

The frontiersmen, peremptorily ordered back to their settlements by Dunmore, were not so happy, by any means. In the first place, they would have felt safer if allowed to destroy the Shawnee towns along the Ohio, as "a blow that should forever intimidate the savages," wrote Foote. In the second, many suspected that Dunmore had "made a deal" with the Indians and set them up for destruction by the Shawnee as prelude to the hostilities of the coming Revolutionary War, in which many western Indians did ally themselves with the British against the American frontiersmen. Gen. Andrew Lewis, for one, "carried with him to his grave a full belief that Dunmore acted in concert with the Indians," commented Foote, espousing a view held by many historians of the period.

Dunmore, in fact, was overly beguiled by his apparent popularity and failed to gauge the anti-British passions already overtaking the Virginia Colony that he commanded in the name of the Crown. With hostilities just breaking out in Massachusetts, he first aroused those passions by seizing the gunpowder in the Williamsburg magazine. Then, with open warfare well underway, Dunmore issued a proclamation urging the slaves of rebellious Virginians to join the British fighting forces—in effect, it seemed, to rise up against their white masters. Forced to flee to the safety of a British warship in the York River, Dunmore led a British flotilla raiding Rebel shore positions and briefly held Norfolk before being defeated in the minor battle of Gwynn's Island in the Chesapeake Bay. The last royal governor of Virginia, he next retreated to New York and then to England.

Cornstalk, in the meantime, proved a friend to embattled Virginia—he refused to join the confederacy of Indians responding to the British call to arms west of the Ohio. He apparently saw a safer and better future for his tribe by aligning the Shawnee on the side of the

Virginians he once had fought so vehemently. That being the case, he visited the garrison at Point Pleasant in 1777 with two Indian companions to warn the Americans of the unfriendly alliance developing to the west . . . and to state his own tribe's more friendly disposition. (Or, say some historians, to warn that he could not hold his own tribe in check despite the peace treaty he had negotiated with Lord Dunmore after the Shawnee defeat at Point Pleasant back in 1774.)

He was held as a hostage while the alerted Americans prepared to defend their frontier yet again. One day, with a shout from across the Ohio, his son Elinipsico appeared, explaining he was worried by his father's long absence. The very morning after their reunion, unfortunately, an Indian party hidden in the foliage on the banks of the Kanawha fired upon two white hunters and killed one of them, a man named Gilmore.

Elinipsico denied having brought the guilty parties with him, but the tragic die was cast. The murdered man's family had been killed years before by one of Cornstalk's own war parties, "and now Indians had just killed Gilmore."

Gilmore, it seems, had arrived at Point Pleasant with Capt. John Hall's company from Rockbridge County; the two men, in fact, were related. Hall and his men now rushed, "shouting," to Cornstalk's cabin.

"Elinipsico hearing their approach trembled greatly. Cornstalk said: 'My son, the Great Spirit has seen fit that we should die together; and has sent you here. It is his will. Let us submit. It is best.' And turned to meet the soldiers at the door. In a moment he received seven bullets in his body and fell without a groan. Elinipsico sat on his stool unmoved. His father's words had calmed his trepidation; his father's death called up in his bosom all his savage stoicism. He received the shots of the soldiers and died without motion."

As a predictable result: "The Shawnees in the war that followed took ample revenge for their chief. The blood of multitudes flowed for Cornstalk and his son; and no man was heard to glory in being the principal or accessory of his death."

☆ ☆ ☆

Additional note: Brig. Gen. Andrew Lewis, a tall, commanding figure once described as "making the earth tremble as he walked," was a veteran of service under George Washington against the French and *their* Indian allies in the 1750s, also in the Ohio region. He served in the Virginia House of Burgesses during the historic pre-Revolutionary period. During the Revolution itself, he had the undoubted pleasure of commanding the force that drove Lord Dunmore off Gwynn's Island— and into historical oblivion. In September 1781, just before the battle of Yorktown, Lewis took ill and died in Bedford County, at about sixty-one years of age, before he could reach his home on the Roanoke River. He was considered such a hero of early Virginia that his would be one of the six secondary figures created as part of the heroic equestrian statue of George Washington in Capitol Square (see pages 192–95).

★

1 7 7 9

That Other Famous Clark

★

"Sir, where is your army?" asked the British commander whose surrender to the lean, red-haired woodsman before him just about doubled the size of a very young America.

"Sir, they stand before you," the American supposedly rejoined, a pointed reference to the 175 bedraggled, half-starved frontiersmen behind him.

While this exchange between an unbelieving British Col. Henry "Hairbuyer" Hamilton and the Virginia-born George Rogers Clark, American conqueror of the Old Northwest, may be strictly legendary, certainly they said *something* to one another. And Clark's defeat of the British at Vincennes is *no* legend. Neither is the 180-mile march by Clark's amateur militia force in the face of adverse wintry conditions.

As dramatically recalled by WFPL (89.3 FM) Public Radio in Louisville, Kentucky, early in 2002, the march through an untrammeled wilderness had been a horror show from the word go. Four major rivers to be encountered en route had spilled ice-cold waters far beyond their streambeds. "Men slog along in water that obscures the path," recalled WFPL as part of its weekly series called *The Chronicles of George Rogers Clark*. "Wading is difficult, and sometimes the water is as high as their chests. To sleep, they must sit down in shallow water and lean against a sapling to snatch a little rest, holding rifle, powder, and supplies to their chests to keep them dry."

By the time they have crossed the Little Wabash, the Fox, and Embarrass Rivers, only the Wabash lies ahead to impede their path to the British-held Fort Sackville at Vincennes, Indiana. Now, they are only eleven miles short of their goal, a stockade fort where British commander Hamilton and his one hundred or so men feel snug and secure. Surely, those pesky Americans wouldn't be crazy enough to mount an assault under such extreme weather conditions!

But wait. Clark? some by now may be asking. *Clark?* Is that the *famous* Clark?

Depends.

Born in Albemarle County, Virginia, on November 19, 1752, George Rogers Clark emerged, unasked, at a crucial time and place of war, *Revolutionary* War, as one of America's greatest early heroes. Tall as an oak, marked by his thatch of flaming red hair, he would try the impossible. He would lead his ragged force on foot through winter's worst weather over partially frozen and flooded terrain to mount the assault against an intimidating enemy bastion . . . and, against all expectations but his own, he would succeed!

He would contribute financially to his crusade against the British out of his own, not-so-terribly-deep pockets.

And after all was said and done, after winning the territory of five future states—Illinois, Indiana, Ohio, Michigan, and Wisconsin—he would spend years struggling to repay personal debts amounting to today's equivalent of many millions of dollars. Compounding his post–Revolutionary War troubles, he would suffer a crippling stroke, then burn his leg so badly in his fireplace that it had to be amputated.

Confined to a wheelchair for the remaining nine years of his life, he found a home with an accommodating sister and her husband—Lucy and George Croghan, whose now-historic Locust Grove home in Louisville is open to the public.

Thus, it was a sad and sometimes bitter end for the once-vigorous frontiersman and farsighted warrior, and yet, what memories he could conjure up as *some* comfort against his years of debilitation.

As an Albemarle native, he was so well known to Thomas Jefferson that Jefferson once offered *him* the leadership of a major western expedition . . . years before it took its ultimate form as the Lewis and Clark

Expedition of 1804–6. As events turned out, of course, make that the Lewis and *William* Clark Expedition, in which the co-leadership role fell to George Rogers Clark's younger brother William.

If George Rogers was so well known in his day as Conqueror of the Northwest, it of course wasn't the same Northwest that later played host to William (Clark) in 1805 and 1806, but rather the Old Northwest, or "Illinois Country," secured by the triumph at Vincennes.

Like his future compatriot George Washington, twenty years his senior, George Rogers Clark came to know the Virginia frontier, then including future Kentucky, as a surveyor. Ever pushing the envelope westward as a young man, he fell in love with the far-flung frontier lands of his day and became known as an avid explorer of that same Kentucky terrain. He fought the Shawnee in 1774 as a Virginia militia captain—in "Lord Dunmore's War" as that little fracas was called. Clark then settled in Kentucky, a "county" of Virginia, and argued in favor of retaining its ties with Virginia rather than establish a new colony to be called Transylvania.

But soon the Revolution was underway, seemingly far away in the East.

What about the "backdoor" West, though? At this early stage of American history, George Rogers Clark volunteered his services as the chief defender of the American West against the combined threat of the British in Detroit and their fierce Indian allies (Hamilton's "Hair-buyer" nickname was no accident, but rather a reference to a standing offer for scalps).

Virginia Governor Patrick Henry and the legislature bowed to Clark's argument that the western flank of the young, struggling America needed protection and made him the frontier commander with a militia major's rank.

Soon armed and promoted to lieutenant colonel, Clark gathered a force of 175 men and marched north in 1778 under secret orders from Governor Henry and a handful of legislators to drive the British and their Indian allies out of the Illinois Country, perhaps even to seize Detroit. Clark never did reach Detroit, but he did seize Kaskaski and then Cahokia and Vincennes, all in the summer of 1778.

Unfortunately, Hamilton stormed south from his Detroit base to recapture Vincennes from the tiny garrison Clark had left in charge of Fort Sackville there. Figuring the Americans wouldn't care to fight again until spring of 1779, Hamilton then sent all but one hundred of his Redcoats and Indian warriors home for the winter months. He and his remaining men discounted the possibility of an American advance across the icy, flooded countryside in February 1779 . . . until Clark's bedraggled little "army" suddenly struck and regained control of Fort Sackville.

As Clark himself later wrote, that advance indeed had been an ordeal. "The water never got shallower, but continued deepening, even getting to the woods, where the men expected land," he wrote. "The water was up to my shoulders, but gaining the woods was of great consequence. All the low men, and the weakly, hung to the trees and floated on the old logs until they were taken off in canoes. The strong and tall got ashore and built fires. Many would reach the shore, and fall with their bodies half in the water, not being able to support themselves without it."

Still, they did reach the enemy . . . and defeat him. And as a reward somewhat more tangible than sweet victory, Clark and his men were given land grants—the "Clark Grant" was the foundation of today's Clarksville, Indiana. The Virginia-Kentucky warrior also founded Louisville, across the Ohio River from Clarksville.

For all that, though, he spent the postwar years a poor man, his land grants insufficient to repay his wartime debts, although Virginia in 1812 finally did award him a lifetime pension of $400 a year—and the second of two ceremonial swords. He died in 1818 at the age of sixty-five . . . four decades after his victory over the British at the age of twenty-five.

1 7 8 1
The Nadir of His Fortunes

Now picture this: No sleep for thirty-six hours, having ridden his horse into the ground, Thomas Jefferson had no choice but to heave the saddle onto his shoulder, leave the horse behind, and trudge on to a nearby farmhouse in search of help. Not far away, the enemy was rampaging through his capital city and burning buildings.

It was the beginning of a long, low period in his life, a period that would be the nadir of his fortunes. Within months, British dragoons would be swarming through his beloved Monticello, and he would have to defend his actions as governor of Virginia, deal with accusations of cowardice, and, finally, endure the lingering death of his wife, Martha.

But first, there would be these two hellish days in January 1781 when the Sage of Monticello was governor of Virginia and thus leader of a rebellious British colony with only a ragtag, ill-equipped militia to defend itself and no money to pay for fortifications, arms, or well-trained troops. Situated at center between North and South, the Virginia of his stewardship had yet to become a keystone to the war of revolution being fought both above and below . . . but now, war indeed was about to sweep into the Old Dominion itself. For this would be the year when Washington, Lafayette, "Mad Anthony" Wayne, and Cornwallis all would be tilting in Virginia, but not quite yet. Just now, a peace-loving political philosopher was serving as governor of a Virginia that had sent its best young men to fight with armies elsewhere, that offered the enemy an inviting, lightly defended coastline to the east and a remote, even more difficult to defend frontier stretching to the Mississippi River in the west and the Great Lakes to the northwest. Just now, in January, even as Cornwallis was pressing northward in the Carolinas, up the James River came a British fleet carrying sixteen hundred professional soldiers led by the notorious American turncoat Benedict Arnold.

It was a relatively small force, but strong enough under the circumstances to seize Richmond. The state legislators scattered to their homes, leaving Governor Jefferson on his own in a town with little to no defenses. Calling out the few militia and local forces he could scrape together, Jefferson ordered them to remove and save what public stores they could. Meanwhile, there was his family to consider.

Leaving the city at one in the morning, he rode some miles to Tuckahoe to move Martha and their children another eight miles up the river, where they would stay out of harm's way with friends. But then he had to turn back to the capital to deal with the desperate situation there—if he could.

His goal was Manchester, on the south side of the James opposite Richmond, which had replaced Williamsburg as the capital only the year before. He was within sight of the new capital—in 1781 no more than a town, really—when his exhausted horse gave in and collapsed.

Shouldering the saddle, the governor trudged on to the nearby farmhouse, where he borrowed a colt to carry him on into Manchester. By then the British were ransacking Richmond, burning buildings, including those housing tobacco and food stores.

It could have been worse. In two days Benedict Arnold and his men were gone—Jefferson was able to move back to his capital.

Weeks later, with spring in the air, Cornwallis came barreling into Virginia. This time, the General Assembly *and* the governor vacated Richmond, withdrawing to Charlottesville. Cornwallis ordered his tough subordinate Banastre Tarleton, known as the "Hunting Leopard," to go after both parties with dragoons and mounted infantry. As the British hastened toward Charlottesville under a bright moon, militia Capt. John "Jack" Jouett saw them passing Cuckoo Tavern in Louisa County. Realizing their intent, Jouett took to a horse incongruously named Prince Charlie and rode little-known back trails over rough terrain for five and a half hours before pulling up at Monticello's doorstep at four-thirty in the morning to warn Jefferson of the coming danger.

Jefferson quickly sent off an unwell Martha, their children, and several assembly members who had been staying at Monticello as guests. Strengthened by a glass or two of Madeira, Jouett then rode down the mountain into Charlottesville to warn more legislators who were staying at Swan's Tavern in the village.

Tarleton, in the meantime, had stopped briefly at Castle Hill, the Albemarle County home of Dr. Thomas Walker, the noted explorer and friend to the Jefferson family. Tarleton sent a detachment to Monticello, where Jefferson waited until the last minute, packing papers and seeing valuables put away by his servants. Despite being warned that the detachment was on its way, he lingered on dangerously. But then, taking a second look at Charlottesville through his telescope, he finally saw dragoons in the streets below. He at last made the appropriate use of a waiting and previously saddled horse.

Down in the village, the alerted assembly members made plans to reconvene across the Blue Ridge, in Staunton, and rode off as quickly as they could. Seven, however, were captured by Tarleton and his dragoons, among them Daniel Boone.

Up on the little mountain, the intruding British stayed about eighteen hours but made no attempt to ransack or damage Jefferson's mountaintop home. Both Jefferson and his beloved home had escaped physical harm.

☆ ☆ ☆

Slipping from one crisis to another, Jefferson next found both his leadership abilities and his personal courage under question. Blaming him for the wartime resources that Virginia lacked, some legislators proposed replacing Virginia's democratically chosen governors in times of war with a strongman possessing dictatorial powers—to get necessary things done. In a secret vote in the House of Burgesses, Jefferson's supporters managed to defeat the notion.

But now the assembly unanimously agreed to conduct an official "inquiry . . . into the conduct of the executive of this state for the past twelve months," a terrible blow to Jefferson's pride. The case against Jefferson was based largely upon the invasions of Virginia by Cornwallis and Benedict Arnold—and the unfortunate gossip suggesting that Jefferson had been less than courageous in respect to the Tarleton episode.

To deal with the inquiry, which began about the time his term as governor ended, Jefferson sought and won election to the House of Burgesses in the fall of 1781—now he could rise and respond to the charges as a member of the legislature himself. Before the matter could end, though, there came the electrifying news in October of the Cornwallis surrender at Yorktown, turning point of the Revolutionary War. And in December, more good news for Jefferson—total vindication by the legislative committee looking into the allegations against him. No information had been obtained, said the committee chairman, beyond rumors, and the rumors themselves had proved groundless.

Then came a unanimous legislative resolution thanking Jefferson for "his impartial, upright, and attentive administration of the powers of the Executive, whilst in office," and saying the General Assembly wished to declare it held a "high opinion" of Jefferson's "ability, rectitude and integrity, as chief magistrate of this Commonwealth."

All well and good, we might think today, but not for Jefferson himself. As biographer Saul K. Padover put it, he "sulked" for more than a year. "I find the pain of a little censure, even when it is unfounded, is more acute than the pleasure of much praise," he told a friend. And to James Monroe he said, months after the fact, only "the all-healing grave" would cure the "wound on my spirit."

Never again, he also vowed in the aftermath of the legislative inquiry, would he return to public life, to political office. This from a man still destined to serve as minister to France, secretary of state, vice president, and third president of the brand-new nation he and his Declaration of Independence had been so instrumental in creating.

☆ ☆ ☆

Before "moving on" to those new heights of historic achievement, however, Jefferson would face the greatest personal loss of his life.

Just thirty-eight in 1782, Virginia's own Renaissance man in many ways was quite content to live in semi-isolation atop his little mountain, in the Italianate, partially domed villa of his own design, airy and spacious inside and looking out at the world below from windows facing every direction. As Saul K. Padover wrote in *Jefferson: A Great American's Life and Ideas:* "The windows in the house were open to every breeze that blew from the misty pale blue of the Blue Ridge and the darkling green of the surrounding hills." And it was here that a visiting Frenchman, the Marquis de Chastellux, found "a man not yet forty, tall, and with a mild and pleasing countenance. . . . An American, who without ever having quitted his country, is at once musician, skilled in drawing, a geometrician, an astronomer, a natural philosopher, legislator, and statesman." And, for that matter, a homeschooler to boot.

In the spring of 1782, Jefferson's wife, Martha, thirty-three years of age, was, as they say, "heavy with child." She already had borne five children in the past ten years . . . with only two still surviving. Her sixth child, a baby girl destined to die in just two years, would be born in May. Already somewhat fragile, Martha never recovered from what would be her last childbirth.

For four months, wrote biographer Padover, her husband "never left her bedside." He nursed her "with desperate tenderness." And when she finally expired in September, he fainted dead away. "For three weeks, he kept to his room, a silent being, tortured with sorrow. Night and day he walked incessantly up and down his room, alone with his wild thoughts, as if he had lost his reason."

When he finally did venture out, "it was to mount his horse and ride into the mountains, aimlessly rambling along unfrequented paths, a solitary man weeping for his beloved."

With time, though, he evidently realized his three surviving daughters—Martha, ten; Mary, four; and Lucy, the newborn—had needs that only he could fulfill. Beginning to tend to those needs, he nursed the girls through smallpox vaccinations at a friend's home but then lingered on uncertainly—the prospect of resuming the quiet life back at Monticello was all too painful. There, of course, he and Martha had lived, there she so recently had died . . . and there, it seems also, she had exacted his promise never to bring a stepmother into the lives of their girls.

In the outside world, though, the Revolution was nearing its end, and talk of a peace treaty was in the air . . . all thanks in large part to the Cornwallis surrender at Yorktown the year before. Up in Philadelphia, the Congress that Jefferson once served with historic distinction was casting about for the right man to represent the still-a-birthing nation in the pending peace talks. Why not send Jefferson, suggested someone— James Madison, possibly. What an excellent idea, was the consensus.

Jefferson received word of the proposed assignment in November and, if not gladly, at least wisely, accepted it. Traveling to Europe for an unknown period of time would be a wrench for the recently widowed father and his children, but he could place the two younger children with an aunt and leave Martha, the oldest, at a good school in Philadelphia. Thus, he decided, he indeed would take up the offer from his one-time congressional confreres.

☆ ☆ ☆

As further events now unfolded, one could say that the dark side of fate was not yet done with Thomas Jefferson. Or so it at least seemed. Armed with his commission from Congress as minister plenipotentiary and peace negotiator, he was prepared to cross the Atlantic aboard the French frigate *Romulus* out of Baltimore. But ice trapped the sailing vessel, and the weeks crawled by . . . into the year 1783. And still the ice held the good ship *Romulus* locked in the harbor.

Finally, at the end of January, word came that the ship might yet sail. Jefferson and his secretary, Maj. David Franks, tried to hurry down to Baltimore from Philadelphia on the wintry roads, only to find the ferry crossings also plagued by ice and the occasional inns en route "miserable." The trip took five days.

When they finally reached Baltimore, the *Romulus* still would not sail. But fortunately so, it turned out for Jefferson, since this latest delay was based upon the grim news that seven British warships were waiting at the mouth of Chesapeake Bay to seize him. "Jefferson, with dry modesty, considered this 'a most amazing force for such an object.'"

As yet more time passed, with Jefferson caught in limbo, neither home nor abroad, word came from Europe that a provisional peace treaty had been agreed to—it soon would be followed by the formal Treaty of Paris ending the Revolutionary War and establishing America as an independent state. Thus, after spinning wheels uselessly for more than three months, Jefferson could only accept the thanks of Congress and return home to Virginia . . . but to what? A lifetime of managing his estate and its slaves by himself, of raising his children by himself?

Not really, and not for long. The General Assembly named him its delegate to the Congress, now sitting in Annapolis, Maryland. Taking his seat in December 1783, he plunged into the work and in a few short months "was regarded as the most influential member of the Congress." He had chaired "most of the important committees, and drafted no less than thirty-one essential state papers," wrote Padover. "Some of these papers have become foundation stones of the American republic."

In May 1784 Jefferson again was named a minister plenipotentiary, this time really to reach France as the base from which he was to help John Adams and Benjamin Franklin develop useful commercial treaties with the European nations. The next year, with Franklin's retirement, Jefferson succeeded his old colleague from the Continental Congress as minister to France. The Virginian's star once more was on the ascendancy, with so much still lying ahead—the presidency, the Louisiana Purchase, the Lewis and Clark Expedition . . . the founding of the University of Virginia. All this and more to come from a man who once had foresworn any further public service whatsoever.

★

1781
Bulldog Seen at Yorktown

★

"The pore General," Martha wrote after a visit to George in Morristown, New Jersey, the summer of 1780, "so unhappy that it distressed me exceedingly." Not only was it a low ebb for George Washington and his Continental army in the struggle for independence from the British, but matters would be turning worse and worse in the months ahead.

By January 1781 the Rhode Islander Nathanael Greene, commanding in the South as probably Washington's best general, was moved to say, "Unless this army is better supported than I see any prospect of, the Country is lost beyond redemption." And Washington himself in April 1781 said, "We are at the end of our tether."

Indeed, every major victory of recent months had not been the Virginian's, but those of the British. First, in 1778, they seized Savannah, and then in 1779 fended off the attempt to take it back. Next, in the spring of 1780, the British seized Charleston, South Carolina, a blow accompanied by the loss of five thousand Americans. The Crown's monolith then took the measure of Horatio Gates at Camden, South Carolina, a debacle for the Americans. In March 1781, the British registered still another victory, albeit a costly one, at Guilford Courthouse, next to Greensboro, North Carolina. All this, and then their fatal blunder—his forces weakened, Lord Cornwallis marched into Virginia.

His Lordship's winter campaign of 1780–81 had been a brilliant one, noted historian Marcus Cunliffe in his book *George Washington: Man and Monument*. "Yet Cornwallis writ in water," added Cunliffe. "Behind him, as he hastened north, south again, and north once more, resistance rose afresh. By May he was in Virginia, where [Banastre] Tarleton almost captured Governor Thomas Jefferson and the startled state legislature. Cornwallis was bold, even brilliant. But he was doomed when, having failed to dispose of agile American forces led by [the Marquis de] Lafayette and ["Baron" von] Steuben, he decided to make for the coast and get in touch with [Sir Henry] Clinton [in New York]."

As every schoolboy knows, Cornwallis chose Yorktown—b-a-a-a-d mistake. "Yorktown was not easy to defend and Cornwallis had fewer than eight thousand men." Not only that, but for George Washington—totally absent from Virginia and busy in the North since 1775—the dominoes all were falling into place. And in his own native state, for that matter. The French were now on hand as his allies against the British on land and, crucially just this moment, at sea.

Thus, Washington was able to march southward from his northeastern haunts with a significantly augmented army. But the key was French Admiral de Grasse, who sailed northward from the Caribbean, entered the Chesapeake, and sailed up the James River to unload three thousand fresh troops at Jamestown Island, then left the bay just in time to engage an entering British fleet . . . and drive it off. Returning to the great bay, de Grasse and a smaller, newly arrived French fleet now commanded the waters at Cornwallis's back—he had no way to retreat from Yorktown on the York River. Nor to obtain supplies or reinforcement.

Now the Cornwallis destiny was writ large for all to see. Washington and the French assembled seventeen thousand men to the Brit's less than eight thousand. As they settled in for a siege, "allied guns and mortars hammered the town." It wouldn't take long. "Outnumbered by two to one and thwarted by a storm in an attempt to escape across the York River to Gloucester Point, Cornwallis lost heart." On October 17, 1781, he sent a note saying he was ready to discuss surrender terms.

With the British defeated at Yorktown, the Revolutionary War was all but won—that *was* the big battle that tipped the scales, although desultory (and ultimately needless) fighting would continue for the next two years, but again the writing was on the wall, plain for all to see. "The remainder of the tale for the British forces, was drab; little by little they packed their bags, evacuated their ports and fortresses, and sailed away. The center of interest had shifted to Paris, where the American commissioners—John Adams, [Ben] Franklin, [John] Jay, and [Henry] Laurens—were getting an even better bargain than they had hoped." The result was the 1783 Treaty of Paris, which formally ended the conflict and confirmed America's emergence as an independent nation among nations, with territories "defined as stretching from the seaboard to the Mississippi, from the Great Lakes to Spanish Florida."

As Cunliffe also noted, an enduring irony of Yorktown, where Washington extracted final victory with the help of the French, is that at the nearby Colonial capital of Williamsburg not so many years beforehand, a young Major Washington of a Virginia militia had been dispatched by a royal governor to warn the French to stay out of the distant "Ohio country" below Canada. In those days, he returned to the frontier and actually fought the French and their allies in the first battle of the worldwide French and Indian War. And he notably was with Edward Braddock in his ill-fated foray against the same foe in 1755.

☆ ☆ ☆

In historical accounts of major events such as the siege/battle of Yorktown, the many small details adding up to the picture as a whole tend to become lost. In the book *Rebels and Redcoats: The American Revolution Through the Eyes of Those Who Fought and Lived It,* edited by George F. Scheer and Hugh F. Rankin, a few such details are recounted:

• Strange but apparently true, a single ball fired by the British at the advancing Americans somehow killed one soldier and wounded two others. With three or four others also wounded, "the [British] execution [against an American unit] was much more than might have been expected from the distance, the dispersed situation of our men, and few shots fired," observed Maj. Sgt. George Tucker. Later, a single cannonball took down four men in Capt. James Duncan's regiment.

• Not so strange, an American militiaman who continually danced atop a parapet in daring defiance of the British gunners, even brandishing a spade in his attempts to snag a British ball, finally was struck and presumably killed. Or, as Duncan stated the case in his diary, "[U]nfortunately a ball came and put an end to his capers."

• When Lafayette learned that his old friend George Washington had arrived in Williamsburg to begin operations against the trapped British, the Frenchman rose from a sickbed and literally rushed into the stern Virginian's arms. He "caught the General round his body, hugged him as close as it was possible, and absolutely kissed him from ear to ear once or twice . . . with as much ardor as ever an absent lover kissed his mistress on his return," reported Major Tucker. In fact, the Virginia officer wrote to his wife, "the whole army and all the town were presently in motion . . . men, women and children seemed to vie with each other in demonstrations of joy and eagerness to see their beloved countryman [meaning George Washington]."

• Imagine Sgt. Joseph Martin's surprise, while huddled with other soldiers close to the British lines on a rainy night somewhat later, to encounter an absolute stranger, unrecognizable in the dark and wishing to pass on ahead, alone, to join a group of sappers and engineers digging a parallel siege trench even closer, *very* close, to the British lines. "The stranger inquired what troops we were, talked familiarly with us a few minutes, when, informed which way the officers had gone, he went off in the same direction." Only when the stranger returned from the exposed forward position with the engineer-sappers did Martin learn the visitor had been George Washington himself.

• When the British discovered the new trench so close to their lines, they responded with mortar fire . . . backed up, you might say, by an apparently mean-looking bulldog. To cite Sergeant Martin's account again: "They had a large bulldog and every time they fired he would follow their shots across our trenches. Our officers wished to catch him and oblige him to carry a message from them into the town to his masters but he looked too formidable for any of us to encounter."

• In sharp contrast to the hidden construction of siege trenches at night, the besiegers occupied their completed new trenches with ostentatious noise and ceremony, a "centuries-old" military tradition, it seems. Wrote Captain Duncan (of Alexander Hamilton's battalion): "The trenches were this day to be enlivened with drums beating and colors flying, and this honor was conferred on our division of light infantry. And now I must confess, although I was fond of the honor, I had some fear, as I had no notion of a covered way and more especially as I was posted in the center with the colors." The British did fire at the Americans, but no one in Duncan's immediate sector was hit. But then, at Hamilton's order, came a "rather extraordinary" maneuver. "We were ordered to mount the bank, front the enemy, and there by word of command go through all the ceremony of soldiery, ordering and grounding our arms." This was craziness, but fortunately for Duncan and his men, the British withheld their fire. "I suppose their astonishment at our conduct must have prevented them," said Duncan, with a postscript that Hamilton, while otherwise "one of the first officers of the American army," in this case had "wantonly exposed the lives of his men."

• And a sad note: While George Washington finally had achieved his greatest and most meaningful victory over the experienced, highly professional British army, his joy was tempered by a great personal loss: His stepson "Jacky" Custis, Martha's son, an aide-de-camp at Yorktown, died there of camp fever.

★

1787
Start of a Hemings Family Saga

★

Why would a family of free African Americans in, say, Charlottesville or Albemarle County, include one or more slaves, also black, among the household members? For instance, the Griffen Butlers of Albemarle County, who in the 1810 county census listed ten free persons and one slave in the household?

As Kirt von Daccke wrote in the 1997 issue of the *Magazine of Albemarle County History,* "In all likelihood the slave listed in the Butler household was a family member or a hired slave."

In the antebellum world of free blacks, it seems, slavery sometimes could be a relative concept. The slave in the house could be a relative or friend awaiting freedom, a hired slave simply living there . . . or even a man, woman, or child who remained a slave in name only, to avoid the implications of Virginia's 1806 law requiring all newly freed blacks to leave the state within a year.

In Charlottesville, some black (or partially black) families living on Main Street, free or slave-in-name, came down from the mountain . . . down to town from slavery at Jefferson's Monticello mountaintop plantation. Some of them were his own kin by marriage, if not blood as well.

According to a careful study by Monticello researcher Lucia Stanton appearing in the same 1997 journal of the Albemarle Historical Society, their story begins with Betty Hemings, a slave once owned by Jefferson's father-in-law, John Wayles of Charles City County, and mother of the slave woman Sally Hemings, by whom, modern DNA testing suggests, Jefferson may have fathered at least one child. Sally, in turn, apparently was fathered by John Wayles, and so Jefferson's late wife, Martha, was Sally's half sister. Betty, the older Hemings woman (and herself thought to be the daughter of a slave woman and a white sea captain), is known to have produced ten children in all. A grandson said six of them were the progeny of the English-born Wayles, an attorney, merchant, and slave trader.

When he died in 1773, he left daughter Martha eleven thousand acres of land and 135 slaves, among them Betty Hemings and all ten of her children.

For the Hemings family specifically, the connection between Monticello and the Main Street of Charlottesville began with Betty's oldest child, Mary Hemings, who had been a household slave for Jefferson and wife, Martha, not only at Monticello, but also at Williamsburg and Richmond when he served as governor during the Revolution.

In 1787, when Jefferson was away serving as U.S. minister to France, Mary Hemings, age twenty-five and already the mother of four children, was leased (yes, *leased*) to Thomas Bell, a Charlottesville merchant whom Jefferson once called a "man remarkable for his integrity."

Staying on indefinitely with the white merchant, she in time had two more children and asked in 1792 to be sold outright to Bell. This was done, but Jefferson kept two of her older children, a boy and a girl, and gave the remaining boy and girl to his sister Anna and daughter Martha.

As one result, Mary had become "the first of Betty Hemings' children to gain her freedom," wrote Stanton. "By this time she and Bell had formed a relationship that was by every indication conjugal, and openly acknowledged." Stanton cited the statement of R. T. W. Duke, who knew Bell, that "with the rather 'easy' morality of those early days no one paid any attention to a man's method of living and Col. Bell lived openly with the woman and had two children by her." They couldn't marry because Virginia law at the time forbade interracial marriages.

Then, too, in this bizarre world of leasing and purchasing human beings, Bell wound up purchasing his own children when he bought Mary from Thomas Jefferson. (And Jefferson presumably was *not* Mary's brother-in-law, as he was in the case of Sally Hemings, because the late John Wayles was *not* necessarily Mary's father.)

As another result of Mary's move into Bell's home in 1787 as a leased slave, wrote Stanton, the dwelling at East Second and Main Street would be "occupied by the descendants of Betty Hemings for just over a century." As part of that hundred-year saga, Stanton further explained: "The descendants of Elizabeth (Betty) Hemings—in bondage and freedom—lived on Charlottesville's Main Street, constructed some of its buildings, and provided much of its entertainment. Her family's fortunes ebbed and flowed . . . some of her grandchildren were heirs, while others were inherited; in some years they were considered white, in others black, and, while one branch of the family lived all their lives on Main Street, their cousins were forced to leave it."

Buying the acre-sized property in 1784, Bell had then added to its "modest" log home and turned its one-time tavern into a general store by the time Mary Hemings entered the picture.

To carry on with the story Stanton unraveled: Bell died in 1800, giving Mary lifetime use of his home and real estate on Main Street and bequeathing other assets to his two "natural" children, Robert and Sarah (called "Sally"). The daughter two years later married Jesse Scott, "the son of an Indian woman and, as he believed, a white Virginian who became governor of Kentucky." (As Stanton says in a footnote, there was a Gen. Charles Scott from Powhatan County, Virginia, who served as an early governor of Kentucky.)

Closer to home, Jesse Scott, now also living in the Mary Hemings household on Main Street, became "a noted musician and composer of dance tunes." He and his sons (Mary's grandsons), well known across the South, played at private affairs, University of Virginia balls, and various spas. ("A violin, sold in Charlottesville at the turn of the century, bore the story that it had been given to Jesse Scott by Thomas Jefferson," Stanton noted. Supposed to have been a seventeenth-century Amati, it since has disappeared from the historical record.)

Continuing with the saga of Mary Hemings, half sister to the famous Sally Hemings, a cold January day in 1827 would be a watershed day for any and all blacks recently associated with Monticello. Jefferson had died in debt in 1826, and now there would be an auction at Monticello of his household belongings. One hundred and thirty slaves were included, a major sale by the standards of the time . . . and one of Mary Hemings's four older children had a vital stake in the outcome. He was Joe Fossett, chief blacksmith at Monticello—and by Jefferson's will freed from slavery, but not until July of that year. He may have taken the name Fossett because his father may have been a white carpenter on the premises named Fossett. Then again, "many of Fossett's descendants believed he was Thomas Jefferson's son."

In any case, he was married to another Monticello slave named Edith ("Edy"), who as a teenage girl had gone to Washington in 1801 with newly elected President Jefferson and borne three babies during his two terms in the White House, one of them apparently the first child ever born in the executive mansion. The father of those children remains unknown today.

By the time of the Jefferson estate sale in 1827, Joe and Edith were married and the parents of seven children all their own. The terrifying complication was that Edith and the children, two to twenty in age, all were slaves about to be sold. But enter now an agent, as it were, of a Hemings protective association—Mary's son-in-law Jesse Scott. Three Fossett children were sold to Charlottesville residents, but Scott was able to step in and rescue Edy Fossett and her two youngest children. (The fate of the other two—Maria and Isabella—is lost to history.)

The family apparently had made friendly financial arrangements with two of the Charlottesville purchasers—those arrangements in the end cost the Hemings clan a loss of real estate and brought about at least one lawsuit but did recover one more child for Joe and Edy Fossett. In the meantime, however, Col. John R. Jones refused to free their son Peter, while a daughter, Patsy, who was sold to a University of Virginia professor, ran away.

As yet another bizarre result, the newly freed blacksmith Joseph Fossett now resided in town with his wife and children living with him *as his slaves.* Because of the state law requiring newly freed slaves to leave within a year, "he was compelled to keep his family in the safety of bondage," Stanton noted. The Fossetts may have lived in a second house on the Bell lot, while his mother, Mary Hemings Bell, Sally and Jesse Scott, and the Scotts' three sons resided in the original Bell home.

In another development, the Fossetts' daughter Betsy-Ann would marry into the neighboring David Isaacs–Anne "Nancy" West family. Isaacs was a white Jew, and West was a "free woman of color . . . who was herself the daughter of a well-to-do white landholder and his slave." Also unable to marry under Virginia law, they openly lived together and had seven children, two of whom "married members of Monticello's Hemings family."

For Betsy-Ann, though, a slight complication—since she was a slave in name, she couldn't legally marry Tucker Isaacs until after she was freed by her father, Joe Fossett, years later. In the meantime, she and Tucker lived as man and wife and had children of their own.

Still to be accounted for, of course, is the most famous Hemings of all, Jefferson's alleged concubine Sally, also a daughter of Betty Hemings. Because of her privileged situation in the Thomas Jefferson household— whatever its exact nature—she had been given "her time" (unofficially freed, that is) by Jefferson's daughter Martha, and thus she escaped the humiliation of the Monticello slave sale of January 27, 1827. Her son Madison Hemings later recalled that he and his brother Eston Hemings "took their mother to live in a rented house in Charlottesville."

By 1832, she was living with Madison and his wife in a home on East Main Street; by the time of a special census taken in 1833, she was listed as free, according to records reported by Ervin L. Jordan Jr. in the 1995 *Magazine of Albemarle County History* and cited by Stanton. Meanwhile, Eston had married an Isaacs daughter named Julia Ann. Now free also, he and brother-in-law Tucker Isaacs may have worked together as joiners from a corner lot that in more recent years was the site of Timberlake's Drug Store.

Farther east on Main Street was Joe Fossett's ironworks shop, and still farther east was a "house of entertainment" operated by musician and gambler Daniel Farley, who may have been Mary Hemings's oldest child, Daniel, once given by Jefferson to his sister Anna. Apparently a free man by 1827, Farley also attended the slave sale at Monticello . . . and, "for one dollar," he bought his own presumed uncle, fifty-seven-year-old Peter Hemings, once a cook and "highly valued brewmaster" at Jefferson's Monticello, but in freedom destined to become a tailor.

What still might be called the Hemings protective association sprang into action again after Farley's death in 1838. He had left his house and lot to his own children, but when the real estate went to public auction a year later, a son of Jesse and Sally Bell Scott stepped in to buy it, Stanton reported.

She explained that the free blacks of Charlottesville "lived in a kind of littoral zone, alternately submerged or exposed by the tides of law and public opinion." Since even the free blacks in antebellum Virginia were denied the right to vote, much less hold public office, or even to attend school, their only means of "achieving security and social standing" was property—"the acquisition, preservation, and expansion of real estate was a critical aspect not only of success, but of survival and the maintenance of family unity." Thus, "a pattern of propertied free blacks working together to maximize security through all the legal means within their power is revealed in the public record, which shows the Isaacs, Hemings, Scott and Fossett family members in frequent legal interaction with each other, as well as with other propertied free blacks."

In time, though, some family members were prepared to move west and leave Virginia behind. Joseph Fossett freed his wife, children, and grandchildren in 1837, and that meant they had to leave within the year. By 1837, too, Sally Hemings had died (in 1835). Madison Hemings, Sally's son, had moved to Ohio, and now his brother Eston would follow suit. Madison had moved into "a rural community of former Virginia slaves located on the border of Pike and Ross counties." Eston and his wife chose Chillicothe, the Ross County seat, as their new home. There, Eston "pursued a dual career as a carpenter and musician." A whiz at fiddling, he led a popular band "playing for the balls of the white population all over southern Ohio."

Meanwhile, "a good many people" in his new surroundings accepted as true the talk that the tall newcomer—"light bronze" in color, according to one acquaintance—was Thomas Jefferson's son.

The Joe Fossetts also moved to Ohio. "By at least 1843, they were settled in Cincinnati, where Joe Fossett pursued the blacksmithing trade with his sons and lived on a city lot he had purchased for $500." With Joe and Edy were four of their children. "Still locked in bondage were James, Patsy, Isabella, and Peter, who recalled, sixty years later, that his master, John R. Jones, had 'promised my father to let him have me when he could raise the money, but in 1833 he refused to let him have me on any conditions.'"

Peter twice tried to run away, at least once with the help of his brother-in-law Tucker Isaacs. Peter's freedom finally was purchased, apparently by a coalition of friends and family. He joined the family in Cincinnati and eventually became a widely known Baptist minister and head of a catering firm. Soon leaving town also were Tucker and his wife, Betsy-Ann Isaacs, first to live in Cincinnati and then in Ross County, where their farmhouse would become a station in the Underground Railroad for fugitive slaves.

Next in the multifaceted Hemings family saga, Eston and his wife, Julia Ann (born Isaacs), moved from Ohio to Madison, Wisconsin, "changing both their surname and their race in the process." Not only that, but, "as part of the white community there, the Jeffersons, as they were now known, gained some prominence." Their two sons served in the Union army during the Civil War, "one afterwards becoming a leading Madison hotelkeeper, the other one of the wealthier citizens in Memphis, Tennessee."

Back in Charlottesville, meanwhile, the Hemings-Bell-Scott descendants, by Virginia's legal definition prior to 1910, also could claim to be white, noted Stanton, since all were more than three-quarters white in their ancestry (three out of four grandparents were white, and Mary Hemings, the fourth, was "of mixed heritage"). Thus, Robert Scott, son of Sally and Jesse Scott, once said before he died late in the nineteenth century at age ninety-six, "We considered ourselves white people."

A well-known local figure by the time of his death, the elderly Robert Scott was on hand to see the postbellum changes taking place as once largely rural Main Street became a bustling avenue of commerce while many other Hemings descendants missed that entire period.

One who *didn't* entirely miss it was an aging Peter Fossett, who returned from Ohio for a brief visit in 1900 as the last of the Monticello slaves to revisit the plantation of antebellum days and its neighboring city.

By then, the original Bell lot on Main Street no longer was in the family; his grandmother Mary Hemings Bell's house had been replaced by the Rosser office building, itself soon to be followed by "Charlottesville's first 'skyscraper,' the eight-story National Bank Building." But Peter Fossett could reflect on another kind of growth as well—on the gratifying fact that the latest generation of his extended family included three groundbreaking local educators: the first black to gain membership in the California state legislature; a doctor; a lawyer; a magna cum laude graduate of Harvard . . . and all of them able to trace their heritage back to his own great-grandmother, to their own great-*great*-grandmother, Betty Hemings, mother of the now famous Sally Hemings.

☆ ☆ ☆

Additional note: Among the related readings cited by Kirt von Daacke in his article are *Slaves Without Masters: The Free Negro in the Antebellum South* by Ira Berlin; *The Free Negro in Virginia* by John Henderson Russell; and *Free Negro Labor and Property Holding in Virginia, 1830–1860* by Luther Porter Jackson.

And by Lucia Stanton: her own study, *Slavery at Monticello,* as well as *Jefferson at Monticello* by James A. Bear Jr.; *Early Charlottesville* by James Alexander; *Thomas Jefferson and Sally Hemings: An American Controversy* by Annette Gordon-Reed; and "A Just and True Account: Two 1833 Parish Censuses of Albemarle County Free Blacks, *Magazine of Albemarle County History,* no. 53 (1995), by Ervin L. Jordan Jr.

1788
Patrick Henry Smelt a Rat

Patrick Henry was so worked up, he unconsciously twisted his wig around his head; diminutive James Madison debated the great issue before them from notes kept in a hat held in his hand.

It was one of those crucial moments when the slightest misstep could have changed history—important history affecting the future of both Virginia and the nation.

Today, we would wonder what was the issue here? Ratify the newly drawn U.S. Constitution? But of course!

In June 1788, however, Patrick Henry, James Monroe, George Mason, and a host of fellow leaders at a state constitutional convention fought tooth and nail *against* ratification. Lined up *in favor* of ratification, though, was another all-star cast: James Madison, George Wythe, Henry "Lighthorse Harry" Lee, popular Governor Edmund Randolph, even convention president Edmund Pendleton. And in *their* collective pocket, figuratively speaking, was an endorsement by George Washington, who had presided over the Philadelphia convention of 1787 that produced the proposed Constitution in the first place.

While George Washington may have chaired that meeting, Virginia's own James Madison had emerged from the closed-door Philadelphia sessions so impressive in discussion and debate over the great charter's far-reaching provisions that he became known as "Father of the Constitution." Patrick Henry, on the other hand, had refused election as a delegate, later explaining that he "smelt a rat." Governor Randolph, who did go, later refused to join the thirty-nine delegates (of fifty-five attending the Constitutional Convention) in signing the foundation document produced at Philadelphia.

George Mason, who also attended, had fought for inclusion of a provision forbidding continuation of the slave trade in the future United States, but he lost that battle. Now, on the state level, he was a leader in the war against ratification, whereas Governor Randolph now was an adherent of the proposed Constitution. Henry, for his part and still smelling a rat, did his passionate best to defeat the ratification proposal . . . and almost did.

His opposition, noted Virginius Dabney in his Virginia history *Virginia: The New Dominion,* "came close to succeeding and could have precipitated a national crisis." The published debates from the month-long Virginia convention of 1788, said Dabney, took up 652 pages, and of these, "136 pages, or more than one-fifth, contain the words of Patrick Henry."

By now a former five-time governor of Virginia himself, Henry of course still was the great orator best known today for his ringing pre–Revolutionary War declaration: "Give me liberty or give me death!"

That was his dramatic pronouncement in 1775, and he still was a passionate debater in 1788, thirteen years later, against any perceived encroachment upon individual liberties. "It was an era," noted Dabney, "when speeches often lasted for hours, even for an entire day. When Henry was speaking, no matter at what length, he seems to have held the attention of those who crowded the floor and the galleries."

The crucial state convention was held from June 2 to June 27 in the newly built Richmond Academy building on Twelfth Street between Broad and Market Streets.

A series of related events had led, first, to the Philadelphia meeting, and now to Richmond. They stemmed from the fact that the Articles of Confederation adopted by the thirteen rebelling colonies toward the end of the Revolution had been too loose, with the colony-states acting for all the world like independent republics, even to the point of issuing their own individual currencies. When Virginia and Maryland couldn't agree on oystering rights along the Potomac River, their joint border, the Virginia General Assembly called for a conference at Annapolis in 1786 to resolve such trade and commerce disputes among the various states. Only five of the thirteen sent delegates, but Congress responded to the mini-convention by issuing the call for the Constitutional Convention that met in Philadelphia the year after the Annapolis conclave. The sole purpose, said Congress, would be to revise the Articles of the Confederation.

As the delegates then filtered into Philadelphia, George Washington was the quick and unanimous choice as president of the convention. Fellow Virginian James Madison kept the minutes of the secret deliberations, notes destined to be published only after his death.

While George Mason fought for an end to the slave trade, Governor Edmund Randolph put forward the so-called Virginia Plan, which would have given larger states (such as Virginia) extra powers, while New Jersey offered its own plan favoring smaller states, with a compromise the final result. The new Constitution and its seven articles then went before the states for ratification, with nine needed to nail it into place as the new covenant among the former colonies.

As the ratification debate unfolded in Virginia the following June, Edmund Pendleton, painfully crippled by a fall from a horse, was chosen president of the state convention meeting in Richmond. Thomas Jefferson, cloistered in Paris as American minister to France at the time, once called Pendleton the ablest debater he had ever encountered, noted

Dabney. Meanwhile, the switch from presumed *anti* to *pro* by the state convention's other notable "Edmund," Governor Randolph, shook and embittered the antiratification forces so much that Mason privately called him a "Benedict Arnold."

The antis may have been doomed to defeat in any case, argued Dabney, late editor of the *Richmond Times-Dispatch* and a Pulitzer Prize winner for his editorials. "The advocates of the Constitution were better organized, they had superior leadership, and they outmaneuvered the opposition from the beginning," he wrote. "Henry and Mason were unable to coordinate their strategy. Henry wanted to attack the Constitution as a whole, whereas Mason preferred to analyze it clause by clause."

Argument over the ratification issue became so heated that some delegates feared Governor Randolph and Patrick Henry might resort to a duel—they didn't. Meanwhile, Revolutionary War hero Henry "Lighthorse Harry" Lee startled many with his vehement attacks against the much older—and widely venerated—Patrick Henry, saying at one point, "I hold his unsupported authority in contempt."

The future of Kentucky, still a part of Virginia, became an issue in the divided convention. The Kentuckians wished to have the backing of Virginia for their right to use the Mississippi River for trade with the outside world, rather than ship all their goods over mountain and valley to the east, but the antis "spread word that ratification would mean relinquishing control of the Mississippi to Spain." As a result, the delegates from the Kentucky counties appeared ready to vote no to the Constitution.

Still others had other doubts, it seems. "Aware that ratification might fail," added Dabney's account, "the proponents shrewdly promised, as the final vote neared, that they would earnestly seek a series of amendments, notably a Bill of Rights. That tipped the scales in their favor." (*Note:* Added to the basic American charter in 1791, thanks in large part to the continuing efforts of one Patrick Henry, the first ten amendments to the U.S. Constitution, guaranteeing free speech, trial by jury, the right to bear arms, freedom of religion, and similar protections, indeed did become the Bill of Rights.)

The time finally came to submit the proposition to a vote, and the learned William and Mary law teacher George Wythe so moved. But Patrick Henry offered a substitute motion that would have "nullified" the Wythe motion. According to parliamentary procedure, that meant the first vote should be on the second motion, thus the pros would vote no and the antis would vote yes—yes to Patrick Henry's substitute.

As the roll was taken, the antiratification forces at first led the count—by as much as twenty-five to twelve at a high point. But there would be surprises as the count continued. For one thing, three of the Kentucky delegates rejected the instructions of their delegation and voted *against* Henry's motion (and thus *for* the Constitution). Tighter and tighter every highly charged minute, the tally reached sixty-nine to sixty-nine. But the count went on, and in the end Patrick Henry's motion was defeated, eighty-eight to eighty.

Now would come the vote that really mattered for the historical record. Would Virginia ratify the new U.S. Constitution, as proposed in the motion by George Wythe? With one of the delegates switching to the pro side for this count, the answer was a clear—but not exactly resounding—yes, by a vote of eighty-nine to seventy-nine.

The fact is, little New Hampshire had weighed in just the week before as the ninth state required for ratification of the Constitution, but prestigious Virginia's affirmation still was important as endorsement for a central government with much greater authority than had been the case under the old Articles of Confederation. As Dabney noted, Virginia at the time was the largest and most heavily populated of all the states. Further, it was a state "whose territory bisected the country from the Atlantic to the Mississippi." If Virginia "had refused to go along," he added, "the future of the nation might well have been in doubt."

☆ ☆ ☆

Additional note: Virginia once included the lands north of the Ohio River and east of the Mississippi, sometimes known as the Old Northwest, but ceded them to the rest of the new nation, thus setting up the future formation of the states of Ohio, Michigan, Wisconsin, Illinois, and Indiana. Fortunately for all, the usually astute Thomas Jefferson was "mercilessly ignored" when he suggested giving those future states outlandish, tongue-twisting names such as Chersonesus, Assensisipia, and Pelisipia, Dabney recalled. Meanwhile, with its ratification of the U.S. Constitution in June 1788, Virginia became the tenth state in the Union. In 1792, meanwhile, the three Kentucky counties severed their ties with Virginia and became a state as well.

★

1794
Medical Marvel Kept Secret

★

Only twenty-five, married barely a year, isolated in a rural log cabin, red-haired Jessee Bennett faced a momentous decision—operate, or likely see either his wife or their unborn child die before his eyes.

The location was tiny Edom, Virginia, west of Harrisonburg; the time was the wintry night of January 14, 1794, and the problem facing the young couple was Elizabeth Hog Bennett's difficult birthing of their first child. Hours after she had gone into labor, it was clear that delivery of the infant was obstructed.

Repeated attempts at a forceps delivery, with Dr. Alexander Humphreys of nearby Staunton looking on, had failed. Normally, the next step would be a craniotomy, or forced removal of the infant from the birth passage by crushing its head, a fatal procedure.

The courageous mother, certain she would die, begged the two men to save her baby by any means possible. Jessee Bennett proposed a cesarean delivery, never before performed in North America. Oh no, absolutely not, vowed the veteran practitioner Humphreys—he would have no truck with anything so risky. When Bennett became more insistent, Humphreys stomped out into the snowy night . . . and left.

But the Pennsylvania-born Bennett, albeit somewhat untried, was himself a physician who had "read" his medicine in Philadelphia, studied in Edinburgh, and completed his training at the University of Pennsylvania. Now, his mind made up, he wasted no time. In minutes, Elizabeth was rendered unconscious by a large dose of laudanum; she lay upon a makeshift table of two planks set across barrels. Two black servant women helped by holding her, and the patient's sister, Mrs. William Hawkins, also assisted.

"With one quick sweep of the knife," as a future historian was to say, the gambling doctor made his incision. Seconds later, he lifted forth the child—a girl.

Taken from the author's article, "A Sharp Knife and Some Stout Thread," appearing in the *Old Farmer's Almanac* of 1985 and reprinted here with permission.

Then, with the remark "this shall be the last," he quickly removed both of his wife's ovaries. By the flickering lamplight, he sewed up the wound with stout linen thread normally used for heavy clothing.

Amazingly, both mother and child would live to ripe old ages, as did Bennett himself, after brief service as an army surgeon in the abortive "Whiskey Rebellion" in his native Pennsylvania; after representing his subsequent Mason home county (now part of West Virginia) as a member of the Virginia House of Delegates; even after figuring briefly as a witness in the treason trial of Aaron Burr in Richmond.

Aside from saving his own wife and child, what Bennett had accomplished that January night could be construed as the first abdominal operation in America, and indeed was, so far as is known today, America's first cesarean delivery and ovariectomy . . . but the nation's medical community had no idea of Dr. Bennett's "triple feat" for another century or so. For many years, in fact, Dr. John Richmond of Newton, Ohio, was credited with the first cesarean for a surgical delivery he performed thirty-three years *after* Bennett's operation.

News of the real pioneer delivery finally was reported in 1891 by Dr. A. L. Knight, a family friend contributing to a history of the Great Kanawha Valley of today's West Virginia, an obscure citation to be followed up nearly forty years later by a report in the *West Virginia Medical Journal* of July 1929. Undoubtedly, Bennett himself could have sped things up, but he is said to have once explained, "No doctor with any feelings of delicacy would report an operation he had done on his own wife."

1 7 9 6
"The Man Himself"

It took some smooth and fast talking by Thomas Jefferson, but the handsome result was perhaps the finest piece of marble statuary to be found in the United States today—Jean Antoine Houdon's white marble statue of George Washington that stands at a central spot below the state capitol's rotunda and hidden dome in Richmond.

It stands there thanks largely to Jefferson, who, as minister to France, supposedly talked a nervous Houdon into crossing the Atlantic by offering him life insurance in addition to a fee equal to several thousand dollars today. It was Jefferson also, not so incidentally, who designed the graceful capitol itself, based upon a Roman temple at Nîmes, France. Its dome is not really hidden—at least not from those looking up from inside and directly below. It's hidden from view from the outside by the classical roofline of the templelike structure.

Art historians and critics consider the Houdon statue of Washington to be extremely fine art, but it is noteworthy also as the only statuary of Washington taken from real life—indeed, taken from a plaster cast of the great man's face, despite his fear of suffocation in the process.

So successful was the Houdon creation that when Lafayette saw it years later, he reportedly exclaimed: "This is the man himself; I can almost realize he is going to move."

The original idea had been for Congress to fund a monumental *equestrian* statue of Washington, but the funding aspect apparently discouraged the national lawmakers. The Virginia General Assembly then decided, in 1784, that Virginia would do the honors for her own native son and Father of his Country—but not-quite-yet first president, since this was only a year after the Treaty of Paris, which officially ended the American Revolution and still three years in advance of the Constitutional Convention of 1787 that would create the basic American charter and the presidency.

The Virginia lawmakers decided upon a less ambitious statue of Washington standing on a four-foot base. According to *Richmond Times-Dispatch* columnist Ray McAllister, Governor Benjamin Harrison, father and great-grandfather of two future U.S. presidents (William Henry Harrison, ninth president; and Benjamin Harrison, twenty-third president), sent word to Jefferson in France to find a sculptor for the job. Enter, then, Monsieur Houdon, who now braved the cross-Atlantic voyage to take Washington's body measurements and apply the plaster face mold at Mount Vernon.

Houdon's fine statue, supposedly replicating the real George Washington's unusually big frame of six feet, two and a half inches in exact detail, took its honored place in the state capitol in 1896, three years before Washington's death.

Treasured ever since its arrival at the capitol, the statue nonetheless shows a nicked marble tassel on G. W.'s cane, thanks to a pair—maybe it was a trio—of warring Richmond newspaper editors who confronted each other at the capitol with the Washington statue somehow caught in between. One party fired a pistol at the other party, and that was it. Off went the chunk of the tassel. "True story," wrote *Times-Dispatch* columnist McAllister on May 15, 1996, the day after the two-hundredth anniversary of the statue's emplacement in the state capitol. "Henry Rives Pollard of the *Richmond Examiner* went after two rival publishers. All three drew pistols, with the statue in between."

Imagine, dispassionate newspaper people!

Meanwhile, reported McAllister, the Houdon sculpture is "so good that twenty-four full-size bronze copies have been made," and, "they reside in places of honor the world over."

It might also be mentioned that Houdon also did a marble bust of Jefferson, and it can be seen today at the Boston Museum of Fine Arts.

1 7 9 9
An Avoidable Death?

It was a bleak December day when a certain gentleman-farmer braved an intermittent mix of snow, rain, and sleet to ride about his riverside property in the northern part of Virginia from midmorning to midafternoon. Rain or shine, it was a commonplace activity for him, but he came down with a cold that very evening. Two days later he was fighting for life.

This was not the first time George Washington had approached death's door. As a young man, according to his various biographers, he had survived deadly smallpox, malaria, and even tuberculosis. He also was laid low several times during his lifetime by dysentery, an illness common in the eighteenth century.

Once, in 1757, he was ill with dysentery for five months. In November of that year, a fellow militia officer wrote to Virginia's Royal Governor Robert Dinwiddie to report that Washington "for upwards of three Months past . . . has labour'd under a Bloody Flux, [and] about a week ago his Disorder greatly increas'd attended with bad Fevers."

Washington soon returned home to Mount Vernon and a regimen of quiet and rest. As late as the following February, however, he had to cancel a proposed trip to the Colonial capital of Williamsburg, thanks to the same long-standing bout of dysentery. "My constitution is certainly greatly impaired," he wrote to an associate. He finally was on his feet again in March 1758—just in time to meet his future wife, the widow Martha Dandridge Custis.

Incidentally, it was not so long before, in 1755, that Washington had risen from another sickbed to accompany British Maj. Gen. Edward Braddock into his disastrous frontier battle with the French and their Indian allies at the Monongahela River near Fort Duquesne, the future site of Pittsburgh. When Braddock was fatally wounded, the fever-weakened Washington proved indispensable in organizing an orderly withdrawal of the survivors. From start to finish of the wilderness fray, he had two horses shot out from under him and took four bullet holes—not in his person, fortunately, but in his clothing.

Once the French and Indian War drew to a close in 1763, George Washington and his bride, Martha, enjoyed a peaceful respite at their beloved Mount Vernon for a full twelve years. Then, in 1775, George Washington was appointed commander in chief of the Continental army, this time to fight *against* the British.

While in winter quarters at Morristown, New Jersey, in 1777, the general came down with an abdominal infection that again kept him in bed for a time, but he recovered. He also survived the many perils of an eight-year war against the British, during which he was absent from his plantation on the Potomac River for six uninterrupted years. After leaving Mount Vernon in 1775, he returned only in 1781—on his way to Yorktown.

There, of course, Washington achieved his signal victory of the Revolutionary War—the surrender of Maj. Gen. Lord Charles Cornwallis. But there, too, he and Martha lost her son, his adopted stepson, "Jacky," to camp fever. While George Washington himself would father no children, he and Martha now adopted and raised Jacky's youngest two children.

Its outcome now all but certain, the rest of the war still lay ahead—the hostilities would not end officially until 1783. Next would come the turbulent politics of establishing the new United States as a constitutional republic. Then, and only then, would Washington serve as the nation's first president—and very nearly die in office. His illness of 1790 also began with all the symptoms of a common cold, but it was influenza, the flu, instead. In fact, flu at the time was sweeping through the young country's first real capital, New York City. Also ailing were Thomas Jefferson, James Madison, Abigail Adams, and her son Charles.

George Washington, still powerful in physique at age fifty-eight, nonetheless lapsed into a serious case of pneumonia . . . to become so ill one of his doctors predicted he would probably die. Contrary to such expectation, however, he rallied later the same day. His fever broke, and he soon was himself again.

Just a year before, Washington had undergone painful surgery for a tumor on his thigh, and that medical episode was such an ordeal he was moved to tell an aide, "I know it is very doubtful whether I shall ever rise from this bed, and God knows it is perfectly indifferent to me whether I do or not." In his later years, additionally, the aging Virginian also suffered the pains of rheumatism, along with the discomfort of ill-fitting dentures (but, historians insist, no *wooden* teeth).

With such a medical history behind him, Washington probably thought little of the sore throat he developed the morning after his long ride about Mount Vernon in the rain, snow, and sleet of December 12, 1799.

He stayed indoors for most of the next day, the thirteenth. He read aloud to Martha and his private secretary, Tobias Lear, after dinner that evening, despite a growing hoarseness.

During the night, he awoke with a burning fever and had difficulty breathing. He now could hardly speak. His condition worsened steadily throughout the day of December 14.

Four bleedings, the first performed by his plantation overseer, did not help.

Arriving at midmorning, Dr. James Craik, George Washington's friend and doctor in war and peace, diagnosed the problem as "inflammatory quinsy," or severe inflammation of the throat, but was unable to stop its raging course.

At 4:30 P.M., Washington instructed Martha to fetch two wills from his desk, selected one and told her to burn the other. Soon after, he told Lear, "I find I am going, my breath cannot continue long; I believed from the first attack it would be fatal."

A while later he told Craik and two consulting physicians: "I feel myself going. I thank you for your attention. You had better not take any more trouble about me; but let me go off quietly; I cannot last long."

About 10 o'clock that night, he weakly said into Tobias Lear's ear: "I am just going. Have me decently buried." He gave instructions as to his burial, looked sharply at his secretary and asked, "Do you understand me?"

When Lear replied yes, Washington said, "'Tis well."

Minutes later, his breathing improved, and he stopped moving restlessly. Martha was at the foot of the bed, and Lear still held his employer's hand. Dr. Craik was in a chair by the fireplace.

The patient now withdrew his hand from Lear's and felt his own pulse. Then his hand went limp.

Quietly, almost serenely, George Washington was gone, his last words on this earth, "'Tis well."

☆ ☆ ☆

Additional note: While George Washington might have died anyway, doctors today would never bleed a patient in his condition. Sadly, the bleedings administered to a George Washington already weakened by throat inflammation may, in fact, have killed him.

1799-1836
Moments of National Grief

As the great ones, the Founding Fathers, began to die off, how did their newly created nation take the news? With considerable grief coupled with reverence, it seems fully evident from a glance at the obituaries that ran in the newspapers of the former colonies.

Virginia's own George Washington, the first in so many things, was, in 1799, the first of Virginia's Big Four to go.

"Sir," wrote a correspondent to the *New York Spectator* on December 16, "it is with inexpressible grief that I have to announce to you the death of the great and good General Washington. He died last evening between 10 and 11 o'clock, after a short illness of about twenty-four hours. His disorder was an inflammatory sore throat, which proceeded from a cold, of which he made but little complaint on Friday. On Saturday morning about 3 o'clock, he became ill."

The doctors then assembled, said the *Spectator*'s informant. "Every medical assistance was offered, but without the desired effect."

Washington's "last scene corresponded with the whole tenor of his life," said this same source. He uttered "not a groan nor a complaint."

In another report, another day, the *Spectator* noted that President John Adams, "with deep regret, announces to the army, the death of its beloved Chief, Gen. George Washington." Adams, the *Spectator* assured, shared in the grief, "which every heart must feel for so heavy and afflicting a public loss." Not only that, Adams surely was "desirous to express his high sense of the vast debt of gratitude which is due to the virtue, talents, and ever memorable services of the illustrious deceased."*

☆ ☆ ☆

Next to die of the Big Four from Virginia who led in the Revolution and in the newly formed nation that emerged, but twenty-seven years after Washington's death, was the venerated Thomas Jefferson. And what symbolic, even exquisite, timing to bow out on the fiftieth anniversary of the very first Independence Day. And then, to be accompanied in death that same July 4, 1826, by his old compatriot from Massachusetts, John Adams! "They were glorious in their lives, and in their deaths they were not divided," proclaimed the *Albany (N.Y.) Argus & Gazette*.

Another voice in the lamenting but wondering chorus was that of the *New York American,* which said, "By a coincidence marvellous and enviable, THOMAS JEFFERSON in like manner with his great compeer, John Adams, breathed his last on the 4th of July."

The exquisite timing, historically, of course struck one and all, and not only because of John Adams's death later the same day. The *Philadelphia National Gazette* reported that Jefferson "expired, at Monticello, on the Fourth of July, within the same hour at which the Declaration of Independence was promulgated in the hall of Congress, FIFTY YEARS AGO."

---

*The obituary references cited here, and obituary information about other famous Americans, can be found at the website www.earlyamerica.obits.

As explained by Jefferson biographer Saul K. Padover in his *Jefferson: A Great American's Life and Ideas,* the dying Jefferson, eighty-four years of age, had fought hard to live until the Fourth. When he awoke the morning of July 3, he had said, "This is the Fourth of July." But it wasn't . . . quite.

When Dr. Robley Dunglison approached with his medicine, Jefferson asked, "Is this the Fourth?" and the doctor replied, "It soon will be."

That night Jefferson was semidelirious. He "muttered about the Committee of Public Safety and that it should be warned." At eleven the next morning, he tried to speak again. Grandson Thomas Jefferson Randolph pressed a wet sponge to his mouth. He lost consciousness, and two hours later, he was gone, the great, multifaceted spirit of America's Renaissance man stilled.

But it was the Fourth. The author of the Declaration of Independence had lived to the day that meant so much to him.

Famously, too, in Quincy, Massachusetts, by one of the most remarkable coincidences in history, John Adams, Jefferson's great compatriot from their days in the Continental Congress of 1776, was dying. Back then, in Philadelphia, of course, they had combined efforts to produce the Declaration—Thomas Jefferson to write it, John Adams to manage its passage on the floor of the Congress.

And true, they had gone through a breach of their great friendship when Jefferson succeeded Adams as president and for some years thereafter, but more recently they had resumed their old friendship, communicating frequently and earnestly by letter.

Now, on July 4, 1826, John Adams's last thoughts were on Jefferson. He didn't know that Jefferson had just died, that very afternoon. "Thomas Jefferson still survives," said Adams at the very moment when, he, too, succumbed.

Quite naturally, it was not a coincidence to go unmarked . . . nor unmourned.

"Two of the great and gifted of our countrymen, the venerated fathers of our Republic, THOMAS JEFFERSON and JOHN ADAMS, are no more!" said the *Albany Argus & City Gazette.* "It is not amongst the least of the events so wisely ordered in the progress of this country, that the Author of the Declaration of its Liberties, and his eminent associate in that duty, should be permitted not only to live, and to witness the prosperous experiment of half a century, but on that day fifty years on which they signed and issued their Declaration to the world, they should be called, both together, from amongst a people so signally blessed by their labours."

Thunderstruck also was the *New York American:* "We remember nothing in the annals of man so striking, so beautiful, as the death of these two 'time-honoured' patriots, on the jubilee of that freedom, which they devoted themselves and all that was dear to them, to proclaim and establish."

Said the *American* also: "It cannot be all chance. It may be permitted for us to believe, that the prayer most natural on such a day, in the mouths of such men, 'Lord, now lettest thou thy servant depart in peace,' was put up and favourably heard."

☆ ☆ ☆

Incredibly enough, whether by chance or by God's will, another of the Big Four from Virginia, this time a Revolutionary War soldier, one-time Virginia governor, and later the fifth president of the United States (after Jefferson and James Madison), also would die on a July 4.

The last of the Revolutionary leaders to serve as president, the last also of Virginia's four early presidents, James Monroe had served at Yorktown under George Washington, had studied law under Thomas Jefferson, had served President James Madison of Virginia as secretary of state and secretary of war at the same time (during the War of 1812). He once owned an Albemarle County farm that today is the site of the University of Virginia, founded by his good friend, mentor, and neighbor Thomas Jefferson. Monroe's home of Ash Lawn–Highland was—and is—situated close to Jefferson's beloved Monticello, just a few miles outside Charlottesville. Each historic site is open to the public today.

Monroe is best known for his "Monroe Doctrine," by which he declared no European power would be allowed to meddle in the affairs of the Americas, North and South. His largely peaceful and noncontroversial years (1817–25) as president became known as the "Era of Good Feelings." As a measure of Monroe's popularity in early America, he was elected to his second term with every Electoral College vote but one.

Unlike Washington and Jefferson (or Adams), however, he did not die at home. Rather, he was visiting a daughter in New York City in mid-1831. The exact day, incredibly, was July 4.

☆ ☆ ☆

With Monroe gone, only James Madison was left . . . for another five years. Notably small in stature, this elderly Virginian would leave a towering legacy, not only as a former president (the fourth), not only as secretary of state under Jefferson, nor as governor of Virginia, but for such a key role in the Constitutional Convention of 1787 that he forevermore would be known as "Father of the Constitution."

Like fellow Virginians Washington, Jefferson, and Monroe, James Madison was elected to two consecutive terms as president, but he unfortunately chanced to be the president in office during the War of 1812, during which the President's House, now called the White House, itself was burned by the invading British. All that, thankfully, was far in the past by the time Madison reached the end of his life on June 28, 1831, at his Montpelier estate outside Orange.

"The death of Ex-President Madison, though an event not unexpected, has produced a sensation in the public mind corresponding with the distinguished talents and exalted character of the deceased," proclaimed a *Journal of Commerce* article reprinted by the *Hartford Connecticut Observer*.

Madison did not die on a July 4, but the *Journal* couldn't resist pointing out that he *almost* did. "Six days added to his life would have carried him to the 4th of July, on which memorable day all his predecessors in the office of President died, with the exception of Washington."

Summing up the final hours of John Adams and all four great Virginians who led in time of revolution, in times of war and peace, the same periodical also pointed out that they had ranged in age at the times of their deaths from George Washington's sixty-eight years to John Adams's ninety-one years, with the average age fixed at "80 years and a fraction." More specifically, the *Journal* article also noted: "The proud but melancholy list, now stands as follows:

	DIED	AGE
George Washington	10th Dec. 1799	68
John Adams	4th July 1826	91
Thomas Jefferson	4th July 1826	84
James Monroe	4th July 1831	73
James Madison	28 June 1836	86"

And so the same proud list still does stand today.

✭ Part 3 ✭
Nineteenth Century

1 8 0 0
Gabriel's Insurrection

But for a single thunderstorm of mammoth proportions one summer's night in 1800, the history of Virginia—and therefore, America—might have turned out quite differently.

Instead of a Civil War six decades later, Virginia might have been torn apart by a real race war, blacks against whites, in the first year of the nineteenth century.

How that would have affected imminent events, such as the Lewis and Clark Expedition of 1804 and later exploration of the American West, is impossible to judge today. But one can suppose . . . suppose the Virginian Thomas Jefferson had *not* become president in 1801, thus setting the stage for his vaunted Louisiana Purchase and the exploits of Lewis and Clark.

In 1800, George Washington had just died. John Adams was president, James Monroe was governor of Virginia, Jefferson was vice president. Slavery prevailed in the South, Virginia very much included . . . and what a complex imponderable it sometimes could be. Here, for instance, a puzzle still troubling us today, was a great man, Jefferson, who had written the Declaration of Independence, but who himself owned slaves. *Owned* fellow human beings as *property!*

And yet . . . there is this picture of Jefferson's return not long before to Monticello, his beloved mountaintop plantation overlooking the town of Charlottesville, from years in France. His slaves hadn't seen their master for five years, and now they rushed down the steep, not inconsiderable hill in a fever of greeting, unhitched the four horses pulling his carriage, and took their places in the traces. Unbidden, the slaves then hauled the carriage up the small mountain. "When the door of the carriage was opened," Jefferson's onlooking daughter

Martha later related, "they received him in their arms and bore him to the house, crowding around and kissing his hands and feet—some blubbering and crying—others laughing. It seemed impossible to satisfy their anxiety to touch and kiss the very earth that bore him."

That same year of 1789, with Jefferson about to serve as secretary of state, a young slave on the Thomas Prosser tobacco plantation outside Richmond already, at age thirteen, had been blacksmithing for about three years. He was growing unusually strong and tall—by 1800 he would be two to three inches over six feet, a giant among men of his era. Gabriel, for that was his name, could read and write, and by 1800 he was used to the small freedoms that came with being hired out for work away from his master's plantation.

Those same freedoms gave him unusual opportunity to move around and make contacts far beyond the plantation, but still he was a slave . . . and it rankled.

The societal stream in which he swam included plantation slaves, hired-out slaves, free blacks, lower-class whites, even a white radical or abolitionist or two. And when Gabriel began singing a song of rebellion, many of them listened. Like Gabriel, they knew the idealistic precepts of the American Revolution. They knew about the endless slave revolts threatening the power structure of Hispaniola (today's Haiti and Dominican Republic) in the Caribbean. It didn't help that in 1799 Gabriel was branded on the left hand for stealing a pig then biting off a good part of his captor's ear. He could have been executed for maiming a white man, but Virginia law allowed public branding if he could recite a verse from the Bible, according to the Public Broadcast System's television series *Africans in the Americas.* "Gabriel recited his verse, and then was branded in his left hand in open court," said the PBS account. He had to spend a month in jail, too.

Once Gabriel was out of jail, it wasn't long before he began building his quiet conspiracy, aimed not simply at achieving freedom but at killing the whites of Richmond and vicinity en masse and taking over their belongings. Bold and clever, he preached a message eventually reaching hundreds, if not thousands, of slaves. Many answering his call busied themselves fashioning scythes into swords, making clubs and spears as primitive arms. But Gabriel and his closest henchmen also made plans to seize modern firearms, powder, and shot from the Richmond arsenal and the state capitol. Gabriel himself stole into the capitol in Richmond on Sundays to inspect its store of arms.

His plan was to set fire to the largely wooden structures in the lower part of Richmond, then attack the whites rushing to the scene to fight the fires. His followers immediately would seize the arsenal and Capitol Square in Richmond, with Governor James Monroe to be held hostage. Gabriel's vision called for rebellion throughout the Commonwealth and indeed in every state that allowed slavery.

And all with no one in the targeted white community the wiser, it seems. White Virginians, wrote Virginius Dabney in his comprehensive history, *Virginia: The New Dominion,* "had been gravely alarmed by the bloody atrocities in Haiti, where slaves had revolted against the French. But they did not suspect the existence in the Old Dominion of this widely ramified plot engineered by a gigantic slave named Gabriel—a plot far more extensive than anything of the sort, before or since, in the history of Virginia."

Gabriel's planned revolt would have been far more sweeping than the rampage led by slave Nat Turner in Virginia's Southampton County three decades later, as Dabney also noted. Gabriel and his chief cohort, Jack Bowler (in some sources identified as Jack Ditcher), apparently had found coconspirators in locales as widespread as Norfolk, Charlottesville, and Petersburg, and in Caroline and Louisa Counties. The startling extent of the conspiracy was testimony, Dabney also wrote, to the "persuasive powers of Gabriel and Bowler, or of widespread yearning for freedom on the part of the slaves, or hatred of the whites, or all three factors combined."

Governor (and future President) James Monroe later reported to the Virginia General Assembly that Gabriel's plan "embraced most of the slaves in the city [of Richmond] and neighborhood, and . . . extended to several of the adjacent counties."

Then, too, according to the online narrative stemming from the PBS *Africans in the Americans* documentary, "while the majority of the men were slaves, the conspirators drew free blacks and a few white workers to their cause. . . . Two French militant abolitionists, Charles Quersey and Alexander Beddenhurst, joined the ranks as leaders. A slave recruit named King, when told of the plot, said, 'I was never so glad to hear anything in my life. I am ready to join them at any moment. I could slay the white people like sheep.'"

When rumors of the slave revolt began to circulate shortly before Gabriel's target date of August 30 for the start of the uprising, said the same narrative, Governor Monroe did nothing. Dabney, however, said that Monroe responded quickly when slaves on the Mosby Sheppard plantation warned their master of the planned massacre, and he in turn alerted the governor. Monroe immediately called out the militia, but that was not the reason for the rebellion's failure.

The fact is, the Saturday night of August 30, Gabriel and his small "army" already were gathered at Brook Swamp just northwest of the city, ready to strike, when the worst thunderstorm in years rolled in and dumped torrents of rain on the Richmond area. In no time, streets, roads, and gullies were flooded, and the bridge over the swamp was washed out. With the rebelling slaves cut off from the city, Richmond was saved.

The storm that stopped the slave rebellion in its tracks, and thus had long-lasting impact on Virginia history, wrote newspaper editor James Callender, was "the most terrible thunder Storm . . . that I ever witnessed in this State."

The conspirators, of course, thought to continue with their plans as soon as the storm waters cleared . . . probably on Sunday evening the thirty-first, but too late. Slaves in two locations, said the PBS account, "cracked under the pressure and told their masters." White patrols and the militia now scoured the countryside in search of the rebels. "Gabriel and Jack Ditcher disappeared. Others eluded capture for several days, but by September 9, almost thirty slaves were in jail awaiting trial in the court of 'Oyer and Terminer,' a special court in which slaves were tried without benefit of jury."

Now began the executions . . . but such harsh reprisal soon raised concerns among Virginia's white leadership. With ten rebel slaves already executed, Governor Monroe wrote Vice President and fellow Virginian Thomas Jefferson asking for advice, the PBS account relates.

"When to arrest the hand of the Executioner," said Monroe, "is a question of great importance."

In reply five days later, Jefferson seemed to agree as he warned, "The other states & the world at large will forever condemn us if we indulge in a principle of revenge, or go one step beyond absolute necessity."

Asking not to be quoted, Jefferson suggested, in essence, shipping out those bad actors not yet executed. Expressing doubt "whether these people can ever be permitted to go at large among us with safety," Jefferson somewhat rhetorically asked: "Is there no fort & garrison of the state or of the Union, where they would be confined, & where the presence of the garrison would preclude all ideas of attempting a rescue."

Jefferson used no question mark to end the thought, which thus came across as a suggested solution.

The fact is, some of the suspected rebel slaves indeed were shipped out—sent to other states. Over a two-month period, an estimated sixty-five slaves were tried in connection with the rebellion; twenty-six were executed by hanging; some were pardoned or found not guilty; one committed suicide by hanging; two escaped from custody; and the remainder went to other locales. The Commonwealth by law had to reimburse the owners of executed or "exiled" slaves for their "value." As a result, the uprising cost Virginia's government $8,900 in such reimbursements.

Gabriel himself finally surfaced, quite literally, by swimming in the James River to the awaiting schooner *Mary* on September 14—apparently by prearrangement, the vessel's captain, a former slave overseer named Richardson Taylor, planned to carry the rebel leader to safety. Ironically, a slave on board the *Mary* turned in Gabriel when the schooner docked in Norfolk. "Gabriel and Taylor were both arrested," adds the PBS account.

If Gabriel had any defense against the accusations piled up against him, it already had been shattered by testimony of the slave Solomon, Gabriel's own brother and coconspirator in the affair. "My brother Gabriel was the person who influenced me to join him and others in order that (as he said) we might conquer the white people and possess ourselves of their property," Solomon apparently told his interrogators.

At Gabriel's bidding, Solomon also said, he had made twelve "scythe-swords." Solomon readily confirmed that the plan had been to attack Richmond, the capitol, the arsenal, the local prison, "the governor's house and his person." Further: "The inhabitants were to be massacred, save those who begged for quarter and agreed to serve as soldiers with them [the conspirators]."

Convicted on September 11 for his role in the uprising, Solomon was hanged the next day. His brother Gabriel went to the gallows on October 10. Bowler also was hanged, Dabney reported. Other sources say rebel slave Jack Ditcher was sent out of state, to New Orleans. (Incidentally, a slave named Jack Ditcher was indicted in 1745 in Amelia County for stealing a purse containing thirty shillings, according to an online genealogical site. He was sentenced to thirty-nine lashes at the public whipping post. If the same Jack Ditcher, he almost certainly would have been seventy or older by 1800, fifty-five years later.)

Meanwhile, suppose the slave rebellion had gone forward the night of August 30. Had the thunderstorm never struck, even a partial success could have wreaked incalculable havoc upon the white power structure of Virginia. A captured Governor James Monroe, for instance, might never have become *President* Monroe, might never have promulgated the Monroe Doctrine. Then, too, with Virginia and possibly the entire South embroiled in an ongoing struggle between rebelling slaves and whites, Vice President Jefferson might *not* have won that multiballot struggle in the House of Representatives in 1801 that gave him the presidency over Aaron Burr by a single vote.

As it was, the thwarted uprising did have lasting impact in the Old Dominion, as Dabney noted in his history of Virginia. Citing the episode's "powerful impact on the minds of the whites in Virginia," Dabney said the uprising and reports of the "increasingly gruesome events in Santo Domingo" combined to cause "a strong reaction against liberalization of the laws covering chattel servitude." As he noted also, local voices in favor of abolition were stilled for some time to come, and "a permanent guard" was posted at the state capitol until the Civil War era. Added Dabney: "The erroneous impression prevails that this antiliberal trend in Virginia did not set in until the Nat Turner Insurrection of 1831 and William Lloyd Garrison's almost simultaneous founding of his wildly abusive journal, *The Liberator.*"

It is worth noting also, of course, that not *all* slaves took part in Gabriel's conspiracy (some, in fact, warned their masters of its existence), and not *all* the slaves initially accused as conspirators were convicted and hanged by a hysterically reacting white society. The added fact is, as Dabney wrote, "Nearly all the great Virginians of the Revolutionary era, such as Washington, Jefferson, Madison, Mason, and Henry, had been in favor of emancipation, provided—and this is important—the blacks, both slave and free, were removed from the state." That, of course, never would, and never did, take place.

As a final note on the unhappy episode, one has to ponder the report of a visiting Robert Sutliff (*Travels in Some Parts of North America, in the Years 1804, 1805 & 1806*), cited in the PBS account, that he encountered a lawyer in Virginia who told him that one of the executed conspirators allegedly told his accusers, "I have nothing more to offer than what General Washington would have had to offer, had he been taken by the British and put to trial by them." It hardly needs saying, though, that Washington never proposed wholesale massacres of the British, and yet . . . Yet the Revolution he, Jefferson, and their colleagues led to victory was imbued with ideals of freedom, liberty, and equality that somehow did not apply to the slaves.

★

1 8 0 1
President at Last!

★

It was a presidential campaign like no other in American history, before or since. For one thing, the Virginian seeking the presidency hardly ever left home. No stump speeches, no campaigning for him! But what vilification he underwent.

Even the widowed Martha Washington called him "one of the most detestable of mankind."

He finally did travel to Washington in November, but only because it was his job, as vice president, to preside over the Senate as Congress convened on Saturday the twenty-third. He and thirty or so fellow party members all would stay at the same boarding house that winter, but that didn't mean he sat at the head of the table. Not by any means. "He must not be allowed to forget that he is one of the people and that all are equal," startled inquirers were told.

He was a Republican by party but a democrat, lower-cased, in political philosophy and avowed principles.

Despite his seeming aloofness, he stood for the common man.

Despite his own aristocratic lifestyle, he championed *the people*. He wanted "every man to have a chance for life, liberty, and the pursuit of happiness," summed up biographer Saul K. Padover.

The trust the common people had in him, added Padover, was "something to marvel at." As the biographer pointed out, the candidate "had literally no contact with the masses, and he sought none." Moreover: "The people who were behind him had never seen him. They had never heard him speak. They had never shaken his hand. And yet to hundreds of thousands of them Tom Jefferson was a symbol of hope."

And yes, the Virginia-born presidential candidate of 1800 was Thomas Jefferson, and what a paradox he and his candidacy evoked, as historians have pointed out for years. "The aristocrat of impeccable taste and of exquisite manners, the hypersensitive gentleman who was shy of meeting with the common people in the mass, was the man who had devoted his life to the popular cause," wrote Padover. "He was the strangest leader of democracy ever known."

None of which is to say that he left the outcome of his candidacy to pure chance, without lifting a finger in his own behalf. Oh, no. The tall, lanky Virginian had been a busy man in preparation for the Republican campaign to oust his once great friend and ally in the Continental Congress, now the incumbent president and the darling of the Federalists (some of them, anyway), the sometimes grumpy, somewhat lumpy John Adams of Massachusetts.

In fact, argued Padover in *Jefferson: A Great American's Life and Ideas,* "the way Jefferson organized the campaign of 1800 was a masterpiece of political strategy." He had among his chief lieutenants future presidents James Madison and James Monroe, and he had willing surrogates scattered throughout the fledgling (largely East Coast) nation to speak and act on his behalf. His—and their—planning had been meticulous. "Every move was calculated in advance, with an eye to maximum political effectiveness," wrote Padover. "Each step was carefully weighed by Jefferson's chief aides, particularly Madison and Monroe. No possible advantage was overlooked; no flank left exposed. In every section of the Union, key figures were set in motion by the vice president. They kept in touch with Jefferson by correspondence and occasionally through personal contact."

Despite Jefferson's effete image, this was no parlor game. "The actual work of winning over the voters and of keeping them in line was entrusted to local agitators and political bosses. Jefferson carefully cultivated and inspired these men, writing them letters which contained judicious mixtures of advice and encouragement. They were a tough lot, used to shouting their arguments in taverns and country stores."

The political idealist from Virginia very pragmatically made use of the press at every opportunity. "The engine is the press," he wrote to James Madison, adding, "Let me pray and beseech you to set apart a certain portion of every postday to write what may be proper for the public." In short, what might *sway* the public.

"He planned his campaign from behind the scenes, striking swift, invisible blows," wrote biographer Padover. "When he suggested to one of his lieutenants that he distribute several dozen copies of a certain pamphlet in 'every county comm[itt]ee in the state,' he added a warning that his sponsorship of the pamphlet should be kept secret."

Then, too, whether by plan or typical personal inclination, he as vice president had stood quite apart from the presidency of John Adams. Thus, he could disavow any responsibility for the incumbent's more controversial actions as president. "Not me," Jefferson could argue.

Still, Jefferson the candidate would be the target of rarely equaled vilification, some of it sectional, some of it ideological (simplistically stated, Jefferson's states'-rights view versus the Federalist preference for a strong central, that is, *federal,* government), but much of it rooted in narrow religious intolerance. "He was made the target of such abuse and defamation as was never before heaped upon any public figures in America," wrote Padover. "The Federalists portrayed him as a thief, a coward, a libertine, an infidel, and an atheist."

Much of the criticism came from clergymen. "[M]obilizing their heaviest artillery of thunder and brimstone," the clergy "threatened Christians with all manner of dire consequences if they should vote for the 'infidel' from Virginia. This was especially true in New England, where the clergy stood like Gibraltar against Jefferson."

If Jefferson withstood the firestorm quietly and out of sight (but directing his surrogates to come to his defense), John Adams also stayed home on the farm (literally) and withstood a firestorm of his own. Not only was he assailed as inept and worse ("a monarchist, old, addled, toothless and insane," recalled David McCullough in his biography *John Adams*), by his professed political enemies, he also was undermined by a "High Federalist" faction, led by high priest Alexander Hamilton. Other Federalists were "aghast" when Hamilton released a fifty-four-page "letter" in pamphlet form at mid-campaign that ostensibly supported Adams but at the same time berated him for faults such as his "ungovernable temper." Some of Hamilton's more unbridled language seemed to give credence to talk that Adams was mad, insane.

Both bewildered and embittered by such attacks from his own side of the political aisle, Adams wrote that the Hamilton pamphlet "will insure the choice of the man [Jefferson] he dreads or pretends to dread more than me."

Whatever the reasons, it did turn out that way—Jefferson won the popular vote of 1800, losing only New England to Adams. Even more unhappily for Adams, first official occupant of the President's House in the new federal city, he learned of his alcoholic son Charlie's death on

December 3, the very day the electors met to begin the crucial electoral count that really would determine who would be the next president.

It would be a few days more before all the results were in and a final count could be made. And then . . . what a stunning surprise for all! *Nobody* was president-elect.

Not yet, anyway. The complication was the electoral vote for Jefferson and his supposed running mate, Aaron Burr. Even in the absence of a bonded party ticket in those days, Burr had won the same number of electoral votes as Jefferson—seventy-three in each case. Adams trailed with sixty-five, a respectable count, but in his case no winner. And now, with the unscrupulous Burr refusing to stand aside politely for Jefferson, a Burr-Jefferson contest for president would go to the House of Representatives for resolution.

Adams, in the meantime, told son Thomas Boylston Adams, "My little bark has been overset in a squall of thunder and lightning and hail attended by a strong smell of sulfur," and yet, "Be not concerned about me. I feel my shoulders relieved from the burden."

With Adams now out of the picture, the campaign to replace him would resume, but in a brand-new environment. And an election left up to the House should have been a cakewalk for the dominant Federalists, who of course had opposed Jefferson. But wait . . . vote for the noxious Burr instead?

What other choice did they have? Even Alexander Hamilton and John Adams now espoused Jefferson's cause as the lesser of two evils. The House wouldn't meet on the matter of the unresolved presidential contest until February 11, 1801. Late-sounding to us today, the date still came nearly four weeks before the March 4 inaugural date of that era. (The January 20 Inauguration Day date now in vogue didn't come about until Franklin Delano Roosevelt first took office in early 1933.)

In the interim, Vice President Jefferson had to visit John Adams on government business, a potentially awkward moment for each. Adams apparently tried to smooth things over by saying, "Well, I understand that you are to beat me in this contest, and I will only say that I will be as faithful a subject as any you will have."

To which Jefferson apparently demurred by saying, "Mr. Adams, this is no personal contest between you and me. Two systems of principles on the subject of government divide our fellow citizens into two parties." In fact, "Were we both to die to-day, to-morrow two other names would be in the place of ours." (As is well known, a quarter-century later, on July 4, 1826, both men would die on the same day.)

Adams, hiding his bitter disappointment, politely agreed and said they "should not suffer this matter to affect . . . [their] personal dispositions." And so, for the moment, they parted.

Then came the expectantly fateful date of February 11, when all questions should be resolved in the House. The membership from fourteen of the sixteen states agreed to a rule of one vote per state (two would divide their votes). The balloting took place. And . . . still no president!

Nineteen times in all, the states cast their ballots on February 11, and each time they produced no clear majority. "On February 12," noted Padover, "the ballot was taken nine times, and the result was the same. On February 13, 14, and 16, the House of Representatives voted six times. And the results were identical."

John Adams, not yet departed from the seat of power, told Jefferson he could win quick victory if he only would agree to compromise on some issues and, more pointedly, "not disturb those holding office." Even more pointedly, Adams during this period named Jefferson's old rival (and hated distant cousin) John Marshall to the Supreme Court. "The President also put a number of other Tories, Federalists all, into lesser judicial posts," noted biographer Padover. "These appointments were a contemptuous challenge flung in the face of Jefferson, for the new judges disliked both his person and his ideas."

Meanwhile, Jefferson told Madison he had brushed off "many attempts" to "obtain terms & promises from me." As his response, said Jefferson also, "I have declared to them unequivocally, that I would not receive the government on capitulation, that I would not go into it with my hands tied." The House campaign became so heated, noted Padover, the Jeffersonians warned that a House vote for Burr would mean "an armed uprising in the Middle States." The Republican leader in the House, incidentally, was Albert Gallatin, for whom Lewis and Clark soon would name one of the Missouri River's three forks in Montana—the other two branches would be named for Madison and Jefferson himself.

One of Gallatin's most loyal House allies was Joseph H. Nicholson of Maryland, who was so ill he had to be carried into the House chamber on a litter to vote, again and again, for Jefferson.

After days of growing acrimony between the two sides, the logjam finally gave way. "Under pressure of opinion and upon the urgent advice of Hamilton, some Congressmen shifted their votes, and broke the week-long deadlock," explained Padover. "On the thirty-sixth ballot ten states finally cast their votes for Jefferson and four for Burr. Two voted blank."

Thus was the Virginian Thomas Jefferson elected for the first of his two terms as the third president of the United States.

☆ ☆ ☆

Additional note: Typical of the man and his campaign for president, Jefferson on the day of his inauguration, March 4, 1801, simply walked from his boarding-house quarters to the as yet far-from-complete U.S. Capitol in the equally unfinished new capital city by the Potomac. He took his oath of office—administered by his old enemy John Marshall—and read an inaugural address to an audience of a thousand persons jammed into the Senate chamber. Urging political unity in the wake of the bitter presidential campaign, he declared that actually "we are all republicans; we are all federalists." His manner, wrote onlooker Margaret Bayard Smith later, was as "mild as it was firm."

Then, it was back to the boarding house for a later dinner at the same communal table as usual, under circumstances so informal that a visitor from Baltimore was able to sit right next to the new president of the United States and engage him in amiable chitchat.

Jefferson postponed his move into the unfinished President's House—later known as the White House—until after a visit to his beloved Monticello back in Albemarle County, 120 miles to the southwest. When he did take up residence in the executive mansion, it would be with Meriwether Lewis, future coleader of the vaunted Lewis and Clark Expedition, as his private secretary.

As the most glaring symbol of the Jefferson paradox, however, his White House staff also would include slaves brought north from Monticello. Not only were these the first slaves to live and work in the White House, they would include the teenage girl, Edith, destined to give birth in January 1803 to an infant who quickly died—the first birth and death to be recorded at the historic home of American presidents.

Meanwhile, in reply to a letter from five well-wishers in Providence, Rhode Island, Jefferson thanked them for their congratulations "upon my elevation to the first magistracy of the United States." He went on to pledge, "The constitution, on which our Union rests, shall be administered by me according to the safe and honest meaning contemplated by the plain understanding of the people of the United States, at the time of it's adoption; a meaning to be found in the explanations of those who advocated, not of those who opposed it, and who opposed it merely lest the constructions should be applied which they denounced as possible." In other words, he would be a strict constructionist.

1 8 0 3
Traveling East to Go West

Before traveling considerably west with fellow Virginian William Clark, Meriwether Lewis had to go considerably east, you might say. And March 15, 1803, you might also say, was the very beginning of the historic Lewis and Clark Expedition, since that was the day Lewis left the President's House in Washington and his employ there as Thomas Jefferson's private secretary (and hunter of local game for the dinner table). From then until July 15, Lewis was on the road to one place or another, but all strictly in the East, as he made his preparations for the great journey west the next year.

While the way west might offer no roads, it should be remembered, even the supposedly well-settled East of the early nineteenth century offered only a relative few of its own, and those could be very rough and rudimentary at that.

By the estimate of the Ohio River and Philadelphia chapters of the Lewis and Clark Trail Heritage Foundation, Lewis in that four-month period of 1803 rode at least eight hundred miles "in all kinds of weather on mostly poor trails and rutted roads." Further: "His speed averaged twelve to thirteen miles a day, much of it over the Appalachian Mountains and its foothills. Sixty-six days, two-thirds of those four months, found him in intimate contact with his horse."

What kept him on the go so constantly, and where did he go? The answers start with his first sojourn, which took him to the federal arsenal at Harpers Ferry armed with a helpful letter from Secretary of War

Henry Dearborn to the arsenal superintendent, Joseph Perkins. The letter "asked Perkins to give the bearer such arms and ironwork as he needed," according to the step-by-step scenario developed by the two Heritage Foundation chapters. Lewis got there by riding on horseback an average of perhaps thirty miles a day.

Staying in Harpers Ferry from March 19 to April 14, nearly a month, Lewis purchased essential items such as guns, knives, and tomahawks for at least fifteen men. But he spent most of his time telling arsenal workers how to build an iron-frame boat capable of being dismantled, a creation all his own that was destined to be tested only when the Corps of Discovery struggled past the Great Falls of the Missouri in Montana in a difficult portage taking nearly a month.

For that matter, the rifles he ordered were not your standard, garden-variety weapon. Instead, he ordered fifteen U.S. Model 1803 .54-caliber rifles with barrels just thirty-three inches long. Firing two rounds a minute, these "short rifles" would knock down a deer at a hundred yards. He also would be taking a swivel gun capable of firing sixteen musket balls at one time, a lethal shower of lead. The inventive explorer additionally saw to it that his 176 pounds of gunpowder was packed in fifty-two waterproof canisters made of lead . . . lead that could be melted down to make rifle balls.

Lewis and his horse turned next for Lancaster, Pennsylvania, where he spent another three weeks learning all the tricks and skills that surveyor Andrew Ellicott could pass along in the use of the octant, sextant, and chronometer to determine latitude and longitude in the field. Ellicott and four more "close friends" of President Jefferson, all of them Pennsylvania residents, had agreed to Jefferson's request that each teach Lewis new skills he would need for a successful expedition. Thus, moving on to Philadelphia in the second week of May, Lewis now would receive intense tutoring from botanist Benjamin Smith Barton; mathematician Robert Patterson; paleontologist Caspar Wistar, and physician Benjamin Rush, with each passing along as much of his respective expertise as possible in a short period of time.

In the case of Dr. Rush, a leading Revolutionary War figure who had signed Jefferson's Declaration of Independence, that meant stocking a chest with the most likely medications to be needed on such a long, grueling trip beyond the boundaries of early nineteenth-century civilization. He and Lewis chose Epsom and Glauber's salts; tartar emetic; painkilling laudanum; opium, also a painkiller; as well as borax, nutmeg, cloves, cinnamon, rhubarb . . . and fifty dozen so-called Rush Pills, a purgative also called "Thunderclappers" for its apparently explosive effect.

On a related point, the books that Lewis stocked for his trip would include *Rules of Health,* but they also would range from a four-volume dictionary to eminently practical volumes such as *History of Louisiana* by Antoine Simor Le Page du Pratz; *Introduction to Spheres and Nautical Astronomy* by Patrick Key; *Elements of Botany* by Lewis's own tutor, Benjamin Barton, and *Voyage* by Alexander Mackenzie, the young Scot who ten years before had crossed the continent and reached the Pacific, on behalf of the Canadian North West Company.

In addition, Lewis purchased an estimated thirty-five hundred pounds (more than a ton and a half) of supplies. Anyone looking over the young army officer's shoulder at this point would have realized he was buying supplies for many more than the mere dozen men contemplated by the $2,500 appropriation Congress secretly had adopted, at Jefferson's request, for the exploratory probe into the Northwest. The fact was, Lewis had a letter of credit provided by Jefferson, and before all was said and done, the supplies and equipage needed for the expedition would cost the government $39,000.

Quite expectantly, the supplies Lewis was amassing ranged from trade goods for Indians to a gold chronometer, a surveyor's compass, chains and plotting instruments, plus a good deal of paper and ink for his note-taking, even 193 pounds of dehydrated soup. A very special item, financed out of his own pocket, was an air rifle destined to intrigue more than a few Indians along the way . . . and later to disappear from history's sight.

Obviously needing more than a single horse for transportation at this point, Lewis made arrangements with a military agent in Philadelphia to obtain a sizable wagon, a team of four or six horses, and a drover to transport his acquisitions. While the drover and his wagon then set off for Pittsburgh on June 10, Lewis remained in Philadelphia for another week or so. Returning to Washington on or about June 19, he "tied up loose ends" there through the Fourth of July.

The "loose ends" included a crucial letter—the very missive in which he invited old friend and fellow officer William Clark to join the expedition as coleader with Lewis himself. Then, too, in a not-to-worry letter to his mother, Lewis wrote his regrets that he didn't have time to visit but could assure her that he would complete the expedition in safety and good health.

As he also noted, their next reunion wouldn't come for another year and a half or so. But that's the way it was in those days—people traveling to the frontier, or beyond, often dropped from all sight of friends or family for a year or two. Sometimes, their fate unknown, they disappeared forever.

For the time being, however, Meriwether Lewis's next travel would take him only as far as Harpers Ferry, for a second visit to the federal arsenal there. Leaving Washington on July 5, Lewis discovered at the arsenal on July 8 that his wagon and drover had come and gone as planned . . . but the drover had refused to take on the iron-frame boat, guns, knives, and tomahawks as ordered. He apparently feared the nine hundred to one thousand pounds in extra weight would be too much.

That perhaps was quite understandable. It did take the drover six weeks, in fact, to make the journey from Philadelphia to Pittsburgh (by way of Harpers Ferry) at an average of ten to twelve miles a day on the really good roads out of the Philadelphia area. Soon after leaving Harpers Ferry, however, he hit the Appalachian Mountains, at thirty-two hundred feet high no laughing matter for a heavily laden horse-drawn wagon. With only primitive roads now available, the wagoner was lucky to make a few miles a day.

Lewis, for his part, didn't linger long at Harpers Ferry. He obtained a second wagon to take on the equipage left behind by the first wagon, then set out for Pittsburgh himself on July 9. First passing through what is now Charles Town and Frankfort (the future Fort Ashby), West Virginia; Cumberland, Maryland, and Uniontown, Pennsylvania, Lewis rode at least as far as Redstone Old Fort (today's Brownsville, Pennsylvania), a village on the Monongahela River. He then either rode farther or took a flatboat downstream to Elizabeth, Pennsylvania, a ship- and boat-building center just fifteen miles above Pittsburgh.

Elizabeth was an important stop because it apparently was the birthplace of two large pirogues that would be going on the expedition west with Lewis, Clark, and their Corps of Discovery. Here, by the way, Lewis was on ground familiar to him from his days in the Virginia militia during the Whiskey Rebellion in 1794 and his service as an army paymaster in the area from 1798 to 1800. From Elizabeth, meanwhile, it was on to Pittsburgh.

Ever since turning his back on Washington, D.C., after July 4, Lewis had been traveling west . . . but even as he now reached Pittsburgh on July 15, he still was in the East. Unlike his previous stops, though, this would be a major jumping-off place for the great journey into the uncharted West. Here, at the merger of the Monongahela and Allegheny Rivers, the Ohio River was born, and down the Ohio way to the Mississippi, Lewis and his nuclear corps would float then push upstream to St. Louis. For a long moment, no more overland travel.

As events turned out, however, Lewis wouldn't be able to leave Pittsburgh for another six weeks, thanks to inordinate delays in construction of the expedition's keelboat. Lewis and a small crew finally were able to start their float down the Ohio to the Mississippi River on August 31. Because of a summer drought resulting in low water, however, it was a trip requiring careful transit of shoals, pushing, pulling, and poling through shallow stretches.

As his next stop of note, Lewis moored at what is now Wheeling, West Virginia, on September 7 to load supplies carried overland from Pittsburgh on two wagons. And here, concerned by the Ohio's unusually low water levels and afraid of overloading his existing flotilla, Lewis purchased a new pirogue to carry some of his equipage.

With the Ohio now doing its part (more or less) to carry Lewis to his destiny in the West, there was a brief stop on September 10 to inspect the Indian mounds at Moundsville, West Virginia. Next, at Clarington, Ohio, on September 11, the travelers spotted squirrels swimming across the river. Yes, swimming.

At Marietta, Ohio, where the Muskingum River rolls into the Ohio, September 13 brought added confirmation of the hard labors ahead for the men making up the Corps of Discovery. They had to dig through sandbars of gravel to float the keelboat past. And next, Maysville, Kentucky, apparently was the stop where Lewis on or about September 22 signed up a famous and colorful recruit, John Colter. Going all the way to the Pacific with the corps and halfway back before joining the first mountain men who filtered into the Rockies on the heels of the Lewis and Clark Expedition, Colter apparently would become the first white man to step on ground now known as Yellowstone National Park. He also would achieve legendary status across the western frontier for his escape from a band of Blackfoot warriors by outrunning them in a life-and-death footrace.

Meanwhile, arriving at Cincinnati on September 28, Lewis found two letters from Clark awaiting him. One reported the recruitment of four men and enthusiastically noted what a treasure the newly consummated Louisiana Purchase would be for the young nation. The other simply reported Clark had not yet found an interpreter.

Clark, of course, already had responded in the affirmative to that all-important letter of early summer inviting him to take part in the expedition. "I will cheerfully join you, my friend," Clark had written in reply. "I do assure you that no man lives with whom I would prefer to undertake such a trip as yourself. My friend, I join you with hand and heart."

Continuing to float downriver on the Ohio, Lewis stopped at Big Bone Lick, Kentucky, to search out and box up mammoth and mastodon bones for his mentor, President Jefferson. He wrote Jefferson a letter reporting the details, but the bones would be lost in an accident at Natchez on the Mississippi the following spring.

Next, Louisville, Kentucky, would be a benchmark in the travels of Meriwether Lewis, for it was here on October 14 that he and William Clark joined up. Here, too, the co-captains formally enlisted the core of their future corps—the men Lewis and Clark had recruited up to that time. Even though they were not all from Kentucky, they would be known as the "Nine Young Men from Kentucky."

Now, apparently guided through the falls of the Ohio on October 15 by a pilot, they reached Clarksville, Indiana, named for Revolutionary War hero George Rogers Clark—William Clark's own brother. Both Clarks, in fact, had been living on the western shore of the Ohio since moving earlier in the year from a long-time family homestead close to Louisville.

Eleven days later, the early corps members—including Clark's African-American slave, York—resumed the journey down the Ohio en route to whatever fate had in store for them over the next three years.

On November 11, with winter looming close, they stopped at Fort Massac, Illinois, originally a French fort, later owned by the British then taken over and, in 1794, rebuilt by the Americans. Here, the two expedition leaders began the first of the hundreds of measurements of latitude and longitude they would be making on their epic journey west. Spending six days here, they also poked around old Fort Jefferson (circa 1780).

Almost at their last destination for the year 1803, they next, on November 28 or 29, were at Kaskaskia, Illinois, where the captains recruited more men—and briefly split up. Meriwether Lewis returned to horseback for overland travel to Cahokia, Illinois, and, finally, St. Louis. Clark stayed behind in command of the riverborne flotilla.

They met again, on or about December 8, at Cahokia. In the interim, Lewis had reached St. Louis and met with the lieutenant governor of "Upper Louisiana," and Clark had pulled into Cahokia on December 7. Reassembled, the entire party "set sail," as it were, on December 9 for the final leg of their preparatory journey to take up winter quarters at Wood River, Illinois, opposite the mouth of the Missouri on the Mississippi just above St. Louis.

It was a Monday, December 12, when Clark at last guided the corps flotilla to Camp Dubois, as the Wood River campsite was dubbed, to settle in for a five-month layover before setting out for the real West in the spring of 1804. The party's eastern—and indeed, you might even say, its midwestern—travels were now over. But the period ahead would not be one of pure indolence, by any means. As the chroniclers of the party's preparatory travels also noted, the days ahead would be busy ones for all, but especially for the two co-captains of the corps. "They would construct huts for winter quarters, train and discipline the men, buy additional supplies, attend formal ceremonies transferring the Louisiana Territory to the United States, begin their daily weather observations, calculate travel distances and times, map the meeting of the Missouri and Mississippi, sketch the keelboat and its many modifications, organize the men into three squads, record their contacts with the Indian tribes nearby, and proceed on with every detail needed for successful and safe experiences."

The official beginning of the great Lewis and Clark Expedition into the Northwest would not come until the forty-five-man Corps of Discovery started up the Missouri River on May 14, 1804, but, clearly, it had taken considerable travel and work by all hands simply to prepare for that official and historic jumping-off moment.

1805
Two Girls on a Horse

Here's the proposition: A man, soon to become a famous explorer, visiting Fincastle, Virginia, early in the nineteenth century, meets two young girls, cousins at that, perhaps ten, eleven, or even twelve years of age, sitting astride a horse that has balked at crossing a stream. The man, William Clark of Lewis and Clark fame, thirty-something in age, helps them with the balky horse . . . *and in time ends up marrying both girls.*

Could it really be? *How* could it be?

The key words are *in time,* since, true, he didn't marry them both at once. Nor either one right away.

But the story, handed down for generations in Fincastle and environs, could be true. William Clark did visit there, he did marry both Judith "Julia" Hancock and, at later date, her first cousin Harriet Kennerly. The only unprovable part is the story of the balky horse.

Theory and fact, it's all in author Gene Crotty's small book *The Visits of Lewis & Clark to Fincastle, Virginia.* And in it, Crotty begins his story with a somewhat cryptic statement, to wit: "Fincastle, the Seat of Botetourt County, Virginia, was a village of both fortune and misfortune for Lewis and Clark. Each one discovered 'the love of his life' in this frontier town west of the Blue Ridge Mountains in the early 1800s."

But only Clark, it seems, would be the happier for it, since his proposal of marriage—to Judith, that is—was accepted, and that of Meriwether Lewis to another young lady in town apparently was not. To wit again: "Lewis also courted in Fincastle, but sadly failed in his quest to obtain a mate for life in this fair community. In fact, this encounter was his last serious female entanglement." *Last entanglement* because Lewis two years later in 1809 died young on the Natchez Trace in Tennessee, either by self-inflicted gunshot wounds or by murder.

On a happier note, Clark apparently had passed through Fincastle one or more times before he and Lewis set out west on their historic expedition all the way to the Pacific Ocean and back, in 1804 to 1806. But why?

Since he lived in Kentucky but still had interests in his native Virginia, it would have been natural for William Clark to spend some time in the 1790s and early 1800s traveling back and forth from one to the other. And since he had two good friends from his U.S. Army service in the 1790s who hailed from Fincastle and environs, why not travel through their little hometown in the great valley between the Blue Ridge and the Appalachian Ridge to the west? One of former Capt. William Clark's army compatriots was former Lt. William "Billy" Preston Jr., of "Greenfield," four miles out of town, and the other was former Lt. Benjamin Strother. "Through these two friends," wrote Crotty, "Clark became familiar with Fincastle."

With that much established, can anyone firmly say exactly when Clark met one or both of his future wives at or near Fincastle? It *had* to be before the Lewis and Clark Expedition set off in 1804. If not both future wives, he had to have met Judith before 1804, since he named a western river for her during the expedition, which ran from spring of 1804 to fall of 1806. And Clark, for that matter, was busy with Meriwether Lewis and the core membership of their Corps of Discovery from fall of 1803 until the very moment they all set out upstream on the Missouri River just above St. Louis in May 1804. Thus, he had to have visited Fincastle and met his future wife Judith before the fall of 1803.

Author Crotty surmises that Clark may have visited Fincastle and the nearby community of Amsterdam in the first months of 1803 or in 1802 or perhaps 1801, if not even before 1800.

Clark probably spent time with—and stayed with—his old army buddy Preston, whose Greenfield home was situated between the two communities of Fincastle and Amsterdam. Interestingly, too, thirty-something Billy Preston, during the period in question, courted and then, in 1802, married Caroline Hancock, age seventeen, an older sister of Judith. Clearly, there would have been ample and even repeated opportunity for the visiting Clark to meet Caroline's sister Judith . . . whose age in 1801 would have been ten; in 1802, eleven; and in 1803, just twelve. Whatever her age, whichever the year, Clark came away most impressed with Fincastle's blue-eyed princess, who at five feet four and a half was not quite petite, but unanimously was described as both pretty and bright.

Certainly Fincastle at the time was no Harvard on the Charles— rather, it was a frontier town, the official seat of Botetourt County, which in theory stretched westward across the green wilderness all the way to St. Louis as, allegedly, the "largest county in the [American] colonies." Still, Meriwether Lewis, for one, was so impressed by Judith's education and intellect, he later would be giving her "a complete set of Shakespeare" as a wedding present, Crotty reported in his Fincastle book.

Clearly, too, Clark made no secret of his interest in the young lady . . . at least not in the company of his good friend Lewis. And we can say it was a lasting interest, since the famed expedition had been underway for many months before the two explorers named the Judith

River in Montana, right after they and members of their Corps of Discovery became the first Americans to spot the eastern slopes of the Rocky Mountains in late May 1805, a full year after the corps began its arduous trip up the Missouri River. With the Rockies in sight for the first time, the explorers then saw the mouth of a wide stream, a tributary, off to one side. Taking to his diary later, Lewis wrote: "Captain Clark thought it was proper to call the . . . south waterway Judith's River in honor of Miss Judy Hancock of Virginia." Lewis also made note that the newly named Judith was "much wider" than the Missouri, which by now had become a narrow, cranky stream beset with difficult bends and rocks that slowed the expedition's progress.

More than another year later, late in 1806, the great expedition now concluded, the love-smitten William Clark traveled east from St. Louis for a visit at his sister's "Locust Grove" home in Louisville, Kentucky. On December 15 of that year, he set off east again, with Washington his ultimate destination. "He would pass through Danville, Kentucky, and travel south on the Wilderness Road toward the Cumberland Gap of present-day Kentucky, and then pass on to modern-day U.S. Routes 58 and 11 in Western Virginia," wrote Crotty. "The Wilderness Road led him to Abingdon and then on to Amsterdam and Fincastle stopovers. . . . Here, he would visit with the Prestons at 'Greenfield' and with Col. Hancock's family in Fincastle."

He would have arrived just after—or possibly just in time for—the twin weddings of Judith's cousin Harriet Kennerly (his own future wife) to John Radford and Judith's remaining sister, Mary Hancock, to John Griffin, marriages performed by the same Presbyterian minister on the same day, December 23, 1806, as major social events for the small community. Coincidentally, Meriwether Lewis had passed through town just before the festivities on his way east to spend Christmas with his twice-widowed mother, Lucy Marks, and family at Ivy, outside Charlottesville, before going on to the President's House in Washington for a celebratory reunion with Clark, a number of their new Indian acquaintances, and expedition-sponsor Thomas Jefferson.

Crotty also wrote that Clark was back in Fincastle again in late 1807, at which time he and Judith became engaged, with plans to marry in January 1808. Thus, Judith, born in November 1791, was just fifteen at the time of her engagement and sixteen on the day of her wedding. She—and thus Harriet—may also have been cousins to William Clark, according to the late historian Stephen Ambrose (in

Undaunted Courage: Meriwether Lewis, Thomas Jefferson and the Opening of the American West), but Crotty found no local documentation supporting that contention.

Still to be nailed down is the question of how all three first met. According to Crotty, "Local Botetourt County tradition holds that Clark had rescued 'Julia' and her first cousin, Harriet Kennerly, from a balky horse episode." And more specifically: "This folklore story holds that while Clark was riding his horse on an earlier pre-exploration visit to the Fincastle area, he had encountered the two young girls riding one horse nearby at a small stream. Their horse was balking to cross the stream and they naturally became frightened. Clark dismounted and came to the aid of the distressed girls, and hand-led their horse safely across the stream." By the same story, conveniently enough, the two girls were on their way for a visit to the Prestons, exactly where Clark might have been staying.

So, who knows? It could have happened that way.

What did happen later is known fact, however. Clark's wife Judith, unfortunately, would die young, on June 27, 1820, at age twenty-eight, of breast cancer. The mother of five surviving children, she apparently died at her father's home on the south branch of the Roanoke River while on an extended family visit to her Virginia relatives. Her father, "attorney, congressman, and owner of one of the largest plantation houses in the area," died just three weeks later. They ultimately were buried together in a mausoleum built on a hill behind Hancock's handsome Fotheringay plantation house, wrote Crotty. "Legend holds that George Hancock had been buried in an upright position, whereby he could continue to observe his slave field-workers. The mausoleum stone is visible today from U.S. Route 11, west of the town of Elliston, and is a conversational subject for all visitors traveling in the area."

A year later, Judith and William Clark's ailing daughter Mary Margaret died at the age of seven while staying with her aunt Caroline and uncle William Preston, who now were living in the Louisville, Kentucky, area.

Harriet's husband, John Radford, in the meantime, had been killed in Kentucky in 1817 by a rampaging wild boar. Harriet and her three children then had moved in with Judith and William Clark . . . before Judith's illness and death. After Cousin Judith's death, Harriet became William Clark's second and last wife. Married on November 28, 1821 (the same year that Clark's great friend Billy Preston died), they had two sons, but one of them died in less than a year's time. Meanwhile, William Clark adopted Harriet's first three children. As a result, noted Crotty, Clark "helped raise ten children," including the Shoshone Indian woman Sacagawea's son, Jean Baptiste, carried to the Pacific and much of the way back as a petite "member" of the Corps of Discovery, and her daughter, Lizette.

Clark's oldest son, Meriwether Lewis Clark, a West Point graduate in the same era as Robert E. Lee, married Abigail Prather Churchill, and the first of *their* six sons was Meriwether Lewis Clark Jr., founder of the Louisville's Churchill Downs racetrack, home of the Kentucky Derby.

As for Meriwether Lewis's dashed matrimonial hopes, he and younger brother Reuben came calling in November 1807 en route to St. Louis, where Meriwether would take up his governorship of the Upper Louisiana Territory. The apparent object of his affections was one Letitia Breckinridge, age sixteen, daughter of Virginia Delegate James Breckinridge (soon to be a congressman from the area). "One of the most beautiful women I have ever seen, both, as to form and features," wrote an approving Reuben to their mother after meeting the winsome Letitia.

"Many facts about the encounter of the eligible pair are not known," wrote Crotty, "but seemingly the over anxious Meriwether may have overplayed his hand and chased the young maiden away." On the other hand, she soon traveled to Richmond with her father, and six months later she married a Richmond man. Perhaps the lucky Richmonder had been waiting in the wings all along. In any case, all that was left for Meriwether Lewis to do was to pour out his aching heart in a letter to good friend Billy Preston.

☆ ☆ ☆

Additional note: In the eyes of many historians, Lewis's failure to find happiness and a stable lifestyle in the immediate aftermath of the triumphant Lewis and Clark Expedition intensified a natural disposition to depression and helped lead to his alleged suicide on the Natchez Trace in Tennessee while traveling to Washington in the autumn of 1809. Both his mentor, Thomas Jefferson, and his expedition partner,

William Clark, seemed to accept his state of mind as a causative factor behind the two apparently self-inflicted gunshot wounds that ended his life . . . but there are other theories to explain the death of such a young man at the heights of success.

Excessive drinking and overuse of medicinal opiates may have been contributing factors, say some. Disease such as malaria or syphilis may have driven him to shoot himself without really knowing what he was doing, others have postulated. And then there is the theory of homicide . . . murder.

That is a still poorly investigated possibility that intrigues Lewis family descendants of today who have been pressing the National Park Service (NPS) to allow exhumation of their ancestor's remains for a modern forensic examination that might clear up the mystery of his death. The disturbing fact is, the only known *fairly* close witness to Lewis's activity during the night of his fatal wounding was in a nearby cabin . . . and she gave sometimes conflicting details in her accounts over the years. As one glaring discrepancy, Mrs. Robert Grinder—of the roadside inn or tavern called Grinder's Stand—said she could see Lewis roaming around through the chinks between the logs of her cabin, but recent research has established there was no moon the night in question, and thus she would not have been able to see him in the utter darkness. On the other hand, others said that Lewis just days beforehand twice tried to jump overboard from the riverboat that carried him down the Mississippi River from St. Louis as far as the future site of Memphis, Tennessee, and that he arrived at a military outpost there in a totally deranged state that cleared up after a few days.

As for the murder theory, Lewis family descendant Howell Bowen of Albemarle County—the birthplace of Lewis—says, "The family has always believed Meriwether Lewis was killed and wishes to remove the cloud of uncertainty hanging over the history of this great man." Asserting that more than 168 Meriwether Lewis family descendants back the exhumation proposal, Bowen also says, "There is a great deal of evidence supporting the murder theory, and only speculation supporting suicide."

More specifically: "The majority of historians and other commentators on his death have drawn upon one, or more, of three sources for their interpretation of the facts. All three agree there were two pistols fired, and no one witnessed the firing of the pistols inflicting the mortal wounds."

Still, said Bowen in a recent statement, those same sometimes-conflicting accounts do provide an avenue of investigation, "of scientific scrutiny for persons schooled in the forensic disciplines of anthropology, pathology, and firearms identification." And further: "We have the DNA to identify the remains, and the bones will shed light on his health, tell if there was chronic drug or alcohol abuse as some historians claim, whether he had various diseases as some put forth, and show what traumas the bones suffered at his death."

If nothing else: "We are ready to accept whatever results come from the investigation. We want finality and to have history recorded correctly and not speculatively." As Bowen also said, he and fellow family members would welcome true identification of the remains in the NPS-maintained gravesite, together with the opportunity "to give him a religious burial, which was denied by his unceremonious burial at Grinder's Stand."

1 8 0 6
Murder of "Virginia Socrates"

Still unclear today is whether George Wythe took his poison with strawberries and milk one Saturday night or in his coffee the next Sunday morning. In any case, the illnesses struck the great eighteenth-century legal scholar's household after the Sunday breakfast. Young Michael Brown, a freed black to whom Wythe was teaching Greek and the classics, died quickly. Wythe's cook and housekeeper, Lydia Broadmax, herself a former slave freed by the old man, also became ill . . . but did not die.

Wythe, age eighty, lasted for another two weeks.

His was an agonizing death, and it was murder, a homicide so shocking to young America—and Virginia, where it took place—that President Thomas Jefferson, Wythe's own former student, was moved to say, "Such an instance of depravity has been hitherto known to us only in the fables of the poets."

Who, then, could have "dunnit"?

Could it possibly have been Wythe's teenage grandnephew George Wythe Swinney, already, at his age, known as a wastrel and gambler . . . and yet chief heir to the old man's estate?

Could it have been young Swinney, who alone of the household members in Richmond escaped any illness? Who had been asking where he could obtain arsenic? Whose room in George Wythe's home yielded a cache of arsenic? Who already had forged checks on his great-uncle's bank account?

Who "got off," as they say, scot-free under the very safeguards promised by the legal system that his eminent victim and relative was personally so instrumental in creating? Yes, yes, yes, and yes, it certainly does appear. Not only did young George Swinney elude a double-murder conviction, he was able to thumb his nose at the forgery charge as well.

Even the hapless, dying victim considered young Swinney his murderer, it would appear. Not only did George Wythe suggest the search that uncovered the arsenic in Swinney's room, he also, on his deathbed, drew up a codicil to his will expressly denying Swinney any inheritance.

And yet, the jury that heard the case against Swinney failed to convict.

It seems amazing . . . and even more so when we consider what a towering and hallowed figure the murder victim had been to early America. Often called the "Virginia Socrates," George Wythe had tutored Jefferson in the precepts of law and had remained his lifelong friend and mentor; he had signed Jefferson's Declaration of Independence; he had been a member of the Continental Congress and, earlier, the Colonial House of Burgesses. He had been mayor of Williamsburg. He later had served as Speaker of the post-Colonial Virginia House of Delegates. At the College of William and Mary, he had filled the first chair of law in an American institution of higher learning. He had been a member of the post-Revolutionary Constitutional Convention. He, Jefferson, and Edmund Pendleton had spent three years revising the Virginia legal code. He taught the law to John Marshall, James Monroe, and, later, Henry Clay, among other historical luminaries. He was one of three judges appointed to the Virginia high court of chancery, and as a chancellor for twenty-eight years he had great influence upon the foundations of Virginia law.

After a long residence in Williamsburg, he was forced by his chancery obligations to move to Richmond in 1791, since it now was the state capital. Unwilling to give up teaching, he founded a private law school there. He still was living in Richmond at the moment of his untimely death in 1806.

His death at the hands of a murderer, unsurprisingly, stirred strong feelings throughout the Commonwealth. And what an open-and-shut case against young George W. Swinney. Or so it appeared.

Circumstantially, the case looked airtight. Or did it?

Let's take a look.

According to records of the *preliminary* court hearings on the charges against Swinney, wrote W. Edwin Hemphill in the *William and Mary Quarterly* back in the 1950s, sixteen prosecution witnesses testified against Swinney. One said Swinney had asked him how to obtain rats-bane, or white arsenic. Others said arsenic was found in the garden of the jail where Swinney was held, adding that he had access to the garden as a prisoner, and in his pocket at the time of his arrest was "a heavy substance wrapped in paper." Then, too, there was the arsenic found in his room and on the grounds of the Wythe home in Richmond.

Open and shut?

Unfortunately for all concerned, autopsies on the bodies of Wythe and young Michael Brown were inconclusive. Their stomachs were found to be "inflamed," but that pathology could have been the result of various disorders. No tests were made to prove the presence of arsenic in either body.

Meanwhile, the court records found by Hemphill, a staff member at the Library of Virginia, also were inconclusive—they were from the *preliminary* hearings only, and thus gave no clue to the thinking of the jury that subsequently freed the defendant. Records of the *trial* stage, coming after the preliminary hearings, may have been among those burned when Richmond fell to Union forces at the end of the Civil War.

It seems fairly clear, however, that no one actually saw Swinney administer the fatal poison to the household food or coffee. Conceivably, then, someone else could have been the guilty party. In short, *reasonable doubt* may have prevailed when the jury deliberated over the murder of the man who probably had more influence upon the founding and early development of Virginia's legal system than any other.

As it turned out also, the forgery charges against Swinney simply evaporated. The authorities discovered they had no laws on the books explicitly declaring those actions illegal—an unthinkable omission that the Virginia General Assembly quickly rectified at its very next law-making session.

By then, the highly unpopular young Swinney, beneficiary of his uncle's legal expertise, long since had departed Virginia for vistas, it is thought, to the west. And gone to no good there as well, according to a Richmond source cited by Hemphill. By that account, given fifty years after the murder episode, Swinney traveled to Tennessee, stole a horse, served prison time, and then dropped from sight.

☆ ☆ ☆

Odd Coincidence: When Virginia-born President Zachary Taylor suddenly sickened and died in office in 1850, the stomach illness that apparently killed him first struck right after he consumed strawberries and milk on a hot July 4. For years afterward, it was suspected in some quarters that he also had been poisoned with arsenic. But no such evidence was found when his remains were exhumed and tested for lingering traces of the poison late in the twentieth century.

★

1812
High Praise for a Sortie

★

When the Petersburg Volunteers marched off to war, one hundred or so strong, they would stop briefly to meet a former president, described as a "very homely old man," and they would serve on foreign soil under a vigorous future president. They went off in a flurry of balls and accolades, of oohs and ahhs one fall, only to spend their winter in mud and snow and cold, cold rain. And when all was said and done, they would return only a dozen or so strong.

Further, the survivors would return with their paymaster and their pay nowhere to be found. They would be famous, though, for their key role in the "sortie from Fort Meigs" during the War of 1812.

It was, in fact, September of that year when Capt. Richard McRae and three others were elected as the officers of the volunteer group, described by a Petersburg letter-writer (in the *Richmond Enquirer*) as "the flower of our youth and the best blood of our country."

They began their war on October 21 by marching, marching . . . and eating. Following the presentation of their flag and a round of speeches at Petersburg's Centre Hill, they marched, first, to an encampment a few miles out of town for a dinner given by prominent citizens of Chesterfield County. Then, the next day, it was on to Richmond, with an escort into Capitol Square by cavalry and militia units, to the rousing music of bands, for an official greeting by Governor James Barbour. The *Richmond Enquirer* described the seated dinner that followed as "the most sumptuous and animated feast which we have ever seen."

After a delay while they awaited delivery of their arms, they finally marched out of Richmond on November 2. They were escorted, wrote Lee A. Wallace Jr. in the *Virginia Magazine of History and Biography*, by "volunteer companies of the 19th Regiment, the Governor and other officials, and by hundreds of citizens." They managed to cover eight miles before bedding down for their first night west of Richmond. Then, it would be November 9, a week later, before they would reach Charlottesville, just seventy miles from Richmond, after encountering more hospitality and added groaning boards in Louisa County.

At Charlottesville, of course, what else to do but pay respects at Monticello, where Thomas Jefferson himself was sure to welcome them as well. What they found, though, was not exactly the image of Jefferson we all carry around in our heads today. In a later memoir, Petersburg volunteer Albert Lorrain described the scene this way: "We drew up, in military array, at the base of the hill on which the great house was erected. About halfway down the hill stood a very homely old man, dressed in plain Virginia cloth, his head uncovered and his venerable locks flowing in the wind."

A few of the men made fun of the elderly apparition. "I wonder," said one, "what old codger that is, with his hair blowing nine ways for Easter Monday." Said another: "Why of course, it is the overseer, and he seems to be scared out of a year's growth. I suspect he never saw gentlemen volunteers before."

To this, Lorain added: "But how we were astonished when he advanced to our officers and introduced himself as THOMAS JEFFERSON!"

Still, the distant war awaited, and so, after a brief visit, the volunteers had to move on, and on. Crossing the Blue Ridge, they made their way to White Sulphur Springs in today's West Virginia and then to Point Pleasant on the Ohio River, scene of the great pre-Revolution battle against Chief Cornstalk and his Indian allies of the Old Northwest. "Throughout their journey westward," wrote Wallace, "the company was graciously received, and plied with an abundance of food and drink, to the extent that they passed almost through the state without having to purchase provisions."

Dark days might lie ahead, but still, after a two-week delay on the banks of the Ohio, due to ice on the river, the Petersburg blue bloods still were well fed and feted once they crossed over and then trekked northward to Chillicothe, then the capital of Ohio. Here, "the volunteers were provided quarters in the statehouse, and on December 24 the Ohio legislature sponsored a Christmas Eve dinner for them at Buchanan's hotel. On the following day [Christmas itself], they were given another dinner by the citizens of the town."

From here on, however, the Virginians would encounter far more rugged and even deadly conditions. Ordered to join Virginia-born Gen. William Henry Harrison's Northwestern army at Upper Sandusky, they marched from Chillicothe a day or two after Christmas despite a "northwester" that blew both rain and snow. Fighting mud, ice, and snow virtually the whole way, they marched until January 10 to cover the 110 miles to Upper Sandusky.

The Virginians next were sent forward with others in a forced march January 21 to support Gen. James Winchester's dangerously exposed force at newly captured Frenchtown . . . but too late. On January 23, word came that Winchester actually had been overrun at Frenchtown, with the British and their Indian allies now threatening the rapids on the Maumee River. Thus, the dawn of January 24 found the Petersburg men and their compatriots marching for the Maumee Rapids . . . not exactly marching now, but instead struggling along behind a pack train of 450 horses that had churned the road into a sea of snow and mud. Some found it easier to wade through the swamps alongside the road, but in the incessant chill rain, nobody could travel in comfort. "In this swamp [Black Swamp]," wrote a private in the Petersburg company, "you lose sight of *terra firma* altogether—the water was about six inches deep on the ice, which was very rotten, often breaking through to the depth of four or five feet."

And now came word that General Harrison was falling back from the rapids and must gather reinforcements before advancing again, his ultimate aim to recapture Detroit from the British and then carry the fight into Canada.

By early February, future President Harrison had gathered his reinforcements and moved upriver to the foot of the Rapids, where he was content to establish a holding position. And that meant building a fort to house and defend his two thousand men . . . Fort Meigs, named for Ohio Governor Return Jonathan Meigs. That also meant a siege by the British could be expected at any time.

In February and early March, the Petersburg Volunteers took part in two sorties from the fort, but no action resulted. For now, their worst enemies would be the climate and their living conditions. And it wasn't long before the first Petersburg casualty, a private named Andrew Andrews, was recorded at the rapids. "Conditions within the camp were far from healthful, with mud and water covering the ground, even within tents," noted historical writer Wallace. "Worse still was the lack of wood for fires. As the timber had been cut for a long distance around the fort, wood had to be collected and hauled in by teams, for which there was not a 'bushel of forage.'" By mid-March, two more Petersburg men had died, and others were ill also. As regular army Capt. Daniel L. Cushing observed in a journal entry for March 19, it was "no wonder" so many were "very sickly" after "lying in mud and water and without fire." At least two or three of Harrison's men now were dying every day.

Meanwhile, different state militia groups came and went as terms of enlistment expired and others came to replace them. The Petersburg Volunteers were doubly disgusted when the militia of their own Virginia melted away. In the end, after all the comings and goings, General Harrison in late April would have sixteen hundred Americans manning—and still building—the fort, with the British and their Indian allies expected to lay siege at any moment.

By April's end, the enemy indeed was in position around the fort—approximately 400 British regulars, 470 Canadian militia, and 1,200 Indians, the famous Chief Tecumseh among them. After intermittent exchanges of artillery fire with the Americans, the British settled down to a punishing bombardment of the fort in early May . . . and so, yet another sortie would be necessary.

"May 5 was the momentous day of the siege, and is the date upon which the fame of the Petersburg Volunteers largely rests," wrote Wallace. The arrival of reinforcements from Kentucky outside the fort served to disrupt and distract the enemy, but only briefly. Turning the tables on the attacking Kentuckians, the British and Indians killed many and captured many others. As still more Kentuckians streamed toward the fort and the safety to be found behind its stout stockade walls, they met—and in fact joined—the party sallying forth to engage the Indians on the fort's left flank.

When that force also ran into trouble by pursuing the "fleeing" Indians too closely for comfort, Harrison ordered a sortie against the British battery in a ravine on the right side of the fort, a battery defended by at least four British and Canadian companies and five hundred of Tecumseh's Indian warriors—an estimated 850 in all. Sent against them were some 350 Americans, 64 of them Petersburg Volunteers.

The outnumbered force assembled in a ravine, invisible to the enemy, as General Harrison in person passed "through the ranks giving encouragement" then took up an observation post nearby while his men attacked, reported Wallace.

The fighting that followed was fierce, by all accounts, and out on the hard-pressed right flank of the American line the whole time were the Petersburg Volunteers. "The Indians firing from the woods with considerable effect came very near turning the right of . . . [the] line and getting into the rear, which could have been disastrous," added Wallace. But Petersburg's finest held . . . and held, despite the enemy fire that wounded seventeen of their number, three of them fatally so.

The British and Indians driven back, the one cannon and mortar in their battery spiked, and forty-two prisoners taken, the sortie was considered a success, thanks in large part to the small Petersburg contingent participating. The volunteers had conducted themselves with "intrepidity," General Harrison later reported. More detailed and just as memorable was a journal entry by his engineer officer, Capt. Eleazar Wood, who wrote: "The company of volunteers from Petersburg (Virginia) particularly distinguished themselves by their intrepid and cool conduct, while approaching the batteries under a heavy fire of musketry." To these accolades, an "unknown post rider" added the observation that the Petersburg men had "fought like devils," Wallace also reported.

With months to go in their military service, an invasion of Canada included, that was the high point of the War of 1812 for the Petersburg Volunteers . . . the sortie from Fort Meigs.

To be sure, there were a few after-events: more deaths during the summer of 1813, sadly; a second but short-lived British siege of Fort Meigs in July; General Harrison's crossing of Lake Erie; Oliver Hazard Perry's defeat of the British on the same lake; and Harrison's invasion of Canada. Also highly notable were Harrison's victories at Malden, and in the battle of the Thames in southern Ontario on October 5, 1813; Tecumseh's death; and, finally, an "end to the fighting in the Northwest," as Wallace noted. All in all, a tumultuous year had passed since the volunteers marched out of Petersburg one hundred strong. And now, for the relative few left, it was time to turn for home.

By general orders issued at Detroit on October 17, they were released with flowery praise of their "exalted merits." Together with reference to their blue-blooded background, they, in fact, were *heaped* with praise for their service. "Almost exclusively composed of individuals who had been nursed in the lap of ease," said the general orders, "they have, for twelve months, borne the hardships and deprivations of Military life in the midst of an inhospitable wilderness, with a cheerfulness and alacrity which has never been surpassed."

And now to march on home, justifiably proud of a job well done . . . but at what cost!

First, though, there was the matter of their pay. "They waited for about a week in Cleveland, expecting to receive their final pay," wrote Wallace. But their paymaster, John G. Chalmers, one of their own, never showed up. After a while, the group broke up into desultory "little social bands, in different routes" for the trek home, wrote volunteer Albert Lorrain in his memoir.

Once the surviving volunteers were all back home, they were honored and officially welcomed back on January 8, 1814, to the sound of cannon and a speech by Postmaster Thomas Shore, whose own brother John had died at Fort Meigs. "The pride of Sparta were the heroes of Thermopylae," Postmaster Shore proudly boasted, "the pride of Virginia the heroes for Fort Meigs." Then, too, their old commander, General Harrison, now briefly *President* Harrison, visited Petersburg on March 14, 1817, during his brief interlude as chief executive before he died of pneumonia just a month after his inauguration.

Among the leading lights of the survivors in postwar life were future Lieutenant Governor John F. Wiley, who had been wounded at Fort Meigs, and future Richmond Postmaster Thomas Bigger. The volunteer company's one-time commander, Captain McRae, unfortunately died a mysterious and violent death on a trip to Washington in 1854. In an apparent case of murder, his body was found floating in the Potomac River at the mouth of Aquia Creek with injuries to the head. Meanwhile, the last survivor of the volunteers would be the company's one-time Cpl. Reuben Clements, who lived to age ninety-one before his death in 1881.

As for paymaster Chalmers, it appears he had gambled away the money owed to the volunteers for their military service. As a result, reported Wallace, "Congress, on March 3, 1853, appropriated $10,334.31, to be paid to the survivors, or their heirs." A bit late for most of the Petersburg Volunteers.

✯

1813
Nation's Oldest Governor's Mansion

✯

A quiet oasis in the midst of downtown Richmond's skyscrapers, Virginia's storied, antebellum executive mansion awaits the arrival of the state's latest "first family" every four years. Normally, the historic brick mansion leads a life of staid dignity in one corner of the Old Dominion's steeply sloping Capitol Square, just steps from the capitol itself. But the stately home also has been noted for elegant dinners, distinguished guests, lighthearted children's pranks, times of sadness, even reports of a ghostly young girl dressed in rustling taffeta.

Due to reach its two-hundredth birthday in the year 2013, the Virginia executive residence is the oldest, continuously occupied governor's mansion in the nation, while the neighboring state capitol is the nation's second-oldest working capitol. Because it replicates a Roman temple that Thomas Jefferson spotted in France and used as the basis for its design, the Virginia capitol building became the nation's first public structure in classical temple style.

As in the case of the White House and official homes for the governors of many other states, the downstairs of the historic governor's mansion often is used for public and semipublic (invitational) events or tours, but the mansion also offers its occupants the privacy of a second-floor family apartment consisting of four bedrooms, a sitting room, dressing room, and library.

One upstairs room, traditionally the "governor's bedroom" at the front of the house, often has been used for guests instead of governors. Across the hall is the "Lafayette Room," so named because the marquis in his triumphal tour of the United States in the 1820s apparently slept in the room's canopied bed. A century or so later, Winston Churchill, then a member of the British House of Commons, snuggled under the same bed's covers.

Other history-making guests who have stayed in the Virginia executive residence range from the Prince of Wales, later and briefly King Edward VIII of England (before he abdicated to marry a divorced American woman); Marshall Foch of France; Queen Mother Elizabeth of England; famed aviator Charles A. Lindbergh; Admiral Richard E. Byrd, the noted explorer whose own brother Harry was an official occupant himself as governor, and five U.S. presidents.

Built in 1813, with various additions appearing in the years since, often modernized and redecorated, the old brick home has generated its share of story and legend. Among them, said a state brochure of the 1960s, were unexplained reports of "the ghost of a lovely young girl dressed for a ball in rustling taffeta who has found refuge in the second-floor living quarters."

Churchill, visiting during Governor Harry F. Byrd's term in the late 1920s, left behind tales typical of the eccentric future prime minister of England. Already possessor of a prodigious thirst, Churchill apparently required delivery of a quart of brandy a day while staying at the mansion during the supposedly "dry" Prohibition era. He thus posed an interesting legal problem for his host, its resolution not entirely clear today.

It is said that a prominent Winchester attorney, a friend and adviser of Byrd's, was another guest during the British lawmaker's stay and took part in an elaborate dinner for those in the mansion one night.

The next morning, Churchill appeared downstairs in his bathrobe and saw his dinner companion from the night before, but apparently failed to recognize him. "Here, boy," the famous visitor is reported to have said, "take this quarter and fetch me a paper."

The story is, the paper was fetched.

In an earlier day, a bowl of hot toddy quite legally was laid out every day for the Virginia legislators meeting in the state capitol a stone's throw from the mansion's doorstep.

During the Civil War, Stonewall Jackson's body lay in state in the home's downstairs ballroom. Two years later, during Richmond's great "Evacuation Fire" of April 1865, the neighboring business center of Richmond was ablaze as officials of the Confederate government fled the city, but volunteers who scrambled onto the mansion's roof with water buckets saved it and its small kitchen house nearby—in more recent years a guest cottage—from the leapfrogging flames.

Another day, another era, early twentieth-century Governor Andrew Jackson Montague's thirteen-year-old daughter, Gay, prepared for the battleship *Virginia*'s christening by smashing empty bottles against a brick wall at the mansion. Somewhat earlier, Confederate veteran Fitzhugh Lee's two daughters scratched their names on upstairs windowpanes. Governor Lee Trinkle and family escaped harm from a Christmas tree fire, while Colgate Darden's wife planted a victory garden of vegetables during their World War II stay in the historic home.

A few governors have known the sadness of death while in residence there as well. John Garland Pollard's wife died while he was in office . . . and in residence. Then, too, in the 1960s, Becky Godwin, age fourteen, the only child of Governor and Mrs. Mills E. Godwin Jr., was fatally struck by lightning at Virginia Beach.

At one time, meals for the first families of Virginia were prepared in the two-story outbuilding that is now a guest cottage. The mansion itself, as designed by Boston architect Alexander Parris, once was a somewhat austere box, but time and wear have softened that look. Before the mansion's construction in 1813, Virginia governors occupied a far less pretentious four-room house on the same site. And still earlier, they had to rent their quarters wherever they could find suitable accommodation in the capital city.

☆ ☆ ☆

Additional note: A small cousin to the more illustrious historic structures in Capitol Square at Richmond is the also-historic Bell Tower, a brick structure erected in 1824 to replace an even older wooden structure that housed the "Virginia Alarm Bell." During the War of 1812, the bell signaled the arrival of British warships in Norfolk waters. Earlier, it warned of Indian raids and was used to assemble troops in Capitol Square. During the Civil War, unsurprisingly, the bell sounded the alarm whenever Union forces were thought to be approaching. In more recent, peaceful years, the bell tower has signaled the opening of a Senate or House session in the nearby state capitol . . . to some an alarming thought all by itself.

Parting with His Books

Down Virginia way, Thomas Jefferson was entirely sympathetic and more than willing. He knew all about the fire, he loved his country, he loved books . . . and he *had* books, sixty-five hundred of them, the largest personal collection of books amassed by any one person in the whole country. "While residing in Paris," wrote the one-time minister to France, secretary of state, vice president, and president, "I devoted every afternoon . . . in examining all the principal bookstores, turning over every book with my own hands, and putting by everything which related to America."

His library came not only from France. "I have been fifty years in making it," he explained in the same letter of September 1814 tendering his extraordinary offer, "and I have spared no pains, opportunity, or expense, to make it what it now is." The result, as valued by appraisers of his day, was a collection worth $23,950—a major sum by 1814 standards.

The year, indeed, was 1814, an ugly time of war once again with Great Britain, the War of 1812. So ugly for young America, in fact, the British that very summer had sacked Washington, D.C., burned down the White House, and—a fact often overlooked in accounts of the war—the U.S. Capitol. To add insult to injury, notes the U.S. Senate's website, the Brits fueled the latter conflagration with three thousand books "taken from a small room that served as the congressional library."

That was in August, and when the Senate was able to reconvene— "in temporary quarters ten blocks from the gutted capitol"—an early order of business was to develop a library all over again.

Hearing the call, heeding it, and offering his own personal library, was the thoroughly sympathetic Thomas Jefferson. And not merely for money, although at that stage in life the Sage of Monticello certainly could use it. "Recognizing that the nation lacked spare funds during the war emergency, Jefferson explained that he would accept whatever price Congress wished to pay and would take his payments in installments," wrote Senate historian Richard Baker in his online series, *U.S. Senate Historical Minutes* (see "Historical Minute Essays" at www.senate.gov).

That seemed more than fair to an obliging Senate, which voted unanimously on October 10 to accept the offer at the appraisal figure of $23,950.

There would be no such smooth sailing in the House, however, not when members went over the list of titles and found more than a few books written in foreign languages. Moreover, "some titles, including those by Voltaire, Locke, and Rousseau, seemed too philosophical—too literary—for the presumed needs of Congress."

As the lower chamber's book lovers prepared for a spirited fight, the critics also asserted that in time of war Congress had no business dilly-dallying over an expensive library acquisition, "for which it lacked secure housing" at that.

When the opponents, Daniel Webster among them, failed to cripple the proposal by amendment, their next tactic was to suggest buying the collection but then weeding out and returning "all books of an atheistical, irreligious, and immoral tendency." Friends of the Jefferson collection "conceded that every major library contained some books 'to which gentlemen might take exception,' but argued there was simply no other collection available for purchase to equal this one." And so went the debate, back and forth, often hot and furious.

In the end, though, the friends of the Jefferson library prevailed— "but by a slim margin of ten votes."

Thus, by that same slim margin, was born the Library of Congress.

☆ ☆ ☆

Additional note: As noted by Jefferson biographer Dumas Malone in his *The Sage of Monticello,* no sooner had the retired president disposed of his "superb" library than he "promptly proceeded to assemble another." And this one would be different. "He now laid less emphasis on law and politics than previously and more on history and the ancient classics, which he read in the original until his dying day."

Still, the remaining great work of his postpublic life would be the founding of the University of Virginia, which he himself regarded "as one of the most memorable achievements of his entire life." Perhaps strangely to us looking back today, Jefferson didn't contribute all that much to the presidency "as an institution," noted Malone as well. "His contributions to executive procedure were not perpetuated. In his last years, however, he gave substance to his undying faith in private learning and public education in the form of a library and a university. He never claimed that he was the founder of the Library of Congress, but it was his virtual creation, and his title as father of the University of Virginia is beyond dispute."

Nor was creation of the university all that easily attained. "After three or four years of tedious preliminaries," wrote Malone, "the University was chartered in 1819." Even then, progress—and the necessary funding—could be slow, due to the era's shaky economy on both the state and national levels. "It took him and his supporters six years to make a living reality of the University that existed on paper. During this period there was little or no improvement in the economic situation in Virginia. The state, which lost its primacy in population by 1820, was clearly falling behind in influence and power in the Union."

Despite all obstacles, in the face of legislative sniping, budget problems, and occasional controversy over Jefferson's unusual concepts, his beloved university at last did take shape, did begin to accept students . . . and remains today one of the greatest institutions of higher learning in the nation that Jefferson also helped to create. Central to it even today, both in spirit and in tangible, physical form, is his concept of an "academical village" housing students and their professors together, in close proximity, in community. Physically, architecturally, this means Jefferson's own plan for a campus with the library—again, his gift—housed at one end, at the crown, in his rotunda, a sweeping lawn falling away before it with student rooms and intermittent faculty pavilions, or homes, on either side. In 1976, noted biographer Malone, this central core of the university—where students and faculty still live in close proximity to one another—was voted in a bicentennial year poll of the American Institute of Architects as "the proudest achievement of American architecture in the past two hundred years." No wonder, then, that the farsighted Jefferson wished the epitaph over his grave to cite merely three of his many, many accomplishments—that he was the author of the Declaration of Independence and the Virginia statute of religious freedom, and that he was "Father of the University of Virginia."

1 8 3 9
Birth of an Island

Virginia naturally has suffered its share of hurricanes over the centuries, most of them highly destructive. Camille in 1969 flooded Nelson County and killed an estimated 153 persons. Another, striking in 1897, lasted for sixty hours . . . two and a half days! Another, in 1878, completely submerged two of Virginia's barrier islands off the Eastern Shore. A hurricane in 1846 carved out the Hatteras and Oregon inlets. Even earlier, a violent lashing of the Virginia Tidewater in 1667 apparently widened the Lynnhaven River in the Hampton Roads area.

All told, Virginia through recorded history has averaged one hurricane or tropical storm a year. The average is based upon the occasional "good" years recording no such disturbances, but it also incorporates the "bad" years featuring multiple storms, such as 1893, when seven hurricanelike storms passed through or close to Virginia between June 17 and November 8.

One huge blow, taking place in October 1749, had a startling positive effect still very much in evidence today. Raising the level of the Chesapeake Bay by an extraordinary fifteen feet, it (and, to some extent, a hurricane in 1806) churned up a sand "spit" of eight hundred acres that today is covered with homes, commercial structures, and a segment of Interstate Route 64 as it emerges from the eastern end of the Hampton Roads Tunnel Bridge. Thus born of hurricane fury was the Willoughby Spit section of Norfolk.

Far different, though, was the fate of tiny Cobb's Island, a barrier islet off Northampton County on the Eastern Shore. Washed over, inundated, in the late 1870s and again in 1896, Cobb's Island apparently "started out" early in the nineteenth century as a mere sandbank of a few acres about eight to nine miles offshore. It "evidently had risen directly out of the ocean by some convulsion of Nature," wrote sportsman and Virginia state legislator Alexander Hunter in the book *The Huntsman in the South.*

A transplanted New Englander, Nathan F. Cobb Sr., paid a fellow fisherman the grand sum of $150 and a few bushels of salt for the hopeless-looking property and moved "aboard" with his family, even though the island was far from stable—"and would tremble, so the story goes, like a bowlful of jelly whenever an unusually large and heavy billow struck it."

But Cobb, it turns out, had made a shrewd bargain—his island, purchased in 1839, would grow over the next forty years into "a substantial piece of land, of fully fifty acres, and sea meadows of several thousand more," Hunter also wrote. To be sure, Cobb apparently aided and abetted the process by hauling in tons of topsoil by barge. Amazingly, too, his island would provide fresh water from artesian wells, and the soil that took hold nurtured various vegetables such as cabbages "as big as baskets" and turnips "the size of watermelons," said a descendant years later. Even more happily, Cobb and his three sons formed a salvaging company and made a small fortune by cashing in on salvage from ships that foundered on the chain of barrier islands. That fleeting largess ended, however, with the emplacement of a lifesaving service station on the island.

More important in the long run, sportsmen had discovered Cobb's Island as "by far the finest shooting grounds on the Atlantic coast for wild fowl and baybirds," Hunter wrote in his *Huntsman.* "It was not only the feeding grounds of an enormous number of brant [small wild geese], geese, and snipe, but, being so far out in the ocean, it attracted, as a resting place, vast flocks of migrating birds, and it was literally the paradise of sportsmen."

It wasn't long before island proprietor Cobb and family were deriving a nice, steady income from the visiting hunters . . . not long, also, before it struck the Cobb entourage that they had on their hands the foundation of a stunning resort for both summer vacationers and the seasonal hunters. Alexander Hunter himself was present for the opening of the hostelry the Cobbs soon built as their grand resort, "a long, rambling structure of boards along the line of architecture of the inns of Virginia and North Carolina, which have been built in the same style since the memory of man."

While Hunter liked to poke deprecating fun here and there, he acknowledged that the opening, attended by two hundred additional guests, "made a greater impression upon me than any seaside resort I ever visited." Here's one reason why, though: "The attempt of three simple-minded, honest fishermen [Cobb and two of his sons, apparently] to run a watering-place, without the remotest idea of anything outside of their storm-tossed isle, was certainly unique and rare."

As one facet of their inexperience, Hunter went on to say, they hired a young family friend from the mainland as the hotel clerk. "But he kept no books; he carried the current sheet and ledger in his head, and at the end of the season, he 'skipped,' and left nothing behind save his conscience, and that probably was of small value."

Only two sons joined in the hotel venture; the third, Nathan F. Cobb Jr., at first refused. "Here I is, and here I stays," was his answer, as he pointed to his neat house and fine garden. The younger Nathan Cobb's real interest was shooting wild fowl. Unlike the visiting sportsmen, though, Nathan did his hunting for profit. Describing Nathan Jr. as "the finest shot I ever met," Hunter estimated, "he probably killed more wild fowl for market than any other gunner in America."

Back at the hotel and its guest cottages, meanwhile, something like culture shock soon set in, with "these untutored, unimaginative wreckers catering to the wants of the delicate, refined pleasure-seekers." Neither the proprietors nor the guests really understood each other, it seems. "The guests were, for the most part, fashionable people. When the hotel and cottages were filled at the opening of the season the Cobbs were simply dumbfounded that there were people in the world who could want so much. Livery, telegrams, drainage, laundries, water-pipes were as Sanscrit to these simple-minded men."

The dining experience on Cobb's Island was . . . well, an experience, to be sure. "For example, a guest would call for fish, and a huge sea-trout, some two feet long, enough for a whole family on Good Friday, would be placed on the table. Bread—cornpone the size of a Belgian curbstone would be handed up. Beef—and a collop that would satisfy a Pawnee Indian would arrive. Soft crabs—six at a time would be brought."

Niceties such as condiments, sauces, preserves, and the like "were unthought of there."

"*Withal,*" wrote Hunter (wonderful word, *withal*), there were many, himself among them, who loved the place, who were undiscouraged to see their proprietors sauntering through the ballroom of an evening "in their usual costumes of an oilcloth hat, Guernsey jacket, canvas breeches, and rubber boots reaching to the hip." Contributing to the resort's popularity was the very fact that "the Cobbs were so sincere, so true, so democratic that they treated all alike." Thus, "whether you were noble or serf, rich or poor, famous or unknown, it was all the same to them; and when the visitors left the island it was with regret at the parting."

It wasn't long after the resort's start, added Hunter, that many a sportsman like Hunter would call it "the most famous resort in America for the combined attraction of hunting and fishing; and a week's stay at that place was like taking an ocean trip abroad." He and many others, he declared, visited Cobb's Island "year after year." More precisely, "We went in the spring for the robin-snipe; in the summer for the bay birds, and in the winter for that king of salt water birds, the brant." During the summers, too, the island was a magnet for yachtsmen—"all sorts of craft filled with pleasure-seekers would anchor off the place, and there would be feast, fun, and frolic."

But trouble, big-time trouble, was on its way.

It came with a steady rain that began one October night in the late 1870s and continued for two days, only to be replaced the third night by a full-blown hurricane that rattled and shook the hotel to its footings.

In a matter of hours, the tide swept past its high-water mark, the cottages were evacuated, and all fled to the high ground, where the hotel stood in defiance of the storm. "The angry roar of the waves was now heard, mingled with the scream of the blast, and surely and slowly the black billows advanced; the bath-houses were swept away; next the coastguard's house was torn from its place, and drifted inland. The crowd assembled in the ballroom of the hotel. The women cried and moaned; the men cursed and prayed alternately."

As all by now realized, they were trapped, "like caged rats." The sea came closer and closer.

"About four o'clock in the morning a dreadful sound smote their listening ears. Above the noise of the warring elements they heard the crash of a building, the splitting of timbers, and the falling in of beams and planking. It was [the cottage called] the New York house, within fifty yards of the hotel, that had caved in, the supports having washed away, and the whole fabric sank in an unsightly ruin."

"Old Man" Cobb, inured to many a stormy night from his years on the tiny island, "sat stoically waiting for death." Son Nathan "was bidding his wife farewell," son Albert "sat with his head buried in his hands," and third son Warren drank and played cards with a fishing and shooting guide named Bill Johns.

"At half-past four o'clock the waves lapped the porch; at a quarter to five the steps were washed away, and the beat of the charging rollers thundering on, made the island tremble and rock as if it were in the throes of an earthquake. At five, the fluid in a thin stream trickled through the cracks of the closed door, and then they all thought their time had come."

But no, that was the height of the storm—quite suddenly, the water fell back, and back again, until, by eight in the morning, "the ocean was in its usual place."

Still, there was nothing usual about the sights that greeted the islanders and their guests as they emerged from their overnight sanctuary. "Daylight showed the topography of the island was much changed. Immense sand lines were thrown up, looking like miniature mountains; the ground was covered with driftwood, spars, shells and marine vegetation. All the fences were washed away, as were several cottages."

In sum, it would be "several years before Cobb's Island recovered from the blow." Still, memories can be short, and, "at last patrons were assured that floods, like the eruptions of Vesuvius, never happen twice in a lifetime, so the old place was regaining its prestige."

Was, that is, until another October date, nearly two decades after the big blow described so graphically by Hunter.

In the meantime, the Cobbs had sold their hotel, a cottage called the Baltimore House, and thirty-one acres of the one-time mere spit of sand to a syndicate out of Lynchburg for $18,000, reported Brooks Miles Barnes and Barry R. Truitt in their 1997 anthology *Seashore Chronicles: Three Centuries of the Virginia Barrier Islands.* "The syndicate also agreed to pay $360 per annum for a twenty-five-year lease on the island's fishing, shooting, and bathing rights," they also said in a footnote to Hunter's story on Cobb's Island.

But now came the eleventh day of October 1896. Over the years, the sea had crept from an original five hundred yards' distance from the hotel to within fifty *feet,* according to Hunter. Not a good omen for weathering any major storms.

When the big blow struck on this day, islanders and visitors wasted no time in taking refuge on the upper floors of the various lodgings and residences now dotting the isle. In short order, "some tremendous billows swept clear across the island." It wasn't long before the island itself was "invisible." Then, too: "Immense waves came charging from the ocean at their homes, as if they were serried lines of cavalry. The sand dunes broke the force of the mighty surges, otherwise the houses would have disappeared in the clutch of the ravening waters."

Caught outside, "uttering cries of distress and fear," were various animals, both livestock and pets—"horses, cows, goats, and dogs were all mingled together, and every now and then some wave overtopping its fellow, would catch some animal and bear it across the mainland and drown it in the deep channel at the rear of the island."

With even the high ground soon underwater, "the life guardsmen went from house to house and rescued the inmates one by one, and carried them to the life-saving station." In the face of sixty-mile-an-hour winds, this obviously was, as Hunter said, "a heroic task."

Many of those rescued took refuge aboard several oystering vessels standing by—"where from the decks they watched the homes of their childhood being washed away; not the houses alone, but the very earth was swept away, and all their belongings were engulfed in the insatiable maw of the angry ocean." Just like that, "the island had for the most part disappeared like the fabled Atlantis."

Hurrying to the stricken spot to check on the fate of Cobb's Island in the hurricane of 1896, an unnamed reporter from the *Baltimore Sun* found the Baltimore Cottage to be "a total wreck" and the hotel itself "a complete wreck." How complete was *complete*? "The floors, porches, walls, and windows are all broken up. About three feet of sand stands in the dancing pavilion on the first floor. The barroom, billiard room, bowling alley, and several other small buildings were tumbled down in one heap and broken up so they were of no use whatever."

Luckily, the lifesaving station had been moved 250 yards inland just four weeks before—"which undoubtedly saved the building, and the water stood six feet deep at the former site of the building."

Overall, Cobb's Island had been "reduced" by fifty acres and was left "only about twenty-five in sight at low water." The outlook was a loss "estimated at many thousands of dollars and probably the extinction of Cobb's Island as a summer resort."

☆ ☆ ☆

Additional note: While its resort days had paled, Cobb's Island still was *afloat,* as it were, and in June 1933 noted ornithologist Olin Sewall Pettingill Jr. and his bride, Eleanor, "undertook a combined honeymoon and scientific expedition to Cobb's Island," reported Barnes and Truitt.

While the original Cobbs had moved back to the mainland after the blow of 1896, the honeymooners discovered, a descendant named George W. Cobb now lived on the island in a sturdy house on piles as a warden for the National Association of Audubon Societies. Like his predecessors, he had a deeply tanned face and appeared to have the vigor of a man much younger than his sixty years or so. Sharing the island with only the Coast Guardsmen still stationed there, he welcomed bird watchers in general, he said, and deplored the fact that the sportsmen of the nineteenth century nearly had exterminated the very species they hunted.

Toward the end of the Pettingills' visit, a severe storm one night forced them to take refuge from their campsite in Cobb's house . . . and like so many hapless onlookers of the century before, they saw the battering waves creep closer and closer, saw them knock a nearby outbuilding on its side and then wet the very floors at their feet before the tide suddenly turned and began to recede. The next day, Pettingill was distressed to discover that the storm had wiped out thousands of bird nests, eggs, and chicks.

As the couple packed and said their goodbyes to their usually taciturn host, he said he was sorry they had to leave and urged: "Come back next year. There'll be more birds than ever."

That same summer, though, Pettingill came across a chilling notice in the Audubon Society's publication *Bird-Lore.* "George W. Cobb," it said, "this Association's warden on Cobb's Island, Virginia, lost his life, on August 23, in the severe storm that lashed the middle Atlantic coast." The same report said every building on the island had been demolished, even the Coast Guard station, but editors Barnes and Truitt, whose book included the Pettingill account, said that wasn't entirely true; the station house survived the storm.

Still, the record books say that same hurricane killed eighteen persons in all. According to the Audubon publication, George Cobb's body was not found.

☆ ☆ ☆

Incidental intelligence: In its heyday, the Cobb's Island Hotel advertised rooms at $2.50 a night, $12 a week, and $40 a month. For those munificent outlays, the visitor could expect: "The Grandest Surf-bathing on the Atlantic Coast; Boating, Hunting, Fishing; The Hunter's Paradise." In more recent years, incidentally, a rare decoy waterfowl carved by Nathan Cobb Jr. sold in collectors' circles for $192,500, "the third highest price paid [at auction] for any decoy," according to editors Barnes and Truitt.

1842
First Glimpses of Cadet Jackson

Dabney Herndon Maury's first glimpse of fellow Virginian Thomas J. Jackson came in the South Barracks of the U.S. Military Academy at West Point, New York, one day in 1842. The new cadet entering the barracks, wrote Maury years later, "was then in his nineteenth year and was awkward and uncultured in manner and appearance."

Even so, "there was an earnest purpose in his aspect that impressed all who saw him."

Maury stood there, watching, with A. P. Hill and Birket Fry, like Maury both future Confederate generals. The object of their attention, totally uncouth by their standards, "was clad in gray homespun, and wore a coarse felt hat, such as wagoners or constables—as he had been—usually wore, and bore a pair of weather-stained saddle-bags across his shoulders."

Not terribly impressive? On the contrary, "there was about him so sturdy an expression of purpose that I remarked, 'That fellow looks as if he had come to stay.'"

Maury, a friendly young man, went to greet the newcomer "with such interest and kindness as would have gratified others under the circumstances," but was received "so coldly that I regretted my friendly overtures, and rejoined my companions, rebuffed and discomfited."

More awkward than rude, however, the new cadet from the western half of Virginia soon impressed one and all with his hard work and dedication to duty, Maury included. "His barrack room was small and bare and cold," wrote Maury in his nineteenth-century memoir, *Recollections of a Virginian in the Mexican, Indian, and Civil Wars*. "Every night just before taps he would pile his grate high with anthracite coal, so that by the time the lamps were out, a ruddy glow came from his fire, by which, prone upon the bare floor, he would 'bone' his lesson for the next day, until it was literally burned into his brain."

As a result, "from one examination to the next he continually rose in his class till he reached the first section, and we used to say, 'If we stay here another year, old Jack will be head of the class.'"

Ranking ahead of "Old Jack," however, was another future general of the Civil War era, a bright and popular youngster not yet sixteen when he entered the U.S. Military Academy at West Point, New York.

Still another popular cadet—"a good and kindly fellow whom everybody liked"—was a whiz in horsemanship. "He was proficient in mathematics, but did not try to excel at anything except horsemanship. In the riding school he was very daring. When his turn came to leap the bar, he would make the dragoons lift it from the trestles and raise it as high as their heads, when he would drive his horse over it, clearing at least six feet."

"Old Jack," by contrast, "was very clumsy in his horsemanship and with his sword, and we were painfully anxious as we watched him leaping the bar and cutting at heads."

As for the young cadet who had entered the portals of the Military Academy before celebrating a sixteenth birthday, he apparently excelled in just about all respects—at academics, horsemanship, and swordsmanship.

On the eve of the civil war lying in wait for them all just a few years ahead, his sympathies would lie with the South, it further seems.

By contrast with these and others among his fellow cadets, memoir-writer Maury would be only a bit player in that momentous drama of the 1860s. A bit player, yes, but a historian at heart . . . and what a window on history he did enjoy as he greeted new cadet Thomas J. Jackson in the South Barracks, as he came to know the all-round (but youthful) star George B. McClellan, as he witnessed U. S. Grant's uncanny horsemanship in the ring!

So many personal glimpses. A six-foot South Carolinian, for instance, "every inch a soldier," and yet, "as gentle as he was brave." Like Jackson, like Grant and McClellan, like Maury himself, Bernard

Bee would fight in the Mexican War, then in the Civil War. First, though, court-martialed for some minor infraction toward the end of his second year at West Point, Bee was ordered to stay behind a full day while all his classmates left on summer furlough. As they departed aboard a Hudson River steamboat, they were supposed to toss "a bottle of cocktail" into the river "to comfort" Bee in his enforced solitude.

"Bee liked cocktail, but couldn't swim," added Maury's account. "I, having promised my mother not to drink while at the Academy, swam for that bottle for love of Bee." Maury's swim was taken in vain, as events turned out. No bobbing bottle turned up. "Poor Bee was in sorry luck that day."

Even sorrier luck, of course, was the moment at First Manassas (Bull Run) in 1861 when Confederate Brig. Gen. Bernard Bee was fatally wounded—but not before he turned and exhorted his men to look upon Jackson holding the line at Henry Hill . . . exhorted with deathless phraseology, "There stands Jackson like a stone wall! Rally behind the Virginians!" (Some witnesses alleged, however, that Bee uttered his famous simile in anger because Jackson had made no move to aid him and another hard-pressed brigade commander.)

Going back to the Mexican War of the 1840s, meanwhile, Maury often saw the Union's future Gen. U. S. Grant, up close and personal. "Grant was a thoroughly kind and manly young fellow, with no bad habits, and was respected and liked by his brother officers, especially by those in his own regiment," wrote Maury.

On the eve of the Civil War nearly two decades later, Maury also alleged, future Union Gen. George B. McClellan's "sympathies were with the Southern States, in which were his kindred and warmest friends." (McClellan apparently wrote a letter to Maury in the winter of 1860–61 saying that "while he knew the South was being wronged, and feared that war was inevitable, he would fight, if fight he must, for Pennsylvania, his native State.")

Maury, future founder of the postwar Southern Historical Society, saw a key distinction between his old West Point friends McClellan and U. S. Grant, a distinction that left Grant a hero of the war and the brilliant McClellan bereft of major victory. As Maury put it: "Both men were kindly in nature, both were brave. While McClellan was personally as brave as Grant, and of a higher spirit, he seemed to lack that inflexible decision of opinion and purpose which bore Grant to his great fortune."

In short, Grant was tough; McClellan was not.

★
---

1 8 4 9
"Nevermore, Quoth the Raven"

★

Poetic but melancholy ground just ahead. In a backwater of old Richmond's East Main Street stands a tight little complex of four structures and garden behind an iron gate. Head for the doorway to "the Old Stone House," the oldest standing building in the city. Step inside . . . into the world of Edgar Allan Poe.

By way of the Edgar Allan Poe Museum.

Now, true, he never lived here, never stayed nor slept here, so far as is known. But he could have been to the doorstep, even stepped inside. The Old Stone House was a part of his world, and it's still here.

That's more than can be said for any of the half dozen or so Richmond homes or boarding houses in which he did live or stay at one time or another—all gone now. A bus station took over one such site, a public library another, a federal post office and courts building still a third. And the site of a hotel where the famous writer apparently gave his last public reading, two weeks before his mysterious death in Baltimore, was replaced by a twentieth-century parking lot.

Still, the Old Stone House and its Poe Museum are a part of his old neighborhood, his own poetic but melancholy ground in many ways. Artifacts and mementos of his life abound in the museum. Perhaps his spirit lingers about as well. After all, the museum site is only blocks from some of his boyhood dwelling places and just a stone's throw from the one-time offices of his early literary vehicle, the *Southern Literary Messenger*. And the overall fact is, he spent more of his short lifetime in Richmond than in any other one spot.

It was here, while serving as editor of the *Messenger,* that he first received national recognition as a writer and critic. It was here, also, that the tragic forces of his life and loves were formed and consummated.

In 1811, when Edgar was barely three years old, his mother, British-born actress Elizabeth Arnold Poe, died here of tuberculosis. Because society frowned upon actors in those days, she was buried at the edge of the churchyard at historic St. John's Church, up the hill behind the museum, in an unmarked grave. With their actor-father David Poe nowhere in sight, Edgar and a sister, Rosalie, only a year in age, were orphaned, their future destinies unknown to anyone at the time.

Fortunately for Edgar, tobacco merchant John Allan and his wife, Frances, took him into their home. Another Richmond family took in the girl. They apparently acted in response to public pleas to help the dying mother in her last days, for she was popular in Richmond as a stage actress (who played an estimated three hundred roles during her life), even if social convention could not stand for her burial in consecrated ground.

Young Edgar's informal adoption by the Allans, never legally validated, gave the future writer his middle pen name, although he and his foster father were destined to break off their relationship over quarrels about money.

It was in Richmond, also, in a long-since-obliterated boarding house, that Poe married his cousin Virginia Clemm. She was thirteen and he was twenty-seven. Her mother, already his aunt as sister to his missing father, now became his mother-in-law.

But Virginia in just eleven years herself died of tuberculosis. The cottage the couple and the mother occupied in the Bronx of New York City at the time—the very place, in fact, where Virginia died—has been restored as a Poe museum. In further fact, Poe museums in New York, Baltimore, and Philadelphia all are situated in former Poe dwelling places . . . but not in Richmond, where none survived the march of progress in a constantly changing urban environment.

"Many visitors to the house are dismayed to find that Poe himself did not live here," former museum curator Denise Bethel once noted. "But the Poe Museum has never claimed that he did. What we can say with certainty is that Poe knew the house and probably knew it well, for it [built in 1740] already was something of a landmark when he lived in that [east] end of Richmond."

The small Poe Museum, owned and maintained by the nonprofit Poe Foundation, Inc., is not exactly unknown itself. Thirteen thousand visitors pass through the wooden door of the Old Stone House to visit the literary oasis on East Main Street every year. In addition, books, articles, even an opera concerning the famous Southern writer continue to flow from the pens of various scholars, authors, and admirers around the world—in many cases with illustrations or other help provided by the museum staff, which oversees the largest collection of Poe papers and rare books in existence.

Not only is Poe still Richmond's best-known writer, Bethel noted, "he's the South's best-known writer," and, indeed, "for many other countries he's America's best-known writer."

As one example, Bethel cited the visiting Japanese who come to Richmond and have "never heard of Robert E. Lee, never heard of [Chief Justice] John Marshall," but are curious about only Edgar Allan Poe. As she also noted, "There are mystery writers in Japan who write under the pseudonym of Edgar Allan Poe."

What visitors may see at the museum ranges from a summer-house wall built of brick from the old *Literary Messenger* building nearby, a desk and chair from the magazine's office, various furnishings from Poe homes, other artifacts of all kinds, and photographic reproductions of nineteenth-century British artist James Carling's forty-three-piece set of illustrations for Poe's immortal poem "The Raven." While only the photos normally are on display, the museum owns Carling's originals.

In addition to such mementos, the museum boasts a remarkable model, five feet wide and eighteen feet long, of early nineteenth-century Richmond done in clay by the late Edith Ragland. Built to scale in 1925–26, her creation is replete with hundreds of clay houses, churches, and other buildings, along with the hills and streets of Poe's Richmond. Small signs point out the structures associated with Poe himself.

The model is considered well authenticated . . . but not the oft-tangled story of Poe's life. For here mystery abounds, as perhaps would suit Poe himself, as quite the aficionado of mystery and the macabre. It certainly is known that he was an intense, controversial, and usually impoverished writer, but was he really forced to leave the University of Virginia because of drinking and gambling? And the U.S. Military Academy at West Point also? Whatever became of his father, David? How did the younger Poe come to be found unconscious on a Baltimore street and die just days later, without ever regaining consciousness? And why did he die at the young age of forty? And so on.

For every Poe-related question, another story, explanation, or fresh mystery seems to crop up. Here's one that directly involves the museum, and Poe only obliquely. In 1987, somebody broke into the Poe Museum in Richmond and stole a seventy-five-pound bust of Poe, sometimes called "America's Shakespeare." Four nights later, a stranger in cowboy hat and boots entered a local restaurant called the Raven Inn carrying the heavy bust. He had a beer then departed, leaving the bust, accompanied by a few lines from a Poe poem written on a paper bag.

Here's another: Also in recent years, a thief or thieves broke into the Valentine Museum in Richmond and stole a rare portrait of Poe's foster mother, Frances Keeling Valentine Allan.

And another: For half a century or more, a mysterious stranger slipped into a Baltimore cemetery on Poe's birthday to lay three roses and a half-empty bottle of cognac on his grave. So ritualized was this phenomenon that Poe admirers organized "watchers" to observe the procedure from nearby points without interfering with the stranger . . . without attempting to identify him or her.

As an additional but older mystery, was the widowed Poe back in Richmond to stay when he reappeared there in 1849, just before his death, and proposed marriage to his childhood sweetheart, Elmira Royster Shelton, herself a widow?

Then, too, why did he die . . . did he have to? Was he laid low by a severe drinking bout? Drugs? Or incipient, unsuspected disease, such as epilepsy? Such a mystery was, and is, his death that the museum in Richmond devoted a special exhibit to the issue in 1999, the 150th anniversary of the writer's death. Scholars and Poe devotees held a special anniversary symposium at the Hotel Jefferson in Richmond to explore the many theories on Poe's death. "I have no doubt that one day we will know for sure the cause of his death," said museum director P. C. Moon at the time. "But for now I find it ironic. Poe invented the detective story. And here, 150 years later, his death is still a mystery. It's a mystery he's taken to his grave."

Despite the oft-repeated allegation that Poe never regained consciousness, incidentally, it also is alleged that he uttered these dying words: "Lord, help my poor soul." Those words, in fact, were the title given the Poe Museum's yearlong exhibit about the mystery of his death.

Poe's sister, Rosalie, also raised in Richmond by an established merchant family, wound up so poverty-stricken in her late years that she was reduced to begging in the streets of Richmond and Washington, D.C.

As for their mother's unmarked grave up at the church where Patrick Henry spoke his "liberty or death" line in 1775, society relented in the twentieth century. The Raven Society at the University of Virginia— where Poe had spent all of one session and built up a significant gambling debt before he left the school—and Actors Equity of New York, together with the Poe Foundation, joined forces to erect a memorial to her in the St. John's churchyard. But her real gravesite, like so much of Poe's own life, remains unknown.

☆ ☆ ☆

Additional note: James Southall Wilson explained much of the Poe mystic—and detailed highlights of his literary career—in a biography placed on the Internet by the Poe Museum (http://www.poemuseum .org). For instance, the real story of his academic career:

"After attending schools in England and Richmond, young Poe registered at the University of Virginia in February 14, 1826, the second session of the university. He lived in Room 13, West Range. He became an active member of the Jefferson Literary Society, and passed his courses with good grades at the end of the session in December. Mr. Allan failed to give him enough money for necessary expenses, and Poe made debts of which his so-called father did not approve. When Mr. Allan refused to let him return to the University, a quarrel ensued, and Poe was driven from the Allan home without money. Mr. Allan probably sent him a little money later, and Poe went to Boston. There he published a little volume of poetry, *Tamerlane and Other Poems.* It is such a rare book now that a single copy has sold for $200,000."

English scholar Wilson also noted that Poe joined the army in 1827, "using the name Edgar A. Perry." In his two years of service, he rose from private to sergeant major. He then secured his appointment to the U.S. Military Academy at West Point, but between his army stint and West Point, he went to Baltimore to live with his aunt, Marie Poe Clemm, whose daughter Virginia he would be marrying at a later date.

In the meantime, he published his second book of poetry, *Al Aaraaf, Tamerlane, and Minor Poems.*

West Point turned out to be a fiasco. "After another quarrel with Allan (who had married a second wife in 1830), Poe no longer received aid from his foster father. Poe then took the only method of release from the Academy, and got himself dismissed on March 6, 1831."

Now came *Poems by Edgar Allan Poe, Second Edition,* and, returning to the Clemm household in Baltimore, "young Poe began writing prose tales." Five of them were published in the *Philadelphia Saturday Courier* in 1832. Then, as of the December 1835 issue of the *Southern Literary Messenger,* Poe had taken over as editor of that publication. "Poe's slashing reviews and sensational tales made him widely known as an author," wrote Professor Wilson. In July 1838, *Harper's* published Poe's book-length narrative *Arthur Gordon Pym,* Wilson also noted.

Recently married (in 1836), Poe and Virginia moved to Philadelphia in 1838 to start a six-year period of residency there. In 1844, they moved to New York (where Poe lived at nine different venues in Manhattan alone). After serving as editor of two periodicals in Philadelphia (*Burton's Gentleman's* magazine and *Graham's* magazine), Poe "found work on the *New York Evening Mirror.*"

His *Tales of the Grotesque and Arabesque* was published in 1840, and five years later, "Poe became famous with the spectacular success of his poem 'The Raven.'" Also in 1845, "Wiley and Putnam issued *Tales by Edgar Allan Poe* and *The Raven and Other Poems.*" The next year Poe rented the Fordham cottage where Virginia would die in 1847. "After his wife's death, Poe perhaps yielded more often to a weakness for drink, which had beset him at intervals since early manhood. He was unable to take even a little alcohol without a change of personality, and any excess was accompanied by physical prostration. Throughout his life those illnesses had interfered with his success as an editor, and had given him a reputation for intemperateness that he scarcely deserved."

His own death in October 1849 came after lecturing and reading appearances in Norfolk and Richmond. He was buried in the churchyard of the Westminster Presbyterian Church in Baltimore.

Incidental intelligence: Maintained by the Raven Society at the University of Virginia, Poe's old room on the West Range of the university's famous Lawn has been kept empty (except for period furniture) and sealed off by a glass partition for years as a combined memorial and visitation site for those interested in Edgar Allan Poe.

★

1853

Forgotten Explorer

★

The thermometer in Norfolk registered a mild thirty-eight degrees, but the eddies slopping against the hull of U.S. Navy Lt. Thomas Jefferson

---

Taken in part from the author's article published in *The Commonwealth, the Magazine of Virginia,* Virginia State Chamber of Commerce, Richmond, February 1970.

Page's awkward-looking vessel were cold and wintry gray. It was February 1853, and Page, Virginia's forgotten explorer, was about to sail his radical, untried steamer on a three-year voyage into the uncharted belly region of South America.

In a few weeks, the Virginian and his USS *Water Witch* would be leaving the waters of the South Atlantic to churn up and down the major rivers of South America's little-known midriff—the La Plata, the Paraná, the Uruguay, the Paraguay, and their various tributaries. Thus, he and his sailors would cruise a wild west frontier; hunt strange animals; encounter untamed, sometimes hostile Indians; chart river waters never before seen by white men; open others to steamship navigation for the first time; seek a river entry to mountain-locked Bolivia, and, at one point, "sail" two thousand miles from the sea into the interior of Brazil.

Their exploratory voyage abruptly would end, however, with a gun duel between the lightly armed *Witch* and a Paraguayan fort, an incident "smoothed over" by a display of gunboat diplomacy just four years later.

Not all these developments could be foreseen, of course, as the navy's strange-looking warship got underway from Norfolk. Slim, even sleek-hulled, the *Water Witch* stretched gracefully enough for 150 feet, bow to stern. Tall masts forward and aft acknowledged her sailing heritage. But her silhouette, nonetheless, was one to make most seafaring men gawk. For there, amidships, was an ungainly smokestack, and there, too, on either side, the round hump of a Morgan wheel. An oceangoing (it was hoped), steam-powered side-wheeler fitted with sails, the *Witch* was a rare specimen, if not absolutely unique, as a warship.

Her odd motive power combination would be put to the test sooner than expected, as events turned out. On her first day out of Norfolk, notes the ship's log, a boiler "blew a bolt." Her crew simply banked their fires and unfurled the sails to keep their ship moving southward before the ocean breezes.

The proud Virginian in the captain's quarters, it is safe to assume, would brook no delay in proceeding with his historic mission. A U.S. Navy officer from the age of nineteen, Thomas Jefferson Page, now forty-three, had been so eager to lead his own exploratory expedition that he turned down an offer to sail the China seas with Commodore Colin Ringgold as the latter's second-in-command. Possibly Page was rankled by the senior officer's appointment to command the China survey, for it had been Page, veteran of an earlier, single-ship command in Oriental waters, who proposed the China exploration.

The eighth son (and fourteenth child) of Mann Page, the Virginia explorer of the mid-nineteenth century had been born on his father's Tidewater estate as the latest product of a distinguished Virginia family. His two grandfathers, after all, were Governor John Page and Governor Thomas Nelson Page, the Revolutionary War general from Tidewater who signed the Declaration of Independence. More precisely, explorer Page's father, Mann Page, was the oldest of Governor Page's progeny. Mann Page's wife, Elizabeth Nelson (the explorer's mother), in turn, was the eldest child of Governor Thomas Nelson Jr.

The elder Pages lived at Rosewell, a striking old mansion built on Carter's Creek in Gloucester County on the north side of the York River, but Mann Page founded his own plantation and home at Shelly, across the creek and on the crest of a hill overlooking the fabulous Rosewell, which by some accounts "beggared" two generations of Pages. Unfortunately gutted by fire two centuries later, Rosewell once was considered Colonial Virginia's grandest mansion, grander even than the governor's palace in Williamsburg.

It was still standing and in use when Thomas Jefferson Page was born at nearby Shelly as next-to-last of Mann Page's fifteen children. This Mann Page, incidentally, should not be confused with the earlier Mann Page, father of the governor . . . and the man who actually built Rosewell.

In any case, it was Lieutenant Page whom a navy secretary named John Kennedy selected in the 1850s for the partly exploratory, partly diplomatic South American venture. The Virginian and his crew were to collect specimens of plant and animal life, minerals, and geological samples. They were to report weather and astronomical findings, observe the agricultural and commercial development of the Argentine states, gauge fish production in the rivers, and chart the waterways and report on their navigability.

Then, too, the combined ocean and river voyage would give the vessel's power plant a major test. And the Americans were to do what they could to establish new friendships in the vast, largely mysterious southern continent. In short, like Matthew Perry in Japan, and Ringgold in China, Page was sent to open doors.

Four months after leaving Norfolk, the *Water Witch* turned into the La Plata River's gaping mouth . . . with, it turned out, auspicious timing. Dramatic events in the Argentine Confederation and among its neighbors had set the stage for an unexpectedly friendly welcome.

Two strongman dictators who had previously barred foreign entry to their remote "inner kingdoms" were gone.

In Argentina, the dictator Juan Manuel de Rosas had been defeated by Gen. Justo Jose de Urquiza in a battle for control of the confederation. One of Urquiza's first actions was to dismantle the shore batteries and river chains once blocking the waters above Buenos Aires.

Likewise, in Paraguay, Jose Francia—"El Supremo" to his frightened subjects—had been replaced by a more worldly Carlos Lopez. Both new leaders initially welcomed the *Water Witch* to their internal waterways. And so, after a few delays at Buenos Aires, the sidewheeler began her river explorations in the South American springtime of September.

The *Witch* moved first up the Paraná, a wide, turgid stream that leads to the Paraguay River then branches off to the northeast on a course into lower Brazil. From the masthead of the oceangoing steamer, her crewmen now reported sightings few mariners ever would see. Rolling away to the horizon on either side was a carpet of grassland sometimes punctuated by trees. At times, great bluffs towered above the sixty-foot masts themselves. One officer, Lt. (and future admiral) Daniel Ammen, jotted down notes that still can be seen in his handwritten journal at the National Archives in Washington, D.C. "Only an occasional sail meets the eye," he wrote one day. "The shores are empty and will be for centuries," he added another time. And still a third: "The scattered trees as far as the eye can see over the green sward give the country an appearance of a continuous English park."

For Ammen and his comrades, every sight, every day, every hour, was a new experience, all attended by the excitement of collecting specimens or jotting down observations from a mysterious, seldom-visited part of the world. And, as the *Water Witch* churned northward, there were special highlights. About 3 P.M. one day, Ammen looked up from his perch on a coal barge towed behind the steamer to see, "a well defined cloud which I thought arose from a fire." But then, two hours later, "I was surprised to see the cloud approach in the form of a vast multitude of grasshoppers, which really darkened the air and appeared to extend for miles."

Another time, he noted eighty-foot bluffs on the shoreline "perforated by great numbers of holes resembling those made by swallows and filled by thousands of parrots." The sailors also came across big "tigre" cats, giant deer, and fish so numerous and bold, their drumming against the ship's bottom kept the crew awake at night.

Here and there the explorers visited the large ranches or small settlements to be found along the river's edge. After a three-day stop at the provincial capital Corrientes, eight hundred miles above Buenos Aires, the *Water Witch* swung into the Paraguay River and chugged upstream to Asuncion, primitive capital city of Paraguay. A bit later, the ocean-going *Witch* would ascend the Paraguay to the Brazilian military post Corumba, two thousand miles from the sea and, by distance, the high point of the vessel's river travels.

Both rivers traveled so far, the sailors learned, shared a forbidden shoreline—the banks of the dreaded El Gran Chaco, "the home and almost boundless domain of various tribes of inhospitable Indians," as described by Page. Said he also, in a report to Congress many months later: "This is an extent of country embracing not less than two hundred thousand square miles; and notwithstanding it has been partitioned out by imaginary limits among the different states surrounding it—the Argentine Confederation, Bolivia, Paraguay, and Brazil—the Indian yet roams that vast domain in undisturbed possession. He sallies forth at times to rob the white man, and when pursued finds refuge in the immensity of this region."

Curious intelligence for the seagoing navy's files, but the men of the *Water Witch* had not seen a single settler's home in a fourteen-hundred-mile stretch of river shoreline forming a natural border to the Chaco region. This is not to say that either stream was devoid of life. The steamer often did pass sprawling *estancias* (ranches) and towns on the river banks *opposite* the Chaco shoreline. And shortly after entering the Paraguay, the *Witch* drew abreast of four Paraguayan "warships," their crewmen dressed in red trousers and white shirts. They gave the Americans a friendly reception, and, after an exchange of salutes, the *Water Witch* moved on to Asuncion—to a cordial welcome by President Carlos Lopez himself.

Then came the upriver run to Corumba, a feat that seemed to open a new roadway into Brazil's legendary Matto Grosso region. Exulted Page: "The Paraguay is now made known to the world as navigable into the very heart of her [Brazil's] rich frontier province." But a subsequent attempt to push up the nearby Bahia Negra River all the way to Bolivia was thwarted by an impenetrable "plain of grass seemingly floating on the water," Page also had to report. Even so, as the year 1854 passed into 1855, the Virginian and his crew continued their explorations of mid–South America aboard ship, boat, horse, and even on foot.

They surveyed vast areas of the Argentine territory and traveled a dozen or more major rivers, among them not only the Paraná and Paraguay, but also the Uruguay, Salado, Pilcomayo, and Confuso—with the most dramatic results on the little-known Salado. For here was a stream never fully traveled by Argentina's European settlers, yet it might provide the confederation's western and northwestern provinces a direct water route to the Argentine hub of Buenos Aires. "We were told by those who were supposed to be the best informed that we might possibly ascend about forty-five miles; by some that it took its rise in some of the numerous lakes," Page wrote.

Unable to resist this challenge, Page rented a local steamboat, the ninety-foot *Yerba,* and chugged 360 miles upstream before low water forced him to turn back. He had gone deep into Indian territory, far beyond any white settlements, and proved his point. Oops, *almost* proved, that is. Not yet satisfied, he took to horses and now journeyed *six hundred* miles overland to the upper reaches of the same river. Then, borrowing a small vessel and an escort of eighty soldiers, he started *down* the virgin waterway. Obstacles such as fallen trees and overhanging branches eventually forced the explorers to leave the boat and hike along the shoreline. Not unlike the pioneers of the American West, they were attacked—twice, it seems—by Indians on horseback wielding deadly spears. The Indians were driven off, but not before "they defended themselves most gallantly," Page noted.

His survey at last completed, Page concluded the Salado would be navigable for six hundred miles once cleared of obstructions, perhaps even for nine hundred miles in the high-water season. In short, it truly could be a new highway to the isolated northern settlements, a revelation that stunned the Argentines and raised Page and his men to near heroic stature. "We are lost in wonder and admiration," said the *Argentino Independente* of November 10, 1855. Added the *Commercio de Salta:* "The service they have rendered to the country in revealing to us the existence of a navigable river in that region, which until recently we regarded only as a desert to be feared because of its savage tribes, is inappreciable."

Another major discovery by the men of the *Water Witch* was a deep-water channel near the mouth of the La Plata. The channel bypassed the fortress island of Martin Garcia, from which the rulers of once-independent Buenos Aires had controlled the gateway to the interior.

"This channel is still used as an entry into the Parana delta," noted Brother Robert Wood, S.M., in his article "The Remarkable Voyage of the *Water Witch*" for the April 1966 issue of the Pan American Union's magazine *Americas.*

Meanwhile, relations with Paraguayan President Lopez had not borne up very well . . . in fact, had fallen apart. In further fact, the *Water Witch,* under command of a Page subordinate, had been fired upon by a Paraguayan shore battery of six cannon on the Paraná. The very first shot carried away the ship's wheel, severed the rudder ropes, threw up a shower of deadly wooden splinters, and left helmsman Samuel Chaney mortally wounded. The crew fired back, but their *Witch* was hulled ten times by Paraguayan shot before she could move out of range.

Page, when he heard of the attack, thundered that it was an "outrage unavenged." He beseeched the commander of a U.S. Navy squadron in the nearby South Atlantic to join in a punitive foray against the river fort, but, wisely enough, that decision was bucked to Washington, where it would await Page's return to the United States.

That return was widely ballyhooed, both for the Virginian's accomplishments and the Paraguayan incident. On the latter point, newly installed President James Buchanan, in his first message to Congress, trumpeted a pledge to demand "satisfaction." Asserting that the *Water Witch* was not, "properly speaking," a warship, he said. She was a small steamer merely engaged in a scientific enterprise intended for the advancement of commerce generally. He also challenged Paraguay's territorial rights to the river stretch where the shelling took place, since the river was bordered on one side by Paraguay, on the other by the Argentines . . . and claimed by each.

Satisfaction came three years later when a fleet of twenty U.S. warships sailed up the South American rivers toward Asuncion in a calculated show of the flag. Two ships from the flotilla, one of them the *Witch* herself, pushed on upstream for a tense visit to the capital city, followed by a diplomatic settlement that restored relations between the two countries and provided a $20,000 payment to Chaney's family.

Page himself was on hand as fleet captain . . . and he remained behind to conduct new surveys of the upper Paraguay for another eighteen months.

In the meantime, he already had achieved fame—and a deserved place in history, even if he has been forgotten in recent years. Returning to the Washington Navy Yard in May 1856, more than three years after her departure from Norfolk, his ship, the untried *Water Witch,* had churned some thirty-six hundred miles by river, while Page and his men had covered another forty-four hundred miles on their overland journeys of exploration. "These waters are open to the American flag and their territory to American enterprise," Page declared with obvious pride. And rightly so. After all, he had skippered the first steamer to ply the upper Paraguay. He had explored regions so backward that in one case (that of Paraguay) the population included no doctors and others so forbidding that white settlers of three hundred years' standing had not ventured into them. Further, the scientific data and specimens he brought home revealed species entirely unknown to scholars of the day. Most important, Page had dispelled the notion that oceangoing ships could not reach the interior of the South American continent.

"In refutation of this idea," he wrote, "I need simply state the fact that the *Water Witch,* a seagoing steamer, a man-of-war, though small, of nine feet drought, penetrated into the interior of South America to the distance, from the ocean by the river, of two thousand miles. Ocean steamers of four times her tonnage may ascend these rivers nine-tenths of this distance at all seasons of the year."

Urging his fellow Americans to forge strong ties with their South American neighbors, Page reported his findings and recommendations not only to the navy but also to the public—in a thick book that ran to two editions and a Spanish translation as well.

But now, the American Civil War loomed close—thoughts of Page, the *Water Witch,* and explorations of a South American "Wild West" would vanish in the cataclysm about to come.

Unsurprisingly, Page would cast his lot with the Confederacy. He soon found himself supervising gun batteries at Gloucester Point, not far from his boyhood home, and planning river defenses for his native Virginia. Later, he was sent to Europe to command an ironclad under construction there, but there were many delays. Finally, shadowed by wooden Union ships that avoided his challenge to fight, he brought the metal-clad *Stonewall* to Cuba en route to a Southern port. In Havana, however, he learned the war was over; the Confederacy had fallen.

As a result, Page would return to South America, to the Argentine ranches he had come to love. That decision also reunited him with his second son, John, who at fourteen had accompanied his father on the first *Water Witch* voyage, only to remain in the land of the pampas and marry a young lady from Buenos Aires.

After a time in his old South American haunts, the Virginian moved on to England, where he supervised the construction of four ironclads for Argentina. In 1880, he shifted his base to Florence, Italy, scene of his long wait during the Civil War for delivery of the ironclad *Stonewall.* It had been a sad wait, too, since his eldest son, Thomas Jr., only twenty-five, had died there while awaiting the ironclad's completion with his explorer father.

By the time an aging Thomas Jefferson Page Sr. himself died, in Rome at the age of ninety-one, his surviving children were scattered over three continents—Europe, and North and South America. Although soon forgotten, he had been a major mariner of his age. Adventurer, visionary, gentleman, able commander, defender of the two flags he had served, Page deserves credit as one of Virginia's greatest explorers.

☆ ☆ ☆

Additional note: But what of the strangely shaped, curiously named ship he once commanded, the *Water Witch*? What was her ultimate fate?

Unfortunately, hers was an epilogue troubled enough to give men of the sea a permanent case of the jitters. First, prowling off Cuba for slavers, she was cursed with an outbreak of yellow fever and then quickly was retired from service. Next, with the eruption of the Civil War, she was recommissioned as a Union warship and dispatched to Southern waters.

There, she served adequately enough, taking part in the battle of Head of the Passes at the mouth of the Mississippi and in the capture of Biloxi on the Gulf Coast. But then she became a prize for both rival navies. Standing off Georgia one dark, stormy night in 1864, the *Water Witch* was seized by a Confederate boarding party that approached in seven small boats and subdued her crew in bloody hand-to-hand fighting. And now, it was the Union's turn to scheme for her recapture and the Confederacy's worry to hold her—a concern so strong, she never put out to sea again. She was moved close to Savannah, Georgia, for that city's defense—but not before the capture of a Union raiding party bent on destroying her.

Finally, though, late in 1864, Sherman carried his march to Savannah's doorstep. Rather than give up the *Water Witch* to the enemy, her Confederate masters put the torch to their powder-laden prize. And when the *Water Witch* vanished beneath the roiling waters, her once-famous, vexingly romantic name all but vanished with her.

1854
"You Cannot Exclude Me from Heaven"

When escaped slave Anthony Burns was about to be returned to Virginia from Boston, immense crowds, composed of perhaps fifty thousand persons, lined the streets to watch him walk, in shackles, to a waiting federal ship in the harbor. That was on June 2, 1854. He had been convicted under terms of the new federal Fugitive Slave Act, passed by Congress as an adjunct to the Compromise of 1850. But that wouldn't be the end of his story.

Less than a year later, Anthony Burns was back in Boston. He now was a free man after all, thanks to a black church congregation that raised $1,300 to purchase his freedom.

And so, all was well for the former Virginia slave?

Not quite. Not when his own Baptist church at Union in Fauquier County now excommunicated him for fleeing slavery in the first place.

It's not that long a story.

Anthony Burns, owned by Charles Suttle of Alexandria, already enjoyed a measure of freedom even as a slave. He not only was permitted to hire himself out for work, and then pay the master a fee for the privilege, he also was in charge of four other Charles Suttle slaves doing outside work for hire. A committed Christian since early age, he was a preacher who believed Jesus Christ "came to make us free." Unlike many slaves, he had learned to read and write.

As evidence of the loose bonds allowing him considerable freedom of movement, he was able to escape slavery by slipping aboard a Boston-bound ship in Richmond one day in 1854. When he then attempted to smuggle a letter to a brother still held in slavery by Suttle, their master learned where Anthony was. Suttle quickly made his own way to Boston, found his slave Anthony, and initiated the legal process to claim him as a fugitive covered by the new federal law. Until 1850, many northern states refused to return escaped slaves, but federal law now took precedence.

Still, Suttle's recovery of his slave would not be accomplished without outside interference, notes the website for the Public Broadcast System (PBS) television series *Africans in America* (http://www .pbs.org/wgbh/aia/part4/4p2915.html). As Burns was being held in the federal courthouse at Boston, white and black abolitionists bent on freeing him were meeting in separate quarters. The blacks quartered in the Tremont Temple decided on a march to the courthouse to free Burns—forcibly if so required. Hearing this, the whites at Fanueil Hall also spilled out of their meeting place and marched for the courthouse. Soon, there were two thousand or so protesters gathered in front of the federal building. A group led by the white minister Thomas Wentworth Higginson then battered through an opening with a wooden beam, but was turned back by the guards inside. At some point in the melee, a deputy was fatally stabbed, but Burns still remained a prisoner.

President Franklin Pierce, himself a New Englander, now stepped into the picture by ordering U.S. Marines to help guard the fugitive slave. Then came Burns's conviction under the Fugitive Slave Act and the walk down State Street in shackles, with thousands watching (and two thousand troops guarding), to an awaiting federal ship in Boston Harbor for the journey back to Virginia, followed by only a brief period of further servitude and then his free status, purchased for the $1,300.

All of which leaves the rest of the story.

Hardly had the newly freed Anthony Burns resettled in Boston than he wrote to his old Church of Jesus Christ at Union, Fauquier County, for "a letter of dismission in fellowship and of recommendation to another church." By way of reply, months later, he was sent a copy of a notice in the Front Royal *Gazette* saying, in part:

> Whereas, it has been satisfactorily established before us, that the said Anthony Burns absconded from the service of his master, and refused to return voluntarily—thereby disobeying both the laws of God and man, although he subsequently obtained his freedom by purchase, we have now to consider him only as a fugitive from labor

(as he was before his arrest and restoration to his master), have therefore Resolved, Unanimously, that he be excommunicated from this communion and fellowship of this church.

Done by order of the church, in regular church meeting, this twentieth day of October, 1855.

Burns replied passionately and eloquently: "Look at my case: I was stolen and made a slave as soon as I was born. No man had any right to steal me."

Not only that, his former master was a "manstealer" who "committed an outrage on the law of God; therefore his manstealing gave him no right in me, and laid me under no obligation to be his slave."

Leaving his so-called master and refusing to return, Burns also said, was no disobedience of "either the law of God, or any real law of men."

And further: "You charge me that in escaping, I disobeyed God's law. No, indeed! That law which God wrote on the tablet of my heart, inspiring my love of freedom, and impelling me to seek it at every hazard, I obeyed, and by the good hand of my God upon me, I walked out of the house of bondage."

His words reminiscent of the rhetoric often heard from leaders of the black civil rights struggle of the twentieth century, Burns also declared: "You charge me with disobeying the laws of men. I utterly deny that those things which outrage all right as laws. To be real laws, they must be founded in equity."

And a summary point: "You have thrust me out of your church fellowship. So be it. You can do no more. You cannot exclude me from heaven; you cannot hinder my daily fellowship with God."

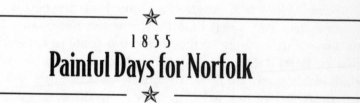

1855
Painful Days for Norfolk

They grew up and went about their lives thinking they were safe from the scourge that had haunted their fathers a generation before. After all, it hadn't struck now for three decades, not since 1826, and here it was the modern, advanced year of 1855, the port city now much cleaner and its streets much better drained than once was the case.

Of course, they did know the dread history of the scourge in their town. They certainly had heard of the outbreaks and the multiple deaths of 1795, 1802, 1821, and 1826. Still, how could anything like that happen again in the year 1855? Their city these days was clean, modern, sanitary.

And so, on June 7, few had any idea of the dire consequences to come with the arrival of the steamer *Ben Franklin,* up from St. Thomas in the Caribbean, even if it had "yellow jack" (as it often was called) aboard . . . with two crewmen already dead.

Ironically, born just four years before and not forty miles away was a child who might have gone far toward saving them, had he only been born and grown into manhood a decade or two sooner.

For now, though, as in the horrific epidemics of the past, the good citizens of Norfolk would have to cope largely on their own . . . with little idea of how to fight the scourge that raged among them like wildfire in a drought-stricken forest. No one realized the real enemy was the mosquito as it flew about the waterfront, buzzed and whined through poor neighborhoods, up and down the commercial streets, into the middle-class residences and even wafting into the "high-rent" sections of the city.

Since she needed repairs, the steamer had been allowed to seek the aid of Page and Allen's shipyard at Gosport on June 19. Just days later the first case ashore turned up . . . said to be a young shipyard mechanic from Richmond. He died on July 8. Several persons in neighboring Portsmouth also were ill. No doubt about it, now. Yellow fever was back in town.

Next, "yellow jack" was tearing through a string of still-unsanitary, overcrowded, run-down buildings near the navy yard. They were quickly evacuated, some of their occupants going to another tenement district, Barry's Row, across the Elizabeth River in Norfolk proper, south of Main. But on July 30, yellow fever struck here also. Again the occupants, sick or not, were evacuated, with the ill sent to a hastily set up treatment facility at Oak Grove.

As some of the Barry's Row occupants then slipped back into their homes, despite the edicts of the Board of Health, the real explosion was only days away. But first an arsonist set the Barry's Row buildings on fire, with a reported eight thousand persons then gathering to watch as they burned down to hot rubble. At this point, though, no great matter . . . it was too late. Yellow fever now seized Norfolk in such a deadly grip that the only remedy was to flee the city . . . and thousands did.

As they jammed aboard trains and steamers bound for safer destinations, however, many of those destinations banged shut their doors for fear that yellow fever was spread by people rather than mosquitoes. That meant the Norfolk refugees couldn't go to New York, nearby Suffolk, to their state capital of Richmond, neighboring Hampton, Washington, or Baltimore. "Fortunately," wrote historian Thomas Jefferson Wertenbaker in his 1931 book *Norfolk: Historic Southern Port,* "Matthews County and the Eastern Shore threw open their doors." Others did the same after seeing Governor-elect Henry A. Wise provide a brave example for his statewide constituency by opening his own home to some of the Norfolk fugitives. He also "equipped his out-houses so as to accommodate as many of the poor as possible."

By August 11, Wertenbaker reported, probably half of Norfolk's population of six thousand had left the city . . . vanished. And now the heroes of the city's worst epidemic ever would make their appearance. Some, like the Reverend George D. Armstrong, would be local people; others, like Annie M. Andrews, a nurse from Syracuse, New York, would come from afar. Much like the rescuers—police, firemen, and others—who rushed into the World Trade Center's two towers on September 11, 2001, these self-sacrificing heroes—primarily doctors, nurses, and pharmacists—rushed from other cities into Norfolk's maelstrom of disease. Here to fight an unseen, totally misunderstood enemy, they came from the cousinly city of Richmond, yes, but also from New York, Savannah, Charleston, Mobile, and New Orleans, herself a frequent victim of yellow fever epidemics. Nurse Andrews was only the first of the medical personnel to come help . . . at high risk to themselves, so high risk that Philadelphia alone lost thirteen would-be rescuers to Norfolk's deadly malady.

"Before the end of August," wrote Wertenbaker, "the city had become a great hospital." Still worse, "the deaths . . . mounted to seventy, eighty, or even a hundred a day." And no one, white or black, high in station or low, was exempt. Before summer's end, the sitting mayor and a former mayor of Norfolk were dead. So were leading bankers and businessmen, plus a member of the Virginia House of Delegates from Norfolk. While any one death, of course, was a loss to family and community, the number of doctors and clergymen who fell victim to the old scourge while tending to the sick was a shock. Reported historian Wertenbaker: "The mortality among physicians was very severe, including ten local doctors and twenty-six out of forty-five who came from other places. Of the eight ministers who were in town during the epidemic, all became ill and four died."

In other words, 50 percent or more in the last two groups died as martyrs to the cause of healing body and soul.

One unflinching hero of Norfolk's ordeal was Connecticut-born George Dodd Armstrong, a Presbyterian pastor in his forties who himself suffered a bout of the fever but who repeatedly visited the sick both before and after his own episode. "Dr. Armstrong gives a heart-rending account of the scenes he encountered in his pastoral rounds," noted Wertenbaker. "In one house, from which a widowed mother and two of her children had just been buried, three other children were ill; in another were two families, all stricken with the fever; at the home of Mr. S., the eldest daughter had had the 'black vomit,' and was upon the point of death; at a nearby home a captain of the marines, his wife, her sister, and one child were dead."

Putting off church services for the duration, the Reverend Armstrong was a familiar sight at the city's cemeteries, where scores of burials went on every day. "We have burials, but no funerals now," he wrote at one point. Accompanying one family to a cemetery, he also said, they arrived at the family's burial plot but found "no grave dug there as yet." The hearse and the family carriages couldn't wait—"all we can do is to deposit the coffin where the grave is to be dug, and, offering a short prayer, there leave it."

Another time, Dr. Armstrong was told forty-three graves had been ordered dug for one day at the same cemetery. "Passing on to the potter's field," added the Wertenbaker account, "he saw large numbers of coffins and rough boxes, 'piled up like cord wood' as high as a man could reach, while close by laborers were at work on a pit in which to bury them."

Still another time, "the supply of coffins gave out, and the bodies had to be interred in boxes, in one instance four to a box," wrote Wertenbaker. "Others were tied up in the blankets in which they died, and carried out to the potter's field, in furniture-wagons, carts, or drays, there to be buried layer upon layer in pits."

For weeks, no end to Norfolk's suffering was in sight. The city was "a living tomb," wrote W. H. T. Squires in a section of the tricentennial city history *Through the Years in Norfolk* of 1936. "The streets were silent and deserted," he also noted. "None save an occasional physician or clergyman passed. All stores and residences were closed."

The port city's waterways were just as "lonely" and undisturbed. "Not a vessel approached these once-crowded shores, save a small boat which ran once daily from Old Point, bringing the mail, medicines, sometimes a physician or nurse, and often with her decks piled high with coffins."

Added the Wertenbaker account: "All through September and until late October the fever raged. In Bermuda Street every house had its sick or dead, while the district north of Black Creek, where dwelt the wealthy and aristocratic, was swept from one end to the other."

When the first frost finally came, killing the as yet unknown carrier of the disease, "Norfolk lay suffering, stunned, still unable to grasp the full meaning of the fearful calamity."

No one knew why the epidemic began when it did, and now, why it came to a dead stop so suddenly. Filthy, unsanitary conditions wouldn't explain the pattern. Neither would person-to-person contagion, except through the mosquito as the vector . . . a theory as yet unexplored, unarticulated.

Once the immediate crisis was over, though, none other than the brave Reverend Armstrong "made some exceedingly interesting observations," noted the Wertenbaker history of Norfolk.

In a book of his own, *History of Yellow Fever in Norfolk,* Dr. Armstrong "dared to express the opinion that the disease was not contagious," added Wertenbaker. And that certainly was the message seen in the Presbyterian minister's passage saying: "I was for more than six weeks almost constantly during the day among the sick, the dying, and the dead . . . yet I did not take the fever until as an epidemic it reached the part of the city in which I lived." Not only that, but "those who resided in the adjoining country, and came into the city during the day only, in no instance that I have heard of took the fever."

Even closer to solving the mystery of the dread disease was his added observation that it had spread "rapidly" in the "direction of the prevailing winds, and but slowly in a direction across the track of those winds."

How close he was to guessing that an insect being wafted here and there by the wind could have been the culprit! As Wertenbaker added in his own history: "Had Dr. Armstrong drawn the proper conclusions from these remarkable observations, had it occurred to him that they pointed directly to the mosquito as the agent of transmission, he might have put the medical fraternity upon the right track a half century before the days of Reed."

By "Reed," Wertenbaker of course meant Dr. Walter Reed, born in nearby Gloucester County just four years before the latest outbreak of yellow fever in Norfolk . . . the same Walter Reed who headed the medical commission that finally solved the yellow fever mystery and virtually eliminated the disease by proving that the mosquito was the carrier.

☆ ☆ ☆

Additional note: Norfolk lost at least two thousand of her six thousand people in the yellow fever epidemic of 1855 . . . and now, with the Civil War about to descend, more grief lay just ahead.

The "normal" effects of a horrendous and fratricidal war would have been difficult enough for the old port city, but few could have expected the punishing dictums of the Union generals who ruled Norfolk with iron fists after the city's Confederate occupiers were driven out in 1862.

The first of them, Egbert Ludovicus Viele, took over a prominent doctor's home for himself and his family and made no move to interfere in the public hanging of a second well-known doctor—a hero of the epidemic at that—who rashly shot and killed a white Union officer marching black soldiers on the street (apparently an inexcusable but spontaneous murder of passion rather than premeditation). Next came Benjamin Butler, already nicknamed "the Beast" for his harsh treatment of occupied New Orleans. His regime put one clergyman to work sweeping streets for a brief period, while Butler in person ordered hard labor at Fort Hatteras for the Reverend Armstrong, recent hero of the yellow fever epidemic, when the "Yankee"-born minister wouldn't "approve of" hanging Confederate President Jefferson Davis.

Then, too, there was the benevolent Howard Association, formed to provide financial support for the orphans whose parents died in the epidemic of 1855. Under Butler, the association funds were seized, even though ten to fifteen orphans still could have benefited from their proper distribution.

1 8 5 6
A Christmas Day Celebration

Climb the mountain slope, part the bushes, follow the old railroad bed to the portals of chiseled stone and . . . hush. Beyond those black, black gates, you're gazing into the heart of a mountain.

Except for the *ping* of dripping water, silence is king here and darkness his queen. Timelessness is their princeling child, a formless creature that takes you by the hand and steps back . . .

And back.

Suddenly, with those hand-hewn walls pressing close, it becomes easy to hear the scrabble of loosened rock. To hear muffled voices, the *thwunk* of the pickax, the scrape of manual drills grinding into hard rock. And to see flickering shadows in the lamplight.

We are in the 1850s. Those bent forms in the half-light are men. Their job, before Nobel invented dynamite, before the introduction of compressed-air drills, is to build a tunnel through Virginia's Blue Ridge mountain range . . . through Afton Mountain, west of Charlottesville.

They are formed into two work parties, and they begin their digging on opposite sides of the mountain, nearly a mile apart, one crew almost seventy feet below the other and both work parties more or less seven hundred feet below the mountain crown.

If they meet in the center as planned, they will have constructed the longest railroad tunnel in the nation. And one of the last built largely by hand. If . . .

But first, they must meet in the center. They must persist despite political and editorial backbiting. They must survive cholera. They must overcome labor disputes and clashes among the predominantly Irish work gangs. They must stumble on despite financial crises, material shortages, and the logistical difficulties of supplying scattered work parties at isolated fourteen-hundred-foot elevations.

And they must survive Afton Mountain's own resistance and treacheries.

If they can keep at it for eight years, and in the process also build three shorter tunnels, a triple-span bridge, and seventeen miles of mountain track, then . . . then, they will have completed an engineering marvel. Then they would link coastal and central Virginia, the Mid-Atlantic region, really, with the lands to the west, not only with the Shenandoah Valley, but also with the Ohio Valley and points beyond.

They had no way of knowing, but their handmade tunnel would do all that and more. It would serve east-west rail traffic for nearly ninety years, into the twentieth century. It one day would be recognized by the American Society of Civil Engineers as a "National Historic Civil Engineering Landmark." And thus, in the 1970s, the long tunnel behind brooding stone portals on the side of a Virginia mountain would join company with the likes of the Brooklyn Bridge, the Erie Canal, and the Mormon Tabernacle as truly remarkable U.S. engineering landmarks.

Claudius Crozet, a French engineer who served with Napoleon in Russia and again in the campaign ending at Waterloo, is the man credited with achieving the impossible in the Blue Ridge Mountains. The tunnel was his conception, his design, his engineering, his responsibility to complete.

As early as 1839, when he was principal engineer at the Virginia Board of Public Works, he saw the feasibility of tunneling the Blue Ridge. But state legislators enamored of a vast canal system had their way. Railroads, then in their infancy even in far-off Europe, were not yet recognized for their potential. So Crozet went his way for a time—to Louisiana as its chief state engineer, then back to Virginia as the first president of the board of visitors at Virginia Military Institute (VMI), and finally to Richmond as head of a new academy there.

By 1849, with Virginia's projected canal system no longer appearing so viable (and other eastern states reaching out to the West with fingers of railroad track), the message finally dawned: Virginia must breach her mountain barriers with the iron horse as well.

The Louisa Railroad just then was approaching the eastern foot of the Blue Ridge. For the next step, a thirty-mile linkup with Staunton west of the mountain wall, the public works agency turned again to Crozet—tall, stocky, at times abrasive toward his critics, even arrogant in manner, but a master at his trade.

The state created the Blue Ridge Railroad for the job of crossing the mountains and appointed Crozet, then sixty, its chief engineer.

His scheme for the crossing at Rockfish Gap was a combination of track mounting steep inclines, switchbacks, cuts into the mountainside, and four tunnels. But the greatest challenge would be the Blue

Ridge Tunnel, designed to extend more than 4,260 feet through the heart of Afton Mountain.

The crew that assembled in 1850 on the western slopes of the mountain at first had an easy time of it, driving into the mountainside at a rapid rate. On the eastern slope, however, the Irish laborers banged into hard rock from the outset, rock so hard it dulled their drill heads.

As a year drifted by, engineer Crozet reported "more than usual difficulties," with "the rock, particularly on the east side, being excessively hard." In that year the tunnel progressed by 755 feet—295 from the eastern slopes and 460 from the western sides.

The Irish workmen living in shanties on the mountainside did have black powder for blasting, even if they hadn't yet heard of dynamite, nitroglycerine, or pneumatic drills.

But Crozet's original, three-year estimate for completion of the tunnel proved overly optimistic. The workers at the western end found themselves in a loosening mix of rock and earth that often gave way over their heads. In addition, their tunnel was under way without benefit of vertical shafts from above that would permit work gangs to drop down into the center of the tunnel's path and dig toward either end.

With such vertical shafts considered technically unfeasible, Crozet had to ventilate his underground works by unique means—a system of suction devices and pipes expelling the fouled air.

Meanwhile, his workers were encountering water that poured into their faces or sent rocks tumbling down as they struck one vein after another. In another unusual engineering feat, Crozet not only sealed off the internal mountain springs as his men advanced but found a means of draining the tunnel works. He emplaced a two-thousand-foot siphon system discharging sixty gallons of water a minute, believed to be the largest such siphon put into operation until that time.

For all his clever strategies, and despite a tight schedule that had the tunnel crews toiling around the clock in three eight-hour shifts a day, the Blue Ridge Tunnel after three full years was far from complete.

Which is not to say the work pace always was so consistent. There were times when construction hazards drove the men back, with many then afraid to resume work. In the summers, many decamped for better jobs to the north.

In 1853, the men at Blue Ridge, who were getting 75 cents a day, learned that tunnel workers in Cincinnati were receiving $1.50 a day. Demanding the same pay, they struck. Work on the tunnel stopped.

When contractor John Kelly answered with $1.25 a day as top scale, many of his men left for Cincinnati.

Those Irish immigrants left behind in time did return to work on his terms . . . but now they were joined by black slaves hired out by their masters, with the caveat that the slaves were too valuable to work in blasting areas. Let the Irish handle the black powder.

In 1854 came another setback—and personal tragedy. Cholera struck in the shanties on Afton's steep eastern slope. As the dread disease spread, 25 of the 150 tunnel workers and their family members died. Eight more died in the shantytown by the tunnel's western portal before the immigrant workers packed up and fled.

Despite such setbacks, the long burrow through the heart of a mountain inched forward in the succeeding months, but often at the rate of less than two feet a day. Somehow, too, the remaining three tunnels also did progress.

But one, the 869-foot Brooksville tunnel, nearly defeated Crozet and his men.

With two-thirds of the Brooksville shaft complete, its workers stumbled into a hellish mix of soapstone and "stiff clay," a composite that crumbled on contact with the air. Then, too, massive mountain slides buried the tunnel's western opening.

Shoring their chamber with timbers then installing brick arches behind them, Brooksville's workers pressed forward—often only at the strong urgings of their overseers. "We can hear rocks falling from an unknown height upon the timbers under which the men are at work, with a rumbling noise resembling that of distant thunder," Crozet complained in one of his reports to the Public Works Board.

In the meantime, the iron bridge and other rail work here had gone forward. In fact, a temporary over-the-mountain spur ran up and then down the opposite mountainsides, but the steep grades were a threat to normal rail operations and would remain a hazard until the four tunnels could be put into use.

Then, in 1855, a new menace: With the economy faltering in prelude to the nationwide Panic of 1857, Virginia's bonds financing the Blue Ridge project fell below par in price. The public works agency no longer could meet its payments. Contractor Kelly and his partner, John Larquey, dug into their own pockets to keep the project going. Thus, by the end of that year, thirteen miles of the seventeen-mile system were complete, as were two tunnels, 538 feet and 100 feet in length.

But Crozet was under attack in the press and by politicians across the state for all the delays . . . and never mind that there was good reason, that there were all kinds of tough engineering and construction problems to overcome

E. J. Armstrong, president of the Public Works Board, provided a glimpse of the problems slowing the work: "Water in streams and showers, extreme difficulty of proper ventilation, treacherous earth, hard flinty rock, fearful slides, and the sudden falling of immense boulders are some of the principal annoyances and perils that have arisen."

By now, the western work gang in the Blue Ridge Tunnel had progressed 1,809 feet, while its counterpart laboring in the eastern section had burrowed 1,718 feet into Afton Mountain. This left "only 746 feet to be perforated," Crozet reported.

As the year 1856 unfolded and the two tunnel segments were drawing closer together, the new question became: Would they really meet in the center of the mountain?

Many of the editorialists and their fellow critics guessed no. Bets were placed as the work now advanced at the rate of seventy feet per month.

Finally, by November 1856, Crozet was able to report the treacherous Brooksville tunnel complete. The first railcars had passed through it. Better yet, with a million bricks devoted to its supporting arches inside, Brooksville had been completed "without injury to anyone."

As for the long tunnel and its two work gangs, hearken to Christmas Day 1856. This was the day, after six years of blind struggle, that the opposing work gangs "holed through." Daylight pierced the Blue Ridge as the two tunnel segments met squarely.

A triumph? Absolutely, but still a newspaper in nearby Charlottesville sourly remarked, "and all hands got drunk."

Why so sourly? Perhaps because another two years must be spent finishing up the Blue Ridge shaft by widening here, shoring up potential weak spots there.

Crozet's enemies were furious at this news. They were even more enraged to hear in 1858 of the specially fitted car frame he squeezed into his elliptical-shaped tunnel. Woefully, it would appear, the car frame failed to clear some tunnel sections. Sputtered the *Lexington Gazette:* "Almost any other man, after an eight-year tug, would have been stupid enough to make the hole big enough for the purpose for which it was designed."

Lost to sight was Crozet's patient explanation that the car frame performed its intended function as planned. It located exactly those knobby projections along the tunnel walls that Crozet needed to identify and then trim off.

The sniping continued even against his Irish laborers, who'd had the temerity to vote in the local elections of 1857. Rejoicing that their work soon would be done (and they gone), the *Staunton Spectator* complained that the workers were "ignorant" and unacquainted with the American form of government, yet they "come out of the bowels of the earth and overwhelm the intelligent, native-born citizens of Augusta [County]."

Still, it wouldn't be long before the critics finally were silenced. The last train to negotiate Rockfish Gap by means of the temporary overland spur struggled up those steep grades in April 1858. The very next day, in an easy, six-minute run, the first train passed through the new Blue Ridge Tunnel, the first of thousands to do so. Crozet's fantastic tunnel, 4,262 feet in length, climbing a grade of nearly 70 feet, built for $488,000, or an average cost of $114.50 per foot, was an engineering legacy destined to remain in service for 84 years, almost a full century.

Built just before the Civil War and in service until World War II, it wouldn't be replaced by a new Blue Ridge Tunnel until 1944.

"No train was ever stuck in the [old] tunnel, and our records show only one train delayed 18 minutes by a small brick fall," reported a spokesman for the Chesapeake and Ohio (C&O) Railway, owner of the tunnel and its east-west trackage, in the 1970s. "You could say that probably everything hauled by a railroad passed through it, including in bygone years C&O's fine fleet of east-west passenger trains."

★

1858
Job for a Thousand Men and Boys

★

George Washington still lived when his native Virginia honored him with the outstanding pedestrian statue in the state capitol by the great Jean Antoine Houdon, but Virginia's next attempt to honor him with statuary would come after his death . . . in somewhat fragile hopes that he would be buried beneath the statuary itself.

Unfortunately for many concerned, including sculptor Thomas Crawford, not all the hopes and plans for this statuary would work out exactly as intended in 1816, the year the General Assembly authorized the erection in Capitol Square of a huge equestrian tableau of Washington on a noble steed, accompanied by six or seven standing figures. It wouldn't be until 1858 that a reported one thousand men and boys, all volunteers, helped drag the massive centerpiece—weighing eighteen tons—up the hill from a dock at the bottom of Seventeenth Street. The dedication of the statue of Washington on his horse then came on the great man's birth date, February 22, a day of ceremony and celebration despite the nasty February weather that prevailed. "Cannons were fired at dawn, each shot honoring one of the 13 original states," wrote Robert Merritt in the *Richmond Times-Dispatch* of August 31, 1986. "Then came a two-hour parade as military units and proud citizens tramped through the mud, acknowledging the women who applauded and waved from the balconies and windows along Main Street."

As Merritt reported also, the Washington statue was only the second equestrian project undertaken in this country, the first being a rendition of Andrew Jackson by Clark Mills for display in Lafayette Park in Washington, D.C., right in front of the White House. Still, the new Virginia statuary came to fruition only after a sometimes troubled history of four decades' duration.

In the first place, after the assembly authorization of 1816, proponents of the monumental statuary gathered only $13,000 toward its cost in the next year, and there the project lingered for another two decades. Finally, the Virginia State Historical Society "prodded the state to raise more money." Next, sculptor Crawford won the commission—and a $500 prize—in a design competition that attracted sixty-four entries. For the job itself, he apparently was paid $53,000.

Like Houdon, New Yorker Crawford, then thirty-five, was no neophyte in the business of public sculpture—he also won the assignment for the twenty-foot bronze "Armed Liberty" atop the U.S. Capitol dome in Washington, as well as fourteen marble statues to be created for the Senate and the main doors to the Senate chamber. So busy was he, in fact, he "kept putting off" his Virginia commission, noted Merritt.

Finally back in his studio in Rome, Italy, Crawford began work on the Richmond project. The sculptor envisioned a central equestrian statue of Washington, along with standing figures of Virginia heroes and a more general, symbolic statue "emblematic of Virginia," added Merritt. "He wisely left the choice of the figures to the state. After much debate, the list comprised Andrew Lewis [hero of the 1774 battle of Point Pleasant], Patrick Henry, George Mason, Thomas Jefferson, Thomas Nelson [Jr., early governor and a signer of the Declaration of Independence], and John Marshall. The Jefferson and Henry statues arrived in 1855, but Washington [astride his horse] took longer."

The fact is, Crawford, now suffering from a brain tumor, was working against time.

Nonetheless, he was able to show off a plaster model of the equestrian Washington in Rome in 1856. It then was shipped northward across the Alps to Munich, where it was cast in bronze melted down from cannons used in the Crimean War, "with zinc added to the molten medal for luster."

According to Merritt also, the sculpture already had caused a "sensation." Its creator "was made an honorary member of the royal academies of Munich and St. Petersburg, Russia."

Later, he was accorded "a similar honor from the Academy of St. Mark in Florence, Italy." Perhaps more meaningful, as Merritt also reported, a writer of the day said the foundry workmen were so impressed, they "would not allow the ordinary laborers to touch the cases in which it was packed . . . but did it all themselves." Not only that, "the roads and bridges were, by order of the king, made free for it to pass over."

The assorted parts to the statue next would travel by barge on the Rhine River to Amsterdam, the Netherlands, and from there by ship to Richmond, where they safely arrived on November 7, 1857. Unhappily, they arrived with the news that Crawford had died the previous month . . . thus he could not be present when his creation was erected in Virginia's Capitol Square and dedicated the following February.

With four of the planned pedestrian figures still missing, modelers in Crawford's studio in Rome completed the Mason and Marshall figures, while Randolph Rogers, "another New York sculptor living in Rome," was given the job of rendering Lewis, Nelson, and "allegorical figures to be placed in front of the six statues." In the meantime, Governor Henry Wise had eliminated Crawford's planned eagles in favor of the allegorical figures, just in case onlookers mistook the noble eagles for Virginia turkey buzzards.

With George Washington already buried at his beloved Mount Vernon, as he himself had wished, it was clear the new Virginia monument, costing an estimated $260,000—in antebellum dollars—would *not* be his burial place after all. Perhaps that was just as well, since the equestrian Washington had not always enjoyed flattering critical appraisal, the feelings of those foundry workers notwithstanding. Right at the beginning, the massive outdoor sculpture drew the ridicule of no less a figure than early American storyteller (and, it so happens, Washington biographer) Washington Irving, who called the monument "foolish and illogical," because it showed Washington "mounted on a very unsteady steed, on a very narrow space, aloft in the air."

On the other hand, artistically good or bad, it may have been inspiration for a teenage Moses Ezekiel, who grew up to become Richmond's most significant sculptor ever. Only fourteen at the time, young Ezekiel apparently was among those attending the dedication of Washington on horseback in 1858. Perhaps he even helped the thousand men and boys pull the massive bronze figure up the long, steep slopes from dockside to the honored place next to Jefferson's classical capitol building.

☆ ☆ ☆

Additional note: Statues, statues, and more statues . . . some on foot, some on horses, but all in Richmond and many with colorful, even tragic, tales behind them.

As a case in point, sculptor John Henry Foley, creator of the equestrian Stonewall Jackson statue in Capitol Square, died before it was unveiled on October 26, 1875. Then, too, after sculptor Joel Hart, a former stonecutter from Kentucky, finished three years of work on his model for a marble statue of the Virginia-born congressional luminary Henry Clay of Kentucky, a ship carrying the model to Italy sank at sea. Starting over to fulfill his $5,000 contract with a duplicate, the unlucky Hart came down with cholera and then typhoid fever.

Conceived as the pet project of the "Whig Ladies of Virginia," supporters of Clay's ill-fated presidential bid of 1844, the Clay statue finally was ready by 1860, but even then it still faced troubled waters. "There was an angry unveiling April 12, 1860," wrote Robert Merritt in his *Times-Dispatch* piece. "Some women had insisted the statue be placed in front of the Capitol or even in the rotunda as a companion to Houdon's [George] Washington, but Gov. John Letcher, a Democrat, refused. He chose a spot near the southwest corner of the grounds, and there the ladies had the marble sheltered in a quaint iron pavilion designed by local architect Henry Exall and made at the Richmond foundry of Andrew J. Bowers."

Seventy-two years later, Merritt also noted, the fifteen-ton roof of the statue's iron shelter "threatened to collapse." Moved indoors to the old House of Delegates chamber in the state capitol, the Clay figure safely remained "in a vacant niche" for another four decades. In 1953, however, it was replaced by a gifted bust of Confederate Vice President Alexander Stephens. "Clay was pushed into a corner, where he has remained ever since."

Meanwhile, Foley's Stonewall Jackson figure had not escaped controversy, delay, and associated problems either. At the behest of a group of English admirers who wished to commemorate Jackson's death at Chancellorsville in 1863 by making a gift of a Jackson monument, the well-known Foley completed a model, "but with the fall of the Confederacy [in 1865] the project was forgotten until 1872, when Gen. Bradley T. Johnson visited England and saw the model."

Both encouraged and discouraged at what he found, the former Confederate general, a veteran of Jackson's Shenandoah Valley campaign, reported the model "was horrible, not at all like Jackson and historically incorrect in all details," but still could be salvaged. "He had photos and a uniform sent to England so that Foley could redo the work, which was completed just before the sculptor's death in 1874."

The post–Civil War legislature of Virginia then authorized a $10,000 sum to see the statue emplaced and then dedicated on October 26, 1875, "with a procession rivaling that accompanying the Washington [equestrian] statue [in 1858]."

Not ever to be forgotten by his native state, Robert E. Lee also— *eventually,* that is—would be granted a memorial statue in bronze, but not until 1932. Money had been the long holdup, it seems. "Governor Harry F. Byrd was authorized in 1928 to raise $25,000 for a bronze of Lee to be placed on the spot where Lee stood in the House of Delegates to receive command of Virginia's troops in the Civil War," Merritt explained. "Byrd was able to raise only $7,000. The state added $10,000, and sculptor Rudolph Evans 'contributed' the remaining $8,000 so that he would be able to undertake a 'labor of love.'"

In addition to these and other memorials in the Capitol Square area, Richmond's Monument Avenue is famous for its monumental works honoring Virginia or Virginia-related heroes, among them James Ewell Brown "Jeb" Stuart at Stuart Circle, Jefferson Davis at Davis Avenue, and Matthew Fontaine Maury, "Pathfinder of the Seas," at Belmont Avenue. As another story behind a significant work of statuary in Richmond, it seems that the Maury piece had been "on its way" since 1888, but little progress was being made until a chastising letter to the editor appearing in the *Times-Dispatch* in 1912 fired up a seventy-eight-year-old reader, Mrs. E. E. Moffitt. According to *Times-Dispatch* columnist Mark Holmberg (January 7, 1996), she "organized a Maury monument association and worked tirelessly to help raise money for the statue, which eventually was sculpted by Richmonder F. William Sievers." Unfortunately, by the time the statue was dedicated in 1931, "Mrs. Moffitt was in the hospital, too sick to attend the ceremony."

In more recent years, Richmond overcame controversy to erect a statue on Monument Avenue honoring pioneer black tennis star Arthur Ashe of Richmond, but then plunged into renewed controversy over a national historical group's emplacement of a statue of Abraham Lincoln and son Tad, commemorating their visit to Richmond on the heels of its evacuation by Confederate forces in April 1865. The statue was placed at the site of the old Tredegar Iron Works, a supplier of munitions for the Confederacy.

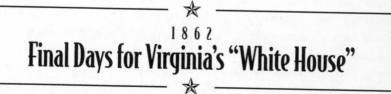

1862
Final Days for Virginia's "White House"

Springtime in Virginia, and at a historic plantation on the Pamunkey River called the White House, an agitated woman half crippled by arthritis stuck a note on the front door telling the oncoming Yankees not to desecrate this old home.

Not asking, but telling.

More precisely, leaving the old family home to the advancing Union forces, Confederate Gen. Robert E. Lee's wife, Mary, addressed her note to "Northern soldiers who profess to reverence Washington." Mincing no words, she went on to say: "Forbear to desecrate the home of his first married life, the property of his wife, now owned by her descendants." And signed it, "A Grand-daughter of Mrs. Washington."

Translated, what she was pointing out in a poignant moment of distress, this spring of 1862, was the fact that George Washington had married the widowed Martha Dandridge Custis right here, at the riverside plantation Martha had inherited from her first husband. Furthermore, the plantation was now owned by a member of the Lee family . . . specifically, by Mary's son William Henry Fitzhugh "Rooney" Lee, left to him by her father, the late George Washington Parke Custis, grandson of Martha Washington.

Mrs. Lee and two of her four unmarried daughters had taken temporary refuge in the old home in the fall of 1861, thus joining Rooney's delicate wife, Charlotte, and a child while the respective menfolk served the Confederate cause as the soldiers they were. All this came after the Lees had to abandon their striking Arlington House plantation overlooking Washington, D.C., from a high hill on the southern flanks of the Potomac River—today, still the high point of Arlington National Cemetery. Once the U.S. Army's Robert E. Lee had declared his true allegiance was to his state of Virginia, the family's Arlington House estate inevitably had been marked for seizure as Federal troops moved into Virginia's northern tier of cities and counties.

Now, a year later, Mary Lee and family were being dislodged by the hounds of war once again. This time it was because of Union Gen. George B. McClellan's Peninsula campaign, which called for a large Union force to move up the Virginia Peninsula lying between the York and James Rivers in an effort to capture the Confederate (and Virginia) capital of Richmond. While McClellan at first moved overland from Fort Monroe at Hampton, he soon would find it convenient to supply his great army from a logistical base closer to Richmond, one best situated on an easily accessible river highway.

The river he initially chose was the York rather than the James, and the landing site for his supplies would be—such bittersweet irony—the Lee family's own White House property on the Pamunkey at the head of the York. Thus, the Yankees were coming, were on their way, with sizable vengeance.

Back in Richmond, meanwhile, Mary's husband, Robert E. Lee, was agitated by her predicament, naturally . . . but what could he do?

He wasn't even a first-rank general. A disappointment to many, he hadn't yet caught fire as a Confederate leader of any great account . . . some people were even calling him "Granny" or "Evacuating" Lee for his seemingly slow and timid performance thus far in the war.

McClellan, though, changed all that . . . that is to say, his troops did, when they badly wounded Joseph Johnston, the Confederate general charged with defending Richmond from the onslaught by McClellan's one hundred thousand troops. With the next in line too ill to take over, fortifications specialist Robert E. Lee was called from his deskwork in Richmond to command the Confederate forces. Then turning unexpectedly aggressive, Lee managed in the series of battles known as the Seven Days' campaign to drive McClellan's superior forces back down the peninsula, thus ending the threat to Richmond for some time. This was history's first view of the *real* Robert E. Lee, who of course was destined to become the leading icon of the entire Confederacy.

Before all those events took place, however, there was that unhappy day when Lee's wife, Mary, and their two daughters had to flee Rooney Lee's White House plantation, which was seized by the Federals— White House Landing then became the huge Civil War depot that Virginia historian Clifford Dowdey once called a "small city of supply."

But now, what of Mrs. Robert E. Lee? Where had she gone next? "Moving not far away to a house called Criss Cross," wrote Mary P. Coulling in her book *The Lee Girls,* "she and the girls watched enemy troops come into the area on May 18 [1862]." At Criss Cross, then, the Federals came across Mrs. Lee, one of them later writing, "Upon our arrival, our reception was not very gracious." The same Yankee officer also conceded, however, "The visit was finally terminated with much more of courtesy on her part than our reception promised."

Next, another move—still behind enemy lines—took the Lee women to another home, but here they were placed under house arrest, noted author Coulling. Then, with McClellan's permission, Mrs. Lee and her two daughters were allowed to pass through the lines on June 10 on their way to besieged Richmond by horse-drawn carriage.

Over the next few weeks, they occasionally saw General Lee "when he made short trips to town from the battlefield."

For the moment, Richmond was saved, but as time and events dictated, not the Confederate cause. And, sadly, not the Custis-Lee White House, "which had been burned to the ground, fired against McClellan's orders by Union troops." As a result, "only two blackened chimneys remained of the frame structure where Martha Custis had married George Washington and where Rooney and Charlotte had begun housekeeping."

Adding insult to injury, the same White House site a year or so later (1863) would be the staging base for a Union raiding party that came upriver, disembarked, and traveled overland to Charlotte's family home, Hickory Hill, in Hanover County. There, in front of Charlotte and, as it happened, her visiting mother-in-law, the interlopers snatched up a badly wounded Rooney Lee, mattress and all, as a prisoner-hostage, returning to the river by way of his own White House property.

"Rooney's exasperation at being captured and forced to leave his weeping wife and invalid mother must have been compounded by seeing the charred remains of his home as he passed the ruined White House on his way to the wharf [the dock used by his captors]," surmised Coulling. (Rooney Lee would recover from his wounds and be released the following year, but his perennially frail wife, Charlotte, and the couple's only two children all had died by then of natural causes.)

With the devastating war over in 1865, Rooney returned to the White House property in New Kent County to begin farming it again. He built anew and hosted a visit by his father, mother, and sister Agnes in the spring or early summer of 1866. In the 1870s, however, he and a second wife moved to the recently inherited Ravensworth estate in northern Virginia, just ten miles west of once-proud Arlington House, by now permanently lost to the Lee family and already a burial ground.

First a popular member of the state senate, William Henry Fitzhugh "Rooney" Lee was elected to the U.S. House of Representatives from the Eighth Congressional District. Not long after, he became ill—only fifty-four years of age, and died at Ravensworth in October 1891.

★

1862

So, Who Captured Norfolk?

★

For the record, the Union recapture of Norfolk in the spring of 1862 can be credited to:

- the elderly general nominally in charge?
- Abraham Lincoln's choice of the invasion beach and his personal stroll on its beckoning sands the night before?
- Treasury Secretary Salmon P. Chase's take-charge attitude?
- an onlooking, low-ranking general who wound up leading the troops at Chase's behest?

The fact is, all four persons contributed, albeit some less than others. And Abraham Lincoln really was on the invasion beach ahead of the troops who recaptured Norfolk for the Union.

For the record, then, the general in overall charge of the projected invasion and seizure of Norfolk that May 1862 was the elderly Gen. John E. Wool, late of the War of 1812 and the Mexican War . . . and by now seventy-seven if he was a day. According to onlooker Gen. Egbert Ludovicus Viele, a mere brigadier, Wool "begged" for command of the invasion force. Oddly enough, it was no War Department that he besought, but Treasury Secretary Chase, who just the evening before had reconnoitered the invasion beach with *his* boss, Abe Lincoln. And Lincoln, carried across the waters of Hampton Roads from Fortress (Fort) Monroe together with Chase and Secretary of War Edwin Stanton aboard the Treasury Department cutter *Miami*, had boarded an accompanying tugboat with Stanton for a closer look at a possible landing spot that Lincoln himself had found on military maps of the area. When the tug nosed right up to the supposedly forbidden shoreline, wrote Harvard historian David Herbert Donald in his biography *Lincoln*, "the President insisted on climbing out on what Virginians called their 'sacred soil' and, in bright moonlight, strolled up and down on the beach." This was at the Ocean View frontage on the Chesapeake Bay just north of Norfolk proper that later became a major beach resort and then a part of a greatly expanded Norfolk itself.

Chase, perhaps unwittingly, had instigated the adventure by deciding to scout the shoreline after "General Wool's command advised that it was impossible to land troops anywhere near Norfolk because shoals would prevent boats from getting closer than a mile to the shore," added Donald's account. Thus, the civilian trio visiting from Washington had completely upstaged the army professionals. And Wool at one nervous point had been in danger of a humiliating dismissal by Chase. "At the last moment," wrote Viele later, "General Wool with much emotion begged the secretary to allow him to command the troops. The Secretary had decided to relieve him of the command of the expedition on account of his advanced age, but finally reversed his decision with the remark that he could not inflict sorrow upon gray hairs."

Lightly opposed as it was, the invasion did not unwind smoothly that early morning of May 10, 1862, despite the reconnoitering of the night before by three of the most exalted officials in the entire Union. For one thing, wrote Thomas J. Wertenbaker in his Norfolk history *Norfolk: Historic Southern Port,* upon reaching Tanner's Creek near the Ocean View landing site, the invading Yankees "found the bridge in flames, and so were forced to make a detour around the head of the creek to the Princess Anne Road."

Still, there was no organized opposition, and the Union troops continued to advance until about four in the afternoon. At that point they had reached a line of Confederate earthworks, but those were deserted, empty of Rebel soldiers, and the guns were spiked. The Union marchers continued unimpeded "until they were within sight of the spires of Norfolk peering through the trees."

Lincoln and Stanton, meanwhile, had remained behind at Fort Monroe, since the major reason for their visit had *not* been a campaign to recapture Norfolk from those who took it earlier in the Civil War, but rather had been consultation, moral support, and, likely, a bit more goosing for Gen. George B. McClellan. Until now, "Little Mac's" grandiose Peninsula campaign, aimed at the seizure of Richmond, had been developing only with great slowness, so far as Washington could tell. Indeed, Lincoln recently had sent McClellan an additional division to bolster the already enormous Union force gathering in the Tidewater area for the drive upon the Confederate capital at the fall of the James.

When Yorktown fell to McClellan on May 3, however, he actually began his "long-planned advance up the Peninsula," Donald noted. And at this juncture, "Lincoln decided to move closer to the scene of operations." He and his two cabinet secretaries, with Viele as an escort, cruised down the Potomac to Fort Monroe aboard the new revenue cutter *Miami* just in time to learn that "McClellan would not join them because his army had just defeated the Confederates at Williamsburg and was pushing them back toward Richmond."

Good news for the Washington visitors . . . and why not now move on Norfolk as well? According to biographer Donald, "The President and his associates decided that the time had come to liberate Norfolk, on the south side of the James estuary, where the hulking [Confederate ironclad] *Merrimac* was sheltered, still a threat to the Union navy."

As for the afternoon events of May 10, Brigadier General Viele later offered a sometimes biting eyewitness account of the Union advance on Norfolk . . . which, it seems, he wound up leading himself. Or was it Treasury Secretary Chase who recaptured Norfolk?

However to mark it down, poor old General Wool was *not* the hero of the day. By Viele's account, the Union had landed two cavalry regiments and two of artillery, "yet not a horse or a gun had been sent to the front."

After Rebel cannon were heard firing ahead, "straggling soldiers now came running toward us with exaggerated rumors of the enemy being in force, burning the bridges, and contesting with artillery the passage of the streams that crossed the road."

To be sure, there was Union infantry on hand as well . . . more or less on hand, that is. "Four regiments of infantry were marching along, uncertain what road to take and unassigned to any brigade; two brigadier generals and their staffs, without orders and without commands, were sitting by the roadside waiting for something to turn up."

What turned up, the sound of cannon booming ahead, was a furious Treasury Secretary Chase. Apparently livid with rage, he expressed to General Wool "in very strong language his astonishment at the condition of things."

Among the obvious questions: Why wasn't someone in charge here? By Viele's account, Wool tried to explain matters by saying he presumed one brigadier "felt some delicacy in assuming command" over the other, while the other also "hesitated to act" while the first was "so near."

"Talk of delicacy!" Chase exploded. "With the enemy firing in front! What absurdity!"

Then calming a bit, he told Wool to send one of the generals to the rear for reinforcements, "and that will settle all questions of delicacy."

When Wool and the prescribed general then fell into a "prolonged discussion" in the "shade of a large sycamore tree," Chase could contain himself no longer. "Losing all patience," wrote Viele in an 1878 issue of *Scribner's Monthly*, "the Secretary exclaimed, 'Two cackling hens!' and turning to me with a voice and manner that would have become [the Duke of] Wellington or [Napoleon's Marshall Nicholas] Soult, he said, 'Sir! I order you in the name of the President of the United States to take command of these troops and march them upon Norfolk.'"

In short time, Viele had deployed one infantry regiment as advance skirmishers and had the remaining troops "moving rapidly down the Norfolk road," as well.

They had gone "some distance" before Wool noticed he was losing his command. "He was not long in overtaking us, however, and on his demand for an explanation from me Mr. Chase assumed the responsibility, after which we proceeded harmoniously toward our destination."

Now came another twist or two in the story of Norfolk's recapture. Just before Viele, Chase, and the entourage would reach a "formidable line of intrenched works" guarding the city, here came "a large deputation" consisting of the mayor and other officials under a flag of truce. "The mayor, with all the formality of a medieval warden, appeared with a bunch of rusty keys and a formidable roll of papers which he proceeded to read with the utmost deliberation previous to delivering the 'keys of the city.' The reading of the documents—which embraced a large portion of the history of Virginia, the causes that led to the war, the peculiar position of the good citizens of Norfolk, and in short a little of everything that could have the remotest bearing upon the subject and exhaust the longest possible space of time in reading—was protracted until nearly dark." Of course, it all was "a most skillful ruse to gain time for the Confederates to secure their retreat from the city."

General Wool still was with the group and nominally in charge. "In the meantime," wrote Viele (with a touch of asperity), "the Confederates were hurrying with their artillery and stores over the ferry to Portsmouth, cutting the water pipes and flooding the public buildings, setting fire to the navy yard, and having their own way generally, while our General was listening in the most innocent and complacent manner to the long rigmarole so ingeniously prepared by the mayor."

The ruse included proposed carriage rides to city hall for the Union officers, for more ceremony, while the troops remained behind. "Falling rapidly into this second little trap, the General accepted and we were driven to the city hall, where some more rusty keys were produced and more formal speeches were made." Several thousands, some of them Confederate soldiers identifiable by their "butternut and gray," milled around in front of the building but apparently offered no opposition.

Then, while Wool was engaged in the "high formalities," added Viele, "Mr. Chase asked for a pen and a piece of paper and wrote an order assigning the command of the city to myself as military governor, which General Wool signed at his direction."

In short order, Secretary Chase said goodbye, took Wool by the arm, and departed.

That left Viele, the new military governor of a captured Rebel city, "the solitary occupant of the city hall, without a soldier within two miles and with not even an aide-de-camp to assist me."

But Viele hardly missed a beat. "Fortunately an enterprising newspaper correspondent had followed the carriages on foot, and him I appointed an aide and dispatched for the troops."

Night had fallen by the time they arrived, but arrive they did. And as Viele placed his men in position by the light of the moon, only posterity could determine who was most responsible for the recapture of Norfolk, Virginia, by the Union.

☆ ☆ ☆

Additional note: This, of course, also was the very night the Confederate ironclad *Merrimac,* trapped upstream at the mouth of the James, met destruction at the hands of its own men to prevent it from falling into the Union's grasp. Viele explained:

"A regiment dispatched to the navy yard was too late to rescue it from almost complete destruction, but it cut off the *Merrimac* from any supplies from either side of the river.

"It was long after midnight before the final disposition of troops was made, and this had hardly been accomplished when, with a shock that shook the city and with an ominous sound that could not be mistaken, the magazine of the *Merrimac* was exploded, the vessel having been cut off from supplies and deserted by the crew; and thus this most formidable engine of destruction that had so long been a terror not only to Hampton Roads but to the Atlantic Coast went to her doom."

Further note: West Point graduate Egbert Viele returned to his civilian profession as a civil engineer in 1863, before the end of the Civil War. He already had served as engineer in chief for creation of New York City's Central Park and as designer of Brooklyn's Prospect Park. Now, before his death in 1902, he would serve as chief engineer for the Pittsburgh, Buffalo, and Rochester Railroad; as commissioner of parks for New York City; as a one-term member of the U.S. House of Representatives, and as president of the Board of Visitors for the U.S. Military Academy at West Point, where his pyramid-shaped tomb of twenty-five by thirty-one feet still is a landmark. A veteran of the Mexican War with service in the American Southwest, he produced a military manual in 1861, *Hand-book for Active Service,* that was used for troop training by both the Union and the Confederacy. He also laid plans for a New York City subway system.

1 8 6 2
Daily Concerns While at War

Beyond the superstars of the 1860s, the legendary generals of Virginia, who else fought the Civil War on behalf of the Old Dominion? Who were the "average" soldiers in the field, always at risk, often in physical discomfort, again and again writing home to loved ones, always worrying about the farm or business left to a hard-pressed wife, some days thrilling to small joys, other days lamenting the loss of their friends. And again, always at risk themselves . . . and knowing it.

When Mary Custis Lee passed from Union lines into Rebel territory to end fifteen months of separation from her husband, Robert E. Lee, Confederate Lt. Robert Gaines Haile Jr. was watching. He saw her carriage at the Meadow Bridge a few miles northeast of Richmond. He wrote home that she had been ill-treated beforehand while virtually under house arrest by the Yankees. And—what a thrill!—he helped smooth the way for her passage from unfriendly to friendly hands.

The mundane . . . the unexpected. That often was the war for the "average" man. Like Lieutenant Haile of the Essex Sharpshooters, Fifty-fifth Virginia, who wove his wartime experiences into both a journal and letters to his wife, Mollie, back home at their Beavers Hill plantation in Essex County. "It will not be very long before I will need some socks," he wrote Mollie one June day in 1862. The next morning, though, it wasn't a matter of new socks. No, this time Pvt. William H. Pound was dying nearby. Dying loudly.

"Mr. Pound, a member of Captain Jett's company, is dying not far from our tents," wrote Haile in his journal for June 11. "His groans can be heard all over the camp."

Private Pound, Haile also noted, "leaves a [w]ife and five little children to mourn for him." Rather than enemy fire, Pound fell victim to disease, to typhoid.

The repeated personal tragedy, the mundane, the unexpected . . . the strange. All a part of the war. Take this entry of June 10 in Haile's journal (*When the Peaches Get Ripe, Tell the Children I'll Be Home: Letters Home by Lt. Robert Gaines Haile, Jr., Essex Sharpshooters, 55th Va., 1862,* compiled and edited by Robert M. Tombes, Haile's great-great-grandson): "The Yankee pickets and ours are on very friendly terms. They are not more than two or three hundred yards apart. I had not been there [at his own unit's picket station] long before one of the Yankees advanced[,] waved his cap and made signs for someone to meet him. I told Fergerson to take a paper and exchange it with him. He went but the man did not have a paper with him. He told Fergerson he would return and get one for him. He also asked how we were off for provisions. Fergerson replied that we had an abundance of everything except coffee[;] that article was not so abundant as one could wish. The Yankee then told him he would bring him some of that two if he would except of it."

And, lo! An hour later the Yankee did return to the scene, "and shure enough brought both paper and coffee."

That same day, Mary Custis Lee crossed the lines, on her way to the Confederate capital of Richmond and a reunion with her husband, Robert E. Lee. Quite unexpectedly, Lieutenant Haile turned out to be a go-between.

"About one o'clock," he wrote in his journal, "two men came rideing down the road waveing a white flag. I immediately started and met them halfway between the pickets. . . . They said they came to pass Mrs. Gen. Lee to our lines and would like to see the officer in charge."

Typical of the South's homegrown units, Haile's immediate commanding officer was a close relative—his own wife Mollie's brother, Capt. Thomas Burke.

After sending word to Burke, Haile simply passed the time of day with the two Yankee officers and a third one who had joined them. "All three seemed to be men of refinement and sence," wrote Haile. "After talking a while, one of them took out a flask and asked me to take a drink. As I was wet and cold, I thanked him and took a good pull at it, found it to be very nice whiskey."

Although the meeting in no man's land was perfectly friendly, none of the conversationalists quite forgot that they were meeting in a time of war—at this particular time, during Union Gen. George B. McClellan's slowly unfolding Peninsula campaign, which, as he neared Richmond, would be followed by the Seven Days' battles. It would be here that Robert E. Lee emerged from relative obscurity as a brilliant and aggressive battlefield commander, much to McClellan's chagrin.

The conversation among the four officers, three Union and one Confederate, continued . . . but now with a bit of an edge to it. "I wanted to know of them how it was that they could claim a victory in the late fight below Richmond," added Haile, "when we had driven them back two miles, capturing their camp and taking a great many other things. They said they would admit we had got the best of it on Saturday but they made up for it on Sunday. Said they buried twelve hundred of our dead for us."

In a follow-up letter to Mollie later the same day, Haile spoke of an even sharper edge to his conversation with the Union officers. "They lie about that," he said in reference to the twelve hundred dead. "I told them they would never take Richmond. They thought differently of course. I told them also I wished the fight would take place tomorrow so shure I was that we are going to give them one of the worst thrashings they have ever gotten. They said if we did they could raise another army as large as the one they now have without any difficulty. I told them yes [but] of Irish and Dutch."

The conversation continued but stopped when Mrs. Lee appeared and was passed over the line. Charles F. M. Bayliss, one of Haile's men and a farmer in civilian life, drove her carriage into Richmond.

Back at his encampment, Lieutenant Haile entered in his journal, "Thus ended a day that I never shall forget."

In his letters to Mollie, Haile mixed together both the minutiae and the important things that might be on a soldier's mind while awaiting battle or on picket duty. He also mentioned the socks; he said his bowels had been "out of fix" for a day or two, and the same was true for half the men in his Fifty-fifth Infantry Regiment. He added, "The Yankees are just as tired of this war as we are and want it ended as much as we do." In one more day, he also noted in a quick postscript the next morning, he and Mollie would be reaching their sixth wedding anniversary.

"How I wish I could spend it at home with you," he said.

Meanwhile, the Fifty-fifth and its Essex Sharpshooters Company had not yet experienced combat . . . but that day was looming close on.

The fact is, explained editor Tombes in a postscript to his great-great-grandfather's letters home, the Fifty-fifth Virginia had been in "retreat" from its one-time encampment at Fort Lowry on Lowry's Point on the Rappahannock River six miles southeast of Tappahannock, to the Fredericksburg area, and finally to Camp Gooch, near Mechanicsville and the Meadow Bridge—and, more precisely, "on or adjacent to present day Henrico High School property on Azalea Ave." A Gooch home, "torn down in the 1960s," was on the site of the school's baseball diamond of today.

The advancing Yankees had destroyed Fort Lowry in April 1862; later the Rappahannock washed away all remnants of the campsite.

During the unit's several moves, the men of the Fifty-fifth "had heard battle, but had never been engaged." All that was about to change, however, in the great struggle at Richmond's doorstep known simply as the Seven Days'.

"It seems to be the impression of all," Robert Haile wrote to Mollie on June 23, "that we are on the eve of a great fight."

But the mundane still was important, as well. "Ask Beazley [a shoemaker back home] to make my shoes," added Haile in the very next breath. He thought he would soon need them. But he also was thinking deeper thoughts. "You must write to me by every opportunity," he pleaded at the letter's end. "I will write by every one that I can get.

"Your devoted husband.

"Ro G. Haile."

As events turned out for Robert G. Haile Jr., and many of his friends and acquaintances after the engagements of the Seven Days', there would be no more letters home.

☆ ☆ ☆

Additional note: After spending a quiet 1861 and early 1862 at the sod bastion on the Rappahannock called Fort Lowry, the Fifty-fifth Virginia had been stationed near Fredericksburg and then near Richmond. As part of a brigade joining three other brigades to form Maj. Gen. A. P. Hill's "Light Division," the Fifty-fifth would be deployed next along the Chickahominy River "just east of Richmond," wrote Tombes. Finally seeing its first real combat at Mechanicsville on June 16, 1862, the Fifty-fifth by war's end would have served through the Seven Days', along with the battles of Second Manassas, Chancellorsville, Gettysburg, Spotsylvania, and Petersburg, editor Tombes also noted.

Incidental intelligence: The ranking Federal officer whom Robert Haile met between the lines the day of Mary Lee's crossing apparently was Archimedes T. A. Torbet, a West Point graduate and commander, in the spring of 1862, of the Union's First New Jersey Infantry. After surviving the Civil War and then serving in diplomatic posts such as that of the U.S. Consul General in Paris, France, he died in a shipwreck off Cape Canaveral, Florida, on August 29, 1880, while en route from New York to Mexico. Oddly enough, Torbet, a native of Delaware, a slave state, briefly had been carried on the rolls of both the Confederate and the Union armies early in the war. He then rose to brevet (temporary) major general's rank as his reward for exemplary Civil War service on behalf of the Union, only to be left with a mere captain's rank in the postwar regular army.

1 8 6 2
The World Around Him

The people of Confederate Lt. Robert G. Haile Jr.'s world ranged from immediate family (wife Mollie and their three children, first and foremost) to siblings (an older brother, John, age thirty-eight, briefly served, but then went home to farm and family, where his wife, Margaret, would go down in family history as the only mother of John's sixteen children), to friends and fellow soldiers of the Fifty-fifth Virginia Infantry and its Company F, the Essex Sharpshooters (organized by Robert's brother-in-law, Thomas Burke, Mollie's brother), to Old Tom, the body servant who accompanied Robert into war.

While many of Robert's fellow soldiers were from his own Essex County, they remained a mixed group in their talents, their backgrounds, their war experiences . . . and, as the Seven Days' campaign outside Richmond and other battles loomed, in the personal fates that lay ahead for each of them.

One of his fellow Essex Sharpshooters, for instance, would make minor history when he saw Stonewall Jackson being carried to the rear after being fatally wounded by his own men in the battle of Chancellorsville. "Great God," shouted 1st Sgt. Thomas B. Fogg, "it is General Jackson!" Fogg himself was killed in battle the very next day, May 3, 1863.

The random chance of war again was proved by the alternate fates of Washington L. Clarke, who joined up at the relatively advanced age of thirty-six and survived the entire war, while schoolboy John Andrew Clarkson joined the Sharpshooters in 1861 at age fifteen and was killed by shellfire in August 1862 at age sixteen while voluntarily taking part in an advance on Waterloo Bridge. Under Robert Haile's command during the Peninsula campaign of 1862, wrote Robert M. Tombes in his compilation of letters home from Lieutenant Haile, the Clarkson youth "earned more trust than men twice his age."

Then, too, the Sharpshooters roster once included Robert F. Mann, elected second lieutenant one day, killed just three days later (at Gaines's Mill, June 27, 1862).

Another two members of the Fifty-fifth Virginia—but this time in Company C, the Middlesex Dragoons—were the doctor brothers Richard Allen Christian Jr. and William "Billy" Steptoe Christian (the latter married to a Helen Elizabeth Steptoe). Richard soon left the Fifty-fifth for detached service at a hospital in Richmond, then became an assistant surgeon. Billy, though, had raised the Middlesex Dragoons and stayed with his unit as its major and then colonel. Known for "coolness under fire," he was wounded during the Seven Days' campaign and once more at Chancellorsville. Captured in July 1863, he headed the hospital at the Union's Johnson Island (Ohio) POW facility for a time. After the war, "Doctor Billy" returned to his medical practice in Middlesex County, later to become county school superintendent, secretary of the county board of health, and, in 1904, president of the Virginia Medical Society.

The future "Doctor Billy" of Middlesex County once excused Haile from taking part in daily drill because of diarrhea, a frequent malady for soldiers in the field. Telling his wife, Mollie, about the minor episode, Haile wrote on June 16, 1862: "When I was in Richmond last I bought a bottle of Forwards cholera drops, said to be good for diarrhoea and dysentery. I took a dose of it this morning and think it has done me good already."

He probably would do even better, he opined, "if I could only get such things as were suitable for me to eat; that is the great difficulty in this sort of life."

Meanwhile, others in Haile's wartime world of the Fifty-fifth Virginia who would become men of relative note ranged from future Tappahannock newspaper editor Albert Micou to future teachers Albert Rennolds and John Temple, to Richard Beale, future member of the Virginia House of Delegates, to Alexander Woodford Broaddus, future treasurer of Essex County.

Another doctor with the Fifty-fifth was Henry Gresham, while Essex County's own Dr. Benjamin Wright, attached to the Ninth Virginia Cavalry, would be the first army surgeon to attend Stonewall Jackson after his fatal wounding by friendly fire at Chancellorsville. "After the war," wrote editor Tombs, "he practiced medicine in Essex County for a time, but gave up the practice because he said he could no longer give placebos to hypochondriacs after having seen so much real suffering." Perhaps he also was recalling the fate of two Essex County brothers by the same name of Wright, Richard F. and William Alfred Jr., both of whom were killed in battle. While Richard survived until September 1864, William as a young captain fought at the battles of Mechanicsville and Gaines's Mill before he was killed while charging a Union artillery position in the battle of Frayser's Farm on June 30, 1862.

Long before the Civil War, the two Wright brothers had been major figures in the world of Robert Haile since their Aunt Matilda had been the first wife of Robert's father, Robert G. Haile Sr.

Even closer to young Robert and wife Mollie, of course, was her own brother Thomas Burke, a farmer from Essex County who originally raised the Sharpshooters company and then served as its commander. After briefly attending Virginia Military Institute in the late 1840s, he organized his Sharpshooters outfit in response to John Brown's raid on Harpers Ferry. Wounded in the arm at Mechanicsville on June 26, he shared William Wright's fate at Frayser's Farm four days later—killed while attacking a Union artillery battery.

For all in the Fifty-fifth Virginia, that battle, a part of the Seven Days' campaign, would be a dramatic watershed. "In less time than it takes to write it," related schoolteacher Albert Rennolds years later, "we were thrown into line and moved forward through the woods which were literally combed with canister [antipersonnel artillery shot]. On reaching the edge of the woods a volley from our men swept the cannoneers from the guns and loading as we go we pass through batteries to be met by a stinging volley from the enemies infantry lying about seventy-five or a hundred yards beyond. We give them tit for tat for a few minutes when the order was given FORWARD! Then, we rushed with a yell, fixed bayonets at a charge and we heard no more of U.S. Regulars until we got to Oxhill [Ox Hill in northern Virginia months later]."

"But, oh!" Rennolds also moaned. "What a loss to the Sharp Shooters. Burke dead. Wright dead. Haile mortally wounded."

Yes, Mollie's husband, painfully wounded in the shoulder, would now undergo the worst days of his life . . . a rapidly ebbing life. Stated another way, of course, this story could have begun from the perspective of Mollie's world, in which so many died so young, her brother Tom and her husband, Robert, included.

With Mollie and two brothers at his side, laid up in the Richmond home of P. J. Barns, Robert lingered . . . and lingered. Nearly a month in all. "Dear Mollie," wrote his sister Lucy on June 6, a Sunday, "how I wish I could be with you and help nurse my dear brother, though I know every thing that can be done for his comfort you all will do—but 'twould be such a gratification to me even to have the privilege of fanning him."

If only she could see him, if only she could know his exact condition, if, if, and if . . . She also wrote, "If I could just hear that the ball was extracted I would be so thankful for this."

But, lodged near his upper spine, it never was, and Robert G. Haile Jr., of Essex County, Virginia, died on July 16, 1862. His world had ended, and Mollie's at the same moment had diminished, never to be quite the same again.

☆ ☆ ☆

Additional note: Also very much a part of Robert Haile's world were the three brothers Latane from Essex County who served the Confederacy in the Civil War. Of the three, the closest to Robert, a friend since childhood and later a brother-in-law through his sister Ann's marriage to a fourth Latane brother, was William Latane, in civilian life a doctor educated at the University of Virginia and Hampden-Sydney Medical College (later to become the Medical College of

Virginia), and practicing in Essex County. With the eruption of war between North and South, William joined the Essex Cavalry as a captain. His brothers John and Henry also would serve the Confederate cause, John as a fellow cavalryman and Henry as a member of Robert Haile's own Essex Sharpshooters.

Just weeks before Robert's own death, his beloved friend William Latane became both a casualty and an icon of the Civil War. Riding with Jeb Stuart in his famous ride around Union Gen. George B. McClellan during the latter's Peninsula campaign (leading to the Seven Days'), William Latane was killed while charging up a hill with fellow members of the Rebel Ninth Cavalry against the Union's Fifth Cavalry at Linney Corners, near Old Church northeast of Richmond. He apparently was the only casualty suffered during Stuart's famous ride around the Union army.

In his compilation of Robert Haile's letters home (*When the Peaches Get Ripe*), editor Tombes added: "Latane's death is remembered in 'The Burial of Latane,' a large (36" by 46") oil painting from 1864 by William DeHartburn Washington." As Tombes also said, "After the war, copies of this painting were distributed throughout the South."

In the meantime, though, news of Latane's death on June 13 was very upsetting to young Robert Haile, so much so, he wrote his wife, "It caused me to spend a sleepless night."

In his journal for June 15, Haile added that he borrowed a horse and rode to the "Cavalry Camp," where he soon found William Latane's brother John. Not until then, it seems, was Haile quite convinced that his good friend from childhood was gone. "As soon as I saw him [John] I knew that his brother was dead," Haile wrote in his journal. "He invited me in his tent. He seemed to be so much distressed I would not ask him any questions concerning the death of his brother."

From John Young, another cavalryman from Essex County, however, Haile did learn the grim particulars of his friend's heroic death. With Latane in command of a squadron of cavalry, he and his men had been ordered to charge Union cavalrymen "drawn up in the road ready to receive them," Haile wrote. "Capt. Latane gallantly led the charge. He fell shot through by two balls. The devil that shot him was killed immediately after wards."

Lamented Haile also: "A more noble, brave, generous, correct man never lived."

Further, he "has been the first one from Essex to fall in defense of our rights and liberties," and, "Many of us may be fated to meet with the same end before this war shall close."

That prediction, of course, would prove all too correct.

★

1 8 6 3
Term As Governor Unrecognized

★

Deep in the heart of Alexandria's highly touted, handsomely restored "Old Town" section rises an imposing brick home rarely noticed by tourists or mentioned by the city's history-conscious promoters. Yet it once was Virginia's state capitol. Sort of . . .

Itself restored in the twentieth century and then turned into an apartment house, the four-story structure at 415 Prince Street with twin arched doorways once, in the 1860s, was the combined executive mansion and statehouse for Virginia Governor Francis H. Pierpont. But this was during the Civil War. And Pierpont, best known as the "Father of West Virginia," headed a puppetlike "restored" Virginia government loyal to the Union, whose troops occupied the old port city. Pierpont spent two years in Alexandria as overseer of a truncated Virginia territory with a rump legislature, and his name still does appear in the state's official government directory—but only as the first governor of *all* Virginia under the Federal rule imposed after the surrender at Appomattox.

His restored government and term in Alexandria from 1863 to 1865 still go officially unrecognized.

Thus, there are those who suggest the old statehouse faded into obscurity in postbellum years because of its Union background. After all, Alexandria basically remained Southern in sympathy after the Civil War, with the Federal row house on Prince Street striking many as an unwanted symbol of a bitter past. Later generations simply didn't know or care that much about the building's past.

Still, Elizabeth Elliott, a twentieth-century owner of the building, once said, "A lot of older people know about it, and they look at it with some awe and say, 'That was the Statehouse.'"

Built in 1806 as a bank, the old structure was restored in the 1950s by the previous owners, Mr. and Mrs. Robert A. Beers of Potomac, Maryland. The handsome results won them the Alexandria Historical Association's restoration award for 1959. Still, the city's history buffs and tourism promoters continued to focus their attention on other points of deserving interest in Old Town, among them the Colonial Gadsby Tavern, Robert E. Lee's boyhood home, the early American Carlyle House, historic Christ Church, even George Washington's "income properties" around the corner from the statehouse. But then, the old statehouse had become private property providing apartments to various tenants. It could be "visited" only from the sidewalk in front.

In a side courtyard darkened by the spreading branches of a magnolia tree, by the way, a painted wooden plaque recalled the old bank's one-time fame, or notoriety, as "Capitol of the Restored Government" during the Civil War.

Most of the Old Dominion then lay behind Confederate lines. The Confederacy itself was headquartered in Virginia's capital city of Richmond. In Union eyes, however, the state capital was Alexandria, and the divided state's business would be done in Alexandria.

Pierpont, born in western Virginia (not yet *West* Virginia), came to the split-Virginia helm reluctantly—and well aware that the Union-occupied city was dangerously Southern in mood. Once, while Pierpont was staying at Gadsby Tavern, Col. John S. Mosby, the Confederacy's legendary guerrilla fighter known as the "Gray Ghost," slipped into town aboard a hay wagon and rode beneath the governor's window. A day later, the Rebel raider sent Pierpont a chilling message: "My driver pointed out your window, and I marked it plain. . . . I'll get you some night, mighty easy."

Mosby never did lay a hand on Pierpont, but it would be months before the new governor brought his wife and children to Alexandria to be with him.

Earlier, the one-time schoolteacher and railroad lawyer had called together the convention of antisecessionist forces at Wheeling that would lead to West Virginia's establishment as a state. According to some historians, an eleventh-hour telegram from Pierpont, elected provisional governor by the convention, was the final argument that persuaded a hesitant Abraham Lincoln to sign the bill creating the new state. But the divorce of the two Virginias left Pierpont in charge of a political stepchild—a shrunken "loyal" Virginia that was no more than a belt of northern counties and two cities, Alexandria and Norfolk.

Before he came to Alexandria and its statehouse, local sentiment had been enflamed by a double shooting that stirred outrage throughout the North and the South. Union Col. Elmer Ellsworth, once an office boy to Lincoln and by now the popular head of the New York Fire Zouaves, entered the city early in the war to remove a Confederate flag flying atop the Marshall House, an Old Town hostelry that since has vanished. By some accounts, the Rebel banner had fluttered defiantly in full view of Lincoln and assembled cabinet members across the Potomac River. And Ellsworth, another of the onlookers, volunteered to take it down.

The flag came down all right, but only after a bloody skirmish on the hotel stairs that saw both Ellsworth and the hotel proprietor, James Jackson, killed. Soon the Federals occupied the city in force; the city teemed with military men, all Union.

According to most historians, Pierpont was fair and considerate in his management of "loyal" Virginia. While he held forth in the statehouse, his rump legislature of seven senators and a handful of delegates met in City Hall and other public places. When the war ended, he shifted base to Richmond and served as governor until 1868. His replacement by a military governor is considered a concession to more radical Reconstruction forces, especially those who opposed a provision Pierpont had secured in the Alexandria Constitution of 1864 giving known Confederates the right to vote.

Today, Pierpont is little known in Virginia, but West Virginia some years ago memorialized him by placing his statue in the U.S. Capitol's Statuary Hall. Meanwhile, his old statehouse in Alexandria fell into run-down, tenement status in the years before the Beers couple purchased it and began their restoration. That effort meant removal of the old brick bank vault still on the first floor, although the vault's massive foundation still would fill most of the basement. A two-story annex of sorts apparently served as the bank's front office in antebellum days and would stay. The Maryland couple also preserved much of the original flooring, woodwork and mantelpieces. However, they couldn't undo one of the structure's most conspicuous features. Ruined by rock-throwing vandals sometime in the past, these were a pair of glass fans over each of the double-arched doorways, each with a gold inscription.

Fittingly enough, one said "Virginia," the other, "West Virginia."

★

1863
Ever Infamous in Norfolk

★

It's a bit late to prosecute, but there is a damning indictment to be drawn from the detailed letter that the one-time *Federal* governor of Virginia, Francis H. Peirpont, addressed to President Lincoln in protest to the harsh rule of Union Gen. Benjamin Butler and his subalterns over occupied Norfolk in the middle of the Civil War.

Norfolk fell to the Union in May 1862 and then was subject to military rule for thirteen months until Peirpont's civilian government of the "Federalized" Virginia territory took over. As explained by historian Thomas Jefferson Wertenbaker in his book *Norfolk: Historic Southern Port:* "When Virginia seceded in 1961, the people of the western part of the state, declaring this action of no effect, organized a government to replace the one at Richmond. They elected Peirpont governor, chose a legislature, congressmen and senators, and received recognition from President Lincoln as the legal government of Virginia."

At first, Peirpont, using an old bank building in Alexandria as his "state capitol" (please see preceding story), had few qualms over the way Norfolk was treated under a military regime that imposed a loyalty oath upon the citizenry. Peirpont apparently approved of the edict granting voting privileges to none but "Union men," Wertenbaker wrote.

With "not more than one hundred" thus qualified, "the mayor, councilmen, and justices were, of course, hostile to the Confederacy, and many of them were Northerners."

In time, though, "some Southern sympathizers took the oath of allegiance, for no ministers, physicians, lawyers, merchants and clerks in the stores were permitted to pursue their advocations without it." As the saying goes, they had to go along to get along . . . but not with any heartfelt change in view. Instead, it was a case, angrily opined the onlooking *Richmond Enquirer,* of: "Take the oath of allegiance or starve!"

In June 1864, however, the arrangement that Peirpont had inherited from the previous military regime backfired on him. The handful of Union men empowered to vote now did so at the bidding of the latest Union general on the scene, Benjamin "Beast" Butler. "In June 1864, by the vote of the Union men in Norfolk, all of them in Butler's power, he overthrew even the pretense of civil government and restored the military regime," added Wertenbaker.

Already notorious for his brutal military rule in federally occupied New Orleans, Butler "regarded the Peirpont government with contempt, and ruled Norfolk almost as though no such thing existed."

In short order, military officers took over the civil courts, "and arbitrary orders were issued to levy taxes on business, [to] open schools, inspect banks and issue licenses to traders."

His regime leveled its guns on the local clergy, too, sending one clergyman, George D. Armstrong, to hard labor at a federal installation nearby, and another briefly to sweeping streets (see pages 183–86).

As one outrage followed another, Peirpont took pen in hand to compose his detailed protest to President Lincoln.

Noting that Butler first was named to command the eastern district of Virginia and North Carolina late in 1863, Peirpont wrote: "I sighed when I heard it—I remembered New Orleans. There was short rejoicing at Norfolk among the ultra Union men, but in a short time the wail of woe came up."

Among the many counts making up Governor Peirpont's indictment of the excesses perpetrated by Butler and his overzealous underlings were:

- Butler's threat of punishment for "any person who used any disrespectful language to any officer or soldiers in the Union army."
- An order "charging 1 per cent on all goods shipped into his [Butler's] military district, to go to the support of the provost marshal's fund."
- The requirement that all vessels leaving Norfolk and environs must pay a fee of $5 to $15.
- A tax on oystermen of 50 cents to $1 per month "for the privilege of taking oysters."
- An edict placing all churches in Norfolk and Portsmouth under control of the provost marshals, the pulpits to be "properly filled, by displacing when necessary, the present incumbents and substituting men of known loyalty."
- Another edict saying churches must be open freely to all officers and soldiers, white or black, with no insult or indignity aimed at

them, presumably meaning no insult to blacks joining traditionally all-white congregations, "either by word, look, or gesture,
on the part of the congregation."

- Further, still quoting from Peirpont's letter to Lincoln: "The
liquor business now stands thus in Norfolk: a few men from
Boston and Lowell, Mass [Butler's home state] have the exclusive monopoly of importing it into the city. . . . The restaurant
keepers pay these Boston men $3 per gallon for whiskey that
costs in Baltimore from 95 cents to $1.05."

- Then, too, taking over the city gasworks, "he sells the gas at
nearly double the price paid in Washington." He arranged for "a
man from Lowell" to come and make repairs at the gasworks for
a $10,000 fee.

- In addition, "Ever since the Union troops occupied the city of
Norfolk and Portsmouth, the military have had possession of
the ferry and boats between the two cities, using them for its
own profit and benefit."

Not even the dogs of Norfolk escaped Butler's greedy eye, it seems.
"On March 7, 1864, an order was issued that every fourth dog in the
Norfolk district be killed," wrote historian Wertenbaker. "This created
consternation until it was learned that any owner could save his dog by
paying two dollars for a license."

Peirpont included the dog fee in his "indictment" as well. "I met a
soldier with a line around a little dog's neck," he wrote. "He was
between a spaniel and the poodle—white wool—but dirty; his chin was
close to the ground, his eyes upturned meekly, and wagging his tail
gently as he went along." A black man watching along with Peirpont
apparently said, "Little doggie, if you don't get two dollars, Marse Butler
will take de wag out of your tail."

Meanwhile, when the Civil War ended with the disintegration of
the Confederacy, the paroled Confederate soldiers returning to home
and family in Norfolk had to endure one further humiliation at the
hands of Butler's provost marshal. "By his order," added Wertenbaker's
book, they were arrested on the street, "dragged before him," and, in the
presence of onlooking whites and blacks, stripped of the buttons on
their uniforms.

As a result of such an aggregate of punishing dictums, noted
Wertenbaker in his 1931 book (seven decades after the fact), "the bit-

terness occasioned by the unnecessary cruelties of the three years of Federal occupation has hardly yet died out." And, no surprise, "the name of Butler will ever be infamous in Norfolk."

☆ ☆ ☆

Additional note: Butler's outrages were recalled yet again in a tricentennial history of the old port city issued in 1936, *Through the Years in Norfolk*. Writing "Book I," or "Historical Norfolk—1636 to 1936," in that volume, W. H. T. Squires not only cited Butler's unforgettable excesses, but was almost as unsparing in his criticism of Abraham Lincoln, who in person had witnessed the recapture of Norfolk from shipboard in May 1862. "Historians," wrote Squires in his twentieth-century treatise, "usually justify the political persecution of reconstruction as due to the anger and vengeance that followed the assassination of President Lincoln." But not in this case, he argued. "No such mitigation may here be pleaded. Federal tyranny was fiercest in Norfolk long before the President was shot. Much of the cruelty here he condoned if he did not encourage. We regret to record that President Lincoln was deaf to every appeal for justice from Norfolk."

And it *is* true that Butler remained at his command over Norfolk even after Peirpont protested, first to War Secretary Edwin Stanton, and then directly to Lincoln himself.

Ironically, Butler, born in New Hampshire but raised in his mother's boarding house at Lowell, Massachusetts, once had been a Democrat who vainly voted—at the party's convention in Charleston, South Carolina, in 1860—for the nomination of U.S. Senator Jefferson Davis of Mississippi for president of the United States. (Yes, the same who later became president of the Confederacy . . . and branded Butler an outlaw for his behavior in occupied New Orleans!) Butler then supported Vice President John C. Breckinridge's bid for president as the States' Rights presidential candidate, also in 1860, the year that Republican Lincoln won the White House in a four-way race that saw the Democrats and the nation itself split over the combined slavery–states' rights issues.

Ironically again, appointed a major general of volunteers by none other than newly installed President Lincoln, Butler soon would emerge as an erstwhile Republican possibly challenging Lincoln himself in the 1864 race for the White House . . . or possibly joining Lincoln's ticket as the GOP's candidate for vice president.

But in 1864, as commander of the Union army of the James, Butler managed to lose face due to his mismanagement of military assignments accompanying Ulysses S. Grant's Virginia campaign, followed by an outright fiasco as commander of land forces in the botched Union invasion of the North Carolina coast at Fort Fisher late in 1864. Butler next appeared on the national scene in the role of a U.S. House member from Massachusetts siding with the Radical Republicans imposing Reconstruction on the South . . . even acting as a floor manager in the House for the impeachment proceedings against the slain Lincoln's successor, Andrew Johnson. In a final self-serving political switch, Butler would be elected governor of Massachusetts in 1882—as a Democrat.

Meanwhile, with the departure of Butler and the return of her young men from Confederate service in the Civil War—those surviving, that is—Norfolk could look to only *somewhat* improved prospects. For now, Reconstruction, riots, and a period of restricted civil liberties still lay ahead. Indeed, noted the city history compiled by Squires, from the first days of the city's yellow fever epidemic of 1855, which killed one-third of the city's population of six thousand, to the end of Reconstruction, with the Civil War period and the Benjamin Butler regime sandwiched in between, the city underwent fifteen terrible years casting "shadows of death, disaster, and despair over this unhappy city."

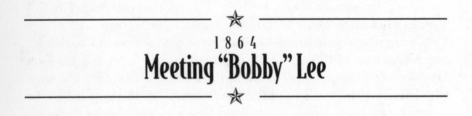

1 8 6 4
Meeting "Bobby" Lee

"I feel as certain of crushing Lee as I do of dying," Ulysses S. Grant allegedly said in those dark, penultimate days of 1864 when his strategy of bludgeoning Robert E. Lee's Army of Northern Virginia into submission was taking terrible toll of Grant's own forces.

Not only were the casualties cause for vilification in the North, at Grant's back, but in Lee he faced a legend pumped larger than life even by the Northern press. And yet the dogged, newly emplaced commander of Union forces was undismayed. On and on he pounded.

As a fellow West Point graduate and veteran of the Mexican War, Grant felt it was to his advantage to have known Lee, the man and the officer, before they were fated to be locked in titanic struggle . . . in one crushing battle after another, roughly along the future path of I-95 through Virginia, from the Fredericksburg area down to Petersburg.

"The natural disposition of most people," wrote Grant later in his personal memoirs, "is to clothe a commander of a large army whom they do not know with almost superhuman abilities. A large part of the National [Union] army, for instance, and most of the press of the country clothed General Lee with just such qualities, but I knew him personally, and knew that he was mortal; and it was just as well that I felt this."

Refusing to bow to Lee the legend, Grant slipped and sidled in one move after another, down the map of Virginia, in the spring of 1864, from one costly battle to another . . . from the Wilderness to Spotsylvania to Cold Harbor and finally to Petersburg. "I propose to fight it out on this line if it takes all summer," he said at one point. He settled, in the end, for a siege of Petersburg, the vital rail hub just below Richmond, capital of both Virginia and the Confederacy, a siege that lasted until spring of 1865—followed quickly by Lee's surrender at Appomattox.

If Grant thought Lee "mortal," he also viewed him as a "large, austere man, and I judge difficult of approach to his subordinates."

In his "sidling" campaign of 1864, marked by staggering Union casualty tolls, Grant felt that his "austere" opponent enjoyed certain advantages, actually.

The Union might have superior numbers, but Lee was defending a familiar countryside—"every stream, every road, every obstacle to the movement of troops and every natural defense was familiar to him and his army." Lee also had the support of the citizenry, which furnished "accurate reports of our every move." Lee, further, had "a railroad at his back," and he needed no rear guard, whereas Grant, advancing ever farther into enemy territory, would be wise to keep an eye on *his* back.

So towering was Lee's reputation when Grant came from the West to take over the Union war effort, noted Grant also, "it was not an uncommon thing for my staff officers to hear from Eastern officers, 'Well, Grant has never met Bobby Lee yet.'"

But then Grant did, and even the ordinary soldier of the South could see the difference between this Union commander and all those who had preceded him in the eastern theater of the Civil War. "Surprise and disappointment were the prevailing emotions," recalled one Confederate veteran of Grant's "sidling" campaign of 1864, "when we discovered, after the contest in the Wilderness, that General Grant was not going to retire behind the river and permit General Lee to carry on a campaign against Washington the usual way, but was moving to the Spotsylvania position instead."

Usually, added George Cary Eggleston of Lamkin's Virginia Battery, the Union fought a battle, retired, obtained a new commander, then had to deal with a fresh Confederate offensive. Not so with Grant, who simply shifted position, *sidled* that is, and spoiled to fight again. By the time of Cold Harbor in early June, "we had begun to understand what our new adversary meant . . . [that] the era of experimental campaigns against us was over; that Grant was not going to retreat; that he was not to be removed from command because he had failed to break Lee's resistance; and that the policy of pounding had begun and would continue until our strength should be utterly worn away."

In short, "He intended to continue the plodding work till the task should be accomplished, wasting very little time or strength in efforts to make a brilliant display of generalship in a contest of strategic wits with Lee."

True, after losing seven thousand at Cold Harbor to Lee's fifteen hundred casualties, Grant gave up the pounding to take a big sidestep, slip around Richmond to the east, cross the James River, and begin his assault on Petersburg, twenty-three miles below the capital city. That was Grant . . . still on the attack. Thus, young Eggleston, well known for his postbellum book, *A Rebel's Recollections,* still had it exactly right. In what many consider the first display of modern war, Grant employed overwhelming resources to wear Lee down, press home his final campaign, and, within the year, win the war for the North. Or, as Lincoln would say, for an undivided Union. Harsh thought that it may be, Grant could afford his huge losses of men, and justify the fact, because he could reach back for replacements, but for every man Lee lost to Grant's juggernaut, there was no replacement. Thus, the outcome could only be a matter of time.

Later, though, whatever Grant thought of Lee, the man or the legend, it largely would be Grant's own intercession that derailed a move to try Lee for treason.

★
---

1 8 6 5
"Awed Stillness" at Appomattox

★

How to describe the scene at Appomattox? Actually, a Yankee onlooker-participant did a beautiful—and highly respectful—job of it.

Once the terms had been agreed to by Generals Grant and Lee, their subordinates had to carry out the mechanics of surrender. Thus, Georgia's Lt. Gen. John B. Gordon would be assigned to lead the long line of Confederate infantry marching uphill toward Appomattox Court House for the dreary symbolism of surrender. And lining the same road would be the victorious Union troops, commanded at the moment by Gen. Joshua L. Chamberlain, who won the Medal of Honor at Gettysburg. And it was this New Englander who wrote so beautifully about what happened next.

From his later (1915) book *The Passing of the Armies:*

> Before us in proud humiliation stood the embodiment of manhood: men whom neither toils and sufferings, nor the fact of death or disaster, nor hopelessness could bend from their resolve; standing before us now, thin, worn and famished, but erect, and with eyes looking level into ours, waking memories that bound us together as no other bond. . . .
>
> Instruction had been given; and when the head of each division column comes opposite our group, our bugle sounds the signal and instantly our whole line from right to left, regiment by regiment in succession, gives the soldier's salutation, from the "order arms" to the old "carry"—the marching salute. Gordon at the head of the column, riding with heavy spirit and downcast face, catches the sound of shifting arms, looks up, and taking the meaning, wheels superbly, making with himself and his horse one uplifted figure, with profound salutation as he drops the point of his sword to the boot toe; then facing to his own command, gives word for his successive brigades to pass us with the same position of the manual—honor answering honor. On our part not a sound of trumpet, nor roll of drum; nor a cheer nor word, nor whisper of vaingglorying,

nor motion of man standing again at the order but an awed stillness rather, a breath-holding, as if it were the passing of the dead.

All the dead, that is, of the entire Civil War.

☆　☆　☆

Additional note: Gordon later served as governor of Georgia and U.S. Senator. "He made a brilliant record in the Confederate army," noted Virginius Dabney in *The Last Review.* "Enlisting at age twenty-nine with absolutely no military experience, Gordon became a brigadier general in less than two years. A born leader of men, fearless and with a commanding presence, he was promoted to lieutenant general before the end of the hostilities." At Appomattox, "it was his unhappy role to command at the surrender of what was left of the Army of Northern Virginia."

Equally distinguished, Joshua Chamberlain returned to his native state of Maine, served three terms as governor and as president of his alma mater, Bowdoin College, for thirteen years, then continued his Bowdoin connection as a lecturer in public law and political science. During the war, he weathered twenty-four combat engagements in all, among them not only Gettysburg but also Fredericksburg, Chancellorsville, and Antietam (Sharpsburg), and was wounded six times. His compatriots feared for his life after one, apparently mortal wound he suffered early in the siege of Petersburg. That is when he was awarded a battlefield promotion to brigadier general by U. S. Grant himself.

1 8 5 9 - 7 0
Robert E. Lee: A Collage

Life presents stages, and for Robert E. Lee, there were several:
1859
Home on indefinite leave but accepting occasional duty stints, the U.S. Army colonel and former superintendent of the Military Academy at

West Point, New York, received sudden orders to proceed with all possible speed to Harpers Ferry, Virginia, to see about a crazed abolitionist who had seized the U.S. arsenal there and taken hostages. Lee, supported by a subaltern named James Ewell Brown "Jeb" Stuart, had to leave Washington so quickly he was still in his civilian clothes a day later as he directed the seizure of the arsenal and the capture of John Brown and his cohorts.

1861

Two years later, home again at his wife's Arlington House estate on the Potomac River overlooking Washington, Lee went into nearby Alexandria—where he had spent a good part of his boyhood—and picked up a newspaper, the *Alexandria Gazette,* which reported that a special state convention assembled in Richmond had voted to secede. The proposal next would go before the all-male, all-white electorate on May 23 . . . but the outcome of the popular vote appeared certain to echo that of the convention. What would this man, native son of Virginia, three decades a U.S. Army officer, son of the Revolutionary War hero "Light Horse" Harry Lee, do? Sit tight and do nothing? Openly, actively, side with his state? Or go with the Union his father had helped to create?

A clue? Months before, he had written to his son "Rooney" Lee, fellow army officer and West Pointer, to say, on the one hand, that "secession is nothing but revolution," but also to say, "If the Union is dissolved and the government disrupted, I shall return to my native State & share the miseries of my people & save in her defense will draw my sword on none."

Another clue? Even before the secession vote, Lee already had turned down proffers to lead the Union army that would be sent to quell the rebelling Southland. By now the Union's Fort Sumter in Charleston (South Carolina) Harbor had fallen under Confederate bombardment. War fever was rampant throughout North and South, but Lee still said he was opposed to secession or war. As for leading the Union's military response, "I could take no part in an invasion of the Southern States," he flatly had declared.

But now Virginia no longer could be a neutral buffer zone between the Union and the secessionist states to the south that had formed a Confederacy. Now, sadly for Robert E. Lee, Virginia, too, would be seceding.

That evening, the Friday night of April 19, in the columned Custis-Lee mansion that was destined to become the centerpiece of

Arlington National Cemetery, he paced an upstairs bedroom deep in thought, then fell to his knees in earnest prayer.

Below, his wife, Mary, crippled by arthritis, waited . . . and did a bit of praying herself.

She probably knew his decision even before he came downstairs about midnight to show her the letter he had written resigning his commission as an officer of the U.S. Army. "It was the severest struggle of his life, to resign a commission he had held for thirty years," she later wrote.

Even more severe struggles were yet to come, as both Lees could easily guess. Answering the call to duty of Governor John Letcher, Robert E. Lee left for Richmond by train Monday morning the twenty-second of April. He would never again spend a night at Arlington; he would not even see his wife for another fifteen months.

Appearing in the old House of Delegates chamber of the state capitol before the Virginia convention that voted to secede, Lee accepted his commission as commander of the armed forces of Virginia and modestly said, "I would have much preferred had the choice fallen upon an abler man." But he also pledged he would devote himself "to the service of my State, in whose behalf alone will I ever draw my sword," an echo to what he had written to his son Rooney months before. Instead of *Colonel* Lee, incidentally, he now was Major General Lee.

For the next many months, his true destiny still hidden from the world, Robert E. Lee would toil rather quietly—in Richmond, for the most part—first for Virginia alone, then for the Confederacy that Virginia soon joined and that he served as chief military adviser to Confederate President Jefferson Davis.

1862

Few realized in the first months of 1862, perhaps not even Robert E. Lee himself, that he was about to emerge as the savior of Richmond . . . and possibly the Confederacy itself. Nor should history give sole credit for his triumph against Union Gen. George B. McClellan in the Seven Days' campaign simply to the fact that Lee was rushed into battle as the replacement for a grievously wounded Gen. Joseph E. Johnston.

The real fact was that Lee, at his desk in Richmond, already had set in place the strategy that allowed the Confederate forces to turn back the Union monolith before it reached and overran Richmond. It *almost* didn't matter whether Johnston, Lee, or some other competent general took over the tactical command in those crucial seven days in June. Thanks to the scenario developed by Lee weeks earlier, the Union was without a force of probably seventy thousand troops that could have been brought to bear in the campaign to seize the Confederate capital.

As Lee had seen the situation, the slow advance of McClellan and his huge army, perhaps 180,000 strong, up the Virginia Peninsula was one threat. But there were others, as well. To the north was the Union's Irvin McDowell opposite Fredericksburg with thirty to forty thousand men; to the west, in the Shenandoah Valley, there was Nathaniel Banks with another twenty thousand men; and in western Virginia, John C. Frémont stood poised with another fifteen thousand men. Thus, McClellan could be joined in his pending assault upon Richmond by another seventy thousand–plus men in a crushing squeeze play that would be well nigh impossible to defend against.

To avoid such a development, Lee advised, the Confederates must slow the overly cautious McClellan as much as possible on the peninsula and create a threat of their own to Washington . . . that is, the *perception* of a threat. Thus, Norfolk, Yorktown, and Williamsburg must be held as long as possible to forestall McClellan, while McDowell must be frozen in place, and Banks and Frémont persuaded to react against the apparent start of a Confederate campaign to seize Washington. To carry out the dissembling strategy, Lee as early as April instructed Stonewall Jackson to initiate action against Banks . . . the beginning, in fact, of Jackson's famous Valley campaign.

The idea was to persuade Lincoln to keep McDowell's force near Fredericksburg free to defend Washington, if necessary, rather than converge on Richmond together with McClellan. As noted by University of Virginia history professor Richard Heath Dabney in the *Richmond* magazine of June 1932, Lee outlined further steps for Jackson to take, "always leaving the details to Jackson, while making it plain that his aim should always be to scare Lincoln into keeping McDowell away from Richmond until Lee was ready to summon Jackson himself to join the army there and help to crush McClellan."

By late May, McClellan at last was moving up the peninsula with "high hopes of taking the city and ending the war." In the Shenandoah Valley, however, Jackson defeated Banks at Winchester and appeared poised for an attack on Washington itself. McDowell of course was held in place as Secretary of War Edwin Stanton frantically wired every state still in the Union: "Send forward all the troops you can, immediately. Banks completely routed. Intelligence from various quarters leaves no doubt that the enemy, in great force, are advancing on Washington."

With Banks sent scurrying across the Potomac, Jackson turned southward, "baffling the attempts of Fremont from the west and of [James] Shields from the east to entrap him." Jackson now was "in position to obey further orders when the time should come."

Soon after May 31, the time would come. With McClellan's command split by a rain-swollen Chickahominy River just to the east of Richmond, General Johnston "attempted, at Seven Pines, to crush McClellan's left wing." The tactic was not entirely successful, and Johnston suffered his incapacitating wound. As a result, "on June 1, Lee was put in his place, and from now on he controlled both the tactics and the strategy of the army."

Appearing to dispatch troops to Jackson's side in the Valley, Lee still kept McDowell at bay . . . still in case of attack on Washington. "But, as McClellan's army had been much strengthened from other sources, Lee ordered Jackson, on June 17, to join him before McClellan could receive further reinforcements. With such skill did Jackson conceal his departure from the Valley that not till he had joined Lee and the orders for battle had been issued did Secretary Stanton discover the true state of the case."

Overall result: "[W]hen Jackson was actually bringing up 18,500 men to Lee's aid, Fremont, Banks and McDowell were keeping 70,000 men away from the scene to guard against an imaginary march upon Washington." In the aftermath, true, Lee did not absolutely crush McClellan's force as hoped, "but he did drive him from the Peninsula and defer the capture of Richmond for three years."

So much also for the critics who had taken in recent months to calling the headquarters general "Granny" Lee.

1863

To Robert E. Lee, the loss of the erstwhile Stonewall Jackson at Chancellorsville, due to terribly mistaken friendly fire in the dark, was so grievous it meant the loss of "my good right arm."

And then, almost precisely coincident with the July 4 celebration of American independence, came the debacle that was Gettysburg. What severe casualties on both sides. What a blow to the Southern cause. What . . . *a terrible mistake?* What could General Lee say; what was his reaction? "Lee's countenance," said a visiting English colonel, Arthur Freemantle, "did not give signs of the slightest disappointment, care, or annoyance, but preserved the utmost placidity and cheerfulness. He rode slowly to and fro, saying in his grave, kindly voice to the men, 'All this will come right in the end; we'll talk it over hereafter; but in the meantime all good men must rally. We want all true and good men now.' They did rally, and even some of the wounded returned with cheers for their beloved commander."

As a personal aside to Freemantle alone, however: "This has been a sad day to us, Colonel; but we can't expect always to have victory." (Chancellorsville, the most recent big battle, *had* been a major victory for Lee and his Army of Northern Virginia.)

To an obviously upset general standing by, so overburdened with emotion, he was "scarcely able to articulate," Lee "cheerfully" said, "Never mind, General; all this has been my fault. It is I that have lost this fight, and you must help me out of it the best way you can."

If there were any faults to find in Lee, the "perfect gentleman," a "thorough soldier," "the handsomest man, of his age, I ever saw," said Freemantle also, they arose "from his excessive amiability."

1864

A low, low point for Robert E. Lee and so many around him. His "right arm," Stonewall Jackson, already was gone. Gettysburg and its horrifying Pickett's Charge already were history; in the west, Vicksburg also had been lost. His son Rooney was badly wounded at Brandy Station and then had been taken captive by a Union raiding party. Rooney's wife (and a child) recently had died. And everywhere he turned, virtually at every corner, the Confederate house noticeably was becoming a shambles. And so, Robert E. Lee bristled angrily when South Carolina's Gen. Wade Hampton approached one day with the relatively minor complaint that Jeb Stuart had placed one of Hampton's brigades under Fitzhugh Lee's command. To which the obviously strained Lee curtly said: "I would not care if you went back to South Carolina with your whole division." Reporting the incident in her famous *A Diary from Dixie*, Mary Boykin Chesnut said the startled Hampton, invariably a fine and astute subordinate, found Lee's manner "mortifying." Chesnut then added, "It seems that General Lee has no patience with any personal complaints or grievances. He is all for the cause and cannot bear officers to come to him with such matters as Wade Hampton had come to him about."

1865

After Appomattox, after weeks of rest, of some recuperation—of some considerable soul-searching as well, no doubt—he rode into Lexington one autumn day in a military coat stripped of buttons and insignia to take over the presidency of tiny Washington College. "He had not come because of a tempting offer, for the fortunes of the little college had never been at so low an ebb," wrote Julia Davis in her history, *The Shenandoah*. "He had come to discharge a responsibility which his conscience laid upon him." He hoped to set an example for his fallen South, to exemplify that life must go on even after defeat, that both he and his former soldiery must go forward in peace. From Lexington, he wrote to wife Mary, "I pray I may be spared to accomplish something for the benefit of mankind and the honor of God."

After chapel services on the small college campus one morning, the school's new president told a woman concerned at his expression of distress that he had been pondering . . .

"I was thinking, madam, of my responsibility to God for all of these young men."

While he may have meant all the young men lost under his leadership during the war, he now had an entirely new challenge before him . . . also involving young men. Instead of trying to win an unwinnable war, he now was to regird a little-known college so destitute it boasted only three faculty members and fifty students. It could pay him a mere $1,500 a year (and provide an on-campus house), but only if enough students would now enroll to wipe out the school's debt of $4,000.

1865–70

During the period of Reconstruction, as whites and formerly enslaved blacks, as Northerners and Southerners, all readjusted to the new order of things—and to each other—often with blatantly unfair treatment, sometimes with violence, frequently with theft and vandalism, wrote Julia Davis also, "General Lee at Lexington stood like a beacon by which men could steer. If he felt regret or sadness, he did not utter it; if he felt critical of the new authorities, he did not say so."

Taking his arthritic wife, Mary, to the spas at White Sulphur Springs in the summertime, he hoped to come and go unnoticed, "but when he first entered the hotel dining room the entire company rose in silent respect."

When a party of Northerners, including the wartime governor of Pennsylvania, was shunned at the springs, Lee insisted on going forward to welcome them. A young lady volunteering to cross the ballroom with him asked, "But, General Lee, did you never feel resentment towards the North?"

"The general stopped under the crystal chandelier. 'I believe I may say, speaking as in the presence of God, that I have never known one moment of bitterness or resentment.'"

To the parents entrusting the education of their sons to him, he said: "Remember that we form one country now. Abandon all local animosities, and make your sons Americans."

1870

For five years in Lexington, noted Davis, the educator Robert E. Lee "guided, built, encouraged, led—and then death came for him, not stealthily, or suddenly but as a last antagonist whom an old soldier might calmly face."

He was just home one evening from a vestry meeting. He stood to "say grace before tea." Unable to speak, he sank down into his chair. "Afterwards he lay quietly in bed for two weeks, perfectly conscious and apparently in no pain, rarely speaking, never complaining."

Nor fighting the coming event.

At the last, though, he was back in the terrible war he wished all others to put behind them. Perhaps he, of all people, could not possibly succeed in that goal.

"Strike the tents," he said at the end. And then, thinking of one of his two generals named Hill: "Tell Hill he must come up."

Later, but not much later, little Washington College would become Washington *and Lee* University.

1 8 6 9
Waterproof Carpetbags for Sale

When Republican A. Linwood Holton of Big Stone Gap campaigned for governor of Virginia in 1969, and won, he was in line to become the first Republican governor of traditionally Democratic Virginia since, since . . . well, since who or when, exactly?

Few asking that question were prepared to learn that the Virginia-born Holton's Republican antecedent was a mustachioed, white-maned "law and order" apostle from New York by the name of Gilbert C. Walker. But, yes, that really was one long-forgotten outcome exactly one hundred years earlier of the turbulent, confused days following Robert E. Lee's surrender at Appomattox, and then the Lincoln assassination—days of bitter feelings, bitter political party splits . . . days when it often was unclear who represented what faction.

A time of coalitions, compromises, even secret Republican seeding among newly freed slaves, the post–Civil War period produced a dizzying assortment of True Republicans, Radical Republicans, Conservatives fronting for traditional Democrats, Freedman's Bureau agents, Funders and Readjusters arguing over Virginia's staggering pre–Civil War debt, aristocratic Bourbons, carpetbaggers, scalawags, and others.

By most standards, however, it appears that Walker, a financier and banker from New York, qualified as Virginia's last Republican governor before Holton took office in January 1970. But even that supposition demands qualification. A True Republican who ran with the support of one-time (and future) Democrats called Conservatives, Walker overcame Radical Republican opposition (which included a black candidate for lieutenant governor) to win election in 1869, a hundred years before Holton's own watershed election victory as a modern Republican.

Adding to the confusion, the historians variously have pronounced Walker effective or not-so-effective as governor, while painting him as both liberal and conservative, the latter in view of his Conservative support and despite (or because of) the early Republican's later appearance in Congress . . . as a *Democrat*. One Virginia biographical tome, recalling his strong "law and order" stand and his encouragement of Virginia's first public schools, gives him the title of "Political Savior of Virginia," and claims that he was the most popular man in Virginia (*a New Yorker?!*) when he took office. In other accounts, by contrast, Walker is depicted as ineffectual, a rumored dissipate who was suspected of profiting financially from his political power.

Typically, Thomas Jefferson Wertenbaker's history of Norfolk (*Norfolk: Historic Southern Port*) and Virginius Dabney's broader history of Virginia (*Virginia: The New Dominion*) offer different views of Walker and his legacy. A native of Binghamton, New York, Walker had moved to Federal-occupied Norfolk during the Civil War. After that, Wertenbaker and Dabney agree, he developed a reputation as a solid, respected banker. Soon, as a candidate for governor in 1869, he appealed to moderate to conservative whites—and a few blacks—as their best hope of defeating an amalgam of Radical Republicans, militant blacks, alleged carpetbaggers, scalawags, and the like. It did Walker no harm to have the support of Confederate Gen. William "Billy" Mahone, the bantam-sized hero of the battle of the Crater at Petersburg.

When Walker won the gubernatorial election of 1869, a great sigh of relief swept the ranks of Virginia whites who had gone through four years of ruinous war, followed by four years of punitive Reconstruction. More visibly, when this "fine figure of a man six feet in height, the picture of health and vigor," appeared on the balcony of a Norfolk hotel, his July 6 election victory fresh in hand, wrote Wertenbaker, he was greeted with "deafening" cheers. He then proceeded to congratulate Virginia "upon her deliverance from 'vampires and harpies,' and promised an honest, capable administration."

For this Yankee, a Republican at that, a local band then, on the heels of the Civil War, struck up *"Dixie"*!

The next day, added Virginius Dabney, the late Pulitzer Prize-winning editor of the *Richmond Times-Dispatch,* "Walker traveled to Richmond and was met at the station by a huge throng, which followed him to the Spotswood Hotel. He spoke to massed thousands from the balcony."

Making his election victory all the sweeter, the coalition behind Walker produced an "overwhelmingly" Conservative General Assembly to work with the new governor, wrote Dabney. "It was a shattering defeat for the Radicals, and for their scalawag and carpetbag cohorts"—so shattering, added Dabney, that "a waggish Charlottesville merchant announced a sale of waterproof carpetbags for anyone crossing the Potomac going north."

The legislature elected with Walker got down to serious business in October 1869, taking up and quickly approving ratification of the Fourteenth and Fifteenth Amendments to the U.S. Constitution, which guaranteed former slaves and blacks in general their right to vote (males only, that is) and equal protection under the law. "Ratification of the amendments," wrote Dabney, "signalized the end of reconstruction, insofar as Virginia was concerned."

While Federal troops would remain in some states of the Deep South until 1877, Dabney added, Virginia was able to bid "a glad farewell" to its designation as "Military District Number One" in

January 1870. "The Federal garrison was withdrawn and the Commonwealth's representatives were permitted to take their seats in the U.S.
Senate and House. Governor Gilbert C. Walker and his government
were given complete control of the state."

But now Governor Walker supported a bill that would allow scattered private purchase of the state's pre–Civil War railroad investments,
an anathema to railroad entrepreneur Mahone. Walker raised the hack-
les of still other key backers by his support for the so-called Funding
Act, which required the state to stand behind its prewar loans that
financed construction of essential facilities such as canals, turnpikes,
and railroads. "By 1870," wrote Dabney, "the debt had mounted to
$45 million. Governor Walker and leaders of like mind in the legisla-
ture succeeded in ramming through the Funding Act, whereby Virginia would pay off two-thirds of the debt. The remaining one-third
would be assumed, it was hoped, by West Virginia."

All very honorable, but the sums needed to pay off the debt left
little money for other government expenses. "The public schools, in
particular, were left with wholly inadequate financial resources." And
the specter of staggering debt set the stage for a string of debt-wary
conservative Democrats, the twentieth century's Harry F. Byrd chief
among them, who would succeed Gilbert Walker, one after the other,
until his GOP descendant Linwood Holton came along in 1969.

It was only in a constitutional revision session of the General
Assembly in the 1960s that the ruling Democrats agreed to abandon
the Old Dominion's by then long-held "pay as you go" fiscal policy and
chart a new course of occasional bonded indebtedness for capital
needs. Significantly, it was a former Byrd lieutenant, Governor Mills E.
Godwin Jr., who called the special session and gave impetus to the
major change in policy—not so incidentally, Godwin would serve a
second term as a twentieth-century governor, this time shedding his
Democratic Party heritage to take on a Republican mantle instead.

Back in the nineteenth century, meanwhile, the voting public had
reacted negatively to the actions of the General Assembly that passed
the Funding Act, defeating all but 26 of the 132 members of the
House of Delegates in the next legislative elections. The newly constituted assembly then repealed the Funding Act, but Governor Walker
vetoed the repeal, and the act stood . . . for the time being.

The debt argument continued, with the less-affluent citizenry of
western and southwestern Virginia opposing the Funding Act and the

more affluent, eastern Virginians supporting it, if only out of "honor." The latter, noted Dabney, "believed that the Old Dominion was obligated to pay every cent of the debt incurred before the war, plus interest, although they felt West Virginia should assume its rightful share."

Opponents pointed out the "colossal and irreparable losses" most citizens had suffered during the war and argued it was unfair for them to carry the burden of payment on bonds largely held by English and Northern investors. After all, they argued, the state's "economy had been wrecked, its currency rendered worthless, and its countryside devastated by the very people to whom a large percentage of the debt was owed."

Said Dabney also: "Most of those who took this view were not asking for repudiation of the debt, but for a reasonable reduction."

As an advocate of the opposite view (and the sale of the railroad securities), Walker became the darling of Virginia's "ultraconservatives or 'Bourbons,'" explained Dabney. But he had lost the favor of Billy Mahone, a growing political power in postbellum Virginia. Walker now saw his influence begin to wane. And in the end, Dabney asserted, even if Walker's role in saving Virginia from the Radicals in 1869 had been "of far reaching importance, some of his major policies as governor were highly debatable, and his personal financial operations were suspect."

As Virginia next reverted to form and chose a wounded war veteran, Gen. James Lawson Kemper of Madison County, to be the next governor, Walker served two terms in the U.S. House—as a Conservative-backed Democrat from the Richmond area—then turned north for a permanent return to his old hometown of Binghamton. Meanwhile, it was a Republican (with black support) who went down to defeat in the gubernatorial race of 1873, setting a trend to last until Linwood Holton came along and broke the political mold a century later.

★

1 8 7 3
Confederate Veterans to the Fore

★

After the passing of the tall New Yorker Gilbert C. Walker as governor, a parade of colorful, strictly homegrown personalities would assume political leadership roles in post–Civil War Virginia—many of them, unsurprisingly, with credentials as Confederate war veterans.

First among them was Governor James Lawson Kemper, who had paid his political dues as Speaker of the Virginia House before the Civil War. While a Confederate general, he had been badly wounded in Pickett's Charge at Gettysburg, and even now, as governor, he often was made understandably irritable from pain caused by an inoperable Union minié ball lodged at the base of his spine.

As for the issues before him in the 1870s, wrote Virginius Dabney in his history of Virginia, Governor Kemper was "more fair minded and objective on the race question than most public men of his day, and while repudiating all notions of 'social equality' for blacks, he stood firmly for their equality before the law."

He showed the courage of his convictions early in his term as governor by vetoing a bill that would have overridden recent elections in Petersburg that placed black candidates in a number of city posts. Not long after, he also insisted that black marching units could appear at the unveiling of a statue of Stonewall Jackson in Capitol Square. Kemper at the same time brushed aside the objections of the fire-eating Gen. Jubal Early and pleaded with him to stay away. As events turned out, Early came, and the black marching units, supposedly due to a scheduling conflict, did not.

On the thorny issue of the Funding Act, Kemper said he would like to see the debt reduced (read here: readjusted), but when the General Assembly took no such action, he felt legally obliged to stand behind payment of state funds to the bondholders rather than divert the money to the underfunded public schools.

With the debt controversy still very much alive, Kemper was followed in office by the "one-armed hero of the Shenandoah Valley," former Confederate Col. Frederick W. M. Holliday of Winchester, who had lost his arm at the battle of Cedar Mountain. Backed by Billy Mahone, as was Kemper, Holliday won election in 1877 without benefit of a single campaign speech, it seems. When the General Assembly then offered him the chance to make history by signing a debt readjustment bill into law, however, Holliday surprised many—and infuriated Malone—by vetoing the bill.

Holliday argued that "our fathers did not need free schools," and to have them now would be a "luxury" that should be funded only by those using them.

Meanwhile, the real and growing power among all the postwar politicians was the diminutive, fastidiously dressing former Gen. Billy Mahone, who, as leader of the emergent Readjusters, wanted to pare down the huge Virginia debt . . . who would go to the U.S. Senate in 1881 as neither Republican nor Democrat, but as a Readjuster. Meanwhile, his fellow Readjusters would take control of the General Assembly and indeed would chop down the $45 million debt to $21 million, with West Virginia still expected to pay off a third.

The debt's readjustment downward came from legislation offered by H. H. Riddleberger of the Shenandoah Valley (himself a future U.S. senator), with the revised bonds to become known as "Riddlebergers."

But it was Mahone who held sway at the controls of a statewide political machine that counted upon major black support and usually was aligned against the political interests of the aristocratic "Bourbons," or Conservatives, who eventually became Democrats by name. And it was the headstrong Mahone, typically, who stirred a political firestorm when he announced he would serve in the U.S. Senate as a Republican.

"This loudly denounced apostasy on the part of Malone was one of the most controversial events of the era," wrote Dabney while also pointing out the Senate was evenly split between Democrats and Republicans when Mahone came to claim his newly won seat. The balance of power of course shifted to the Republicans once Mahone announced that he would align himself with the Republicans in the Senate. In the storm that followed, predictably, the Funders of Virginia called him "a traitor to his state, his section, and his party." But the fact was, Mahone guaranteed himself choice committee assignments and his state beneficial attentions from the majority dominating Congress.

Not that he was so pure in motive, cautioned Dabney. "He was anxious to build a machine that would maintain a steely grip on the state for an indefinite period. His political methods, furthermore, were slippery. In addition, he became increasingly arrogant and dictatorial." Still, "Mahoneism" remained a potent political force in Virginia until the former Conservatives—now once again Democrats—gained control of the General Assembly in the elections of 1883 and then began to undermine Mahone's power. That would be a long process, but he finally was ousted as senator in 1886 as Robert E. Lee's nephew, Fitzhugh Lee, also a Confederate veteran, took office as governor.

With fellow Readjuster Riddleberger also repudiated in the Senate election of 1888, "the Democrats held the governorship, large majorities in the General Assembly, both seats in the U.S. Senate and most of those in Congress," noted Dabney. "Enclaves of Republican strength would remain in southwest Virginia, the Shenandoah Valley, and a few other areas of more limited extent, but the Democrats would retain control of the state government, the legislature, and both Senate seats for more than three quarters of a century." Further, the black vote no longer was "solidly" with the one-time Readjusters-now-Republicans.

Still, Mahone, the son of a Southampton County tavern keeper, was not yet ready to slip away without one more fight. Running for governor in 1889, he kept most of the black vote, but former allies and leaders of his fellow white Republicans—like Mahone, no longer Readjusters— were split over his candidacy. His loss in the gubernatorial election was such a "severe reverse for the Republican party" that "it would be generations before the party regained its influence in Virginia."

When Mahone died in 1895, just six years later, he unfortunately would be recalled by many of his contemporaries as a feisty, often difficult autocrat, but the fact is, he left behind certain very positive legacies. "There would never again be the widespread indifference to the public schools that existed when the little general came upon the scene a few years after the Civil War," wrote Dabney from his perspective as a long-time student of Virginia politics. "Nor would Virginia ever again be rent asunder in controversies over the public debt, with essential services shunted aside while lawmakers, public officials, and business leaders wrangled over the best means of dealing with the problem."

Meanwhile, the U.S. Supreme Court not only approved the Riddle-berger reduction of the Virginia debt, but also, as late as 1918, ruled that West Virginia was responsible for paying off a third of the antebellum debt. It took West Virginia until 1939 to pay off its $14 million share.

1 8 9 0
Dinner Party for "Such a Rebel"

Now picture this: former President Grover Cleveland, the writer Mark Twain, and former Union Gens. Daniel Sickles and William Tecumseh

Sherman, all milling around at a formal dinner held in New York City late in the nineteenth century to honor one Roger Pryor, himself a former general—*Confederate* general, that is.

Confederate general voluntarily turned private, that is.

Former U.S. House member and one-time Confederate congressman, it also seems. And now, late in the nineteenth century, a justice of the New York State Supreme Court.

There's got to be a story in all that . . . and there is.

It almost ended, however, barely before it started—the day in April 1861 when Roger Pryor picked up a container at Fort Sumter, took a swallow . . . and only then learned it wasn't water he had gulped down, but potentially deadly iodide of potassium.

The stomach-pumping that followed was an embarrassment for the fiery Secessionist from Petersburg, Virginia, who had been sent out to the island fortress in Charleston Harbor to help negotiate the formal surrender of the Federal bastion, but he did survive.

As time and the war wore on, the congressman-now-turned-officer also survived honorable and brave action in the battle of Williamsburg and the Seven Days' campaign outside Richmond. He then fought at Second Manassas and at bloody Antietam in Maryland. Well connected socially, it might also be mentioned, he had been offered the "honor" of firing the first shot at Fort Sumter while serving as a volunteer aide to Gen. Pierre G. T. Beauregard at Charleston, but declined. Then, too, after the battle of Williamsburg, he and his wife, Sara Rice Pryor, learned from the highest authority in the Confederacy of his promotion from colonel to brigadier general.

The way she told the story, they were at a reception in Richmond's first-class Spotswood Hotel, an affair also attended by Confederate President Jefferson Davis and his wife, Varina. A crowd gathered to honor Pryor for his performance at Williamsburg, Sara Pryor wrote, was shouting for her husband to come out and make a speech. Said she also:

"This was very embarrassing and he fled to a corner of the drawing room and hid behind a screen of plants. I was standing next to the President [Davis], trying to hold his attention by remarks on the weather and kindred subjects of a thrilling nature, when a voice from the street called out: 'Pryor! *General* Pryor!' I could endure the suspense no longer, and asked tremblingly, 'Is it true, Mr. President?' Mr. Davis looked at me with a benevolent smile and said, 'I have no reason to doubt it, madam, except that I saw it this morning in the papers.'"

Meanwhile, with the uncharacteristically bashful Pryor still among the plants, the Confederate president's wife, Varina Davis, now chipped in with: "What are you doing lying there *perdu* [lost] behind the geraniums? Come out and take your honors."

Another moment that Pryor's wife would recall, also from their wartime sojourn in Richmond, came at the end of the Seven Days' campaign, during which *General* Pryor had fought for days on end. With Union Gen. George B. McClellan's army finally withdrawing, Sara Pryor wrote, "A gray, haggard, dust-covered soldier entered my room, and throwing himself upon the couch, gave way to the anguish of his heart—'My men! My men! They are almost all dead!'"

Months, later, though, after Manassas II, after Antietam, the anguish was over being relegated to foraging duty in southeastern Virginia, far from the great events of the war. Sara Pryor put on a brave face about his mission there, saying he and his men were arrayed "in front of a large Federal force to keep it in check while the wagon trains sent off corn and bacon for Lee's army." Itching for *real* action, however, her husband in late 1863 made the extraordinary decision to resign as general and join Maj. Gen. Fitzhugh Lee's cavalry as an ordinary private.

"Fitz" Lee, Robert E.'s nephew, greeted Pryor in hearty fashion. "Honorable, General, or Mr.," he wrote in a welcoming note. "How should I address you? Damn it, there's no difference! Come up to see me. Whilst I regret the causes that induced you to resign your position, I am glad that the country has not lost your active services, and that your choice to serve her has been cast in one of my regiments."

As the war now moved on to the months-long siege of Petersburg, *Private* Pryor's hometown, he became a highly useful courier and scout for various Confederate generals, up to and including Robert E. Lee.

Trapped in Petersburg along with her husband and Lee's crumbling army, Sara Pryor was stunned to learn one day in November 1864 that her husband had been captured and was being held as a prisoner of war. After a general tapped on her door with the grim news, there came a second officer . . . from Robert E. Lee's own staff.

"Madame," he said, "General Lee sends you his affectionate sympathies."

She glanced out the nearest window. "I saw General Lee on his horse, Traveller, standing at the well. He waited until his messenger returned—I was too overcome to speak—and then rode slowly towards the lines."

Fortunately, Roger Pryor was paroled and returned home unharmed. But then, with the war ending in the spring of 1865, Roger Pryor, like many another Southerner, was left financially ruined. Instead of remaining in Virginia, however, he headed north, to New York City, where he painstakingly began to build a law practice. Eventually able to have his family join him there, he in time became, first, chief judge of the New York Court of Common Pleas, and next, a justice on the New York State Supreme Court.

As Sara later wrote, "The war had left him with nothing but a ragged uniform, his sword, a wife, and seven children—his health, his occupation, his place in the world, gone; his friends and comrades slain in battle; his Southern home impoverished and desolate."

That he "conquered" all such setbacks, she added, "is a striking illustration of the possibilities afforded by our country; where not only can the impoverished refugee from other lands find fortune and happiness, but where her own sons, prostrate and ruined after a dreadful fratricidal strife, can bind their wounds, take up their lives again, and finally win reward for their labors."

Still, it took a remarkable man to overcome so much, to rise to such heights in the realm of his one-time foes, to win such respect and even affection among his former enemies that at a dinner in his honor in 1890, one such former adversary, William Tecumseh Sherman, would come along, throw his hand on Pryor's shoulder, and say, "We would have done all this for him long ago, but he had to be such a rebel!"

1899
Century of Sorrows

For Richmond, capital of Virginia, capital of the Confederacy, the nineteenth century often seemed a long string of disasters or near disasters, beginning with the specter of a widespread slave revolt in 1800, moving on to the murder of the widely revered George Wythe in 1806, and then by no means ending with the collapse of the Confederacy and occupation by the Union army in 1865. Not at all . . . still to come after that disaster was the physical collapse of the visitors' gallery in the House of Delegates with scores killed and injured.

Flood, fire, even war, you name it . . . Richmond in the nineteenth century went through just about every kind of calamity conceivable except for severe earthquake or widespread pestilence.

It was only pure chance, in the form of a soaking thunderstorm, that quelled Gabriel's Insurrection of 1800, just in time to avoid a major bloodletting among both whites and blacks, to no one's advantage. As it was, the discovery of the slave conspiracy led to tight restrictions on the state's slave population in general (see pages 115–21).

Another shock for the city and state was the murder by arsenic poisoning of the great law professor George Wythe in Richmond in 1806 by his nephew (see pages 140–43).

Just five years later, Richmond was left reeling by a calamitous theater fire that killed U.S. Senator Abraham B. Venable, Governor George W. Smith, and seventy other persons the day after Christmas, 1811. Either the scenery caught fire or a recently moved chandelier caused the blaze. Either way, Governor Smith apparently was overcome after dashing back into the building in an effort to rescue others. "The victims were buried in a common crypt at the very spot where the theater stood," recalled Randy Fitzgerald in the *Richmond Times-Dispatch* of October 24, 2001. Architect Robert Mill's Monumental Church was built at the site, "and you will find its columns on the left side of Broad Street, in the midst of the MCV [Medical College of Virginia] buildings, in the block before the street is intersected by I-95."

A list of the dead can be seen at the doorway; the crypt is in the church basement.

As always is the case, though, life went on, but with fire an ever-present danger. Fire in fact struck again in 1853, destroying the Virginia Woolen Mills, damaging Haxall Mills, and costing four hundred workers their jobs. Fire also hit the state penitentiary . . . but fortunately no one was killed or injured. In 1855, however, an explosion in the Pump Shaft coal mine in outlying Midlothian killed fifty-five men. Another twenty had been killed in a Midlothian coal mine just the year before. Mother Nature, rather than man's mechanical means, then took a hand in January 1857—several persons died as a snowstorm stilled outdoor activity with twelve-foot drifts.

Then, from spring of 1861 to spring of 1865, came the local, state, and national disaster known today as the Civil War. As the casualties mounted, wagon trains carrying the wounded filled Richmond's streets. Holding eight to ten thousand patients at its peak (and serving seventy-six thousand in all), the largest military hospital known in the history of mankind was developed on Chimborazo Hill. Long parades of mourners for the dead also filed through the streets. Among the most notable casualties of the war, Jeb Stuart died of his wounds in a Richmond home. Another emotional shock came when little Joe Davis, the five-year-old son of Confederate President Jefferson Davis and his wife, Varina, fell to his death from an open porch at the Confederate White House. Earlier, Gen. James Longstreet was called back from the front as disease, in the form of scarlet fever, struck his four children and killed three of them.

At other times, notably during the Seven Days' battles of 1862, the war crept right up to Richmond's doorstep . . . and the wounded poured in. After the battle of the Seven Pines (Fair Oaks) early that June, wrote the teenage diarist Constance Cary, "ambulances, litters, carts, every vehicle that the city could produce went and came with a ghastly burden; those who could walk limped painfully home, in some cases so black with gunpowder they passed unrecognized." The city streets, she added, "were one vast hospital."

It was a time when city residents repeatedly heard the "wailing dirge of a military band preceding a soldier's funeral." Said she also: "One could not number those sad pageants: the coffin crowned with cap and sword and gloves; the riderless horse following with empty boots fixed in the stirrups."

Even when the battles were far away, it was a city in constant turmoil, under emotional siege, a city of visiting Confederate heroes; a city one moment of high hopes and the next, of dashed hopes, followed by more of the funeral dirges and riderless horses; a city of escaping slaves and shrinking supplies of luxury goods, even basic foodstuffs. And the wounded, always the wounded.

The pain and suffering would end with a final burst of agony in early April 1865 as the Confederate government fled Richmond just days before Lee's surrender at Appomattox, as fires set by the fleeing Confederate forces burned through downtown Richmond, and as the dread Yankees filed in, extinguished the fires, and gradually restored order, albeit as an unwelcome occupying army.

Hardly had the streets been cleaned than double, triple, even quadruple disaster struck again . . . and all in the single year of 1870. As one event sufficient to cast a pall all by itself, the venerated Robert E. Lee died in 1870. Then, too, fire hit the Spotswood Hotel at Eighth and Main, a landmark often mentioned in Civil War histories and diaries. Eight killed. And further, in a year previously marked by drought, the worst flooding of the James River since 1771 destroyed twenty homes, covered low-lying areas, made a wreck of Mayo's Bridge, knocked out the gas- and waterworks, and killed many.

What else could go wrong? Richmonders found out at 11 A.M. on Wednesday, April 27. At the state capitol, the gallery of the original House of Delegates chamber was packed with spectators expecting a dramatic legal battle to unfold in a special session of the State Supreme Court being held in the chamber below. That third-floor area of Jefferson's capitol itself was jammed by participants and more onlookers. At issue in these last days of Reconstruction were the competing claims of two men to the post of city mayor. One, newspaper publisher Henry K. Ellyson, co-owner of the *Richmond Dispatch*, had been elected by a city council appointed, in turn, by the General Assembly. But refusing to bow out was the mayor appointed earlier during the Federal occupation of Richmond.

Before the high court could convene, however, a girder "gave way with an awful crash," reported Ellyson's own *Dispatch*, "and precipitated the spectators who were in the gallery of the court-room to the main floor, and the additional weight in one single moment's time crushing the court-room through."

As the *Dispatch* added in graphic terms, "The mass of human beings who were in attendance were sent, mingled with the bricks, mortar, splinters, beams, iron bars, desks, and chairs, to the floor of the House of Delegates, and in a second more, fifty-five souls were launched into eternity."

The final toll that emerged actually was 62 killed and 251 injured. As Tom Campbell reported in the *Times-Dispatch* of October 15, 2000, the nineteenth-century *Dispatch* in effect blamed "outdated construction methods" conceived and implemented "before anyone thought so many people would ever assemble there at one time." The collapse, it also turned out, did *not* start with the gallery but rather beneath the third-floor legislative chamber itself. "The main wooden girder under the courtroom had snapped in the middle, causing the floor to buckle and leaving the gallery suddenly unsupported," added Campbell. "Many survived the fall but smothered under the bodies of other victims."

The same legislative chamber rather famously had been turned into a courtroom, *federal* this time, early in the century for the treason trial of Aaron Burr, vice president during Thomas Jefferson's first term as president (1801–5), with Chief Justice John Marshall presiding. Here, too, Robert E. Lee was welcomed and sworn in as commander of Virginia forces in the first days of the Civil War.

Still ahead for the shaken city in the next few years after the capitol disaster were even more troubles. In 1872 and 1873, reported Campbell also, several workers were killed "in collapses during the 22-month construction of [a] Chesapeake and Ohio Railway tunnel under Church Hill." In just one cave-in, he added, a half dozen houses were "swallowed." Included were the study and kitchen of the rectory at historic St. John's Church, where Patrick Henry delivered his famous "Give me liberty or give me death!" speech.

In 1875, an earthquake physically shook the city "with severe shocks of 20 to 30 seconds each," but only as an event frightening city residents and visitors.

Even now, the century of disasters wasn't quite through with Richmond yet. In 1877, a James River flood just as bad as the flood of 1870 swept through town, again wrecking Mayo's Bridge. In 1882, thirty-two or more miners were killed "in explosion, fire in [the] Grove Shaft coal mine in Midlothian." This, fortunately, would be the last of the deadly explosions that had plagued the Midlothian mines since 1816.

In town that same year, fire destroyed a "half-dozen factories and the Richmond and Petersburg Railroad Bridge over the James River."

Aside from physical disaster, meanwhile, Richmonders and their fellow Virginians, their countrymen as well, could hardly forget that the same nineteenth century had been ushered in on the heels of the shock created by George Washington's death in December 1799. Still to come in the century's early years, predictably but with attendant sadness, would be the deaths of Washington's fellow Virginians, Founding Fathers, and early presidents—Thomas Jefferson, James Madison, and James Monroe. Together with Washington, they constituted one-half of Virginia's proud claim to furnishing the nation an unequaled eight presidents in all. And, further, their deaths marked an end to the glorious eighteenth-century era in which Virginians led the way in proclaiming and winning independence from Great Britain and then establishing a democratic republic unequaled in world history for its combination of lasting stability and guarantees of individual liberty for all.

☆ Part 4 ☆
Twentieth Century

Babes in Incubators

What would Capt. John Smith and company have thought? A wild animal show. Monstrous, metal-clad, and steam-driven warships standing just offshore. A Wild West show. Even a live-babies-in-incubators show!

All this, and more, a lot more, made up the Jamestown Exposition of 1907 in celebration of Jamestown's three-hundredth anniversary. And surely, the redoubtable Captain Smith and his contemporaries of 1607 would have been floored to see what three hundred years had wrought in the virgin land they first settled. As just one item, the great naval fleet assembled in honor of the anniversary would have been mind-boggling to any Englishman of Captain Smith's era.

The same seventeenth-century Englishman would have been equally astonished by some of the more zany elements of the twentieth-century Old Dominion's response to the historical milestone. The building housing babes in incubators, for instance, generated more return visits than any other enclosed exhibit, according to the Norfolk Public Library System. Visitors fascinated by live babies in incubators "returned to the exhibit repeatedly in order to watch tiny, premature infants from the local area thrive and become healthy babies."

And, yes, it all did take place in Norfolk, after a strong lobbying effort at the General Assembly quashed Richmond's aspirations to be home for a grand and ambitious three-hundredth birthday celebration.

The Jamestown Exposition that emerged on isolated Sewells Point on the outskirts of Norfolk was ambitious in concept and often grand in execution. Starting from scratch, the promoters created a miniature city of buildings representing various states, offering amusements, or serving educational purposes. Among the latter was the Negro Building, created by and for the black community of Virginia to show off the advances of blacks in America since the first African Americans arrived on U.S. shores in 1619—at Jamestown, of course. The great educator Booker T. Washington, born a slave in Virginia before the Civil War, spoke at the building on "Negro Day" at the exposition.

John Smith would have been stunned, since he had returned to England before the first blacks arrived in America. At the same time, the proud and unabashed use of the term "Negro" was perfectly ordinary and acceptable in 1907 but would be startling and unacceptable to many among us today in the twenty-first century.

Whatever the terminology in use at a given time, the large columned structure had a short history of its own. "The building was designed by W. Sydney Pittman, a graduate of Tuskegee and Drexel Institutes," says the library system's online presentation. "The building was erected under the auspices of the United States Government, and Mr. Pittman was the first African American whose design had ever been accepted by the government."

Meanwhile, the "most successful" of the exposition exhibits was the building marked, "Battle of the *Merrimac* and *Monitor.*" Located on the exposition's "Warpath" midway, "Battle" offered a replay of history's first battle of ironclads, which took place in nearby Hampton Roads during the Civil War. "On several days, the box office receipts at this amusement exceeded those of the Exposition gate," says the library site. Even though nearly three million persons visited the mile-long exposition frontage at Sewells Point, incidentally, the overall "gate" was a disappointment to exposition officials.

Among the exposition's other standing exhibits was an exhibit on the San Francisco earthquake and fire of the year before 1907. This simulation of that city's utter destruction was "reproduced with astonishing accuracy," noted the public library system in its online presentation (http://www.npl.lib.va.us/sgm/oldlobby/archives/james.html). Still another exposition attraction of great interest was a ground-level concrete relief map of the Panama Canal forty yards in length and twenty yards in width. Tiny ships, inches in size, "cruised" the canal.

This, too, would have been a surprise to John Smith and his crowd.

Perhaps more understandable to them would have been the "children's school farm," a concept first established in New York City in the late 1800s. Here, at the exposition, each of sixty children from Norfolk, Portsmouth, and Newport News "was given a 4 x 12-foot plot of land entirely under his or her charge, from the planting to the harvesting."

Even more happily for John Smith, the Smithsonian Institution had weighed in with a "tableau of twenty-two life-sized figures portraying Capt. John Smith trading with Indians for corn." And further: "The costumes were reproduced with historical verity, and the corn was grown from seed carried to New York by the Tuscaroras in 1711."

Quite a contrast was the Ferrari Wild Animal Show featuring live lions, tigers, bears, panthers, wolves, and snakes in hourly performances. As part of the show, a woman named Seleca danced among lions seated on pedestals. More live entertainment came from the Miller Brothers' 101 Ranch from Bliss, Oklahoma, a Wild West show featuring demonstrations of steer roping and sharpshooting or staging reenactments of stagecoach robberies and Indian raids. Still another of the amusement exhibits was "Hell Gate," described as "the thriller of the Exposition" for its "precipitous waterfall, snakes, lizards, bats, and other eerie creatures [that] abounded in this turn-of-the-century haunted kingdom."

All this, and Mark Twain and Teddy Roosevelt, too—President Roosevelt to open the exposition on April 26, 1907, and Twain among its many distinguished and famous visitors.

The exposition facilities were not completed and in full operation, however, until mid-September. After that point, noted Thomas J. Wertenbaker in his history of Norfolk (*Norfolk: Historic Southern Port*), visitors were greeted by "an interesting and beautiful spectacle."

From 1900 on, unsurprisingly, plans had been laid to commemorate the establishment of the first permanent English settlement in America, as Wertenbaker also noted, but the road ahead would be rife with unexpected, sometimes risky, twists and turns. "Many took for granted that the exposition would be held at Richmond, but a delegation of prominent citizens from the Norfolk section appeared before the [General] Assembly, and carried the day for Hampton Roads."

The legislature acted in 1902 to grant the exposition company a charter, but with the stipulation that it must raise $1 million in capital stock for the venture by January 1, 1904. As of the afternoon of New Year's Eve, 1903, the exposition organizers were $100,000 short of the goal, but community leaders who gathered at the Norfolk Board of Trade that evening narrowed the shortage to $5,400.

Then, shortly after eleven o'clock, came news that a group meeting in Newport News had pledged $5,000. That left just $400 to reach the million-dollar mark by midnight. Fittingly enough, M. D. Lowenberg, director general of the exposition, pledged the final amount, "and the great project was saved."

Meanwhile, former Governor Fitzhugh Lee, a popular Civil War veteran and nephew of Robert E. Lee, had been appointed president of the enterprise, but in the midst of promoting it and fundraising, he suddenly died. That was in 1905, and now others carried on with the great project commemorating Virginia's very start.

And quite a project it would be. "It was no light task," wrote Wertenbaker in his history, "to erect a miniature city on this isolated spot [the exposition's 347-acre site on Sewells Point], to lay down a boulevard ten miles to Norfolk, to pipe drinking water, to build piers, to provide lights and telephone service, to make streets and pavements, to erect a group of beautiful and permanent buildings, to set out flowers and shrubs." The much-delayed result, though, was indeed memorable, as he also noted:

> The two great government piers, shining white against the water of Hampton Roads, were united by an artistic arch to form a basin called Smith Harbor. To the south was Raleigh Square, leading up to the Court of Honor, with its sparkling fountain and its two lagoons, and beyond was the stately administration building. The central group of buildings included structures devoted to art, to machinery and transportation, to food, to medicine, to manufactures and liberal arts, to mines and metallurgy, to marine appliances. To the south of the administration building was the Lee Parade, and beyond this the military encampment. To the right and left, facing Hampton Roads were the state buildings, many being replicas of historic structures—the Old State House, for Massachusetts; Independence Hall for Pennsylvania; the Bullock House, for Georgia; the Carrollton Mansion, for Maryland. The dignified buildings, the thousands of lights, the avenues set with trees and bushes; the waving pennants, all set off by the broad expanse of Hampton Roads, presented a picture of rare beauty.

If the Jamestown Exposition failed to make money for its promoters (and even went into receivership shortly after its closing in November 1907), was it, then, a failure? Wertenbaker argued no, that it succeeded in showing off progress in the Virginia Tidewater while also underscoring the potential of Norfolk's harbor and the great Hampton

Roads watery expanse in general. And it kicked off a significant building boom for Norfolk proper.

More pointedly, in a few short years, the 347-acre Sewells Point site of the exposition would become the foundation of the Norfolk navy base and air station, today the largest naval facility in the world. And guess what became of a dozen and a half of the "statehouses" that once were major attractions at the exposition. What else, but form the core of "Admirals Row" at the naval base?

1 9 0 9
A Challenging Presidential Foray

The extraordinarily robust Theodore Roosevelt presidency featured many challenging activities, such as hiking, riding horseback, boxing, tennis, climbing the cliffs of Rock Creek Park, even swimming across the Potomac, to say nothing of T. R.'s occasional forays as a big-game hunter. As seen in his youthful "cowboy" days on his own western ranch or two, T. R. was not one to give up any sport, challenge, or cause easily, whether it was foot-jousting with Army Chief of Staff Leonard Wood after going blind in one eye, breaking precedent by having Booker T. Washington in for dinner at the White House . . . or continuing to ride horses after life-threatening accidents.

In one such case—in 1885, long before he became president—Teddy Roosevelt was fox-hunting near his Long Island estate at Oyster Bay. His horse failed to jump a five-foot fence but instead fell and rolled over the twenty-seven-year-old Roosevelt, mashing him against stones on the ground. The result was a broken left arm and a badly cut-up face. Undeterred, T. R. climbed back aboard his steed and continued the hunt, albeit somewhat behind his fellow riders. "I looked pretty gay, with one arm dangling, and my face and clothes like the walls of a slaughterhouse," he wrote in a letter to Senator Henry Cabot Lodge. He went out to dinner that same night and the next day spent three hours walking in the woods, he added somewhat boastfully.

Another time, but now as president, he was riding a horse new to him in Rock Creek Park, and it balked when he tried to ride up the embankment from the creek. "That the president likes to have his own way with horses as well as with men is accepted now as a fact," wrote presidential aide (and U.S. Army Capt.) Archie Butt, "so he tried to wheel the horse about again, which he succeeded in doing but the horse wheeled again, and in doing so went over backward and both fell into the creek."

This time, T. R. managed to avoid a broken arm, a lacerated face, or like injury. "Fortunately, the water was deep at that point and no great harm was done, but it would have been serious had the water been more shallow," added Butt in a 1908 letter to his mother.

Typically, even after falling off the Rock Creek cliffside, T. R. kept on riding horses, hiking, or climbing, often going forth alone, except for his aide Butt, each of them carrying a pistol for T. R.'s protection.

Typically again, T. R. was not in the least discouraged from tennis when struck in the head by an errant ball, fired at high speed by Archie Butt himself. Wrote Butt to his mother on this occasion:

"I hit him a heavy blow on the head with a ball the other day and began to apologize when he stopped me and said:

"'If I hit you, Captain, I am not going to apologize, so you just bang away at me as much as you like and say nothing in the fray.'"

None of which activities, demands, challenges, responses, or what-have-yous quite prepared Butt, or anyone else associated with the Teddy Roosevelt White House, for his proposal one day to indulge in a grueling horseback ride to Warrenton, Virginia, and then back in the teeth of a winter gale.

Having challenged American military personnel, including high-ranking officers, to take a horseback riding "test" as a part of their required physical fitness, Teddy Roosevelt in the last weeks of his presidency felt it incumbent upon himself to set an example. For once, he didn't really want to display his own toughness, but he apparently felt he had no choice. At least that's what Butt had to say in a letter to his sister-in-law, Clara Doughty Butt (Mrs. Lewis F. Butt).

It was January 1909, and in March of that year, fellow Republican William Howard Taft would be taking over the reins of power from Teddy Roosevelt. The announced ride to Warrenton and back, a hundred-mile excursion, all on horseback, was to begin with a wake-up call at 2:30 A.M., January 13. Butt would be spending the night in the White House itself for convenience's sake. "I would enjoy the night there if it was an entire night and not a mere chip off one," he wrote to Clara the day before the great ride. Said he also, with obvious foreboding: "We have had good weather for the last few days. It was that which decided the president to go tomorrow, but the bulletins this afternoon are predicting a blizzard, and the wind is howling on the outside now."

On the night of the twelfth, as Butt was trying to read himself to sleep a bit after ten o'clock, Roosevelt returned from a dinner and came knocking on Butt's door. His aide told this part of the story in a letter to Clara penned on January 14, the day after the scheduled ride. "He came ostensibly to say a word of welcome, but in reality what he came to say was this: 'I suppose I will be criticized again, Archie, for making a spectacular play for the benefit of the public, but I don't think you know how I dread taking this ride at this time; but you would understand if you could see the protest from people against my last order prescribing the test for the navy. I believe it has done so much for the army and will bear much greater fruit later that I would undergo any hardship myself to guarantee the continuance of the order.'"

As T. R. also said that night, he was afraid "a great coterie of both the army and the navy are only waiting for me to leave the White House to deluge the next president with applications to modify the order."

The ride that T. R. had proposed for himself, Archie Butt, and the White House physicians Presley M. Rixie and Cary T. Grayson, both of them navy officers, would have been challenging under the best of conditions. "I had never ridden more than forty miles at a time," Butt wrote to Clara, "and while the president had ridden as much as seventy, yet it was in good weather and over good roads and on good horses."

Despite all such misgivings, on the part of T. R., Butt, or anyone else, the planned affair would go forward.

Five minutes after his conversation with President Roosevelt, Archie Butt was asleep in his White House bed, "and the next thing I knew he was hammering at my door to get up."

They breakfasted on bread and "a considerable amount of rare steak," plus two cups of coffee for T. R. After a quick examination of the latter's heart by Dr. Rixey, and a few medical punches "here and there" on the presidential body, the party got under way at the black hour of 3:40 A.M. Teddy Roosevelt, fifty years of age, rode a familiar horse named Roswell, and Butt started out aboard his "old faithful," a horse named Larry. It would be a long, cold ride, and there would be other horses during the day.

"We started on a dog trot down Pennsylvania Avenue and made the bridge in ten minutes," wrote Butt. "But, oh, the wind was cold!" For the moment, though, no blizzard was in sight, and the roads were at least "fair."

For the first six miles, the party made good time. At Falls Church, however, the roads turned bad—"they had been deeply furrowed and cut up since the last thaw and snow, and had simply frozen in this way." Losing time now, the group pushed on to Fairfax City, today, like Falls Church, a bustling northern Virginia suburb of Washington. Here, at the Fairfax Court House about 6:20 A.M., T. R. and Butt undertook their first change of horses. Unfortunately, through a misunderstanding of orders, a favorite T. R. bay mare named Georgia had been sent back to her stables. Clearly disappointed, T. R. moaned that he had hoped to ride Georgia "as a matter of sentiment if for nothing else."

But that was not to be, and the party moved on, now at a "brisk trot," with Centerville the next destination.

Passing Centerville about 7:20 A.M., T. R. and Butt changed horses again at Cub Run, two miles farther toward Warrenton—"and the change for the president and myself," noted Butt later, "was for the worse; for the horses we got in exchange for the ones we were on were rough, slow, and mine was vicious."

By now, of course, they were passing the Civil War battlefield of Bull Run (First and Second Manassas). That, quite naturally, provoked pointed discussion. "He [T. R.] joked Admiral Rixey about the Virginia roads and wondered what the old vets would say if their spirits could come back to earth and see him riding over Bull Run road with three rebels, as he called us." As New York–born T. R. well knew, Butt was from Georgia, and the two navy doctors riding with them were from Virginia.

The president fell into reminiscences about his mother, herself a Bulloch from Georgia. "I can see her now," he said fondly, "when, in order to show my resentment to her for some disciplinary measure she enforced, I would pray for the success of the Union forces or, as I was wont to speak of them, the 'Yankees.' She always heard our prayers at night, and when I could not vent my anger any other way I would close my prayers with asking God to bless the Yankees. And when we wanted anything which she could not give us we often resorted to the stratagem of calling on God's blessing on the rebels, too. This frequently secured a respite for us from bed for another half hour."

All the while that T. R. was talking, the quartet rode on southward, more or less on the line taken in modern days by U.S. Route 29, known in northern Virginia as Lee Highway. "By the time we reached Gainesville," wrote Archie Butt, "we all felt that the trip would be a success. Each had measured his strength, as it were, and knew about what we could do."

Still an unknown, though, was the weather, thus far no problem, although the sun had broken through the cloud cover only once briefly.

Stopping outside Warrenton for another change of horses and then encountering a road all cut up and furrowed, the riders realized they would be lucky to reach their destination by the planned hour of 11 A.M. "We took advantage of every good stretch, however, to gallop, and just as the town clock struck 11:00 we entered the main thoroughfare of the town."

Warrenton wasn't expecting a presidential visit, but "several persons" spotted T. R. and soon had spread the word. "In less time than it takes to tell it there had gathered upwards of a thousand persons in front of the old Warren Green Hotel," wrote Butt the next day, "and I was detailed to go out and see them."

After Butt paved the way, telling the good citizens of Warrenton that T. R. was "as anxious" to meet them as they were him, Roosevelt made his appearance, and "they gave him a rousing cheer."

The first president to visit the Virginia town since New Englander Franklin Pierce, T. R. then delivered a short speech, "and shook each one by the hand, I presenting each by name just as I would do at the White House, and to each he had some special word to say."

The friendly encounter ate up the clock, naturally, and now the riders had to bolt their lunch in order to start back to Washington in timely fashion. Just for the record: T. R., overweight and prone to high blood pressure, had soup and drank two cups of tea.

They left Warrenton at 12:15, and for more than an hour Archie Butt had to contend with a mean-spirited mount. "I had a horse which fought the bit the whole way," he wrote, "and once when I got off to look after the girth on the president's saddle I was fifteen minutes getting back on again. He would plunge and rear, and once he struck at Doctor Grayson and came near putting him out of business. Finally I made a flying leap for the saddle and made it."

The next horse Butt rode wasn't a prizewinner either. Nor was T. R.'s, it seems. "Admiral Rixey was on a fine animal of his own, and he set the pace at a jog trot, which was all right for him, but it was hell on the president and myself, who were riding about the roughest troop horses which Fort Myer [the U.S. Army cavalry post in Arlington] could turn out."

The next change of horses, accomplished at Cub Run, south of Centerville, produced better results for the tiring travelers. Taking Rixey's place at the lead—by presidential order, that is—Butt now set the pace "by walking slowly when the roads were bad and galloping like mad when they were good." This way, he insisted, "we made better time, although one is not supposed to." Furthermore, "this pace had the effect of resting us up when very tired and when galloping to warm our blood and exhilarate our spirits."

But now came the blizzard, and they were riding right into its teeth. It came from the north, wrote Butt, "in the shape of a blinding sleet storm, and this storm was continuous from this point to Washington." With the wind "blowing a gale," he added, "the ice cut our faces so that I thought mine must certainly be bleeding." It wasn't long before completion of their journey home looked very, very doubtful for that day, but they pressed on anyway, since "every mile covered now was that much made certain."

Relatively speaking, they kept up a fast pace to Fairfax, where a final change of horses would reunite them with their steeds of the early morning—good old Roswell for T. R. and faithful Larry for Archie Butt. A welcome change at that . . . except that, due to the wintry blast assailing them all, Roswell blindly trotted into a ditch. Fortunately, the T. R. favorite kept his footing and was able to avoid injury to himself or his rider. The president, for that matter, was proceeding quite blindly himself, "for the ice would cake on his glasses so that he could see nothing ahead of him." He simply placed his trust in Roswell . . . and, of course, the man in the lead, his faithful aide, Archie Butt.

On and on they went, by now quite wearily, to be sure. But progress was being made, if slowly. Then, at Falls Church, "we began to trot, for the roads were better, and, strange to say, by the reflected lights of Washington, nine miles away, we could keep fairly in the roads." Even better, "enough snow had fallen with the sleet to make them fairly safe, so we trotted the entire way into the Aqueduct Bridge [today's Key Bridge into Georgetown]."

There a carriage ordered out by Butt awaited the party. The smooth, paved streets of Washington might not be safe underfoot for the horses, he had thought, and so he had told an orderly out in Fairfax to telephone instructions into the White House . . . but T. R. balked at this. Despite his thoroughly bedraggled state, he had a course to finish, and finish it he would. "By George," he said, his black riding jacket, fur collar, and broad-brimmed black hat coated with ice, "we will make the White House with our horses if we have to lead them." And with that they crossed the bridge and turned in the direction of the Executive Mansion, where T. R.'s wife, Edith, anxiously was watching for the group from a window in daughter Ethel's room.

Minutes later they hove into view, and "by the time we alighted, she was standing in the doorway to welcome us."

For Archie Butt—likely for the ice-covered T. R., too—it was an enchanting moment. "It was a perfect picture. She had on some light, fluffy evening gown and I don't believe that Doll[e]y Madison, even in her loveliest moments, ever looked more attractive than did Mrs. Roosevelt at that moment, standing there, framed in the big doorway with the strong light on her and the wind blowing her clothes in every direction." Then, "Mrs. Roosevelt had us come in and gave us each a julep, which was the first drop of liquor any of us had during the entire ride."

The next day T. R. addressed an admittedly sore-bodied ("stiff," he wrote to Clara) aide with a triumphant note to be "filed" as part of the Archie Butt record.

"On January 13th, you rode with me from the White House, Washington, to the inn at Warrenton, Virginia, and back, a distance which we have put at 98 miles, but which I am informed was 104. We covered the distance between 3:40 in the morning and 8:40 in the evening, including an hour and a quarter at Warrenton and five or six minutes at each of the places where we changed horses."

Still for the record, T. R. methodically listed each of the horse relay stations, while also noting that after the first phase of the hundred-mile ride, the horses were "ordinary cavalry horses, and two of yours were hard animals to ride, which materially added to the fatigue of the trip so far as you were concerned."

Then, too, the weather conditions "materially increased the difficulty of the ride, for from Centerville in a blinding sleet storm drove in our faces, and from Fairfax Court House in we were in pitch darkness going over the frozen roads through the sleet storm."

And, a final point to be made of the entire affair: Since all had returned in "fine condition," despite all the various handicaps cited, T. R. now was happily convinced that his test for army and navy men was "not excessive."

Which undoubtedly is what he thought in the first place.

1909
Unwitting Catalyst for Reform

Virginia running back Archer Christian's mother reportedly had this uneasy feeling, a strong premonition that kept her in a hotel room and away from her son's game against Georgetown University in Washington, D.C. It was November 13, 1909, just three years since the college football reformers of 1906 thought they had made the game safe.

Sadly, as the afternoon unfolded, Archer Christian's experience in the Georgetown game would go far toward showing them to be wrong—and his mother's premonition of personal disaster to be proved right.

As told in John Sayle Watterson's definitive study, *College Football: History, Spectacle, Controversy*, it really wasn't clear how or why the eighteen-year-old Christian suffered a fatal head injury in the Georgetown game. Still, taken together with the recent death of an Army player at West Point, his unhappy fate immediately rekindled demands in some quarters to end the college game altogether and in others to consider still more reforms, still more rule changes.

At the core of the long-standing football controversy was—should have been, actually—the phenomenon called mass play, by which big blockers advancing alongside the runner pushed and/or pulled him forward. The reforms of 1906, stemming from a rash of serious injuries and deaths among college and high-school football players, had failed to eliminate the mass-play offensive tactic.

A freshman and a halfback, Christian certainly did incur his injury on a running play, but it may not have been a mass play. As Watterson noted, accounts by eyewitnesses and newspapers of the day differed. But all would have agreed that young Christian "was enjoying the best game of his young career." The Virginia halfback repeatedly sliced through the left side of the Georgetown line at the tackle position, and by the second half "had kicked a field goal and then scored the team's third touchdown, to put the Orange and Blue ahead 21–0."

But then came his last and fatal plunge, again off the left tackle position. "Escorted by blockers, or 'pushers,' on either side and one man to block in front, Christian again broke through the Georgetown left side for perhaps eight yards, but then the gap quickly closed. Christian abruptly toppled back across a Georgetown player as others fell on top of him. When the players got to their feet, the Virginia halfback remained prostrate. Carried to the sidelines, he appeared barely conscious. 'Oh, I'm suffering, Pop,' he said to the trainer. 'Please do something for me.' He then slipped into a coma."

Suffering hemorrhaging of the brain, he died early the next day. And now came the competing accounts of just how he was injured. The *New York Times* blamed the injury on mass play, Watterson noted. By that view, "Christian's teammates had dragged him across the line, then he had stumbled." Next, "just as he was getting to his feet, several Georgetown players converged on him and knocked him on his back."

Question: Was the *Times* relying for details upon the reports of stringers or other news agencies, "rather than its own reporters"? Whatever the case, the *Times*'s story on Christian's solitary injury shared page 1 of the Sunday editions on November 14 with a disastrous out-of-town explosion spreading mayhem among many victims.

Back on the stunned University of Virginia Grounds, the student newspaper *College Topics* denied the mass-play reports of "several papers" and asserted that "the death-dealing play was not one of the dangerous mass formation maneuvers, and twenty-one players did not heedlessly pile on the injured player."

The *Baltimore Sun* weighed in with a report, wrote Watterson, indicating that Christian "might have attempted one of his patented backward dives, a maneuver that had little to do with mass play."

Soon to be heard from also, Virginia Coach John Neff later said the injury took place "well beyond the line of scrimmage" and insisted the play had been an unembellished running play with no pushing or pulling by teammates. Still, Christian had run off tackle so often in the game, the Georgetown defenders no doubt were primed to swarm in his direction as he once more emerged from the line into their secondary.

Perhaps he tried to gain extra yardage with a spin and backward leap, and most likely he wore no helmet—not all players did in those days.

Perhaps his timing was off a beat, or perhaps he had become too weary to brace himself before the Georgetown tacklers smothered him in a reverse sort of mass play of their own. However it happened, the head injury he suffered was fatal. And now came the recriminations and the question: What next for college football?

Naturally, Georgetown and the University of Virginia canceled their remaining games for the season. So did the University of North Carolina, which had been scheduled to play Virginia at the end of the season. But those were only short-term responses. What about the long haul? Should college football be canceled, period?

The fact was, two highly visible gridiron deaths now had taken place in shockingly short time—not only that of Archer Christian on November 13, but also of Army tackle Eugene Byrne in a game with Harvard just two weeks before. In addition, two weeks before that, Navy quarterback Edwin Wilson was so badly hurt in a game against Villanova that he would lie "near death for nearly six months."

All this could mean the death knell for college football itself, but should it? Certainly, these latest unfortunate incidents gave the critics of football fresh impetus in their argument against the game. Georgetown, in fact, did cancel its football program outright for the time being.

But Virginia's President Edwin Alderman, keen on the game as both a builder of character and an outlet for youthful restlessness, wasn't ready to take that route. "While the Virginia president lamented Christian's death, he managed to find ways to defend football in a public statement published only three days after the accident," wrote Watterson. "'A boy cannot play football successfully,' he declared, 'without the use of self-denial, self-restraint, or resoluteness, or of patience, of well-ordered attention, of loyalty to a cause, of a distinct form of unselfishness.'"

Wrote Watterson also: "By banishing football, colleges would suffer a calamity, if for no other reason than the lack of diversion in small towns like Charlottesville."

Perhaps new and now all too compelling for the Commonwealth of Virginia at large, this was not a new issue at all. A revolution in rules for college football had emerged in 1906 after years of broken bones and heads on gridirons across the nation, accompanied by growing controversy that peaked in 1905. The consensus by 1906 was that most such injuries could be blamed on "the collision of heads and bodies near the point at which the ball was snapped," wrote Watterson in his history of the game. "Old grads who had played in the 1870s and 1880s looked back nostalgically to a period before the bunching of players near the center, a golden age of kicking and broken field runs, when serious injuries seldom occurred."

By 1906, the reformers saw the need "to redirect play so that running, throwing, and kicking would become more common, a game in which teams would take advantage of the open field." The idea was "to rewrite the rules so that grinding line play would be less profitable and that penalties would discourage foul play."

Among the new wrinkles that emerged was the requirement for the offense to gain ten yards in three plays to keep the ball and go for another ten yards; establishment of a "neutral zone" between the two teams; a shorter game of sixty minutes instead of seventy; and the addition of a fourth official to spot and enforce rule violations. Also to be forbidden was "hurdling," the practice of bodily heaving the ball carrier over the opposing line.

Left unremarked, untouched, though, was the use of bruising mass play to bull through the opponent's line.

Still, the new neutral zone would be a welcome innovation. "Previously, the teams had lined up so close to each other that officials could not see the pushing, holding, and slugging that occurred before the play. By defining a neutral zone, the officials could spot infractions, especially the sparring that occurred between linemen before the snap."

With such new rules in effect, noted Watterson, "football enjoyed a brief vacation from controversy." But only from 1906 to 1908, and even then not all was well. "People who recalled the brutality of football in 1905 or the corrupt practices of coaches and alumni did not necessarily drop their opposition to football simply because the rules had changed. The debate over football still stirred just below the surface and required only a catastrophic event to bring it to the surface."

The fact is, hardly noticed, the number of deaths in college football "jumped from two to six in 1908." On a more positive note, the number of deaths on high-school gridirons dropped "to a record low of four," but serious injuries among high-school players shot up from twenty-four to fifty-one.

Why weren't the new rules eliminating, or at least reducing, those tolls? One major reason: the mass play. "Simply put, the juggernaut of players blasting through the line posed a danger to the vulnerable linemen." In the East, "where coaches preferred running plays to the forward pass," the situation was aggravated by widespread use of the fake pass to encourage the defenders in the secondary to play back, off the line. "Then the ball carrier would come smashing across the weakened tackle position, often accompanied by men on all sides to push and pull him through the defense."

The continued risks of football suddenly came to the fore again in 1909, with serious injuries and deaths striking during major, highly visible games between well-known teams such as Virginia, Georgetown, Army, Harvard, Navy, and Villanova. Significantly for the rules-makers, Army's fatally injured Byrne had been the target of one off-tackle plunge after another by a powerful Harvard team. Ironically, Virginia's ill-fated Archer Christian, who apparently had broken into the open beyond the line of scrimmage on his fatal run, didn't really fit the same mold of injury from mass play.

Still, he was yet another casualty of the game, and now the rule-makers had to gather once more in an attempt to make the game safer . . . to placate a worried, questioning public as well.

The result, coming in 1910 and thereafter, was a series of rule changes finally outlawing mass play, enhancing the appeal of the forward pass, and in general creating the modern game of football. Also important: protective gear for the players, such as the all-important helmet, became a commonplace feature of the game. Even today, of course, injuries and deaths still do occur on the gridiron since football is a rough contact sport . . . but in general the game is far safer than it once was, thanks in large part to the unwitting "sacrifice" made by earnest young men such as Edwin Byrne of Army and Archer Christian of Virginia in 1909 and the years immediately before.

☆　☆　☆

Additional note: One critic of University of Virginia President Alder-man's hopes to keep football alive and well was one-time Virginia student John Singleton Mosby, more recently of Civil War fame as a Confederate guerrilla leader in the Shenandoah Valley. By now seventy-five years of age and almost quietly practicing law in Washington, D.C., Mosby considered football too violent and "unsuited to higher education," Watterson's book also recalled.

Well known as he was, Mosby didn't carry the weight of a real Virginia alumnus, since he had been sent packing, and even had gone to jail in 1851 for responding to a fellow student's bullying by shooting him in the neck. The "irascible" Mosby's views on the football controversy became known through publication of a letter he wrote to a friend in Charlottesville, but Alderman was not the slightest bit dissuaded from his view that football could be a positive part of college life.

In that view, not so incidentally, he was joined by still another one-time Virginia student of note, Princeton University's former president and New Jersey's governor-elect, Woodrow W. Wilson. To be sure, the Virginia-born future president did object to the mass-play tactic, but otherwise he, too, was well known as a friend to football.

1912
Surviving the Titanic

The most amazing stories to come out of the sinking of the *Titanic?* Virginia has two.

First, the story of Frank Aks, short, sweet, incredible . . . and still a bit mysterious, since we don't quite know why an absolute stranger threw him overboard, right over the rail of the sinking luxury liner.

How the man did it is pretty simple. Frank Aks at the time, the night of April 14, 1912, was a mere babe in his mother's arms. The stranger simply snatched the infant away from her and tossed him over the rail. But why? Accounts vary. Surely this was not a zany attempt at saving the child, was it? By one story, the hysterical stranger actually did shout he was saving the baby. More ominous, but also more likely, was Frank Aks's own version that the stranger, as a man, had been denied access to one of the ship's few lifeboats—only sixteen plus four collapsibles, when there should have been more than sixty for the 2,228 passengers, plus crew members, aboard the huge liner. The age-old seagoing rule for such calamities of course was women and children first. Thus turned away, perhaps even "thrown back" bodily when he tried to climb into the lifeboats, said Frank Aks himself many years later, the stranger shouted something like, "Women and children first? I'll show you!" And with that he wrenched the infant from Leah Aks's arms and threw her baby overboard.

So far as Frank's mother knew—for days to come—her helpless child landed in the North Atlantic waters, waters so icy cold they were dotted with palatial icebergs like the floating castle that had scraped along the long hull of the "unsinkable" *Titanic* just minutes before.

Aks and his mother, quartered in the cheap steerage cabins below decks for forty dollars each, were on their way to join his father, a tailor who recently had immigrated to Norfolk. About 11:40 that fateful night, Mrs. Aks "heard the scraping" of the iceberg along the side of the ship. Frightened, she rushed out of the steerage section with her babe in her arms. "She was one of the first ones out of steerage up on deck," said a grown-up Frank Aks years later. She was fortunate, since so many of the passengers in steerage, men, women, and children, were among the 1,502 who drowned in the sinking of the *Titanic*.

The man who snatched away Leah Aks's baby boy, just ten months old, may have been one of the victims. "There were reports that the villain was clubbed and shot by outraged crew members," wrote *Richmond Times-Dispatch* reporter John Witt in 1988, "but Aks was never able to confirm the stranger's fate."

Meanwhile, how on earth did the infant Aks survive his toss overboard? As Aks himself one day would tell the audience of *Ripley's Believe It or Not* radio show (and often relate in other venues as well), he had landed in the lap of another woman as she sat in a lifeboat about to pull away from the sinking ship. Stunned at first, she hugged him close to keep him warm as the lifeboat was rowed away.

On the deck above, the infant's hysterical mother refused to climb into a lifeboat by herself. "Mother was in a state of shock," explained her son later. "She believed she had lost her baby. She had to be pushed into a lifeboat. She had no desire to live. She didn't want to meet my father and tell him his son was dead."

By daylight, with the *Titanic* consigned to the deep four hundred miles off Newfoundland, the occupants of both lifeboats were taken aboard the liner *Carpathia*, which had raced to the scene as quickly as it could.

At first, Leah Aks had no idea her baby was safely aboard the *Carpathia* with her. As three days passed, she remained numb with grief. But then came the moment when she encountered a woman holding a baby. Would Leah Aks, not noticing, have passed on by?

We'll never know, because her infant son spotted *her.* "Every breast-fed baby knows his mother," said Aks later. "I recognized her when we passed and reached out for her."

But that still wasn't the end of his mother's ordeal.

The woman holding her son, a stranger, turned and darted out of sight among the hundreds overcrowding the rescue ship.

Added reporter Witt's account: "Mrs. Aks begged the captain for help. The woman was found and summoned to his cabin, where she reportedly said, 'He's my baby. He fell out of the sky.'" Mrs. Aks then was able to identify the child as hers by describing a birthmark on his chest, "and the story had a happy ending."

In later years, by now a leading expert who lectured on the sinking of the *Titanic,* Frank Aks acknowledged, "People always ask why the good Lord saved me," and he would say he didn't know. "If I heard somebody tell that story, I wouldn't believe it," he freely admitted. "I have led a very charmed life."

He spent that life quietly enough in Norfolk, where he was in the salvage and auto parts business for many years until his retirement. In 1988, with only eight other *Titanic* survivors still living worldwide, Aks was able to report, "I am seventy-seven years old, and I am the baby of the bunch."

After his death in 1991, his widow, Marie, said his rescue from the *Titanic* always was his favorite story . . . and understandably so. "Sometimes I asked him why he thought he was saved from the *Titanic,*" she also said. "And he said, 'I know. It was because my children had to have a father.'"

☆ ☆ ☆

Some survivors said they felt only a mild jolt, but for Richmond's Robert Williams Daniel, the hour of 11:40 P.M., April 14, 1912, brought "a terrific crash." The mighty *Titanic* "quivered," he said, "and the lights went out." He had been in his cabin, in his berth and dressed in his nightclothes when the collision with the iceberg came.

More than a hour later, noted *Richmond Times-Dispatch* reporter Bill McKelway in an eighty-fifth anniversary piece appearing April 15, 1987, the Richmond-born international banker stood behind a railing on the sinking ship next to Pennsylvania and West Virginia coal scion Lucian P. Smith. They stood there watching the lifeboats pull away . . . with who knows what foreboding thoughts on either man's mind. Daniel, only twenty-seven, was still single, and Smith, also a young man but just married, was on the final leg of a round-the-world honeymoon. His bride, Eloise Hughes Smith, of Huntington, West Virginia, was in one of those lifeboats.

Neither man could know it at the moment, but Lucian Smith was fated to go down with the ship . . . and Robert Daniel just months later would be marrying Smith's young widow, Eloise.

But first, there is the mystery of how Daniel got off the ship and was himself rescued—an episode not totally clear even today.

In a newspaper account published just days after the maritime disaster, Daniel was quoted as saying: "Oh, I can't tell you what happened. I hardly know myself. I was in my nightclothes. I grabbed something and uttered one prayer. Then I went over the side of the boat—over the side of the boat."

Overcome with emotion, he paused to light a cigar, then explained further: "After waiting for an interminable time with a collapsible boat in my hands, I felt the *Titanic* sinking under my feet. I could feel her going under at the bows. The storage batteries furnishing the light again gave out, and there was darkness. I tried to wait a while, but I suddenly found myself leaping from the railway up in the air and it felt an eternity before I hit the water. When I came up I felt that I was being drawn in by the suction, and when I felt a cake of ice near I clung to it.

"For five hours I battled with ice cakes, and when I saw other boats coming near I almost gave up." But he didn't and he was rescued. . . . He was given new life, but for the rest of that life he would be marked, and not always comfortably, as a *man* who somehow joined women and children in surviving the sinking of the *Titanic*.

But all that, clear or not, came later. In the interim, what led him to those final moments before he somehow left the sinking ship?

Rushing to an upper deck, "almost naked" after the "terrific crash," he also related, he found scores of people "fighting and shouting in the dark," but then "they got the storage batteries going and gave us a little light." Capt. Edward J. Smith's calming instructions, shouted over a megaphone from the bridge, helped to restore order as well. Before that, "men and women fought, bit, and scratched to be in line for the lifeboats," said Daniel. "Look at my black eye and cut chin. I got those in the fight."

Somewhat later, said the *Titanic* survivor, "as the passengers got into the boats, the women were thrown in if they did not move fast enough. An officer jumped in to command, and the boats were swung from their davits and down into the water.

"Hundreds, it seemed, did not wait for the lifeboats. They could see there was no chance for them, and they jumped overboard."

Which apparently is what the dazed Daniel did as well.

Eloise Hughes Smith, in the meantime, was safe in her lifeboat but in an agony of worry over her husband, last seen and heard urging her to leave the sinking ship while she could. He had strapped a life belt on her beforehand and tried assurances that everything really was all right, that the ship would *not* sink. But then there came a moment when he became more serious.

"Then Lucian took me to one side," related the nineteen-year-old bride later, "and said that he never before had thought of invoking the 'obey' part of our marriage vow but that he felt he must exact it then. He said I must get in the boat. And obey orders always.

"I went to Captain Smith and told him I was alone and asked him if my husband could go with me. 'Women and children first,' he replied.

"Lucian hit him on the back, I think, and said, 'Good boy. Don't think I would ever take a woman's or a child's place.'

"Then he helped me fix the boat, kissed me, and said, 'I will see you later. I will be there in a minute.'

"The last words I heard him say were, 'Keep your hands in your pockets so they won't get cold.'"

If Eloise's harrowing tale seems perfectly clear, Daniel's story, noted *Times-Dispatch* reporter McKelway, was "loaded with contradictory details—at least as reported by hordes of journalists set on finding (or creating) as much drama as possible."

Undisputed, though, was his blue-ribbon family background, which included a prominent attorney as his father and among their ancestors Edmund Randolph of Virginia, the nation's first attorney general, as well as a U.S. Supreme Court justice of the Civil War era. Young Daniel himself often traveled to Europe and lived at the time in Philadelphia.

Returning to the horrific final moments for anyone aboard the stricken *Titanic* the night of April 14–15, 1912, McKelway summed up: "Daniel somehow managed to get free of the ship, last for hours in thirty-degree water wearing little more than his underwear and his watch, and eventually make it aboard the principal rescue ship, the *Carpathia,* around daybreak."

McKelway cited a newspaper account reporting that the *Carpathia's* surgeon recalled seeing four men "mentally unconscious of the fact that they had been rescued" and appearing at first like "four dead men." One of them allegedly was Daniel, "delirious" and "clothed only in a woolen sleeping garment." The doctor gave the Richmonder his own shirt.

At one time, too, Daniel was quoted by the *Washington Post* as saying he jumped overboard, with a life preserver, just five minutes before the *Titanic* went down. "I waited until every woman was off the boat—until I had done everything I could do," he said.

When he hit the water it was "icy" cold. "The shock was fearful. I realized that I could survive only by getting my blood into good circulation, and I lashed the water in an effort to get away from the *Titanic.* I managed to get two or three blocks away, and after two hours, when I was quite resigned to going down, I was picked up by one of the boats that I had helped to load."

By this account, it was Eloise's own lifeboat (and, it seems further, that of Mrs. J. J. Brown of "unsinkable Molly Brown" fame). Daniel later said the young widow Eloise Smith "seemed inconsolable" over the loss of her husband, Lucian. Although she herself may not yet have known it, she was pregnant with her late husband's only child, who upon his birth would be named Lucian Junior.

Robert Daniel, in the meantime, may have observed Eloise's shattered state aboard the *Carpathia,* since in other accounts neither Daniel nor Eloise Smith mention their being together in the lifeboat. "Somehow," wrote McKelway, "Daniel is not listed as a passenger on any of the ship's lifeboats, but it seems from most accounts that he was picked up in the water and may have been overlooked."

Certain it is, though, that both were aboard the overtaxed *Carpathia* as it chugged its way to New York. And there, when the ship docked on April 18, the *Richmond News Leader* reported, Daniel debarked carrying a fainting Eloise in his arms. Said the headline over the same story: ROBERT DANIEL LANDS FROM CARPATHIA HALF DEAD AND INCOHERENT. Relating his story at dockside, Daniel "reeled and was caught by several men who had gathered about him," McKelway also reported.

Twenty-eight months later, Robert Daniel and Eloise Hughes Smith were quietly married at the Little Church Around the Corner (officially, the Church of the Transfiguration) in New York City.

But theirs would *not* be a romantic story with a happy ending. Their marriage ended in divorce nine years later. He remarried twice and she three times. Both died in the year 1940, about eight months apart.

☆ ☆ ☆

Coincidental fact: Eloise Hughes was the daughter of a congressman from her West Virginia hometown of Huntington, and Robert Daniel in a later marriage would sire a future Virginia congressman, Robert W. Daniel Jr., who, like his father, lived at the seventeenth-century Brandon plantation on the south side of the James River below Richmond.

As should also be mentioned: The long list of 1,500-plus *Titanic* victims would include Teddy Roosevelt's faithful and highly capable aide, Capt. Archie Butt, an able aide also to T. R.'s White House successor, William Howard Taft. By all accounts, Butt was said to have been a gallant and helpful hero aboard the stricken ship to the very end. (See "A Challenging Presidential Foray," pages 263–70.)

1912
Boomtown Days for Hopewell

Environment? Who ever heard of it way back when . . . when little Hopewell, the munitions town that sprang from a cornfield in 1912, reached a dizzying population of forty-five thousand by the middle of World War I, just a few years later? When its workers wore wool

Most of this story appeared in the author's *Washington Star* article of September 20, 1976, with contribution by John Sherwood.

clothing on the hottest summer day because cotton might spark off and blow the place up? When the wrong chemical-bearing wind would turn garments hanging on a clothesline into rags?

"Wonder City" it was called back then. Even "Wizard City" was applied to this previously innocuous village at the corner of the Appomattox and James Rivers that so suddenly became a boomtown boasting the world's largest guncotton plant. That overnight attracted an international medley of hard-fisted, pistol-packing workers who whored, drank, and gambled with abandon. Who, when time permitted, slept in a hasty, tarpaper-shack city with wooden sidewalks built over mud holes and quicksand.

It was Dodge City all over again, with steam-driven trains instead of cattle drives pulling into town by the hour. From three dozen nations, the workers poured into Hopewell, stepping off as many as thirty-seven trains a day. The result was a brawling, lawless town so notorious the *Detroit News* sent one of its top writers to recap it all. And he wrote:

"Never will there be . . . such an amazingly unreal, bizarre, screamingly funny, gloriously optimistic town as Hopewell.

"Fortunes that turned men's heads were made there in a few days simply by buying and selling lots. Fire swept the town, and it sprang up again from its ashes; no one can even say how many were shot in brawls; martial law was proclaimed because Hopewell just could not be good." Rather, it was a hardened sinner with "a rich background of crime and disaster, of gold, of lawlessness, of perilous work and perilous play."

And there was the key, the extremely dangerous work, the high pay to compensate for the risks . . . and with a world war on, numbers that multiplied every day. Money of course was the magnet for the growing mobs that crammed into the few square blocks that were Hopewell's bedroom. Tarpaper shacks with corrugated roofs sat on land that leaped in value from $12 an acre to $100 a foot. Some entrepreneurs rented out beds—three men a day to a single bed.

It was Du Pont that established a dynamite plant at the once-sleepy river town (population fewer than a thousand) in 1912. It was the Great War in Europe breaking out just two years later that turned Du Pont's guncotton plant into the world's largest, one that handed out a daily payroll of $75,000 and at its peak produced 1.5 million pounds of explosives a day.

Hard on the heels of immigrant workers hungry for the town's big dollar came a wave of card sharks, prostitutes, strong-arm men, and various sharpies after the same dollar. Adding to the brew was Prohibition, which took effect in 1916 and quickly made bootlegging Hopewell's second major industry. Then, too, the army's Camp Lee (Fort Lee nowadays), situated right next door, teemed with young soldiers made wild and reckless by the prospect of fighting in the trenches overseas.

They say the only law and order in town was behind the Du Pont gates, an area patrolled by a small army of ninety armed guards. They say Du Pont bought land for churches in an effort to quiet down the restless labor force. They say Du Pont built three villages for its employees, replete with schools and playgrounds. But it all happened so fast, they also say. And it is a fact that Du Pont had 230 bunkhouses within its gates housing 15,305 workers.

So many people were new to town, it also is said, only thirty-two persons out of the booming city's thousands were eligible to vote in the city council elections of 1916. And, they say, a local laundry became a still operation turning out a thousand gallons of illegal booze a day.

Heady, heady days. Daily pay by Du Pont, and everybody thinking—with some justification—that his work was winning the war against the "dirty Hun," too. Then, on November 11, 1918, came the armistice ending the war. In one week, Du Pont closed.

In one week, Hopewell died . . . and did *not* go to heaven.

In 1920, neighboring Camp Lee closed its doors, too. They would not reopen until 1940, on the eve of World War II.

Hopewell's population fell to 1,397. By 1925, they say, Hopewell could boast only twenty-three citizens with taxable incomes to report.

In more recent years, Hopewell achieved a steadier population of twenty-two thousand or more. Aside from favoring the nickname "Chemical Capital of the South," it's a far different town. But some of those boomtown shacks are still visible on the cityscape. They appear in places still called "A Village" or "B Village." They've been nicely spruced up by now with window shutters, shrubbery, and siding. Yet, some locals as late as the mid-1970s still were arguing over ownership of properties the World War I workers left behind in their pell-mell exodus.

Nor was the Du Pont pull-out the only economic calamity to befall Hopewell between the two world wars of the twentieth century. For a while during the Great Depression, Hopewell appeared to have rebounded to some extent, with Tubize Artificial Silk Co., pioneers in rayon, in town and employing 4,200 workers. But disaster came in the form of a strike in 1934. One morning at four o'clock, two hundred to three hundred men scaled the fences and drove two hundred other workers off the production line. Tubize laid off nineteen hundred workers the very next day, then left town.

Still, there was some solace in the form of Allied Chemical, which came to town to produce nitrate of soda, a fertilizer that helped pull American farmers out of the depression. Best of all, Allied stayed. Operating two large plants in Hopewell by the 1970s, it was the city's biggest employer, with some thirty-five hundred workers on the payroll. Also contributing to the "Chemical Capital's" newfound economic footing were Continental Can, Firestone, and Hercules Powder—occupying eleven hundred acres within the city limits, employing seven thousand men and women, and handing out $97 million annually in paychecks.

Their stacks—at the joining of the James and Appomattox Rivers, eighteen miles southeast of Richmond—smoked, fumed, and spewed smells that Hopewell had known for years . . . and hardly noticed.

But then the term *environment* suddenly entered the picture.

In the mid-1970s it was discovered that the pesticide Kepone, a chlorinated hydrocarbon, had been leaking into the air, water, and ground in and around Hopewell. As a result, the James River and its marine life had been affected, bird populations apparently had suffered, Kepone particulates were found in air filters as far as sixteen miles from the production site—and worst of all, workers were suffering severe toxic effects from exposure to the compound. There were fears, too, that Kepone might prove to be a cancer-triggering agent as well.

As investigators—and the press—descended upon Hopewell, it turned out that Kepone originally was produced by Allied at Hopewell and at other places, but in the mid-1970s, it was produced at an old gas station by a subcontractor, Life Science Products. Until workers at Life Science began to turn up ill, no one had paid much attention to the white Kepone clouds that occasionally billowed across the street from the gas station, infiltrating the sandwiches the workers ate for lunch on-site. As the case moved into the courts, with one revelation after another, Hopewell constantly was in the news for better than a full year.

Still a blue-collar town dependent for its economic life on the big chemical plants, Hopewell didn't care for that kind of attention. "There would be a lot of starving sons of bitches in this town if them stacks wasn't smoking," Hugh Brown, an instrument mechanic at Allied, told *Washington Star* reporter John Sherwood in September 1976. "It's a damn fine town to live in. The economy is good. It may seem like a baddy to some people, but them stacks make money. The plants here pay on Tuesday, Wednesday, and Thursday because they can't haul this much money in town on one day."

In close agreement was Allied utility man Charles Gill, who said: "I don't feel the chemicals are any more dangerous than any other stuff we're exposed to. We smoke, we drink. It's all bad for our health. It's a great place to work. We're required to wear safety clothing. There are very rigid safety programs."

In short, "If you have to have industry, you have to put up with certain things."

Chiming in was Steve Gorkiewicz, who had just earned $700 for the week (including overtime) making sulfuric acid at Allied. "Why should we bite the hand that feeds us?" he said. "A bunch of EPA [U.S. Environmental Protection Agency] nitshits that don't know their ass from a hole in the ground come down here and drive us crazy. This environmental stuff is driving me up the wall."

Indeed, added Gus Robbins, retired editor of the *Hopewell News,* "there would be no Hopewell, period, without those chemical plants. They're our bread and butter. Almost everyone benefits in one way or another from the industry here. It's a way of life with us."

As Robbins also said, Hopewell was "essentially a workingman's town." And, obviously, many a Hopewell workingman in 1976 was more than willing to say, "*Kepone* truckin'."

1917
Pulled Out of the Fishbowl

In a wheelchair five decades after it all took place, James Euin Gordon, age eighty-two, Company E, 318th Infantry, Eightieth Division, still wasn't about to forget. "Never got a scratch. But I've had men killed on either side of me. Three times, wounded and killed."

With minor differences, this article by the author first appeared in the *Washington Star* newspaper on July 5, 1973.

Never did forget. "There's four of us who left Madison County together, and we left two of them in the Argonne Forest and one in the hospital."

James Euin Gordon of tiny Etlan, Virginia, was twenty-seven back then. Woodrow Wilson was president, and the bloodiest war the world ever had seen was their war, the First World War. A blindfolded official in Washington and a number pulled out of a fishbowl on a slip of paper sent the Madison County farmer to war. And who knows exactly what carried him through the Artois Sector, St. Mihiel, the weeks-long battle of trenches at Meuse-Argonne . . . carried him all the way back home again, unscathed?

"Gas? Never got it. I was living cautiously a little bit.

"I always would scent along, like a dog scenting a trail. The gas would lie on the ground like fog in the woods, pockets of it. Whenever I got a little smell of it, I'd slap my mask on."

Gordon's number in the first draft lottery for World War I was 258. That was the number that would send him to war.

But first it was just one of 10,500 numbers in the fishbowl that stood on an oak table in Room 226 of the Old Senate Office Building, Washington, D.C., on July 20, 1917.

Blindfolded, Secretary of War Newton Baker reached into the bowl at 9:49 A.M. and, at random, pulled out a gelatin capsule holding the slip of paper bearing the number for the first lot of draftees—number 258.

All across America, trembles and thrills rippled through every draft precinct populated by at least 258 men registered for possible military service. The "258s" would be the first to go. Some would survive, some would not.

The drawing was recorded by those newcomers to the "media," the motion-picture men. The Senate room was filled with dignitaries, other reporters, and tellers. A senator assigned to pull out the second draft number was so nervous that his hand had to be guided into the bowl.

In his rural home on the eastern slopes of the Blue Ridge, James Euin Gordon was unaware of all the fuss in the nation's capital. But he knew about the war in Europe, and he wasn't reluctant to go.

Later in the summer, the court clerk told him he didn't have to go. As the oldest of three brothers, he could stay home on the farm and a younger brother could go. "You can fill out these papers if you aren't a-going," the clerk told him.

"I told him I was a-going. I was going to volunteer anyway. We had a country worth fighting for."

James Euin Gordon went first to Camp Lee, Virginia, nowadays, *Fort* Lee, for training. And there, before embarkation with the American Expeditionary Force (AEF) for duty in France, he encountered men who were convinced they would die in the trenches "over there."

His lieutenant, brandishing a letter from his mother and saying he would never see her again, was one. Two others were Gordon's companions from Madison County, Robert Utz and Jessee Tanner.

All three died in the horrors of the Argonne.

Gordon, though, never did feel he would be left behind. "I said I don't feel that way. I'm a-coming back."

The battle of the Argonne lasted from September 26, 1918, to November 6, five days before the armistice that came in the eleventh hour of the eleventh day of the eleventh month.

Gordon went back and forth with the waves of doughboys charging the Hun in his trenches, charging into barrages of fire and dropping like the fall leaves of the Argonne Forest.

And at the end, Gordon was the first infantryman to enter an "office" in the German fortifications. He saw a nameplate on the safe and pried it off with his bayonet. It said "von Hindenburg," the name of the German general.

But another American soldier or officer—later, Gordon wasn't sure which—came along and said, "You'd better give me that." For some reason, the Virginian did.

For many years after, he searched and advertised for the mysterious soldier in hopes of retrieving the nameplate, but to no avail.

The men of Gordon's decimated E Company came back to Camp Lee in Virginia for homecoming parades and discharge, and one day the sergeant beckoned to James Euin Gordon. "How many 'Old Boys' do you reckon we brought back?"

Gordon wasn't sure. He knew there weren't many left of E Company's original 250 men, but he didn't know the attrition had been anything like the sergeant's next statement. "He said we got thirty-seven of the 'Old Boys' left."

"Old Boy" Gordon went home then to his Madison County community, married, and raised three boys and six daughters. His boys fought in World War II and Korea. Two were wounded, but they all three came back . . . as he did.

Gordon and his wife, Lelia, lived in a modest brick home on a hill, close by the farm he worked in the decades after the Great War. At eighty-two in 1973, he was confined to a wheelchair, but he remembered it all clear as a bell.

He pointed to the framed letter from Gen. John J. "Blackjack" Pershing, General Order 38-A, a farewell to all the departing men of the AEF as they left France and its new fields of white crosses. "General Pershing wrote me a letter," he sighed. Then, recalling the great battle at war's end, he had another thought. His Eightieth (Blue Ridge) Division, he said, "was the only division called three times in the Argonne."

1921
School That "Bad Sam" Built

Not yet known as "Bad Sam," he was only sixteen when he turned up in a West Virginia logging camp and earned a job as "lobby boy"—or peacekeeper among the sometimes hot-tempered loggers. Young Sam Hurley, left on his own at an even earlier age, quickly tamed the older men by subduing the camp bully with an iron poker. In the years ahead, he became known as both a fearless brawler and a crack shot often subject to challenge by would-be rivals. According to a local history written by a Kentucky judge: "He was beaten and bruised with rocks and clubs, stabbed with knives, shot with revolvers and guns. His rivals were also bruised, beaten, shot, cut, and killed."

Obviously, this hard-drinking roughneck of the Appalachian Mountains had not the remotest connection with any peaceful, wholesome activity such as, say, a Sunday school picnic.

He could be on the right side of the law, however.

He became so well known in the tri-state area of southwest Virginia, Kentucky, and West Virginia that a federal revenue agent once enlisted his help in an effort to capture a notorious band of bootleggers and whiskey-makers. By the same story, the band already had killed three U.S. deputy marshals. Hurley and the agent met eight of the lawbreakers in a mountain pass one midnight. The "revenuer" was wounded in the first exchange of shots, but when the smoke cleared some 250 rounds later, "Bad Sam" was the only man still standing.

He was charged with murder but was acquitted by a federal jury sitting at Covington, Kentucky.

As a step toward a quieter, more normal life, he married at age twenty-two and became a father of seven . . . but for a time he still was a hard drinker. That ended for good after he narrowly missed his own son with a careless shot from a pistol he thought was unloaded. "I almost killed that child," Hurley told his wife, Jane Looney Hurley, an orphan herself. "If I keep this up, he will grow up doing the same thing."

Instead of carousing, "Bad Sam" now became a *good* Sam. He began appearing at small churches in and around his home in mountainous southwest Virginia. He helped them organize Sunday school classes, a glimmer of a certain promise made many years in the past.

That past, even before his logging camp days, had included lone wanderings in the mountains of eastern Kentucky after his father died and his mother couldn't afford to keep her son at home. Only ten, Sam went from house to house seeking work in exchange for food. One night, sleeping under leaves in a cavelike hollow under a rock outcropping, he trembled at the wail of a mountain lion. Terrified, he prayed to God to keep him safe. If God would do so, he promised, he would create a home someday for abandoned children like himself.

Now, years later, having been taught to read and write by his wife, Sam Hurley became a lumberman and building contractor. He was so successful, a friend remarked, "Sam Hurley could turn money out of a rock." He also achieved political fame in traditionally Democratic Buchanan County by winning election to clerk of the court as a Republican. He, in fact, built the courthouse at Grundy, the county seat.

Without quite realizing where their actions would lead, Hurley and his wife had taken nine orphaned children into their home. One day a homeless boy seeking similar help turned up at Hurley's courthouse office in Grundy. Heavy in heart, Hurley had to turn him down—there simply was no room for him at the already crowded Hurley home.

Later, Hurley saw the same child sitting forlornly on the courthouse steps. With his childhood promise to God in mind, "Bad Sam" suddenly knew what he had to do. That very afternoon he began liquidating his holdings to finance the beginnings of a home and school for orphans, to be called Grundy Academy. Today, Hurley's remarkable legacy is the Mountain Mission School of Grundy, Virginia, both a home and a school for an average 230 children, ranging in age from infancy to twenty or so. More than twenty thousand lucky youngsters have passed through the trim campus on Slate Creek, all of them rescued from deprivations ranging from poverty to abuse at home, the death of parents, or abandonment.

Operated as a nonprofit charitable organization, the school that Sam built accepts no government funds, charges no tuition, and yet provides its young wards with food, housing, health care, clothing, and an education—right from the nursery through grade twelve.

"Mountain Mission School functions as a full child-care facility (home, church, school) for children with legitimate needs regardless of the child's race, age, color, or creed," says the school's literature. The "church" part means "students study Christian ethics along with every academic discipline, thus enriching and enhancing their education in a way unavailable to the children in public school." The school's racially diverse students have come from foreign countries, Washington, D.C., and nearly all the fifty states, but many "have had roots in Appalachia."

Uniquely, too, the school subsists entirely on donations from churches, business groups, charitable organizations, and individuals, including its own graduates—90 percent of whom go on to college.

To meet needs such as foodstuffs for the thirty thousand monthly meals at Mountain Mission, contributions range from money to "in-kind" gifts of food, clothing, and other useful items, even baby wipes. From ninety-one-year-old cattle farmer Arthur Clark in Kentucky came packages of fully dressed beef. Similarly, the Interfaith Knitting Group of Leisure World, Maryland, gave boxes of hand-knitted hats, mittens, and scarves for the children at Mountain Mission. Other groups, too, numerous to mention, have contributed their time and energy in helpful, hands-on work such as painting, cleaning, and landscaping.

As former school president Charles M. Sublett, a Church of Christ minister, once explained, "God multiplies our efforts." He recalled that when the school nearly foundered on the rocks of the Great Depression, President Franklin D. Roosevelt, an admirer of Hurley's, had a hand in arranging the loan that enabled the school to avoid foreclosure. And it's been that way ever since . . . the world has given and given over the years since the Hurleys began their school for needy children in 1921.

Fittingly enough, Hurley family members have been in the school's leadership ever since. Sublett was the Hurley couple's son-in-law. Likewise, James M. Swiney, president of the school as it entered the twenty-first century, is married to Hurley's granddaughter Charliece . . . and *their* daughter, Cynthia S. Rodda, succeeded her father as president of the school in mid-2003. "Husbands and wives, one generation with another, the pattern is set," said outgoing president Swiney in a newsletter announcing his daughter "Cindy's" selection as president-elect. "We work together. It is the family tradition."

Both Charliece and Cindy, of course, are themselves Mountain Mission graduates.

☆ ☆ ☆

Additional note: The telephone rang in Charles Sublett's study at Mountain Mission School one day some years ago. "Can you take another eight children?" asked the minister at the other end of the line.

"My goodness, no," said Sublett, then president of this school with a mission. "We don't have any room."

Still, he couldn't help but ask: "What's their problem?"

"I buried their father three weeks ago, and I'm burying the mother today," replied the far-off clergyman.

Just days later, the eight orphaned children took their places in Mountain Mission's red-brick residential halls just outside Grundy. Ever since Sam Hurley decided to act on his childhood promise to God, it's been that kind of school.

1925
"Watch Out, She's a-Coming In!"

They sing of the Rock Island Line and of John Henry, the steel-drivin' man, but they sing no songs, not even a verse, about the ten-car work train that lies a-moldering deep down beneath a double-named Richmond hill. There was nothing else to do, it seemed in 1925, but seal one

From the author's article in the *Washington Star*, May 9, 1976.

end of the tunnel beneath Church Hill and, nearly a mile away, cap the other end beneath Chimborazo Hill.

Thus the four-thousand-foot burrow in the middle of Richmond would remain the final resting place for the C&O work train, its locomotive and at least two railroad workers never again seen after a cave-in caught them all in the Church Hill Tunnel.

By some accounts, there may have been more laborers trapped in the collapse, but only "R. Lewis" and "H. Smith"—the only form in which their names survived—were known to be lost.

Engineer Thomas J. Mason died as well, his body found sitting bolt upright in the engine cab. Fireman Ben F. Mosby managed to crawl out but died of the burns he suffered from scalding steam.

So, there were at least four gone—and a train. But there were survivors, more than a hundred of them, who fled the collapsing tunnel that rainy day, who never forgot that afternoon of October 2, 1925. Never forgot the thud of the first bricks falling from the tunnel roof. Never forgot the sharp crack and roar that followed. Or the sudden darkness as the lights winked out. The hiss of escaping steam.

Never forgot the screams and the mad scramble to get out.

One of the first men to emerge from the tunnel, according to local newspaper accounts, was laborer Lemy Campbell. He had heard the strange clunk of a fallen brick, had looked up and seen many more showering down.

He had seen them hit the electric light lines strung through the tunnel, had seen the lights jump and flicker . . . and he began running at the sharp crack of a break in the roof.

Mosby the fireman was at the rear of the locomotive with engineer Mason. They were about to back the engine out of the tunnel after dropping off their ten-car load. Mason, an affable railroad veteran with nine children, was due for a transfer the next day. This probably would have been his last trip into the tunnel.

Mosby also noticed the shower of bricks.

"I yelled, 'Watch out, Tom, she's a-coming in!'" Mosby told rescuers later. "Then there was an awful crash and steam squirted all over me. I scrambled out and found an opening and began to crawl."

Mosby lived long enough to tell his tale. And to request of his coworkers: "Phone my wife. Tell her I'm not hurt bad and not to worry."

Apparently Mosby got out by slipping beneath the train itself, then by crabbing his way along the crawlspace beneath the cars.

Outside the tunnel, he was placed in a taxi vacated by an arriving reporter. He went to the hospital, and in seven hours he was dead.

Meanwhile, the railroad and the city were wheeling up their rescue forces. Nobody could be sure how many men might be buried with the train, which had been trapped at least a hundred feet from the west end of the tunnel and at last sixty feet below ground. About 125 men had been in the tunnel for repair work. The C&O now mustered a force of three hundred for the digging, while Richmond City police formed lines to hold back the crowds of onlookers.

A spectator was Edward M. Eck, then twenty-six and an employee of the C&O's traffic department, later a chief clerk in the same department. "You stand around and watch and hope and pray," Eck still recalled fifty years after the cave-in. There really wasn't anything more for the onlookers to do. Few of the railroaders or the spectators thought the men trapped inside had much of a chance.

Still, the rescuers did their best. They at first dug from both ends of the collapse, digging with hand tools. Up on top of populous Church Hill, a lengthy twenty-foot dip in the ground surface indicated a 250-foot section of the tunnel had collapsed right below . . . but far below.

But the rain fell and fell, and the crews digging into the saturated muck caused earth slides. A steam shovel carving into the hillside above the west tunnel entrance succeeded only in collapsing the sides of the tunnel section beneath the heavy machine itself.

The rescue effort then shifted to crews attempting to dig three vertical shafts, each one three feet square, straight down from the hilltop into the tunnel.

The digging began on the same Friday as the collapse and continued for days after. A roll call of workers known to have been in the tunnel turned up the two missing names, Lewis and Smith. But rumor persisted for many years that ten to fifteen more men, newly hired, may have been inside as well.

If true, it's not clear why their families or friends did not report them missing.

Of course, Engineer Mason was known to be trapped in the tunnel. His wife, later to be married and widowed again, stopped by to watch the digging. Many years later she recalled, "As fast as they would take one shovelful out, two more would fall in. Finally, they took me away."

That was the trouble with the hillsides above the tunnel, an engineering marvel that was punched through Richmond's great mound of Church and Chimborazo Hills combined. Created within ten years of the Civil War, the tunnel was used for only a short time, then abandoned to small boys who liked the adventurous shortcut from the city's Shockoe Valley to the far side of Chimborazo.

It was for shoring-up work that the big repair force was in the tunnel that October day, although some say the day's rains drove some of the men "indoors" from other work, sent them scurrying past the tunnel portals to get out of the rain.

Meanwhile, the middle of the three rescue shafts from the hilltop moved more rapidly than its two partners, but still, this was slow work. By Sunday the leading shaft was twenty feet deep. By Monday, thirty-three. By Tuesday, forty-two.

Only two men could dig at a time, and they naturally had to ship the dug-out clay upward with every inch gained. They were shooting for the locomotive and Mason, but no one knew how close they might come. Or if he had taken shelter and might still live.

Eight days after the tunnel collapse, the middle shaft broke through. The diggers hit the coupling between the engine and the first car behind it. They cut through and crawled forward to the locomotive cab by way of the protected crawlspace under the monstrous railroad equipage.

And now their lanterns focused upon an unearthly sight. It was Mason, sitting with lifelike rigidity in his seat. He had been pinned there, apparently at the moment of the tunnel collapse, by the engine's reverse lever, and he was dead. They had to cut his body free from the jammed lever before lifting it up the shaft for proper burial.

With Mason's death confirmed and the remainder of the tunnel section obviously in full collapse, the rescuers gave up hope of finding anyone else alive. Abandoning the two missing workers, train, tunnel, and all, they filled in the long cavern with sand and sealed both ends with concrete. It was early 1926 by the time they finished the job.

Today, there is hardly a clue to the old railroad tunnel and its work train that lie far beneath the feet of the tourists who throng to St. John's Church on top of Church Hill, site of Patrick Henry's "Give me liberty or give me death!" speech; who visit the Civil War exhibits on the nearby crown of Chimborazo, once the site of a major Confederate hospital, a high brow also once fortified for the defense of Richmond from the dreaded Yankees.

⋆

1932
Reunion to End Reunions

⋆

They came on seven special trains from the deeper South. "They were in their eighties and nineties, most of them too feeble to walk in parades, a goodly number with a missing leg or empty sleeve," wrote Virginius Dabney more than fifty years after he, himself, witnessed the last great reunion of Confederate veterans in their old Confederate capital of Richmond, an event evocative of misty eyes and a lump in the throat.

"A fifteen-year-old drummer boy who enlisted near the end of the war was eighty-two in 1932," Dabney added in his 1984 book *The Last Review.* And most of the aged veterans, "white haired and grizzled," were older than that. Dabney knew what they looked like and how old they were because he was there, in person, covering the nostalgic event as a young reporter for the *Richmond Times-Dispatch,* the same newspaper he later would serve as a Pulitzer Prize–winning editor.

For members of the United Confederate Veterans (UCV), it was to be their forty-second and last major reunion. And what more fitting a venue for such a farewell review than Richmond, whose highly visible Confederate statuary recalled "a pantheon of heroes to be venerated with an almost religious fervor"?

And what tales these old vets had to tell—"in hotel lobbies, at the encampments, everywhere that two or three men in gray are assembled," reported the *Times-Dispatch* at the time. For instance,Col. Edward C. Wilson, an elderly Texan, related that he, his three brothers, and their father all joined the same Louisiana regiment. Detailed to spy duty disguised as a black produce peddler, the Texan boldly visited Federal encampments to collect "valuable" intelligence. One time, though, "he ventured into a Union officer's tent, and a Yankee soldier slapped him for his audacity." Worse, the slap "brushed off some of the charcoal which begrimed his face, and he was straightway clapped into prison."

Escaping from the Yankees, he rejoined his outfit in time for the battle of Gettysburg, but there, he was recaptured. Concerned about his father and three brothers because he had seen one brother fall, he was given temporary parole to search the battleground. He then found the bodies of all four family members. "Such tragedy affected even the hearts of enemy officers, and he was permitted an extension of parole to accompany the bodies back home for burial."

He dutifully returned to Yankee hands . . . but then he escaped all over again.

Also an attendee of the Last Review was a sprightly looking Maj. John Crowley of New Orleans, described by the *Richmond News Leader* as "a secret dispatch rider for President Jefferson Davis during the War between the States."

Crowley, eighty-eight in 1932, claimed that he crossed Union lines thirty times disguised as a black girl. He won his dangerous job after presenting himself to Davis in person, "with a tattered dress and market basket, his face and hands stained with walnut." Davis, it seems, "was himself deceived and immediately added him to his couriers."

But now came an "epochal" assignment for Crowley, the *News Leader* also reported. "He was entrusted with a message to the British minister in Washington, whose aid the South sought to enlist." That meant a high-risk journey of more than six hundred miles from the first Confederate capital at Montgomery, Alabama, and all by horse-back—almost. He first encountered Union lines below Alexandria, and to get through them, he abandoned his horse, found a mule, "and rode into camp singing lustily."

The disguise as a loudly singing black girl passed muster with the Union officers, who stopped and questioned the courier-in-secret before allowing "her" to go on.

"Crowley delivered his message and then returned to Richmond, to which the Southern capital had been removed. There he was rewarded with a captain's commission and assigned to [Robert E.] Lee's headquarters. Afterward, he crossed the lines into Washington twenty-three times before his ruse was discovered."

Sentenced by a drumhead court-martial to be shot, he was saved by a group of sympathetic women in Washington who apparently persuaded Secretary of War Edwin Stanton to intervene, due to the fact that Crowley was only a teenager at the time. President Lincoln commuted his death sentence, and Crowley was remanded to an Ohio prison camp. He then was released after becoming ill.

Among other tales he still lived to tell in 1932, it seems that Crowley by 1864 had become an indispensable part of the Jefferson Davis household at the White House of the Confederacy in Richmond. By his own account, he was right there in June when the presidential couple's last child, their daughter "Winnie," was born. He said "he was the first person outside of the family who kissed the infant." As an added historical footnote, reported the *News Leader:* "He also claims to have coined for her the famous sobriquet, 'Daughter of the Confederacy.'"

In 1889, as a final connection with Jefferson Davis, Crowley "was one of the guards who accompanied Jefferson Davis's body from New Orleans to Richmond for burial"—in the city's historic Hollywood Cemetery—the *News Leader* account added.

The colorful Crowley also appears in Virginius Dabney's book as "an especially lively participant" in the "grand parade" of the Confederate veterans attending the Last Review at Richmond in 1932. "Holding tightly to the banner of the South, he insisted on riding part of the time astride the hood of the car in which Virginia's adjutant general, S. Gardner Waller, was traveling. But when the parade passed the [Confederate] statues on Monument Avenue, Major Crowley dismounted and saluted each one."

The Richmond gathering of 1932 was a last showing for most of the still-living "old men who fought long years before at Spotsylvania's Bloody Angle or the siege of Vicksburg, rode with Forrest's daring cavalry, or wrote their names on history's scroll in Pickett's Charge at Gettysburg." The excitement and pace of events during their four days in Richmond "had left a goodly number exhausted," Dabney also noted in his reminiscing book.

"After 1932 there would not be enough survivors of the Civil War to hold another Confederate convention that could be called a major reunion in the usual sense," he added.

Not to be forgotten and still to come, though, was the "gathering billed as the final reunion of the United Confederate Veterans." It took place in 1951 in Norfolk, another Virginia venue. And out of the "twelve or more" veterans still living that year, three showed up, ages 104 and 105. "The meeting was held in conjunction with the convention of the Sons of Confederate Veterans," with "hundreds" of them in attendance.

Among the three, one, John Salling of Slant, was from Virginia, but William Joshua Bush of Fitzgerald, Georgia, was "the liveliest," wrote Dabney. "I can hear good, I can see good, I can taste good, and I can kiss any damn woman who wants to be kissed," he declared with apparent gusto. "His wife felt it necessary to admonish him several times: 'Hush, Daddy, stop that cussing.'"

But it would be the Virginian Salling who lived the longest of the three, the longest, it is claimed on his behalf (a claim disputed in some quarters, true), of any Confederate veteran of the Civil War.

1 9 3 4
Explorer in Trouble

Far from home, far from friends or family, far from anyone else in the whole world, utterly alone in the midst of a polar blizzard, "Dick" of Virginia's Tom, Dick, and Harry family was trapped. It would be so easy now to die. So quick, and nobody ever to know exactly how or why.

Noon was twilight here, and twilight, noon. The Antarctic's Ross Ice Barrier simply is that way by mid-May, with winter just around the corner. "The noon twilight was dwindling to a mere chink in the darkness, lit by a cold reddish glow." And now the polar night settles in, the bottom of the world becomes totally still, empty, "the soul of inertness." And then, "out of the deepening darkness comes the cold."

Soon it would be sixty-five below zero (Fahrenheit) as Adm. Richard E. Byrd took his usual walk—seventy-two below the next day. All his surroundings so still . . . for now.

At the moment, the great Virginian explorer of the North and South polar regions may have been the best known of the Byrd brothers. Brother Harry, a former governor of Virginia, recently had been elected to the U.S. Senate (in 1932) and was not quite yet the political institution he later would become. Brother Tom had stayed home in the Berryville-Winchester orbit to manage the family's apple orchards and other business interests. Richard, on the other hand, had been in the public eye since he and Floyd Bennett made the first-ever flight over the North Pole in 1926. He then led the expedition of 1928 establishing the first "Little America" base camp at the South Pole. And after that, in company with Bernt Balchen, he flew over the South Pole. By the age of forty-two, Richard Evelyn Byrd (U.S. Naval Academy graduate of 1912) was a rear admiral, holder of the Navy Cross for heroism, and a bona fide national hero.

Just now, though, he was utterly isolated, and when the polar storm struck, not even the most outstanding résumé in the world, not his nor anybody else's, would be of much help.

It was May 1934. "Days when the wind brooded in the north or east, the Barrier became a vast stagnant shadow surmounted by swollen masses of clouds, one layer of darkness piled on top of the other," he would write in his book *Alone.* "This was the polar night, the morbid countenance of the Ice Age." Or, another way to describe it: "One could almost hear a distant creaking, as if a great weight were settling."

And this, days later, was to become the polar storm, the polar blizzard, he almost didn't survive.

How to describe *that?* "There is something extravagantly insensate about an Antarctic blizzard at night. Its vindictiveness cannot be measured on an [instrument] sheet. It is more than just wind; it is a solid wall of snow at gale force pounding like surf."

And worse yet: "The whole malevolent rush is concentrated upon you as upon a personal enemy."

Add to all this the cold, of course. Sixty-five below, seventy-two below, whatever the temperature, today, tomorrow, the next day, he still had to go outside on a regular basis—going "topside," he called it—to check his weather-gauging instruments. He lived, alone, in a shack below the snow cover, burrowed deep in the snow strata. And knowing the wintry blows would come, he had done his best to "armor-plate" his abode. "I carried gallons of water topside and poured it around the edges of the shack. It almost froze as it hit. The ice was an armor-plating over the packed drift [snow heaped against the sides of his shack]."

Inside while the winds howled and the bottom side of the planet creaked of its own weight, it was practically hot. By comparison, that is. "Reading in the sleeping bag . . . I froze one finger, although I shifted the book steadily from one hand to the other, slipping the unoccupied hand into the warmth of the bag."

Then came the day that May, the polar night upon him, the deep, deep cold upon him, the "insensate" blizzard blowing and thus upon him also, the day when he ventured topside to check the instruments outside. All alone still, and without thinking, he allowed the trapdoor simply to fall shut behind him.

He allowed it simply to drop rather than see his entrance tunnel fill up with the frantically dancing snow.

He didn't think because he was met by a "blinding smother" of snow, his breathing suddenly a struggle because of the snow stuffing his nose and mouth like so much cotton. And, too: "To see was impossible. Millions of tiny pellets exploded in my eyes, stinging like BB shot."

Afraid of being blown right off his feet, he crawled on hands and knees to the anemometer (wind gauge) pole, but found it impossible to wipe clear the contact points. "The wind cups were spinning so fast that I stood a good chance of losing a couple of fingers in the process."

There wasn't much else he could do but go back inside. Obviously, it wouldn't be safe to stay outdoors any longer than necessary, not in this gale. And so, he did crawl back to the entrance to his subsurface hut. Careful in every move he made, he did find the crucial trapdoor. He found it "completely buried," but managed to push away the accumulated snow with his heavily mittened hands. He took hold of the handle and . . . pulled.

It didn't open. It didn't yield the slightest bit. It was like welded iron.

Disbelieving, he yanked hard. No go again.

Now standing to bring all his strength to bear, grasping with both hands, he didn't simply pull. He heaved. And heaved.

Still, nothing. Not a tremble.

By now, he wasn't merely alarmed. "Panic took me then, I must confess. Reason fled. I clawed at the three-foot square of timber like a madman. I beat on it with my fists, trying to shake the snow loose; and, when that did no good, I lay flat on my belly and pulled until my hands went weak from cold and weariness."

This, then, so far from springtime in Virginia, really was *alone*.

And it was ironic, too. For weeks he had been afraid of somehow being trapped *inside*. Now, he was trapped on the outside.

And more irony: "Just two feet below was sanctuary—warmth, food, tools, all the means of survival. All these things were an arm's length away, but I was powerless to reach them."

Suddenly he thought of the ventilator pipes, a mundane thought that steadied his nerves for the moment. One of them indeed was close by. He put his face to it, saw the light in the shack below and even felt the warmth rising up. Perhaps he could rip it out and use it as an awkward digging tool. But no, it wouldn't budge.

How about kicking in the roof windows? But again no, they were under the snow—"two feet down in hard crust, and were reinforced with wire besides."

Finally, it came to him! A week before, digging snow, he had cast aside a shovel near the "front door" of his burrow. "I had stabbed a shovel handle up in the crust somewhere to leeward. That shovel would save me. But how to find it in the avalanche of the blizzard?"

Lying down like a child making snow angels, feet extended and hands gripping the edges of his hatch, he swept his legs to one side and then the other in search for the shovel. And when he did strike it, he embraced it eagerly, for here was salvation!

Triumph surely just seconds away now, he inserted the handle under the U-shaped handle of the trapdoor. Surely, the leverage he now could exert would spring free the stubborn hatch.

Surely . . . except that exert as he would, the trapdoor remained tight and fast.

Back home in Virginia, they never would know exactly how he died. By the time they found his remains, if they found them, the ice locking tight his trapdoor might be all melted and gone. Why didn't he go into his refuge from the winter storms? they would wonder. Here he was, after all, right at the door. Surely he hadn't been lost. He knew exactly where he was. . . .

Never mind, Virginia, he did have one more trick up his sleeve. And not much time to try it, since all he had on in the way of clothing was a "wool parka and pants underneath my windproofs."

Suppose, he thought, well aware of the time factor, in fact, already well chilled . . . suppose he left the shovel handle where it was and simply slipped beneath it? That is, lie face-down and wriggle his shoulders and back up underneath the shovel's good stout handle. And then heave like nobody's business. Get his back into it.

"Then I heaved," he later was able to write, "the door sprang open, and I rolled down the shaft."

Hallelujah! Saved after all! "When I tumbled down into the light and warmth of the room, I kept thinking, how wonderful, how perfectly wonderful."

So wonderful, in fact, he was able to outlast the elements (barely), return to civilization, write his book, and, in gratitude for his survival, work for international peace in the years leading up to World War II. Once the war broke out, however, the veteran navy man and explorer served his country on secret missions in Europe and the Pacific. He survived that experience as well, living until his death in Boston in 1957.

☆ ☆ ☆

Additional note: Admiral Byrd's narrow escape from death the day he was "locked out" of his snow hut was not the only moment of peril he faced in this, his third expedition to Antarctica. His lone vigil of five wintry months ended with a rescue as he was close to death again, this time from carbon monoxide poisoning. By then he had written these words in his diary: "If I survive this ordeal, I shall devote what is left of my life largely to . . . help further the friendship of my country with other nations of the world."

1939
Start of a National Treasure

No other person; no library, school, or institution; no government; no power on earth, can ever duplicate the unique national treasure that just one man, Clifton Waller Barrett, amassed in a lifetime of loving effort and then turned over to his beloved school, the University of Virginia.

When it comes to American literature, the first two hundred years or so of *meaningful* American literature, this one-time shipping magnate left only scattered crumbs for others to nibble on while he gobbled up the main course—first editions, hand-penned manuscripts, or letters authors wrote to family, editor, agent, or fellow author. "I've been collecting now for thirty-one years," he once said. "I estimate I've acquired books at the rate of 12,000 a year, or 1,000 a month, or 250 a week, on the average." That was in July 1970, and he still had two decades of collecting to go before his death in 1991.

Over all five decades of activity, he spent millions putting together a collection now considered priceless in value . . . a national treasure that cannot be bought or sold. Or duplicated, since Barrett's exhaustive collecting, matched by a bottomless pocketbook, simply preempted the field.

Thus, Virginia can boast the richest, most complete and academically stunning repository of American literature in the world. Not just first editions, but *rare* first editions, such as books signed by authors to their mothers; not just letters, but all kinds of formal or casual scribblings by all kinds of authors. And the manuscripts . . . oh, yes, those manuscripts showing the raw creative process employed by American authors, from the earliest to the literary giants of the twentieth century. And all right here, at the visiting scholar's fingertips. Then, too, the most complete collections of Robert Frost and James Branch Cabell, various Edgar Allan Poe works, ranking assemblies of Carl Sandburg, O. Henry, Richard Harding Davis, Stephen Crane, prized pieces from Ernest Hemingway, Mark Twain, Willa Cather, John Steinbeck, John Dos Passos, and F. Scott Fitzgerald; even Louisa May Alcott's account books—again, all in Barrett's collection, all tucked and stowed away in the lower confines of the University's library.

The fortunate visitor or scholar given a tour may see the inky manuscript of Walt Whitman's handwritten *Leaves of Grass,* complete with the marginal pinholes from where he pinned his pages together. Or the handwritten sheaf of paper that gave us "Rip Van Winkle" and companion tales of the Catskills by Washington Irving. Or a certain manuscript wherein the author scratched out his character Jim's name in the second paragraph of page 1, to insert the words "a certain tall soldier."

And at the top of the same page, written clear as day in the author's own hand, is his title: *The Red Badge of Courage,* and, on the next line down, his subtitle, *An Episode of the American Civil War.* The period right there, incidentally, was his. Then, on the next line, came: "By Stephen Crane" (Uppercase *B* his.)

But these, plus the manuscripts for John Steinbeck's *Grapes of Wrath,* Ernest Hemingway's *Green Hills of Africa,* and similar gems are only the tip of the iceberg. The collection covers American literature from its start to the present—twelve hundred authors in all—with greatest focus upon the years 1775 to 1950. The collection is so deep, it not only includes the literary giants of America, it also contains key works by "many significant, lesser-known writers."

As examples of the last group, the brochure touts Joel Barlow (1754–1812), "whose poem 'The Hasty Pudding' exemplifies early attempts to create a national and uniquely American literature," along with Susanna Rowson (1762–1824), "author of *Charlotte Temple,* the first American bestseller"; Charles Brockden Brown (1771–1810), "whose gothic romances influenced Nathaniel Hawthorne and Edgar Allan Poe"; and Phillis Wheatley (1753–84), "a former slave and the first important female African-American poet."

The collection's preeminence was clear and already long established before Barrett's death in 1991. "You can take almost any of the important authors, really, and with very few exceptions, the collection here is extensive," William H. Runge, rare book curator at the university library, said as early as 1970. "You'd almost have to come here if you're working in American literature now."

"What excites me most as curator of this marvelous library," says Michael Plunkett, current director of Special Collections, "is its vibrant use." Not a day goes by, he says, without contact by students, faculty, literary researchers, biographers, or publishers inquiring about "some book, letter, or image."

Also in 1970, Barrett, a mild-mannered, bespectacled grandfather, took the time to explain how his unparalleled collection began small . . . almost by chance. "I've always loved to own books," he started out. "The very possession of a book to me was a very desirable thing."

As a young steamship company executive, he added, he often spent lunch hour browsing secondhand bookstores near his New York office. One summer day in 1939, a friendly clerk showed him a first edition of Booth Tarkington's novel *Cherry,* handsomely done up in a red morocco slipcase. Until then, Barrett had given no thought at all to *rare* books. But the sight of Tarkington's obscure novel somehow stirred the Virginian (a native of Alexandria). "The whole thing was kind of an attractive package," he recalled. He bought the book, slipcase and all, for $4.50. By the end of the year, he had filled two bins with additional finds.

Even then the neophyte collector had no grand design in mind. But an old friend, and former teacher, did. "Why don't you make it your business to gather the first complete and inclusive collection of American literature," suggested James Southall Wilson, a professor of English at the university.

And that did it. "I was sold," said Barrett. "That scheme just seemed overpowering."

Barrett immediately cleared out his book bins, plunged into studies of bibliography, tutored himself in the most remote aspects of American literature, and took to the book trail.

It wasn't long before rare-book dealers and rival collectors learned that a hard-driving newcomer had burst into their ranks with the competitive zeal of a corporate giant. Armed with ready cash and a fast-acquired knowledge of his quarry, the new hunter of books was buying at a pace that left them breathless.

Despite the edge that personal wealth gave him over less-well-heeled collectors—and often over established libraries—Barrett attributed much of his success to pure luck, to "being in the right place at the right time."

Once, he strolled into a favorite book emporium and discovered its owners and a lawyer discussing a rare prize to be sold as part of an estate. The attorney was holding bids, as yet unopened, from the nation's most prestigious libraries, among them the Library of Congress. But the lawyer agreed to take a sealed bid from Barrett as well. When the envelopes were opened later the same day, Barrett's bid of $27,500 gave him possession of Whitman's *Leaves of Grass,* left behind by a deceased dealer in New York City's Fulton Fish Market.

Imagine the price that same, 376-page sheaf of small, yellow copy-paper pages could command today!

Another essential requirement in rare-book collecting, Barrett said, "is patience, the feeling that in time the most rare book will turn up."

When Barrett began collecting, Edgar Allan Poe's one-time school in Charlottesville had assembled impressive materials by the influential writer on its own. But thirteen Poe "rarities" still were at large, among them the manuscript of his famed *Tamerlane.* "We got them all, one by one, over the years," said Barrett with the editorial "we" that peppered any discussion of his bookish exploits.

Once, too, Barrett held back when an auction rival bid $3,500 for the original copy of Robert Frost's *Twilight,* the New England poet's first booklet of poetry. Realizing his mistake, Barrett asked the purchaser, a collector from Arizona, if he would sell the item for a quick, tidy profit. The new owner refused. Eight years later, at the urging of Frost himself, Barrett tried again. This time he obtained the slim booklet by buying his rival's entire Frost collection for $21,000. This was a coup . . . and a major factor in making Barrett's the most complete Frost file known. The exchange came on the eve of the Barrett Library's dedication at the university in 1960—and close friend Frost, one of those on hand, spent thirty or more minutes studying the earliest printing of his verses for the first time in decades.

Barrett's collection of course ranges far beyond Poe and Frost. Not only did he gather manuscripts penned by famous American authors—please add James Fenimore Cooper, Oliver Wendell Holmes, Bret Harte, Tennessee Williams, even the mysteriously disappeared Ambrose Bierce to that crowd—but the letters he gathered ranged from a thousand such epistles written by Richard Harding Davis to more than one hundred each from Henry Wadsworth Longfellow and Nathaniel Hawthorne.

One of the book hunter's successes was to collect some five hundred authors "in depth," meaning almost everything in printed or written form relating to them. Commenting after the dedication of the Barrett Library at Virginia in 1960, Herbert Cahoon, curator of autograph manuscripts at the Pierpont Morgan Library, said the collection even then contained, "insofar as it has been possible to assemble them, all fiction, poetry, drama, and essays published by an American in book form up to and including the year 1875." Moreover, for the years after 1875, it held "a very nearly complete collection of the works of every major American writer, as well as those whose achievements were not of first rank but who, nevertheless, occupy a place in the literary history of the Republic."

Despite his Virginia background, Barrett certainly didn't favor southern literature in his selections . . . not while collecting seven ranking New England authors so completely that, in the view of Cahoon, "No research on these authors can safely be undertaken without consulting the material in the Barrett Library." And who were the seven? Merely Hawthorne, Longfellow, Holmes, Henry David Thoreau, Ralph Waldo Emerson, James Russell Lowell, and John Greenleaf Whittier.

Likewise, whimsy and juvenile literature have their place in the Barrett firmament, among them *The Wizard of Oz* and *Mrs. Wiggs of the Cabbage Patch*. A sentimental speciality that emerges again and again is the collector's admitted "weakness for books inscribed by authors to their mothers." In this vein, Emerson, Twain, Holmes, Herman Melville, Thoreau, and F. Scott Fitzgerald are represented. Not to be left out, here also is Anita Loos's *Gentlemen Prefer Blondes*, with the author's fond inscription to both her parents.

The dedicated man who gathered these and so many more examples of literary Americana came from an Alexandria family known for its devotion to both the arts and public service. Clifton Waller Barrett's father, Robert South Barrett, was a diplomat and editor-publisher of the venerable Alexandria *Gazette,* one of the nation's oldest newspapers. The collector's mother, Annie Viola Tupper Barrett, was a poetess. In addition, Grandmother Kate Waller Barrett was a pioneer distaff physician, famous sociologist and philanthropist.

As a boy, Barrett walked the historic streets of Old Town Alexandria, many of them originally laid out by a youthful George Washington, and many of them lined with Colonial- and Federal-style homes still surviving the once busy port's days as a center of Virginia's—and young America's—cultural and political life. Countless times, too, he wandered the city's waterfront, once home port to a grandfather's Potomac River shipping fleet.

Barrett graduated from old Alexandria High School as valedictorian of the class of 1917 and winner of the school's literature medal. At Virginia, before World War I interrupted Barrett's studies, Professor Wilson became a friend and lasting influence on the young scholar's life.

Barrett's first full-time job, coming after the end of World War I, was with the Munson Steamship Lines in New York. Twelve years later, he and a friend founded a shipping firm of their own, the North Atlantic and Gulf Steamship Company. In the twenty-two years before Barrett retired, North Atlantic's fleet grew from a single vessel to more than six hundred. In the interim, Barrett had become an expert on sugar transport—during World War II, he served his country as the War Shipping Administration's sugar director. And it was Barrett who averted a wartime sugar "famine" by insisting that Cuban sugar could be ferried to Florida ports by barge.

But book collecting by then had emerged as Barrett's first love; at the age of fifty-three, he left the shipping business to devote his full time to the world of letters. When interviewed by this writer some years later—in 1970—his blue eyes sparkled as he warmed to his favorite topic. Amazingly, after thirty years of collecting, he could recall the exact price he paid for almost any of his acquisitions, the year he obtained it, its latest valuation—and the invariable story that went with it.

One tale he related with obvious relish explained the safe delivery of the early bestseller *Charlotte Temple* by Susanna Rowson into his hands. A London dealer unearthed the long-sought prize in a provincial English bookshop then rushed to the United States, and a likely sale at Harvard University, with his find—but he traveled by ship because he was afraid to fly. In New York, however, a blizzard had wiped out ground transportation to Cambridge, Massachusetts. He still would not step foot on an airplane, and the ship providing his return passage to England was about to sail.

"He had to unload," recalled Barrett with a boyish grin. The London book dealer turned in desperation to a New York dealer, and the New York dealer had Barrett on the telephone within minutes. The result was another coup for the Virginian.

Another time, also marked by a heavy snowfall, Barrett received word that a dealer was prepared to part with a truly stunning literary prize. It was New Year's Eve, and the Barretts were due at a formal dinner in just a few hours, but Barrett rushed to the seller's office anyway. By now a snowstorm had crippled transportation in New York City, so Barrett next trudged nearly two miles to the Pennsylvania Railroad Station to hop a late-running commuter train to Long Island and his home there.

At his suburban station, he found that his car wouldn't start, so he hiked another mile in the snow, the bulky package still under his arm. When he finally reached home, his wife reminded him they had been due at the dinner an hour earlier . . . and asked what was in the package. "Just a book," he said, tossing his new acquisition on the couch. "I might have known," she fondly commented as they rushed off.

What it was, was the manuscript for *The Red Badge of Courage.*

After retirement from the steamship business, Barrett maintained an incredible pace . . . not all of it related to book collecting. For one important thing, he and his wife, the former Cornelia Corinne Hughes of Birmingham, Alabama, had six children and a fast-growing collection of grandchildren. Then, too, while still living in the New York area, he served as a New York City art commissioner. Moving to Charlottesville, home of his beloved University of Virginia, the Barrett couple lived at Arcadia, a striking home built around a domed library in which the collector of Americana kept his own private collections of Spanish, French, and Italian literature. A reader of all three languages, he was able to skim along at a thousand words per minute in English.

A great fan of Thomas Jefferson, founder of the university and an accomplished gardener, Barrett maintained a Jeffersonian garden of local renown. In addition, whether in New York or Virginia, he collected abstract, nonrepresentational art.

At one time, one place or another, he was one of six experts selecting books for the library at the John F. Kennedy White House; he served on the university's Board of Visitors; he was president of the scholarly Bibliographical Society of America and head of the exclusive Grolier Club; chairman of the Columbia University Libraries Association and the Pierpont Morgan Library Fellows; an honorary trustee of the New York Public Library; founder of the Associates of the University of Virginia Library; a board member of three major historic shrines, including Mount Vernon and Jefferson's Monticello, and four college boards aside from Virginia's.

He was honored as a Laureate of Virginia after his death, and while still living was elected to the university's chapter of Phi Beta Kappa

When his collection was dedicated as the Clifton Waller Barrett Library of American Literature, University President Edgar F. Shannon Jr. pronounced the donor's stunning gift as "almost incredible" in value. "The monetary value, which is one kind of index, has been placed in the millions," said Shannon, himself an English scholar. "But its great value to us lies in the fact that generations of men and women, through their study of these books and manuscripts, will live with great men."

As for why Barrett decided to give away his hard-won literary treasure, he would only say: "I don't care; I'm not looking for personal aggrandizement, because I'll be dead and gone."

He also noted that a university is no better than its library.

Modest as he was affable, Barrett frequently pointed out that Virginia had assembled impressive Americana all on its own, before and after he came along—most notably, former writer-in-residence William Faulkner's entire literary estate and the Tracy W. McGregor Library, an unequaled collection of southeastern U.S. historical materials also housed in university library. Still collecting after dedication of his library in 1960, meanwhile, Barrett added fifty thousand items over the next decade or so, while spending an average of $100,000 in each of those years, he estimated.

As always, his fabulous luck prevailed. At a Charlottesville cocktail party, Barrett was approached by retired Prof. Quincy Wright, who asked how extensive a collection Barrett had accumulated on the poet Carl Sandburg.

It was only "adequate," Barrett admitted.

But not for long. Wright, it developed, was the son of the mid-American poet's first printer and patron. As a boy, Wright had set type for Sandburg's earliest works. Now, he was willing to part with rare first editions of those volumes, several manuscripts, and a set of previously unknown letters.

The exchange that followed gave Virginia a Sandburg collection second only to the material that the late poet had bequeathed to the University of Illinois in his home state.

The Sandburg story was typical of Barrett's amazing career in letters. But then so were accounts of his encyclopedic knowledge of his quarry, his tireless attendance at book auctions, his close reading of galley proofs for new book-dealer catalogs, and the early morning telephone calls that would nail down a literary trophy while fellow collectors still were asleep.

The magnificent result was the treasure that Barrett built—a vast slice of the nation's heritage, a priceless gift not only for Virginia's academic community, but for Americans everywhere.

1943
No "Folly" After All

"It was just in a field," Daphne Webb of Arlington recalled years later. "One day we were all sitting at our desks and the wall behind us caved in—the fresh cement poured down like molten lava. We jumped over our desks and ran for our lives."

Eggs in those days sold for thirty-one cents a dozen and milk for fourteen cents a quart. Overseas, the nation's men—"our boys"—were fighting World War II. And on the home front, things sometimes could be a little bit crazy . . . especially at the construction site for the world's largest office building.

Buses, for instance. Bus service to the first completed sections of the vast structure was often inadequate. The drivers often missed the new roads into the site, clouds of dust hovered everywhere, and long lines formed at the bus stops. "Girls would smack each other over the head with their purses to get into the buses," recalled Marie Owen of neighboring Washington, D.C.

Leo Urbanske Jr., a young telephone installer back in the early 1940s, later would recall stringing the overhead telephone lines to newly placed desks at night, only to find incoming workers had shifted their desks the next day. "Those wires were every which way," he said in 1967, by then twenty-five years older and chairman of the Arlington County Board. "You could hardly pick your way down the aisle."

Still another veteran of the construction period was Roy B. Pruitt of Arlington, a timekeeper back in the forties working out of an engineers' "shack" at the construction site. One morning, he couldn't find the shack. "During the night they had taken a bulldozer and moved it," he explained years later.

Overseas, bannered the *Washington Star* in April 1942, JAPS REACH LASHIO; CHINA ROAD DOOMED. In all the tumult, scant notice was paid on April 30 when a handful of Ordnance Department workers moved into Section A of the Pentagon—that strange, once-upon-a-time hotly disputed structure rising on flat swamp- and farmland in Arlington previously occupied by the old Hoover Airport. Daphne Webb, Marie Owen, and scores of others began work in "offices" often lacking any divider walls. The telephone lines dangled from ceiling fixtures and reached for desks like so much seaweed. More than twelve thousand construction workers, laboring around the clock, still had to complete the remaining four "wedges" of the vast, five-sided building. One section had not even been started as of April 1942.

By January 1943, though, the $83 million Pentagon officially was opened as a new home for workers in seventeen of the War Department's widely scattered buildings. Then the world's largest office building in square footage (more than 6 million gross and 3.7 million net), the Pentagon had risen in just sixteen months. An enclosed city with its own police, fire, hospital, and commercial services, even its own moving men—serving a "population" of sometimes twenty-six thousand and even up to thirty-five thousand workers, military and civilian—the great five-sided structure registered its own births and deaths long before the terrorist attack of September 11, 2001. For instance, the first known suicide at the Pentagon came during World War II when an enlisted man jumped to his death from a fifth-floor window.

Aside from the personal tragedy involved, his leap raised thorny legal issues for federal and Virginia authorities debating which government should take charge of the body. While the officials argued, recalled early Pentagon workers Rose C. Butera and Marie Owen, the suicide's body lay in the Pentagon's five-acre central courtyard from morning to midafternoon.

Under the unrelenting impetus of the war, the same women said, they worked fourteen- to eighteen-hour days with no letup.

And, if the war was fought on a historically unprecedented scale, the statistics associated with construction of the Pentagon—a vital part of the U.S. war effort—also were cosmic in scale. The Pentagon's construction force pounded 41,492 concrete pilings into 5.5 million cubic yards of fill for the foundations. The construction army processed 680,000 tons of sand taken from the nearby Potomac River for the 435,000 cubic yards of concrete eventually molded into the Pentagon form.

The final result, on a twenty-nine-acre site, was a five-story (plus mezzanine and basement), five-sided structure faced with Indiana limestone and enclosing five concentric rings connected by ten "spokes," or corridors. Outside were two hundred acres of lawn and terraces plus an initial sixty-seven acres devoted to parking. Inside, the corridors ran for 17.5 miles in all, but no office was more than seven minutes' walk from another . . . and usually less. "It's a very simple system," said Armor H. P. Taylor of Alexandria, an air training administrator stationed at the Pentagon in the 1960s. "Whoever designed it put a lot of foresight and effort into cutting down the time between stations."

Surprisingly, the sprawling Pentagon complex, now famous throughout the world, once was known as "Somervell's Folly." The derogatory reference was to Brig. Gen. Brehon B. Somervell, who, as chief of construction for the army's Quartermaster General's Office, dreamed up the radical pentagon concept one weekend in mid-1941 as the best way to gather scattered War Department personnel under one vast roof—but only temporarily, mind you—instead of going along with a proposed District of Columbia site for separate Navy and War Department buildings. Now, more than sixty years later, the U.S. Navy also is headquartered in the Pentagon, along with the Army and Air Force. Today, too, the complex not only is considered a permanent home for the defense establishment, but it also is more fondly known by sobriquets such as "Puzzle Palace on the Potomac" than it is as anybody's "folly."

It wasn't long after its construction, meanwhile, that the Pentagon housed the world's largest telephone system, along with the world's largest pneumatic tube system (fifteen miles of tube was the estimate in the early 1960s). At the start of the twenty-first century, four decades later, the official Pentagon website on the Internet offered a few more staggering statistics. To wit: The Pentagon's twenty-three thousand employees traversed thirty miles of access highway and express bus lanes every weekday, to say nothing of the Washington, D.C., area's metro subway system, simply to get close to their place of work. "They ride past 200 acres of lawn to park approximately 8,770 cars in 16 parking lots; climb 131 stairways or ride 19 escalators to reach offices that occupy 3,705,793 square feet. While in the building, they tell time by 4,200 clocks, drink from 691 water fountains, utilize 284 rest rooms, consume 4,500 cups of coffee, 1,700 pints of milk, and 6,800 soft drinks prepared or served by a restaurant staff of 230 persons and dispensed in 1 dining room, 2 cafeterias, 6 snack bars, and an outdoor snack bar" in the center court.

Impressively also, more than 200,000 telephone calls were made daily through phones "connected by 100,000 miles of telephone cable." Then, too: "The Defense Post Office handles about 1,2000,000 pieces of mail monthly. Various libraries support our personnel in research and completion of their work. The Army Library alone provides 300,000 publications and 1,700 periodicals in various languages."

Cleaning the internal rabbit warren of offices required a systematic approach, quite naturally. Thus, in the 1970s, Benjamin E. Jackson of Washington, D.C., rode up and down the Pentagon corridors aboard a motor scooter while supervising a nighttime force of 309 cleaners that included all kinds of "specialists." As explained by Howard J. Pavel of Falls Church, the Pentagon building manager at the time—and thus Jackson's boss—the night force and a daytime crew of eighty-eight more cleaners were divided into "custodial laborers, squad supervisors, and shift supervisors."

Going into greater detail, Pavel defined a few of his cleaning army's specialists: "Some are rug people—all they do is vacuum rugs," he said. "We have our high-level cleaners, people who clean above the eight-foot level. We have lampists, as we call them, who clean out those [90,000] light fixtures and repair them. They get to every fixture once a year. We have zone cleaners, primarily women, who are assigned 21,000 square feet of office space every night."

Outside the office spaces but still inside the outer walls, sweepers, buglike in appearance, swept and buffed the corridor floors, while outdoors more sweepers brushed clean the vast parking lots surrounding the Defense Department headquarters. Inside again, venetian blind experts cleaned the venetian blinds in a special "laundry" on a carefully planned, rotating schedule.

It is tempting to say that routine cleaning and maintenance of the Pentagon has been carried on with military precision ever since the giant structure's earliest days.

Since those days the very name of the vast structure has become a household word known around the world as reference to America's military establishment in general. Then, too, over the years since the Pentagon's official opening in January 1943, the five-sided structure on flat Virginia ground witnessed the triumphant end to World War II, along with the Korean War of the 1950s, the Vietnam War of the 1960s and 1970s, the Persian Gulf War of the 1990s, the Iraq War of 2003 . . . but only once did any hostile force bring a conflict directly to the military nerve center itself—in September 2001, when terrorists crashed a hijacked airliner into the Pentagon, with heavy loss of life resulting.

On a far lighter note, it should be noted here that there is *no* truth to the old saw that a Western Union messenger boy entering the Pentagon's vast office spaces one day during World War II wasn't seen again . . . until he emerged with full colonel's rank.

Quite true, though, is an often-forgotten entry in the résumé of Maj. Gen. Leslie Groves, the man who supervised creation of the atom bomb as head of the super-secret Manhattan Project. The fact is, General Groves first came to public attention as the man who supervised construction of the Pentagon in the amazing time of just sixteen months. Moreover, notes the Pentagon website, the $83 million cost was an investment returned "within seven years."

★

1944
Grim Tidings for Bedford

★

The word didn't come until weeks later. It would be a Monday morning in July when Elizabeth Teass sat down at the teletype machine in Green's Drug Store and signaled the Western Union office in Roanoke that she was up and running. Back came the shocker: "We have casualties."

Imagine. So long after.

All over the country, the folks back home had been following the progress of the Allied invasion of Normandy. D-day and the landing on Omaha Beach on June 6 already were history . . . weren't they? Well, not quite.

There had been the casualties—so many, it took until now to sort them out and send the notifications.

And somewhere in the fair land there would be a community, probably a small town, that would have lost more young men on D-day in relation to its overall population than any other.

As fate would have such things, that town would be Bedford, Virginia, close by the eastern slopes of the Blue Ridge, population thirty-two hundred.

Not all the War Department telegrams would arrive that first day, just seven, eight, maybe nine. But before it was all over, Bedford would be staggering from the news that twenty-three of her sons, nineteen of them members of Company A, 116th Infantry Regiment, 29th Infantry Division, had died in the Normandy invasion, most of them right on the beach . . . the now-legendary Omaha Beach.

Boarding the small boats for the final assault were twin brothers from Bedford. As Roy Stevens, a tech sergeant back then, later would explain, his brother Ray stuck out his hand as they were about to split up and climb into different assault boats. But Roy didn't take his brother's hand. He reminded his twin they had agreed to meet at the Vierville-sur-Mer crossroads, inland from the beaches. Roy said that's still what they would do. "And he just sort of dropped his head. He had a feeling that he wasn't going to make it, and he just kept telling me that."

Going into the beach under a firestorm of German resistance, Roy's boat hit a sunken obstacle and sank. Nearly all aboard drowned, dragged down by the weight of their gear, but not Roy. Inflating his Mae West life vest, he floated for an hour and finally was picked up and carried back to England.

It would be another four days before he could return to Bloody Omaha . . . return and look for his twin brother, Ray. What he found was a hastily dug grave. "That has haunted me quite a bit since that happened, because I should have shaken his hand."

In Bedford, the grim telegram came weeks later to tell their mother, Martha Jane Stevens, that Ray wouldn't be coming back . . . except for his reburial.

For Martha Jane Stevens there was at least that.

But not for fifteen-year-old Lucille Hoback's family. "I remember well the devastating impact on my family when we received telegrams two days in a row stating that my two older brothers were killed or missing in action," said the married Lucille Boggess in more recent years. The first dreaded wire came on a Sunday morning forty-five days after D-day as the family prepared for services at their small-town church. "The doorbell rang and it was the sheriff. The telegram said, 'Private Bedford T. Hoback has been killed in action.'"

Instead of their leaving for church, the church congregation came to their house that morning.

The following day, the next telegram was a "missing in action" notification. This time it was her brother Raymond. His body never would be found, never would come back home.

And yet, forty-five days before, on June 7, 1944, D-day plus one, a West Virginia soldier "walking on a beach in France," came across a pocket Bible. He found a name in it, Raymond Hoback's mother's name. After a spell he sent it to her, saying, "By now you have probably heard from your son and he is fine."

Of course, he wasn't . . . and the Hoback family never would know how the Bible survived (with no water damage) when its owner didn't.

He had been wounded, some of the other Bedford men recalled, but not all that badly, they didn't think. Had he been left on a stretcher too close to the water's edge and an incoming tide? How did he and the Bible become separated? Questions, questions . . . so many questions left unanswered.

Another Bedford man had been with the twin Stevens boys when they separated and Roy said he probably wouldn't make it through the Normandy landing. A first lieutenant, he was Elisha "Ray" Nance, quite likely the first of the Bedford men to come home since he was wounded right at the outset and then shipped back Stateside.

When the A Company commander, Capt. Taylor Fellers, stepped out onto French soil, he was killed on the spot, Nance later related. All twenty men in the captain's assault boat also were killed, and command now fell to Nance. Coming into the beach twenty minutes later with the company headquarters personnel, "five of us," he found no one left to command. So many already had been killed, "the company didn't exist."

Not that he had much time to take over. "I went down. I don't know how I got across the beach." There was no time to think as incessant German fire swept the beach. Anyone standing was likely to get hit. "The first sergeant, the radio operator, and the foot messenger were killed beside me. The recon unit got in front of me and I yelled at them to scatter, and a mortar shell landed on top of them."

Nance had been hit in the thumb and a leg. But that wasn't his overriding concern. "There wasn't anybody in front of me. There wasn't anybody left behind me. I was alone in France."

Of course, he really wasn't. A sergeant came along and somehow carried Nance, piggyback, out of the fire zone. He next went to a hospital in England and then eventually home to Bedford. "I wondered what people thought," he said in recent years. "There he is, and there they are? He's here, and my son is over there, dead? I never did find out."

Returning home to a postwar career as a rural mail carrier, he couldn't quite shake the ghosts of D-day. Ray Stevens's family was on his mail route, reported Scripps Howard News Service columnist John Lang in July 2000. "Mrs. Stevens came out each morning," he said. "She'd ask me what happened over there; where was her Ray?"

As Lang also explained, the Bedford men were Virginia National Guardsmen. That explained why there were so many men, even relatives, from one community in one outfit. Indeed, their Blue and Gray Twenty-ninth Division was a National Guard outfit made up of men from Virginia, Maryland, and the District of Columbia; their 116th Infantry Regiment once was the Confederacy's Stonewall Brigade of Civil War days, and before that a militia outfit dating back to frontier days, the French and Indian War, the Revolution, and the War of 1812. On D-day, further notes a regimental online history, four 116th rifle companies were among the first troops to hit the Normandy beaches. "In those early hours on the fire-swept beach, the 116th Infantry Combat Team, the old Stonewall Brigade of Virginia, clawed its way through Les Moulins draw toward its objective, Vierville-sur-Mer."

Despite the smothering German fire, elements of the 116th's Second Battalion, "battered but gallant," managed to break loose from the beach, climb past the embankment, and fight its way to a farmhouse, which immediately became a command post. "The 116th suffered more than 800 casualties this day," says the same online history. And for its share of those eight hundred, little Bedford, Virginia, beneath the shadow of the Peaks of Otter, acquired the unenviable badge of honor that made it, by act of Congress, the home of the National D-day Memorial, a ten-acre statuary park memorializing the sacrifice not only of the Bedford men but of all Americans who stormed ashore at Omaha and other Normandy beaches that historic morning in 1944.

1944
Rosa Parks Preempted

A quiet Sunday morning in Gloucester County, and nobody on this particular wartime day in 1944 was thinking homebound revolution. A Greyhound bus pulled up, and Irene Morgan, age twenty-seven, dressed in her Sunday-go-to-church clothes, climbed aboard and settled into an aisle seat four rows from the back.

The young black woman, on her way to Baltimore to see her doctors as a follow-up to a serious operation, quite properly had taken a seat in the so-called colored section of the bus.

As the bus rolled northward on U.S. Route 17, with occasional stops to pick up additional passengers, it began to fill up. Then came the critical moment. "When a white couple boarded, the driver turned to Morgan and ordered her and her seat mate to the far back of the bus," reported Bill McKelway in the *Richmond Times-Dispatch* of August 4, 2000. And right there, although little noted for many years, began a revolution of sorts . . . a new day for those heretofore relegated to the back of the bus. Some of them, anyway.

Irene Morgan had refused to move.

"I paid for my ticket," she later said. "I was where I was supposed to be. Why should I move?"

And there she sat, not budging.

It was a brave thing to do. "It was a troublesome time," wrote McKelway in his coverage of a Gloucester County "Homecoming for Irene Morgan," held five decades later. "Newspaper stories carried items every few weeks about blacks who had been similarly defiant and as a result had been jailed, shot, assaulted, or forced off buses in the dark of night. Soldiers were frequent victims."

None of that kept the young black woman from sticking to her guns that Sunday morning.

As the passengers "looked on in silence," there was a delay while Middlesex County Sheriff R. Beverly Segar was called to the scene.

When the elderly sheriff, standing by her seat with a deputy in support, served Morgan with an arrest warrant , she tore it up and "tossed it out the window." Added McKelway: "She also managed, in the words of the state Supreme Court, 'to kick the sheriff three times on his leg.'"

Actually, there was more graphic physical contact than that, it seems. "They never should have put their hands on me," Morgan said. "That's what got me so mad."

Eighty-three years of age herself by the year 2000, married name Kirkaldy, a great-grandmother and a resident of New York, she said she kicked the sheriff "where it would hurt a man most." And she didn't mean the shinbone.

Picking up the civil rights story again, McKelway noted, "Two days later, with Richmond lawyer Spottswood W. Robinson III by her side, Morgan was found guilty of resisting arrest and fined $100."

More significant, she was fined another $10 on the charge of failing to move to the back of the bus.

She appealed . . . eventually to the U.S. Supreme Court, with Thurgood Marshall as her lead appeals attorney. Not so very incidentally, Robinson was destined to become a federal circuit court of appeals judge, and Marshall would reach the highest bench in the land as a Supreme Court justice. Both black attorneys were prominent and highly successful advocates in the civil rights struggles of the 1950s and 1960s.

But this was 1944 . . . actually, 1946, by the time the Supreme Court ruling came down, a decade before the world would hear of Rosa Parks and the Montgomery, Alabama, bus boycott over the same back-of-the-bus issue. Only, this was *interstate* bus travel, and Montgomery was *city* bus travel. Thus, the highest court in the land could, and did, easily rule in Morgan's case as a federal issue. And the six-to-one ruling of June 3, 1946, said the Virginia law calling for segregated seating on interstate buses was illegal; it interfered with interstate transportation.

Not all that widely publicized at the time, the ruling should have meant no more back-of-the-bus seating for interstate bus travelers . . . that is, if and when enforced. Thurgood Marshall called the ruling "a decisive blow to the evil of segregation and all that it stands for." Echoed a page 1 photo caption in the Richmond *Afro-American* newspaper:

"Her Fight Ends Jim Crow." Also exultant was the banner headline above: JC [meaning Jim Crow] BUS TRAVEL OUTLAWED. Beyond that and some sporadic publicity here and there, Morgan's action didn't garner nearly the headlines accorded the civil rights activists of the fifties and sixties. Her name was no household word. Nor was the somewhat narrow ruling always strictly enforced nationwide.

"Left for another day," explained McKelway, "was the deeper issue of whether segregation was constitutionally flawed." Some states, in fact, would claim that their segregation laws were *not* affected by the federal ruling.

So, it wasn't *all* bus travel, true, but Irene Morgan Kirkaldy had broken a major, long-standing barrier, nonetheless. "She was a true pioneer, an early pioneer whose role seemed to get lost," commented civil rights historian Taylor Branch at the time of her recognition by Gloucester County in 2000.

At that ceremony, Morgan alternated between "a few tears of emotion" and a "beaming smile" as a parade of "county officials, college administrators, and politicians thanked Morgan for what is recalled as a selfless act of heroism that chipped away at the country's onerous color barrier," McKelway wrote. Janine Bacquie, a granddaughter proudly looking on, said: "It's time to let people know. Until now, she has preferred to let it be part of her past. But she's excited that people care and are paying attention."

Said Morgan herself: "My thought has always been that it was more important to just get on with your life, to move on and put the past behind you. I never thought to bring attention to myself."

As for that Sunday morning in July 1944, "I did what I did because it was right."

1952
Start on a Foxhole Promise

With German mortar shells dropping around his foxhole shortly after the Allied landings on the beaches of Normandy, France, on June 6,

1944, University of Virginia dropout Carl Stark of Alexandria made a solemn bargain with God. "I said if I get out of this mess, that's what I'm gonna do. I'm going to be a doctor in a rural area and spend my life helping people."

Surviving the war, he did do exactly that . . . in so many different ways.

But first, his deceptively none-too-illustrious background, as recounted by *Richmond Times-Dispatch* reporter Rex Bowman on Sunday, June 30, 2002:

Born in Poughkeepsie, New York, to a nurse and a barnstorming pilot, Stark spent part of his boyhood in Holland, where his father taught flying . . . and Stark learned the Dutch language. "He moved to Alexandria to finish high school," added Bowman's account, "and when World War II broke out, he was having the time of his life as a flunking student at the University of Virginia. College officials told him his happy-go-lucky attitude and his grades would be forgiven if he joined the army, so he did."

It wasn't very long before he found himself in that foxhole just outside the Normandy village of St. Mere-Eglise, a key objective of the American forces just landed on Omaha Beach. It wasn't long before those mortar rounds dropping all around *suggested* that quick promise to God.

With the war over in 1945, Stark returned home and wangled his way back into the university, earned a medical degree, and "received his physician's license in 1952," added Bowman. But what now? "I just wanted to be a doctor in a small country town, the kind you read about," Dr. Stark would explain later. "I had never lived in one, I never visited one. But I just wanted to go into a family practice and treat people for everything, from cradle to grave."

He happened upon Wytheville in southwest Virginia, related reporter Bowman, liked its look, and accepted a local bank's offer of "money to set up practice."

Roughly three thousand childbirths, two hundred or so tonsillectomies, and "countless house calls in floods and blizzards" later, Carl Stark, age eighty, died in his Wytheville home one Wednesday morning in the spring of 2002, fifty years after his arrival.

To friends and neighbors, he had become a fond and familiar figure all those five decades "as he jauntily walked down the town streets with his stethoscope around his neck or jutting out of his jacket pocket." All those years, too, "he greeted many people by name, having brought a good percentage of them into the world."

But there was more than merely (*merely?!*) doctoring, so much more, that Stark did for his adopted community. Hardly had he arrived in 1952 than he "set about putting his stamp on the town and the surrounding area." Just ten years later, he began a stint as mayor that would last from 1962 to 1990, nearly three decades in all. As just one accomplishment of his dedicated leadership, he "persuaded local governments to work together and helped create the Mount Rogers Planning District Commission, serving as its first chairman."

Not only that, but, "according to many, it was Stark who persuaded the federal government to align Interstate 77 so it intersected Interstate 81 in Wytheville, making the town of eight thousand a crucial transportation hub."

And more yet. "Stark also led the effort to rid Wytheville of its outhouses, helped secure $20 million in grants over the decades, brought water and sewer pipes to the nearby hamlet of Ivanhoe, and established the region's Head Start program to help poor children."

But hold on, still more.

"He volunteered his labor to every local organization that needed help: the Masons, Shriners, Lions Club, American Legion, and Veterans of Foreign Wars. He also preached as a lay minister."

Could it be a big surprise, then, that he, at one time or another, also had reached beyond Wytheville itself to serve as president of the Virginia Municipal League; president of the Medical Society of Virginia; chairman of the Virginia State Parks and Recreation Commission; president of the Great Lakes to Florida Highway Association; district governor of Lions Club International, and Virginia coordinator of community operations for the American Association of Retired Persons? According to Bowman, Stark once explained his philosophy that a leadership position in such groups made it easier to help people. "If you can't get it done through channels," Stark had said, "just go ahead and become the leader and get it done."

Wrote Bowman also: "A slender slip of a man, Stark was nonetheless a giant, and his passing marks the end of an era here [Wytheville] because Stark literally reshaped the landscape of this corner of Southwest Virginia."

It hardly needs adding that this small-town hero's life, "one continuous effort to live up to his bargain with God, is worth remembering."

★

1958
Massive Resistance at Work

★

If Virginia's school desegregation crisis of the 1950s and 1960s were to be viewed through a keyhole, the eye's focal point would be the sleepy-looking, innocuous-seeming town of Farmville, seat of Prince Edward County.

For this location not only was a party to the U.S. Supreme Court's historic school desegregation decision of 1954 but also the state's most extreme example of refusal to bend before the federal court edict.

For here not only did the public schools close from 1959 to 1964 rather than allow both black and white students to attend class together but here, a "lost generation" of blacks finally would be granted honorary high-school diplomas half a century later—in 2003.

"R. R. Moton High School" the diplomas would say . . . and it was at Moton, arguably, that Virginia's school integration nightmare (nightmare, controversy, civil rights achievement—call it what you will, it was a struggle for all concerned) really began.

Fifty years after the fact, radio talk show host John Watson would recall his role in a student strike of 1951 protesting the poor, over-crowded conditions at the county's traditionally black high school, where one class was taught in a school bus.

It was his job to go home, call the school, and pose as a Farmville merchant complaining that a number of students were playing hooky. As the students had hoped, school principal M. Boyd Jones immediately left the school grounds to deal with his young "truants."

With Jones unable to interfere, "students led by sixteen-year-old Barbara Johns could stage a strike protesting conditions at their racially segregated school," reported Kathryn Orth in the *Richmond Times-Dispatch* of April 22, 2001. The strike that April day in 1951 led to a protest march up Main Street to the county courthouse, to a student walkout of two weeks in all . . . and "ultimately led to a lawsuit that became part of the Brown vs. Board of Education case and the 1954 U.S. Court decision that struck down racially segregated schools as unconstitutional." In effect, said the high court at the time, separate was not equal.

As the courts, school boards, and state officials then jockeyed back and forth over the issue of public school racial integration, Virginia finally found itself poised in the late summer of 1958 to close down public schools rather than allow any black child to attend classes in a traditionally all-white school.

"Virginia's massive resistance machinery, which the State has had in readiness for two years now, is about to get its first workout," wrote Mary Lou Werner in the *Washington Star* of September 1, 1958. "One integrated student is all it takes to set in motion the legal mechanism Virginia adopted to bar Negroes from white schools."

The mechanism she cited was mandated school closure, whether local authorities wanted to take such drastic action or not. Writing a few days later as part of the coverage that earned her a Pulitzer Prize in reporting, she also noted, "Barring last-minute legal delays, the threat of closed schools is imminent in Arlington, Charlottesville, and Norfolk."

All three localities, she explained, were under court orders to end segregation in their schools. "As soon as an integrated assignment is made—by local action or court order—State law automatically closes the school involved. The law is explicit. There is no room for uncertainty about what it means."

Few were happy to be at such a crossroads in public policy, but that's where Virginia stood for the moment. "The long legal battle ushered in by the Supreme Court's desegregation decisions has brought Virginia the role of leader of Southern 'massive resistance.' It is face to face with the prospect of closing some schools, or permitting integration."

To be sure, the machinery of massive resistance was destined to break down . . . within months, actually. But first, in the fall of 1958, public schools indeed were shut down in the face of integration orders—in Norfolk, Charlottesville, and Front Royal. An estimated thirteen thousand students found their public school doors locked. (Ironically, in a sense, it was the white schools that were closed, whereas the black schools in the same localities could operate as before.)

With more court action threatening and the state's all-white political leadership rethinking the disastrous massive resistance policy, the school closures lasted only for a short time. By 1959, as Orth was able to write in her *Times-Dispatch* story of 2001, "black students were admitted in Arlington and Norfolk without protest from state leaders, and the policies [the state's anti-desegregation laws) effectively came to an end."

But not in Prince Edward County, where the Board of Supervisors simply didn't budget money for the public schools, which then all, whether traditionally black or white, closed their doors. The white students then quickly switched to a private academy organized by their parents.

The situation lasted for five long years, 1959 to 1964, during which a "lost generation" of blacks (and a few whites) had to find school opportunities elsewhere . . . or miss going to school altogether. "Black parents scrambled to provide for their children, in many cases sending them to live with out-of-state relatives to continue their educations," wrote Orth and Jamie Ruff in a shared *Times-Dispatch* article of May 15, 1994. "The Quakers helped some black students by placing them in homes across the country. . . . When it became clear the Prince Edward schools might remain closed for some time, the Quakers arranged for about seventy children to attend integrated schools in other states."

Unhappily, most of the county's 1,780 students "had nowhere to go," except for classes run by volunteers in churches. U.S. Attorney General Robert F. Kennedy "helped launch the privately financed Free School Association in 1963, providing classes for about 1,700 blacks and a few whites." Even so, "when the public schools finally reopened a year later, many blacks never returned."

Calvin Bass, appointed to the county school board in 1954 and later its chairman, said he and his colleagues tried "to operate public schools as long as we could operate racially segregated public schools." And the county did go all the way to the Supreme Court in an effort to maintain the old "separate-but-equal" system . . . under which the white public schools were awarded twice the budget of the black schools, according to the *Times-Dispatch*.

"Charlie Pickett, elected to the Board of Supervisors in 1960, believes county leaders merely reflected the will of the people" said the same article. "'They wanted the separate system,' he said."

As school board member Bass well recalled, feelings ran high in those days. "I had people who would rather walk across the street than speak to me," he said. Apparently his hope of keeping the schools open was seen as being in favor of integration. "I had my life threatened. That gives you an idea how intense feelings were."

Today, the old Moton school building has been replaced by a new one, and the old plant is now a museum and designated a National Historic Landmark by the federal government.

John Watson, who made the phone call in 1951 that lured Moton principal Jones out of the school while the students organized their strike, was still proud of their accomplishment fifty years later. "Looking back we can see the significance," he said. "We were the only school where the strike was carried out by the students. It really was student led."

He also carried vivid memories of the conditions that led to the student protest, to the lawsuit, to the U.S. Supreme Court ruling against "separate but equal." His old high school in 1951 had no gym, cafeteria, or lockers, he recalled. "I was all for the strike. I was on the football team. We would visit other schools, and they had lockers. When they visited us, they would laugh at us. We had no showers, no gym. The players had to change in the tarpaper shacks" (three wooden classroom structures covered by tarpaper and heated with stoves).

Watson always had the sneaking suspicion, by the way, that Moton's Principal Boyd Jones recognized his voice, distinctive enough to make the adult Watson a prizewinning radio talk show host . . . a strong suspicion that when he called the school to say some Moton students were playing hooky, Mr. Jones merely "played along."

★
---

1 9 6 7
Lessons for a South African Visitor
★

The news in 1967 rocked the world. Who, just a few years before, would have thought it ever possible? What an incredible concept: Amputate—that is, take out, remove—a living person's heart and replace it with another . . . with a dead person's heart! How could it be?

And yet that was the news from South Africa, where Dr. Christiaan Barnard had done exactly that. At a hospital in Cape Town he had performed the world's first human heart transplant.

The fact is, pure chance made Cape Town the locale of the medical milestone instead of Richmond and its Medical College of Virginia, a groundbreaking medical institution already noted as a pioneer in kidney transplantation. "Only a mismatch in blood types" kept MCV's

Dr. Richard R. Lower from performing a human heart transplant the year *before* Dr. Barnard's feat, noted Beverly Orndorff in the *Richmond Times-Dispatch* in 1988. "In 1966 a potential heart donor became available at the same time a potential heart recipient was in the hospital, but their blood types differed and Dr. Lower said he decided not to perform it" (the unprecedented operation).

Why at that point in time would a surgeon in Virginia even consider taking on such an extraordinary procedure? Well, the further fact was, at Stanford University in the 1950s, Dr. Lower and Dr. Norman Shumway had been the first surgeons to perform heart transplants on dogs as vital research that "led directly to the first human heart transplants a few years later," added science writer Orndorff.

Lower came to MCV in 1965, wrote Orndorff also. "He was recruited by the late Dr. David M. Hume, MCV's surgery department head chairman and pioneer in kidney transplantation, to start a heart transplantation program. Dr. Lower continued research here [Richmond] on transplanting hearts in dogs."

Meanwhile, South Africa's Christiaan Barnard wasn't exactly operating in a vacuum as he prepared to make medical history with the first human heart transplant late in 1967. Guess where he spent several months earlier the same year?

Exactly. At the Medical College of Virginia, where he had planned to learn about kidney transplants but also "watched Dr. Lower and his team perform some dog heart transplants." After visiting Stanford, Dr. Barnard returned to South Africa, and the rest is history.

Back in Richmond, according to Dr. Michael L. Hess, later head of the MCV heart failure–transplant program, "this obviously incensed . . . the late Dr. David Hume." But Dr. Lower laughingly said he was "sort of relieved" that Dr. Barnard performed the first human heart transplant, "because he got all the heat." His point was the worldwide publicity that greeted Dr. Barnard, his patient, and the donor.

As science writer Orndorff also pointed out, however, MCV's first heart transplant, which came in May 1968, wound up thrusting Dr. Lower himself into the glare of intense publicity—and at the center of a "long, historic court case two years later."

Explained Orndorff: "The family of the donor charged that Dr. Lower and other surgeons took the donor's heart while it was still beating, and thus under the existing law at the time, took it before the patient was legally dead.

"The patient had no brain function, but brain death was not included in the legal definitions of death anywhere in this country at the time.

"A Richmond Circuit Court jury decided, however, that brain death could be a criterion of death and as a result of that landmark case, laws were changed throughout the nation to include cessation of brain activity as a definition of death."

The decision was critical to the entire organ transplantation field, Orndorff pointed out, "because . . . a potential donor's heart and other organs could be maintained in good condition, until shortly after transplantation, as long as the brain-dead donor was kept on a respirator."

☆ ☆ ☆

Additional note: Twenty years after the Medical College of Virginia began its heart transplantation program, Dr. Lower announced he would be leaving MCV and the medical field in early 1989 to operate a cattle ranch in Montana. Not so incidentally, the MCV heart transplant team by that time had performed hundreds of heart transplants in humans, with "around a 93 percent one-year survival rate, and probably 65 to 70 percent five-year survival rate," Dr. Hess said in mid-1988.

Incidental fact: Another early heart transplant recipient at MCV, during the initial period of research on the procedure, was a giant baboon that long would be remembered because the animal wouldn't take its postoperative medication unless it was dissolved in beer.

1968
Life with a New Heart

When Louis B. Russell Jr., a barrel-chested industrial arts teacher from Indianapolis, looked into the mirror the last few years of his life, he saw

From the author's article in the *Washington Star* of January 13, 1971.

a friendly bulldog face, somewhat grizzled, bejowled, and black. And he often wondered, "Why me?"

Still, if heart transplants were to become a successful surgical procedure for the desperately ill, *somebody* was destined to become the longest-living recipient in the early history of such replacements. And for the better part of six years, thanks to surgery performed on Russell at the Medical College of Virginia (MCV) in August 1968, he was *it,* the longest-living heart transplant recipient.

The thirty-fourth person to undergo cardiac transplant surgery worldwide, and only the second to receive a new heart at the Richmond medical facility, the forty-two-year-old Russell acquired his new organ from a seventeen-old Virginia youth, also black, who had been fatally shot in the head just hours before.

Once apparently dying of heart disease, a rejuvenated Russell next became an incredibly active missionary for heart associations, patients facing major cardiac surgery, and their doctors. Returning to MCV for a semiannual checkup early in 1971, he explained that he wanted to give back. "I needed help once, several times in fact, and people helped me," he said. "This family, they decided at once to give me their son's heart."

He also was quick to credit his doctors and nurses, adding, "I feel that I owe people things."

Giving back meant a life busier than he ever had known before. At home in Indianapolis, his day would begin with coffee and rolls for breakfast, then the ten-minute drive from his home on Washington Boulevard to Joyce Kilmer Junior High School, where he carried a full schedule of industrial arts classes—but packed them into the mornings to be free for all his speaking engagements in the afternoons and evenings before church, school, and civic groups, at the rate of ten to fifteen a week. Russell also served on the board of directors for the Indiana State Heart Association. In 1971 he was chairman of a statewide fundraising drive. In addition, Russell worked with mental health groups and often talked with prospective surgery candidates.

A post as a lay chaplain with the Indianapolis police force gave him still another opportunity to help others. "I use this position to work with kids in the community," he said. "So many people want to label the police officers pigs, and they aren't. They're just human beings."

Russell even traveled from time to time in surrounding states to address various organizations and spread his messages of cheer, often at his own expense. He also spent time answering his mail, a good ten to twenty letters a day, among them queries from college students writing papers on transplants.

Before August 1968, however, Russell was desperately ill and could indulge in none of these activities. He was tired, despondent, and depressed, he recalled. He had suffered his first heart attack in 1961 and his second, a bad one, in 1965. By 1968 he was gripped by a progressively worsening series of frightening heart failures.

He entered St. Francis Hospital in Indianapolis in June 1968. "This was the last trip to the hospital I was going to make—until I came here [to MCV]," he said. His cardiologist, Dr. Robert Chevalier, a graduate of MCV, made the arrangements for Russell's transfer to the Virginia medical school, already established as a pioneer in kidney transplants and one of the first hospitals attempting cardiac transplants as well.

"I came here July 26, and they operated August 24," Russell added. "Of course, you have to wait for the donor, too. They had a few false alarms. Then they came to my room on a Saturday morning about 3 A.M., woke me up, and told me they had an approved donor and they were preparing me for surgery that morning, and took me down about 20 minutes after 9."

As Russell spoke, he alternately sat or lounged on his bed in MCV's fourth-floor Clinical Research Center. His voice husky, he puffed on several cigarettes. He smiled and laughed freely.

At that time, twenty-eight months after his surgery, he weighed just over two hundred pounds and stood five feet eleven and a half in his stocking feet. Once, he carried 230 to 240 pounds. His doctors in 1971 wished he weighed twenty pounds less—and, of course, that he didn't smoke!

They had reduced him to 163 pounds before the surgery and, despite his arrival in a wheelchair, frequently made him walk.

And then came the fateful morning he had been waiting for . . . hoping for. And yet, going to the operating room, Russell recalled, "I was tired, I wanted to get it completed, I just wanted them to do *something*. I didn't care what happened. I just thought, if it works, fine. If it doesn't, well."

Later, when he came to, Russell was aware only of an overpowering thirst. "I wanted a drink of water. I was giving everybody fits because I couldn't get one."

That night his wife, Thelma, a department store buyer, was permitted to wave at him from the door of the recovery room. In two days, Russell was walking again. By Thanksgiving 1968 he was home—but not before making his first postoperative speech, an address to students at John Marshall High School in Richmond.

"I stood there shaking like a leaf," he said. After that, of course, he made hundreds of speeches. Even when in Richmond for his semi-annual checkup in early 1971, he squeezed in appearances before a local Shriners group and a Baptist church assembly. "My basic theme," he explained, "usually is love, concern, and involvement." He also did his best to discourage attitudes of hate, negative thinking, and prejudice.

As Russell sat on his hospital bed talking, the public address system sounded a hornlike alarm and issued the emergency code for the cardiac team on duty that day. "Shhh . . . ," said Russell. "That's up here. Cardiac arrest."

Nurses bustled around the room of a young woman two doors down the hall. One called out, "Get the EKG [electrocardiogram], get the EKG!"

Russell left his bed, stepped out in the hall, and watched the scene with obvious concern. He resumed talking only after doctors crowded into the stricken woman's room.

In his first twelve months with a borrowed heart, he went on to explain, he had survived four episodes of potentially deadly rejection. By January 1971 he was obviously happy to say, it had been sixteen months since he exhibited symptoms of rejection, the usual nemesis of heart transplant patients.

Filling in the rest of his life story, Russell said he was the son of a retired Baptist minister and he had worked at a variety of jobs—newspaper hawking, shoe-shining, foundry work in his native Terre Haute, Indiana—from the age of eleven until he was graduated from Indiana State Teachers College in 1954 and entered teaching.

He was the father of four children, two girls, two boys . . . but as a result of his historic operation he had acquired a second family, that of his heart donor. In fact, Russell talked about the youth from Providence Forge, Virginia, as if he had known him. He and the donor's family kept in touch, he said. To the slain teenager's mother, "I'm just another married son living away from home," Russell said. "She says she sees her son living in me."

Meanwhile, Russell welcomed the publicity generated by his status as the longest-lived heart transplant recipient. He said his celebrity status helped him deliver his messages of prevention of heart disease or encouragement for its victims. And, as one result of the ripple effect from his publicity, he often discovered he had helped people he knew nothing about. A mother wrote him to say his example inspired her son to try lifesaving corrective surgery even though he was terrified of the prospect. "She writes, 'Thanks for saving my son's life,'" said Russell, "and I didn't even know about it."

In his travels as the world's longest-living heart transplant recipient, Russell willingly submitted to all kinds of questions from his audiences. He assured many that he lived without pain or discomfort. But there always was the man or woman, he added, who would hem and haw, shuffling their feet and hesitating. He always knew what was on that inquirer's mind. He or she wanted to know if his sex life had changed with a seventeen-year-old's heart in his forty-five-year-old body, said Russell . . . without offering an answer.

But there still remained the one question that even he couldn't answer. Why him? "That's my question," he said. "Often I look in the mirror and ask myself, Why me? Out of all the millions and millions of people, why did I get into this position?"

The only reply Russell could offer was: "God is totally responsible for the success I had. He worked through these surgeons. They deserve a lot of credit, but the top credit goes to God."

☆ ☆ ☆

Additional note: Although Louis Russell died in 1974, six years after his transplant, he still lives on in the hearts of the many whom he helped. He also is memorialized in ways both tangible and intangible. Among the more tangible monuments to his name is an elementary school in Indianapolis named after him. And among the intangible, the local teachers union bestows an annual Louis B. Russell award to an outstanding teacher, while the American Heart Association gives an annual Louis B. Russell award to an individual noted for working with minority and "underserved populations." The award is given in honor of Russell's work as an association volunteer, "actively spreading the message about heart disease prevention in the minority community."

✲

1 9 6 9
Night the Mountains Fell In

✲

At dusk that August night in 1969, a light patter of rain began to fall on the mountains and hollows at the head of Virginia's James River Valley.

The weather bureau had predicted a heavy downfall because of a hurricane that had socked the Gulf Coast earlier, but up here, this far to the north, no one was overly concerned.

In tiny Massies Mill, a Nelson County hamlet of about sixty persons, Gail Bowling and her young brother John had no fear of staying alone while their parents were out of town for the night. Their grandmother, eighty-four, was bedded down in her trailer behind the house.

The patter in the foothills of the Blue Ridge soon turned into a steady drumbeat of heavy rain.

Still, few gave Hurricane Camille more than a passing thought. A killer when it struck the Gulf Coast several days earlier, the tropical storm clearly had lost its punch.

Passing over Kentucky on its way to Virginia, Camille gave the neighboring Bluegrass State a relatively light, two-inch dousing.

There was no reason to expect trouble, although the mountain folk of Nelson County often talked of the day when the "mountains might fall in on us."

Bessie Campbell, seventy-four, another Massies Mill resident, spent a quiet evening in her home on a grassy slope next to the picturesque Tye River.

In Rockfish, some distance away, Fred Wood, a retired carpenter who always kept a worried eye on the stream by his home, put finishing touches on his new barn before going inside the house for the night.

In Huffman's Hollow on Davis Creek, near the Nelson County seat of Lovingston, members of the Huffman clan also bedded down—most of them for the last time in their lives.

As the night hours passed, the outside world unaware, sheets of rain flailed the mountainsides, hills, and slopes. Swollen waters appeared in

---

From the author's account in the *Washington Star,* August 19, 1970.

gullies, creeks, and rivers. Mud, then trees, rocks, and boulders were sliding downward. Whole mountainsides were loosening.

Beyond the rain-swept area, no one realized.

Even the next day, scattered reports only hinted at the devastation wrought by eight to ten hours of rain. Two drownings were reported in Nelson and Amherst Counties. Charlottesville reported nearby roads blocked by mudslides. From the western part of the state came reports that a pair of trains had been halted because of washouts.

But still, no one really knew.

In the hollows and valleys, their communications cut off, villagers and mountain people had spent a night of peril, incredible havoc . . . and death.

Many of them had been awakened by the sound of water rushing beneath their beds.

At Massies Mill, Gail Bowling and her brother scrambled to carry household goods upstairs from the flooded ground floor. Soon, the water was too deep to continue. They huddled together on the second floor. Out back, Grandmother's trailer had vanished.

Rescuers found it two hundred yards downstream the next morning. Somehow, the elderly woman inside had survived.

Not far away, Bessie Campbell didn't dare move from her second-floor haven. The water downstairs was neck-deep. It wasn't until daylight that she discovered her house had been washed 150 feet from its foundation. Her son-in-law, astride a horse, carried her to safety.

At Rockfish, Fred Wood and his wife fled their low-lying home with a metal box of valued papers. As the waters kept rising, they climbed higher and higher on the steep mountain slopes during the night. By daylight, standing under pine trees, they could see that their homestead—house, new barn, and outbuildings—had been swept away.

Back in Massies Mill, Virginia Napier, her husband, and grandson spent most of the night on their knees in prayer and singing hymns while the Tye River flowed relentlessly through the ground floor.

These were the lucky ones, however. Scores of survivors later told tales of houses, autos, and giant trees tumbling downstream before their eyes. They knew many of their neighbors had not escaped. No one yet knew just how many.

James Huffman, away from his Davis Creek home when the flood-waters struck, would be burying his wife, three sons, two grandchildren, his father-in-law, and a brother-in-law. Still, there were some miraculous rescues and escapes. A small girl was plucked from a bale of hay on the rampaging Maury River. At Buena Vista, a man and his wife ran from their home seconds before it collapsed with a thunderous roar.

Also at Buena Vista, officers of the Virginia National Bank were stacking vital records on furniture in a back room when the front window broke and a surge of water rushed in. The bankers swam through their lobby to a staircase leading to the second floor.

Even in distant Louisa County, Chester Dadaza, fifty-seven, was sucked out of his trailer when he opened the door during the night. As the raging South Anna River hurtled him downstream, he managed to snag a tree limb and drag himself to safety. He was to remain in the tree for more than forty-eight hours.

In some areas, "harmless" Camille had spawned twenty-seven inches of rain in eight hours, one of the nation's rarest cloudbursts, a phenomenon theoretically expected once in a thousand years. The impact in Nelson County alone was compared to that of two nuclear explosions.

The area's topography itself had changed. Whole mountainsides were gone. Rivers were flowing along brand-new routes, and piles of debris cluttered the countryside.

Worst of all, more than 150 persons were dead or missing, among them, 30 or more children.

More than two hundred miles of road were impassable. About 140 bridges had been washed out. Thirty landslides covered major sections of U.S. Route 29, the artery linking Charlottesville to Lovingston and then Lynchburg to the south. One of those segments stretched for three miles.

Railroad lines were destroyed. Property damage to roads, schools, homes, factories, business places, and rail lines came to $113 million. Road damages alone accounted for $20 million.

Governor Mills E. Godwin Jr., who visited the area six times in the days after the flood, pronounced it Virginia's worst natural disaster . . . ever. The havoc, he said, "defies description." President Nixon declared the James River Basin a major disaster area.

The rescuers and relief workers found bodies for weeks, not only in the immediate area but also far downstream in the major rivers affected. One was found among the jumbled pews of Grace Episcopal Church at Massies Mill. Bulldozers clearing hummocks of debris turned up many others.

The area's hardy people and an army of helpers began the task of rebuilding. The state sent in an emergency force of highway construction workers. The Army Corps of Engineers and the U.S. Navy's Seabees pitched in. Mennonite volunteers from as far as Canada arrived to take part in the work, some staying for more than a year. And in that first year alone, the state spent more than $5.5 million in restoration work, and the federal government spent another $26.4 million. According to Virginia's Office of Civil Defense, the American Red Cross provided an additional $1 million, while the Mennonite Church contributed $150,000; the Catholic Church, $54,000; the Salvation Army, $24,000; the Virginia Jaycees, $85,000; the state's lumber manufacturers, $75,000, and their contractors another $30,000 in relief efforts, contributions, goods, restoration work, and building materials.

"There were hundreds and hundreds of people who came in and worked," said Marge Sherrod, a state disaster assistant. Among still other groups contributing to the gigantic cleanup effort were the Lions, the Rotarians, the Loyal Order of the Moose, the Masons, and the Virginia Council of Churches. The Red Cross rebuilt 34 homes, repaired another 267, and provided new household furnishings for 386 families.

The Small Business Administration granted some $12.5 million in emergency loans. The Department of Housing and Urban Development (HUD) provided low-cost mobile homes. A Richmond radio station's campaign bought a fleet of used cars for the flood victims.

In less than a year's time, Bessie Campbell lived in a new white house by the Tye River, thanks to the Red Cross and Mennonite workers. In Rockfish, Fred Wood and his wife had a new house by Christmas 1969, funded again by the Red Cross and built by Mennonites. Devastated Route 29 was reopened late in September 1969, but work continued on the remaining road damage.

A year after the natural disaster, tall corn covered the meadows that were inundated twelve months before. High-school boys practiced football on fields that had served as landing pads for army relief helicopters. "Because of the wonderful expression of concern on the part of churches, organizations, and agencies, Nelson County is near recovery," the Reverend Wilfred E. Roach of Grace Episcopal Church in Massies Mill was able to tell Red Cross workers.

But he meant only *physically* near recovery, since his county alone counted its human toll at 125 persons lost.

In a saga never to be forgotten in Nelson and adjoining areas, one chapter was closed within a year's time by the Virginia General Assembly's passage of a special law declaring anyone still missing from the floods to be legally dead.

☆ ☆ ☆

Additional note: How could the disaster of Camille have caught everyone, even the weather experts, by surprise? Afterward, weather bureau specialists said they had no reports of the rain even after it started. The meteorological "state of the art" equipment in 1969—greatly improved since—was unable to predict a deluge in such concentrated form over such a small land area. Indeed, until the so-called remnants of Camille reached Virginia on a fateful path northward, the dissipating hurricane did not encounter the atmospheric conditions needed to spawn a brand-new killer storm. While rushing to install a much-improved flood warning system and flood-control works in central Virginia, the experts of course couldn't promise such a storm would never strike again. They could only hope for more timely warnings for the general public, improved control of flooding in the area . . . and an always alert public.

☆

1972
Day on the Job at Dulles

☆

For R. Dan Mahaney, it was just one of those days. In one vast parking lot, a man was stricken with a heart attack. Down the long access road from the northern Virginia suburbs immediately next to Washington, D.C., airport police were in pursuit of a fleeing warehouse thief. And fast approaching the two-mile-long runways was a "plane in trouble."

There were two or three other crises popping at the same moment, but Mahaney, manager of Dulles International Airport in the early

---

Based on the author's article in the *Washington Star* of April 30, 1972.

1970s, soon forgot them. As Dulles finally was achieving its predicted volume of air traffic, his was a seat that could become hot on moment's notice. In his job, the critical decisions of one day soon replaced those of the last.

A Trans World Airlines flight out of Phoenix hijacked and heading for Dulles? No choice. Bring it on.

"Every day is new; every day is different," said the husky Irishman from the coal fields of Pennsylvania. "You never know what's going to happen next."

He was seated behind his large desk in a softly carpeted and draped office on the ground floor of the main airport terminal. It was quiet and for a few moments there were few interruptions. But telephone messages were piling up on his secretary's desk in the next-door reception room.

Upstairs in the soaring terminal that Eero Saarinen created, several hippies seated on the cold floor were singing. Passengers were lining up for flights to Paris and San Francisco. In the swank Portals restaurant, late-afternoon travelers sipped on cocktails. A young soldier and his wife were leaving with their infant. The soldier's cap was too big for him, and an empty baby bottle trailed from his slender fingers.

Across a concrete apron, two Boeing jumbo jets, whalelike even at a half-mile distance, were waiting to swallow their Jonahs.

Elsewhere in the complex that many call the world's most fabulous airport, twenty-seven hundred personnel—U.S. Customs inspectors, airline reps, firemen and policemen, cooks, bankers and store clerks, air traffic controllers—moved about their respective tasks. In addition, of course, airline crews came and went by the hour . . . by the minute, really.

This was Mahaney's world, his job, even his only hobby, he related. And day by day, hour by hour, one thing did come after another. It could be the private plane with landing-gear trouble. Foam the runways, goes out the order. Stand by with crash vehicles. Or deer wandering the runways? Get out the deer rifles. Or a traveler, slightly soused, calling to complain he got his coat sleeve wet fishing for the good-luck coins that other travelers toss into the main terminal's indoor reflecting pool. Or a complaint about a meal served in one of the airport's eateries. Even a taxi passenger's lament that the cabdriver wasn't all that nice on the long drive out (thirty to forty minutes) from the District of Columbia.

But wait . . . even at busy Dulles, as at any other large international terminus, there could be the really tough problem. And, as always, out of the blue. This time, one June afternoon in 1971, it was a hijacked airliner . . . one of the most dramatic airliner hijackings in history. This little problem dropped into Mahaney's lap while he was at lunch with members of a Dulles promotional committee. The word was that an Arizona man had commandeered a TWA jet and was demanding a $100 million ransom for the safe return of the plane and its passengers.

Meanwhile, the entire unwelcome package was headed straight for Dulles.

As events turned out, the flight from Phoenix indeed did reach Dulles and land there—twice. The first time was to pick up the $100,000 that TWA hurriedly withdrew from a local bank, and the second time was for the remaining $999,900,000 of the $100 million demand. For the second landing, airport manager Mahaney helped round up the mailbags that were placed at one end of a runway for the hijacker. But the bags contained no money, and two of Mahaney's handpicked airport police officers shot out the tires of the rolling jet from a crash truck that raced up behind the big airliner.

When it jolted to a stop, and passengers burst out of the aircraft on the emergency exit chutes, FBI agents climbed aboard and captured hijacker Arthur G. Barkley in a wild melee that left both the hijacker and pilot Dale C. Hupe with gunshot wounds.

It had been Mahaney's plan to render the aircraft inoperative with the deer rifles his policemen kept in a locker near his own office. "In times of emergency," he said months later, "*your* thoughts are as good as the next guy's. If you think it's right, go ahead and do it."

Meanwhile, on a loftier level, he took note of architect Saarinen's grand scheme to separate the terminal from the aircraft . . . and send out the passengers in mobile lounges. (Nowadays, however, the mobile lounges tend to go to outlying smaller terminals.) Mahaney said he himself "laughed" when he first heard of the Dulles concept, but he soon became a convert. "The laughing days are over," he explained. "Saarinen always said the day would come when you stop attaching airplanes to buildings, and the plane will be parked in remote areas, and today [the 1970s] this is happening."

As he also noted, the giant 747 jumbo jets and the wide-bodied DC-10s called for new ways of handling their huge number of embarking or debarking passengers. "The 747, the DC-10—these are what Dulles was built for," he said. "The 747 starts in a new era, this is really the era that Saarinen was thinking of. This is what separates the men from the boys in airports."

Once called a white elephant and initially shunned by many of the air carriers after its debut in 1962, the $106.5 million airport finally had shown healthy growth in air traffic volume by the early 1970s. "We're just slightly over two million passengers a year now," Mahaney could boast. The traffic increase he cited, most of it coming from international air service, was itself an 11 percent jump over the previous year's total. And the new totals, coming on Mahaney's watch as manager, were just enough to begin action on the first expansion of Eero Saarinen's famous terminal building—by the addition of some 620 lineal feet to its original 600-foot length.

In more recent years, with that addition now an accomplished fact, new outlying terminals (concourses), a huge parking garage, and other facilities also have appeared on the Dulles map. Moreover, passenger volume at Dulles reached a staggering twenty million a year by the first years of the twenty-first century.

☆ ☆ ☆

Additional note: Named for former Secretary of State John Foster Dulles, the futuristic Dulles International Airport (renamed in 1984 as Washington Dulles International Airport) took shape in the late 1950s and early 1960s on a rural site of ten thousand acres in Fairfax and Loudoun Counties, twenty-six miles west of Washington, D.C.

As stated in a history provided by the Metropolitan Washington Airports Authority (MWAA), at www.mwaa.com/dulles, the unusual size of the site "allowed for an airport, the first in the country designed for commercial jets, to be buffered from its neighbors." To assure the future airport a proper greenbelt a thousand feet in width, its developers planted a million and a half tree seedlings around the air facility. "Only 3,000 acres of the 10,000 acres were graded for the new airport, and boundaries were established at least 8,000 feet from the end of all runways," notes the MWAA history.

While all that was environmentally welcome, it was architect Eero Saarinen's striking design of the terminal and 193-foot control tower that stirred the public's imagination and created a landmark known around the world. With the terminal building's soaring roofline and the control tower as a startling punctuation mark next to it, Saarinen succeeded in his stated goal of finding and conveying the very "soul" of a major airport that would be in use for decades to come. Indeed, his design won the 1966 First Honor Award given by the American Institute of Architects.

Dulles went into operation with a pair of north-south runways stretching for 11,500 feet each. Situated 6,700 feet apart, they were 150 feet wide. A third runway, northwest-southeast in direction, ran for 10,000 feet and also was 150 feet wide. All three runways boasted an additional 25 feet of paved shoulders.

More noticeable to the average air traveler, however, was the innovation called a mobile lounge—the lumbering, big-wheeled vehicle that transported up to 102 passengers directly from the terminal to a waiting aircraft on the apron half a mile away. "This protected the passengers from weather, jet noise and blast, and also eliminated long walking distances," says the MWAA Internet history. "Because of the mobile lounge, passengers had to walk only two hundred feet once they entered the terminal until they were seated in the lounge for the short trip directly to their aircraft."

Dulles was formally dedicated on November 17, 1962, by President John F. Kennedy. The first commercial plane to land at the new airport was an Eastern Airlines Super Electra on a flight from Newark, New Jersey, notes the MWAA website.

Two figures provide a measure of the airport's progress since: In its first year of operation, Dulles served 52,846 passengers all told, all year. In more recent years, the passenger volume has been on the order of 55,000 passengers *every day.*

1 9 7 5
Pesticide in Their Veins

Moving swiftly in the water, *Pomatomus saltatrix* carried an angry appetite behind the cruel jaws as he coursed the big bay, cruised the river mouths, and snapped up small water animals and lesser fish. He was able to range from one end of the bay to the other—from Baltimore to Portsmouth, Virginia—in a single day.

A predator of the first order, he was a magnificent animal. Nearly four feet long, almost twenty-five pounds in weight, he made a sleek, greenish-blue projectile as he relentlessly searched for food.

Had he been endowed with matching intelligence, of course, the blue fish would have realized his own chief predator—man—had been strangely absent lately.

At Solomon's Island, Maryland, on the Chesapeake Bay, charter-boat captain Bill Hall was reviewing his disastrous summer. Only two fishing parties had chartered his thirty-eight-footer since July 6. "I've lost twenty-six parties that I can document," he moaned. "I've been put out of business as a charter-boat captain."

Similarly, in Norfolk, the Sterling Oyster Company, a thriving seafood market for fifty-five years, quietly closed just before Labor Day. "People just stopped coming in," explained Rick Taylor, who said he had "poured every cent I had" into his purchase of the fish market in 1975, just the year before. "Business had dropped a bit after the report of Kepone in oysters last winter. But then the reports that blue fish were 'hot' came in, and there just wasn't any business anymore."

As Rick Taylor indicated, the alarm over the pesticide Kepone had spread after toxic illnesses had turned up among workers at the small Life Science Products plant in Hopewell, Virginia, far upstream on the James and Appomattox Rivers. (See "Boomtown Days for Hopewell," pages 273–77.) Soon after the Life Science discovery in July 1975, investigators realized that Allied Chemical Corporation's huge agricultural division plant, situated next door to Life Science, also had produced Allied's patented pesticide Kepone in intermittent batches since 1966. Unfortunately, production discharges sometimes went directly into a creek leading to the James, with no prior filtration treatment, according to later testimony in a federal district court.

Officials at the Virginia Institute of Marine Sciences (VIMS) estimated the James River might hold as much as one hundred thousand pounds of the pesticide in its muddy bottom—enough, said one VIMS official, to contaminate "trillions of fish."

Faced with such heavy pollution of Virginia's historic James River, Governor Mills E. Godwin Jr. acted in December 1975 to close the river downstream from Hopewell, as well as its estuary leading into the

Chesapeake Bay, to all forms of fishing, a tremendous economic blow to an estimated thirty-five hundred watermen and others who derived their living from the river and its marine life. By the next summer, the ban had been partially relaxed, but not entirely . . . and of course it was too late to put a cork in the publicity bottle.

Key to all this was human consumption of seafood products. The dangers were Kepone's known toxicity and the fear it could cause cancer in humans. Making matters worse was the chemical compound's tendency to persist in the environment or in animal tissue. As Virginia's state epidemiologist, Robert Jackson, explained: Eat a little bit today, another bit tomorrow, plus a third bit the third day, and you wind up "with the accumulation of all three doses."

Frightening, also, a recent National Cancer Institute study had indicated that Kepone, a chlorinated hydrocarbon similar to DDT, could cause liver cancer in rats and mice. With such possibilities in mind, the federal Environmental Protection Agency (EPA) worked up Kepone "action levels" for various marine species—technical warnings they shouldn't be marketed when above one level or the other, depending on the fish involved. Thus, the cut-off level for finfish such as the popular blue was .1 part per million (ppm); for shellfish such as clams and oysters, .3ppm; and for crabs, .4ppm.

According to Jack Blanchard, head of the EPA's Kepone task force, the first recommendation from his agency's toxicologists had been to allow zero tolerance in the case of finfish—the hard-hit, often-protesting seafood dealers of the region would have been surprised to know the zero tolerance level was eased specifically to lessen the economic impact on their fishing industry. According to Dr. Jackson, however, the EPA action levels were no assurance of safety. "It only means that based upon currently available data, they [EPA] cannot justify taking the material off the market at levels below that."

What it all boiled down to was the fact that Kepone was a new environmental and health threat not fully understood—no one really knew how much Kepone was either safe or dangerous in terms of human consumption. The EPA's Blanchard was frank to say as much. "We can't set a safe low level because Kepone is a carcinogen," he said. "We don't know its mechanism of action—whether one 'hit' sets off cancer, or whether there's a [longer] dose-response relationship."

As might be guessed, the James was closed because most of its marine life at first was found to be at or above the EPA action levels—

in some cases, far above. Various specimens taken from the river's estuary and the lower Chesapeake Bay near the mouths of the James, York, and Rappahannock Rivers also were above the EPA guidelines—among them, bluefish, flounder, trout, and croakers. While random fish with low Kepone levels turned up in Maryland's portion of the vast bay, state officials said no "action level" fish were among them.

In hard-hit Virginia, however, the seafood industry challenged the governmental guidelines and began a public relations campaign aimed at restoring a positive image to Virginia-grown seafood products. The federal Food and Drug Administration also had weighed in to the Kepone environmental snarl with a report saying that tests on fifty to sixty fish shipments from Maryland and Virginia markets showed *no* composite samples with action-level Kepone in them. "We have no data to indicate there is any reason to refrain from eating fish," said an FDA spokesman.

Still, government scientists suggested that worried consumers might reduce any Kepone levels in their cooked fish meals by boning the fish, removing their heads and fatty tissue, and pouring off the cooking oils. Additionally, the EPA's Blanchard suggested broiling or poaching to extract body oils.

Dr. Jackson, in the meantime, took sharp issue with a Kepone "fact analysis" issued by the Virginia Seafood Council. "Since many of your readers have a seafood intake way in excess of the average, the level that should be allowed in their seafood should be well below the action level," he bluntly warned. Proof in the pudding? As Jackson previously had reported, about twenty persons who had been steady consumers of James River fish turned up in 1975 and 1976 with low but detectable levels of Kepone in their blood.

☆ ☆ ☆

Additional note: Twenty years later, the Kepone scare along the James River corridor had lessened dramatically, but still, the *Richmond Times-Dispatch* reported in 1995, "the river's bottom is laced with Kepone." After the river was closed to fishing in one form or another for thirteen years, "state officials estimated the cost to the public, including lost revenue to watermen, at tens of millions of dollars." Health officials still advised against habitually eating fish from the James River.

As better news, though, "Officials say Kepone's threat is diminishing as the poison is covered by new sediment washed from upriver."

The same anniversary report by Rex Springston also recalled that the cost of the environmental disaster to Allied (now known as AlliedSignal Inc.) included penalties in federal district court equal to $13.2 million—$5.2 million as an outright fine, and another $8 million as a donation establishing the Virginia Environmental Endowment. The latter has been providing money for environmental projects of all kinds ever since.

As Springston recalled also, investigators back in 1975 "found Kepone in air, soil, and wells" in the Hopewell-James River corridor areas. Thoughts of dredging the estimated hundred thousand pounds from the river bottom "were abandoned when costs were estimated at more than a billion dollars."

Not only did the pesticide build up in the consumer's body tissue, it built up in the river food chain. "Bottom-feeding fish consumed Kepone with their meals," Springston noted. After that, "bigger fish eat smaller Kepone-tainted fish, and the poison moves up the food chain to fish eaten by such creatures as eagles, ospreys, and people." Fortunately, the new layers of sediment covering the river bottom by 1995—and even later—made it less likely that the bottom feeders would have direct access to the poison, but state officials still feared the consequences if a major hurricane came along and churned up the layers of mud lying along the bottom of the river channel.

Meanwhile, the costly ban on fishing in the James River was lifted in 1988, although consumers still were advised against frequent consumption of its marine life over a long period.

1 9 7 6
Gaffe by a Queen

Here's a Freudian slip if there ever was one. The queen of England, a direct descendant of King George III, publicly forgetting that the

Declaration of Independence (from England, of course) was one of the three lifetime achievements for which Thomas Jefferson most wanted to be remembered. And of all times and places to be so forgetful . . . in his "hometown" of Charlottesville during the American bicentennial ceremonies of 1976!

Queen Elizabeth II is a lovely lady, though, and her heart no doubt was in the right place when she said—at the University of Virginia on July 10, 1976—that Jefferson would have preferred to be remembered as father of the university, "rather than for his authorship of the Declaration of Independence, a document which changed the course of history."

To the contrary, in the epitaph Jefferson himself composed just prior to his death in 1826, he said he wished most of all to be remembered as: "Author of the Declaration of Independence, of the Statute of Virginia for Religious Freedom, and Father of the University of Virginia."

As can be seen, he listed the Declaration first and "father" of the university last on his very short list.

Few seemed to give the queen's gaffe much thought, if indeed it was noticed at all during her bicentennial-year visit to Charlottesville. The crowds attending her every public move were strictly friendly as she toured both the university grounds and Jefferson's mountaintop home, Monticello. Gaily dressed in a green-and-white silk print, Queen Elizabeth II, a direct descendant of the very king whom Thomas Jefferson chastised so severely in the Declaration, was welcomed by Gov. Mills E. Godwin Jr., by more than a hundred members of the Virginia General Assembly, and by crowds ranging from forty to fifty thousand in number.

She moved smilingly through a day that took her from a ceremony on the Lawn of Mr. Jefferson's school to a luncheon in its recently restored Rotunda, the campus centerpiece designed by Jefferson.

Children perched on tree limbs were among the estimated eighteen thousand persons lining a roped-off pathway up the center of the famous Lawn as the queen strolled from the site of the brief welcoming ceremony, at one end of Jefferson's "academical" village, to the Rotunda at the top of the Lawn. The queen and her husband, Prince Philip, the Duke of Edinburgh, often paused to shake hands with nearby onlookers, some of whom carried signs with friendly greetings such as "God save the Queen" or "Welcome to Virginia."

In the ceremony moments before, she presented Godwin a devisal, or copy, of the coat of arms used by the Virginia Company of London, sponsor of the Jamestown settlement. In return, Godwin presented the queen with a set of leather-bound books by Jefferson biographer Dumas Malone. In his welcoming remarks, Godwin noted that Virginia was named for the visiting queen's namesake, the Virgin Queen Elizabeth I. He also declared, "In the hearts of all Virginians there will always be an England."

For her part, the queen asserted that the long-standing partnership between Britain and America "has its roots here in Virginia." That partnership, she elaborated, began with the arrival of the Jamestown settlers 369 years earlier. The queen also noted her own distant kinship with George Washington and took pains to speak of Jefferson as "the intellectual driving force behind your Revolution." Then came her minor historical gaffe, but the day's events moved ahead in any case.

After the presentations, the queen and her husband paused briefly to see one of the student rooms on the Lawn. They were shown the simple bedchamber by two student residents of the Lawn, a young man and young woman.

Noting their genders, Prince Philip jokingly asked if they lived together in the single bedroom—and drew a testy look from the queen.

Again, the day's events moved ahead anyway.

At the luncheon minutes later, the royal party was served by student waiters and waitresses who served up a tasty meal of cream-of-asparagus soup, curried chicken salad, and baked Virginia ham with hot biscuits. Pool reporters attending (that is, watching) the luncheon said the queen ate sparingly.

From there it was on to Monticello and a tour of Jefferson's magnificent neoclassic brick home overlooking Charlottesville. And now came gifts. For the queen, a pair of silver goblets based on a Jefferson design.

She and Prince Philip met members of the Virginia General Assembly at the rear of the restored mansion, pausing here and there to shake hands or to chat briefly. It no doubt was confusing to the queen to have Delegate Earl Bell of Loudoun County introduced to her—facetiously, to be sure—as the "Earl of Loudoun."

From there, the queen and her party motored to the local airport for a fast flight to Providence, Rhode Island, where she would be hosting President and Mrs. Gerald Ford aboard the royal yacht *Britannica*.

★

1 9 7 6
New "Byrd Machine"

★

This Byrd was different. Unlike his late father, Harry Flood Byrd Jr. didn't hold the reins of political power in Virginia. He was only remotely connected with the once-dominant "Byrd machine" that ruled Virginia from governor's mansion to county courthouse for so many years. Indeed, the time came when he wasn't even a Democrat.

His only organization, it appeared after three election triumphs, was the crucial one that trooped to the polls every six years to elect and reelect him as a U.S. senator.

It was an army with only one general and few officers. It controlled no political territories. It awarded no judgeships, boardships, or commission seats. It anointed no candidates in the style of the old "organization" days when his father, Harry Flood Byrd Sr., and his Democratic Party forces forged an unbreakable chain of command extending from both the Senate and the governor's office to Virginia's most far-flung courthouses.

"Little Harry," as he often was called, eschewed his father's party and the "tantamount" politics of his father's heyday. "Tantamount" meant that to be nominated and running in a general election with the Byrd organization's blessing was tantamount to election. The senior Byrd, who arrived in Washington in 1933, simultaneously with Franklin D. Roosevelt, also was a power in the Senate, where for many years he held sway as chairman of the Senate Finance Committee.

All that changed in 1965 with the retirement of the elder Byrd from the Senate seat he had held for more than thirty years. He then died a year later at the age of seventy-nine. In the interim, "Little Harry," still a Democrat in name and an eighteen-year veteran of the Virginia Senate, was appointed in his father's place. He then won election in his own right in 1966 to fill his father's unexpired term.

That done, even more changed when A. Linwood Holton was elected in 1969 as the first Republican to gain the governor's seat since the Civil War era a century before. And then in 1970, Harry F. Byrd Jr. stunned Virginia's political world by announcing as an independent, running again, . . . and winning his second U.S. Senate election, all without the help of either political party. Thanks to their combined opposition, in fact, he won in a three-way race . . . by an outright majority rather than a mere plurality, as usually is the case in such affairs. He followed that triumph with yet another victory as an independent in the bicentennial year of 1976, this time defeating a single major-party nominee, Democrat Elmo Zumwalt, the former chief of naval operations, as well as a minor contender, northern Virginia businessman Martin Perper, a self-proclaimed "Republican independent."

When he was appointed to his ailing father's Senate seat in 1965, the younger Byrd had explained beforehand, he decided against carrying the older Byrd's double "burden" of conducting Senate business while also exerting control over the state's internal politics. Following his father's footsteps on the body's Finance Committee, "Little Harry" said his choice was day-to-day Senate business.

Fairly clear, however, was the fact that his own "organization" did have its allies and "treaties." Allies such as the one-time Byrd Democrats who fled to the resurgent Republican Party of Virginia, most notably former Democratic Governor Mills E. Godwin Jr., who served as governor again in the 1970s as a Republican. And treaties such as the happy understanding by which that same Virginia GOP declined to challenge Byrd when he sought reelection in 1976 as an independent for the second time. Or treaties such as the equally happy arrangement (for Byrd) that allowed him to caucus with Senate Democrats in organizing the national legislative body.

Thus, the "organization" of the younger Harry Byrd was one barely visible to the naked eye—between elections. It was needed, and appeared, only when he was embroiled in his latest campaign.

Take the case of his 1976 campaign, his last run for the Senate. After giving him nearly 54 percent of the vote in his 1970 race against the two major-party nominees, the Virginia electorate this time awarded him a whopping 57 percent as he overwhelmed Admiral Zumwalt, Byrd's only serious challenger in the 1976 race. Rolling up heavy margins across the lower three-fourths of the state, Byrd captured all but two of Virginia's ten congressional districts. As expected, those were northern Virginia's suburban Eighth and Tenth Districts—a pair of hotly fought battlegrounds where two liberal Democrats won reelection to the U.S. House, and Democrat Jimmy Carter made a strong showing in the presidential voting.

"All we wanted to do was to fight 'em to a standstill up here," said political consultant J. Kenneth Klinge, a highly gratified strategist aiding the Byrd forces in 1976.

Byrd's margin of victory was all the more significant in two other areas that Democrat Zumwalt's organizers had looked upon with fond hopes—the navy-oriented Virginia Tidewater section, encompassing Norfolk and other naval base sites, and the mountainous southwest. Along Virginia's coastal zone, ranging from the Eastern Shore to the Carolina border, Byrd easily took the First, Second, and Fourth Districts. He also brushed aside Zumwalt's would-be claims to the southwestern Ninth District.

Two districts, meanwhile, gave Byrd margins of more than two to one. They were the Fifth, incorporating much of the Old Dominion's Southside—an old Byrd organization stronghold, and the younger Byrd's home-port Seventh, incorporating the Central Piedmont and the Upper Shenandoah Valley. (In 1970, incidentally, he had carried nine of the ten congressional districts.)

At a markedly low-key victory party in Winchester on election night of 1976, Byrd insisted his second election triumph as an independent wasn't personal at all. "I regard it as a mandate for a philosophy of government," said Byrd, who, like his father before him, was noted as an opponent of deficit government spending. Silver-haired and apple-cheeked, again like his father, Byrd was beaming as he added, "I dedicate myself for the next six years to represent all the people of the state in bringing the Virginia philosophy of government to Washington."

By the time Byrd retired from the Senate after completing that same six-year term, the father-and-son combination of "apple-cheeked" Byrds had served a combined total of fifty years in the U.S. Senate, from 1933 to 1983. Then seventy-eight, the younger Byrd walked away from the Senate as the only member elected twice as an independent. A newspaper publisher by background, yet again like his late father, "Little Harry" then settled down to write a book, titled, appropriately enough, *Defying the Odds: An Independent Senator's Historic Campaign*. Its subject was his 1970 campaign in particular, voted by the Associated Press as Virginia's top news story of the year.

In his book, Byrd noted that as one immediate effect of the dramatic break with his Democratic Party legacy, quickly followed by election victory as an independent, "the Republicans benefited."

Thus, his triumphant break with the past "made it easier for conservatives like Mills Godwin to move from the increasingly liberal Democratic Party into the Republican Party." In 1973, Byrd also noted, Godwin was again elected governor, "this time as a Republican."

What it all boiled down to was an "accelerated" (his own word) movement of the Old Dominion's considerable conservative forces—troops of the old Byrd Organization—into the ranks of the resurgent Republican Party, with a true two-party political system resulting. The conservative-liberal ideological split once played out within Democratic Party ranks now was a political-party split instead, with first one party, then the other to dominate Virginia politics in the years ahead.

★

1 9 7 8
Love Affair with Virginia

★

Mills E. Godwin Jr., age sixty-three and removed by a political eon or two from his days as a young FBI agent and country lawyer in tiny Chuckatuck, left the office of governor of Virginia in January 1978 with a rare mosaic of memories. Among them would be the portrait of Patrick Henry, Revolutionary Virginia's first governor, that hung above the mantel in the third-floor governor's office at the state capitol. Another memory, though, would be of the barbs thrown by political enemies, not only liberals who didn't see eye to eye with the conservative Godwin, but also those in the Democratic and Republican Parties who found fault because he switched parties midstream in a highly successful political career.

As a result of the switch, he now could step down as the only governor in modern Virginia history to serve two terms, first as a Democrat and then as a Republican. In *all* the post-Colonial history of Virginia, not so incidentally, only his icon Patrick Henry came even close, at just short of five years in the office, of matching Godwin's eight years as governor.

Another piece from the mosaic reflecting Godwin's political life was a small figurine of an elephant, symbol of the Republican Party.

When Godwin, now a Republican, returned a second time to the third-floor executive's office in January 1974, he found his immediate predecessor, A. Linwood Holton, had left it for him. Also a historic political figure, Holton had come into office as the first Republican elected to it in a hundred years . . . since the Civil War, really. And now, in 1978, the retiring Godwin would be leaving the same figurine on the office mantel for *his* successor, John N. Dalton, also a Republican.

Virginia's modern constitution forbids the chief executive to succeed himself for consecutive terms, but Godwin managed by serving immediately before Holton and again immediately after, with four years in between. Seeking the governor's chair under those conditions meant vilification by some Democrats and at least initial distrust among some Republican leaders when the switch came about in 1973. One GOP congressional district chairman cried on the floor at the party convention that nominated Godwin that year.

Then, too, Godwin's first term was marked by unexpected sadness. Godwin and his wife, Katherine, lost their only child, fourteen-year-old Becky, when she was struck by lightning at Virginia Beach while the governor—then still a Democrat—was attending the strife-torn Democratic National Convention of 1968 in Chicago.

More happily for history buff Godwin, a strong apostle of free enterprise and admirer of Virginia's early heritage of national leadership, being governor a second time meant the major satisfaction of serving simultaneously with the celebration of the nation's bicentennial in 1976.

Serving twice as governor inevitably invited comparisons, and some criticism, of one term versus the other. And there were major differences: In his first term, becoming known as Virginia's "Education Governor," *Democrat* Godwin was a leader and innovator, and in the second, *Republican* Godwin was more noted for his holding actions in the face of one crisis after another. But then circumstances had changed significantly.

The first time around, the governor's mantle meant leadership as Virginia adopted its first state sales tax, then assigned the new revenues to educational improvement. He also orchestrated the creation of a statewide system of community colleges, plus a network of four-lane arterial highways. The late Governor Godwin was at the helm during revision of the state constitution to meet modern needs, and he helped nudge the state away from its hallowed pay-as-you-go fiscal tradition that eschewed loans in the form of bond issues for capital needs.

All this was ironic for a political figure who began his legislative career in 1948 as an upstart challenger defeating a follower of Virginia's once-dominant "Byrd organization" but who soon became a chief lieutenant for U.S. Senator Harry F. Byrd Sr., and in that role became a leading spokesman for Virginia's "massive resistance" campaign against court-ordered public school integration.

His second gubernatorial term was ironic, too, because Godwin's conversion from an increasingly liberal Democratic Party aligned him and other Byrd forces with a Republican Party once rife with anti-Byrd sentiment. In that second term, meanwhile, Godwin faced a crisis in overcrowded state prisons, the national energy crunch of the 1970s, the worst drought in forty years, a hurricane (but nothing like Hurricane Camille of 1969, during his first term), floods, the worst winter in a century, the environmental disaster caused by the pesticide Kepone, a national economic recession, and faltering state revenues.

In his own words, the accomplishments of his first term were "relatively easy because the mood of the times was with us." By 1974, however, "both the mood and the economic situation had changed drastically." He readily conceded that his reactions to crisis after crisis failed to produce "raving headlines." Still, his stewardship of Virginia's rocky fortunes in the mid-1970s won editorial plaudits throughout the Commonwealth as he prepared to step down a second time. The overall theme was what one major newspaper called the "quiet accomplishment" in his second round as governor.

Just reaching the political pinnacle of a second gubernatorial term after switching parties had been a noteworthy accomplishment all by itself: Godwin had to defeat the Democratic Party's liberal standard-bearer of the era, Henry E. Howell Jr., despite the impact on Republican candidates everywhere of the still-unfolding Watergate scandal and of Spiro Agnew's recent resignation as vice president. It was a difficult political assignment, but Godwin managed to carry the 1973 gubernatorial election anyway—by the slim margin of just fifteen thousand votes statewide. A colossus among his political contemporaries, Godwin campaigned with his head often shaking from a nervous disorder but with an unforgettable voice of thunder.

As governor a second time, Godwin had to make a host of controversial decisions. He opposed federal directives to further desegregate Virginia's public colleges, rather than accede to imposed "quotas." He closed the historic James River and its tributaries to fishing because of Kepone contamination of the great waterway . . . and reportedly cried over that tough decision. He vetoed funds the General Assembly awarded for a northern Virginia metro rail project, and he initiated a suit to invalidate collective bargaining agreements between northern Virginia government employees and their respective public agencies.

Stepping down from a second round as governor meant a few lifestyle changes. Now, he joked, he must once again learn to drive himself after a second four years of auto travel strictly by limousine driven by a state trooper escort. Overall, for that matter, he would be ending a period of thirty years in public offices ranging from delegate (Virginia House of Delegates) to state senator to lieutenant governor to governor (twice). Thus, his leave-taking also meant a final farewell to the still-Democrat dominated General Assembly in the last days of his gubernatorial term, its ranks so changed that only House Speaker John Warren Cooke remained as a colleague from Godwin's first year in the House of Delegates in 1948.

There were, in fact, tears on the normally impassive Godwin's face after he kissed his wife and hustled her out of the House chamber after that farewell. Moments before, he had told a joint session of the House and Senate it would be impossible for him ever to "quench the glow of a lifelong love affair with Virginia." Stepping down meant leaving the helm, he also said, while "believing my duty done, my charge fulfilled."

☆　☆　☆

Additional note: The remaining twentieth-century governors of Virginia, each a success story himself, were (in addition to Godwin's successor, John N. Dalton): Democrats L. Douglas Wilder, the first black elected a U.S. governor; former Attorney General Gerald Baliles; and Charles S. Robb, President Lyndon B. Johnson's son-in-law; and Republicans George Allen, son of professional football coach George Allen; and former Attorney General James Gilmore. Democrat Mark Warner would be Virginia's first twenty-first-century governor, while both Robb and Allen became U.S. senators (with Allen taking over Robb's seat after defeating the Democrat).

1978
Tantamount Politics No More

For the once totally moribund Republican Party of Virginia, the numbers game of 1978 was a phenomenon, sensational . . . compared to days not so long gone by. And the event attracting such hail and hearty numbers was itself unprecedented for the once sickly GOP.

To chose a U.S. Senate nominee, an unheard-of eight thousand delegates and alternates rushing to Richmond for the Republican State Convention of 1978 actually had a viable set of potential candidates to chose from. Never before in the state party's history had its members had an opportunity to choose among such political stars as a former GOP governor of Virginia; the former head of the national bicentennial observances of 1976; a second in command of the Republican National Committee, and a bright young state senator eager to make his mark, too.

For that matter, never before in the state party's history had so many GOPers turned out for such a mammoth political convention. By the same party's standards of just ten years before, much less twenty or more, this alone was an amazing feat.

Republican veterans scattered across the Commonwealth still could recall the many years in their own lifetimes when they would call a local party convention "and get together in a phone booth." A state convention was a mere multiple of the phone booths.

Senate contender A. Linwood Holton—a former GOP governor of Virginia, amazingly enough—embellished the old phone booth story with the recollection of flipping a coin with others to see "who had to run" one year or another against the totally dominant Democrats.

In many ways, though, the change was all Holton's own fault, since he was the first Republican to break the Democratic Party's century-old hammerlock on Virginia's governorship. That was in

1969, and by 1978, Virginia was on its third Republican governor in a row.

All this was a dramatic departure from the decades when the famed Democratic "organization" headed by Senator Harry F. Byrd held an iron grip on public offices in Virginia ranging from the state capitol in Richmond to the lowliest courthouse post in the most remote sections of the Old Dominion. Those were the days, political observers often pointed out, when the name of the game in Virginia politics was "Tantamount"—when winning nomination at a statewide Democratic primary or convention for any office was tantamount to election in the general election to follow. (See previous story as well, please.)

Also astonishing as record numbers of GOPers gathered at the Richmond Coliseum in 1978 was the fact that GOP trailblazer Holton wasn't even considered the favorite in the four-way sweepstakes for nomination to the U.S. Senate. Not by a long shot. As his own strategists were willing to concede on the eve of the convention, he appeared to be running no better than second in the four-man field.

Running ahead by just about everybody's estimate was party conservative Richard D. Obenshain, a former state GOP chairman who also had been second in command at the party's national level.

On the other hand, party moderate Holton was considered to be behind, ahead, or running neck and neck—take your pick—with former U.S. Navy Secretary John W. Warner, the former administrator also of the nation's bicentennial in 1976—and, as simply *everyone* knew, husband of actress Elizabeth Taylor. By any advance count, meanwhile, those three—Obenshain, Holton, and Warner—were running far in advance of a well-liked and widely respected dark horse bringing up the rear, State Senator Nathan Miller of Rockingham County. Even Miller, as a bright, articulate young man, reflected the change in the Virginia party's fortunes as a candidate symptomatic of the bright young people now beginning to rally behind the GOP banner.

Symptomatically, too, one of that crowd, state Senator J. Marshall Coleman of Staunton, in 1977 narrowly nosed out another relative youngster, Delegate Wyatt Durette of Fairfax, to grab the nomination for attorney general in the most spirited GOP struggle to date for that always unreachable post. Not only that, Coleman won the office as the first Republican ever to win it in a general election.

The fruit of all such previous labors, however, and the latest proof of the Virginia GOP's political "arrival," would be the looming state convention of June 1978. Party chairman George McMath, a former General Assembly member from Virginia's Eastern Shore—and, incidentally, like many other Republicans, himself a former Democrat—laid out the startling dimensions of the pending meeting a day or two beforehand. More than seventy-five hundred delegates had been chosen in hometowns all over Virginia for the honor of nominating the party's standard-bearer in the 1978 Senate race, he said. Fairfax County alone would be sending fifteen hundred persons to the weekend convention. Overall, in terms of convention delegates, it would be a record turnout for the Virginia GOP, for any party in Virginia . . . for any state political convention in U.S. history, so far as the experts could say.

The seventy-five hundred or so delegates traipsing to Richmond, plus alternates, plus family and various hangers-on, somehow would squeeze into twenty-three area hotels and motels boasting three thousand rooms, McMath also said. The coliseum housing the GOP fraternity would seat twelve thousand souls.

Keynoting the vast party meeting would be National GOP Chairman Bill Brock. In addition, Governor James Edwards of South Carolina, the first Republican to win *that* southern state's executive post in a century, would be the speaker at a party banquet the Friday night before the nominating session on Saturday. Virginia's own Republican governor, John N. Dalton, of course would be addressing the eight thousand delegates and alternates expected to take seats on the convention floor on Saturday as well.

In a way, they could all thank Dalton for the record crowds, the long restaurant lines in town, or for just being there, for Dalton more than ten years before had helped to develop a change in the official party plan allowing up to five GOP delegates to share one convention vote. The idea, explained Dalton, was to open party doors to as many participants as possible without spending taxpayer dollars and heavy campaign funds on a statewide primary to nominate GOP candidates. But whoever dreamed back then of 7,500 or more warm bodies sharing the 1978 convention's 3,081 votes?

The result of all the ballyhoo, and a subsequent personal tragedy, would be a watershed year in the history of Virginia politics.

Party leaders going into the convention were predicting it might go to three or four ballots before settling upon the GOP contender for the Senate—instead, raucous, colorful, but largely good-natured throughout the day and evening, the convention went through six ballots before choosing the GOP standard-bearer. The hoopla included former Navy Secretary John Warner's unveiling of sailor hats for his staff and committed delegates. Then, too, his wife, Elizabeth Taylor, stopped convention business with her entrance at the coliseum late on Friday—dressed nautically in jeans, a short-sleeved pullover, and a sailor hat. The convention's temporary chairman, State Senator Herbert Bateman of Newport News—himself a recent recruit from Democratic ranks—was forced to interrupt his announcements while the delegates stood and applauded what he called "this most charming distraction."

In the convention's keynote speech, meanwhile, National GOP Chairman Brock noted claims by Virginia Republicans that theirs apparently was the largest political convention in U.S. history. According to Brock, a former U.S. senator from Tennessee, he had seen record Republican turnouts all over the nation in his fifteen months as chairman, but, he declared, "Nowhere have I seen anything like Virginia."

As for the real business of the monolithic convention late that day, former Governor Holton bowed out after seeing his delegate count steadily slip in the first three ballots. That left the field to Obenshain, Warner, and Miller—Obenshain still the front-runner, as expected, but Warner, a newcomer to many in the Virginia GOP, running a surprisingly strong second.

After three more ballots, Miller bowed out. Warner, gaining all the while, remained in second place . . . but Obenshain finally had taken the nomination by winning the 1,540.51 votes needed for victory, and then some. Thus, after the state's Democrats met in Williamsburg the following weekend and chose former Attorney General Andrew P. Miller as their nominee for the Senate, it looked like an Obenshain-Miller contest in the fall.

But not so. Sadly, Obenshain later that summer was killed when his small airplane crashed outside Richmond. A somber, largely conservative Republican Party State Central Committee then turned to John Warner, somewhat suspect as a possible moderate and still new to many party regulars, to carry Obenshain's dropped banner. With the help of Obenshain's campaign leadership, his own staff—and, bottom line, the electorate, Republican John Warner then won the Senate seat in the general election of 1978, and he has held it ever since, up until this writing in 2003. (He and Elizabeth Taylor parted company, however, shortly after he took his U.S. Senate seat.)

★

1993

Passing of a "World Citizen"

★

Upon his death, he was the first person to lie in state in the governor's mansion in Richmond since Stonewall Jackson. In time also, he would join Robert E. Lee, Jeb Stuart, and Jefferson Davis on Monument Avenue—his monument joining theirs, that is.

He also won at Wimbledon in 1975, a historic first.

To gain that distinction, he had to beat the other best of the worldwide crop that day, top-seeded Jimmy Connors.

In Richmond years earlier, his father was the caretaker for a large, segregated playground, the largest of its special kind in the city.

They lived next to the playground and its four tennis courts.

The tennis perhaps would have come about naturally, but, by some accounts, it had a jump-start when Ron Charity, arguably the city's best black player, stopped practice one day, walked over, and asked the seven-year-old boy, "Would you like to learn how to play?"

Little Arthur Ashe would and he sure did.

But first, summertime coaching by another key benefactor, Dr. Walter Johnson of Lynchburg, would provide another jump-start for the young tennis aspirant, as would spending his senior year of high school in St. Louis for still more tutoring in tennis.

Despite the barriers of racial segregation that limited his tournament opportunities—and thus, topflight competitive experience—he then earned a tennis scholarship to UCLA, became the first black to win the NCAA singles title, and landed a berth on the U.S. Davis Cup team at the age of twenty as its first black player ever. Over the next fifteen years, he would win twenty-eight of his thirty-four Davis Cup matches.

But Arthur Robert Ashe Jr. was busy all those years at other tennis venues as well. Turning professional in 1970, he soon won the Australian Open, and in 1972 he became the first American player, white or black, to salt away more than $100,000 in tournament earnings in one year. The first black male to win a U.S. Open, he then achieved the same milestone by defeating Jimmy Connors at Wimbledon in

1975. Destined for a lifetime score of thirty-three worldwide tournament victories, Arthur Ashe at his peak was ranked one of the world's top five tennis players for thirteen years in a row. For the year of 1976, he was ranked number one in the world.

So much for the stats, and the breakthroughs, a combination that by itself made Arthur Ashe a historic figure both in the world of tennis and the world at large. But there was more, much more, to the Arthur Ashe story, including his care for what the breakthroughs meant and his terrible, terrible bad luck.

A small but typical incident: At Wimbledon one time, little-known George Seewagen of Bayside, New York, the varsity tennis coach at Columbia and 1969 U.S. amateurs winner, was scheduled to play his first-ever Wimbledon match—against four-time Wimbledon champ Rod Laver of Australia—and Seewagen was understandably nervous. According to John McPhee's "Centre Court" chapter in his book *Pieces of the Frame*, Arthur Ashe quietly went to Seewagen and said, "You'll never play better. You'll get in there, in Centre Court, and you'll get inspired, and then when the crowd roars for your first great shot, you'll want to run into the locker room and call it a day."

According to McPhee also, Seewagen hoped to win at least two games against the incomparable Laver, and he did.

Arthur Ashe also operated, and gave of himself, on a larger, even worldwide scale as well. He was a leader in the formation of the Association of Tennis Professionals (ATP) and served as ATP president in 1975–76, noted Brad Herzog in his book *The Sports 100: The One Hundred Most Important People in American Sports History*.

Obviously cognizant of his own beginnings, Ashe spent time off the courts writing the book *Hard Road to Glory: A History of the African-American Athlete*. He lobbied against apartheid in South Africa, where he was once denied permission to play (but later his presence was allowed on local courts). A founding member of Artists and Athletes Against Apartheid, he once, in 1985, was arrested in a demonstration in front of the South African embassy in Washington, D.C. Overall, as both tennis player and black pioneer, there is no doubting the truth of Herzog's statement that Arthur Ashe "inspired a generation of blacks to take up a previously uninviting sport."

But suddenly, out of the blue, came disaster for the trailblazer—in July 1979 he suffered a heart attack, followed by a quadruple coronary bypass six months later. Emerging from that experience wan but wry, he said with a touch of humor, "The doctors say I will live to be one hundred, but they won't put it in writing."

As events turned out, he needed a second bypass operation in 1983, but the really unfortunate outcome this time was the AIDS virus he contracted from a blood transfusion . . . without knowing about it until he underwent brain surgery five years later.

Not that these physical and health setbacks completely sidelined the star player, not at all. He as of 1980 began a five-year stint as non-playing captain of the U.S. Davis Cup team. He spent nearly $300,000 to have researchers help him develop a three-volume history of black athletes. He formed the African American Athletic Association. He taught a college course called "The Black Athlete in Contemporary Society." Typical of Ashe also, once he was stricken himself, he started up the Arthur Ashe Foundation for the Defeat of AIDS. Somehow he also had found time to launch the Arthur Ashe Institute for Urban Health and to put his broad shoulders behind the American Heart Association, the United Negro College Fund, and a "U.S. foreign policy think tank, TransAfrica," Herzog also noted. In addition, Ashe turned out a personal memoir, *Days of Grace*.

To many, *grace* indeed was his hallmark, in bad times and good. In the HBO documentary *Arthur Ashe: Citizen of the World,* television personality Bryant Gumbel said: "He was an ambassador of what was right. He was an ambassador of dignity. He was an ambassador of class." Among others who knew him well, according to *Richmond Times-Dispatch* reporter John Packett, former New York Mayor David Dinkins noted: "It is through tennis that he got a lot of youngsters to do better. To believe in themselves. To learn discipline, and on and on. His interest was not so much in just producing good tennis players, it was in producing good people."

In similar fashion, former Virginia Governor L. Douglas Wilder, the first black ever elected governor of Virginia or any other state, said: "The thing that is spoken mostly about Arthur, in addition to his prowess as a tennis player, was his deep, insightful observations on humankind, justice, self-reliance, education. I think his stature grows with each passing day."

Unfortunately, as the 1980s gave way to the 1990s, his days were severely numbered. After addressing the United Nations on World AIDS Day, Ashe maintained his dedication to the causes he believed in, but at greater personal risk than anyone quite realized. Arrested in

Washington at a protest on behalf of Haitian refugees, Ashe suffered another heart attack soon after. Weakened by that event and his AIDS condition, he succumbed to pneumonia and died on February 6, 1993, just months short of his fiftieth birthday in July.

Back in his hometown of Richmond, in the meantime, there were those who felt that Arthur Ashe, self-proclaimed "citizen of the world," perhaps should have stepped off the national and world stages to give Richmond a bit more of his personal attention. Or . . . should Richmond have done more for him? Virginia Union University's retired Professor John Watson, who once helped introduce a very young Arthur Ashe to the finer points of the game, summed up that very quandary in Packett's *Times-Dispatch* piece of February 6, 2003, the tenth anniversary of Ashe's death.

"People have often wondered why he never did much for the local community," said Watson on the one hand. "As far as buildings are concerned. As far as putting money into the local community. . . . Why did he not come to town and train people to do what he had done, as opposed to going to California or St. Louis or other places to do what we thought he should have done here?"

On the other hand, said Watson, "there's so much good that he's done that it's difficult to say he has no legacy here." And Richmond, in fact, could do more to memorialize its connection with Ashe, perhaps a tennis facility named for him. "Something familiar, something concrete associated with Arthur Ashe and what he means to everybody," Watson added. "We don't have that." As Packett noted in the same story, Ashe is well recognized in the nation's most prominent tennis venue of all. "At the U.S. Open in New York," wrote Packett, "the main arena is named Arthur Ashe Stadium. In 2000, the United States Tennis Association [USTA] dedicated the Arthur Ashe Commemorative Garden at the National Tennis Center. Arthur Ashe Kids Day has preceded every U.S. Open since 1992."

Then, too, "in Philadelphia, the Arthur Ashe Youth Tennis Center works with kids. Similar programs can be found in New York, Chicago, and South Africa."

And further: "He and Charlie Pasarell formed the National Junior Tennis League [NJTL] in 1969 to give inner-city kids the chance to learn about the game." In 2002, "the program helped nearly 200,000 children in more than 900 programs nationwide, according to the USTA. Serena and Venus Williams, the world's top two female players, participated in the NJTL when they first began playing organized tennis in Los Angeles."

And so on . . . nationwide and even worldwide, various programs and facilities recall the contributions of Arthur Ashe. But then, in certain respects, so does the Richmond community. In Richmond proper, the Arthur Ashe Jr. Athletic Center is a popular and well-known facility for high-school and college events, while Henrico County's Arthur Ashe Jr. Elementary School is another kind of memorial to adjoining Richmond's famous son. And so is the twelve-foot Arthur Ashe statue on Monument Avenue (twenty-eight feet in height, counting the base), born in controversy and added to Monument Avenue's stone-cold parade of all-Confederate figures in 1996.

"We are not against the statue," said one protester at the time of the statue's dedication. Identifying himself as a member of the Sons of Confederate Veterans, he added, "We just don't like the location."

Aside from the arguments pro and con, all now moot, Paul Di Pasquale's sculpture of Ashe quite appropriately shows him carrying a tennis racket in one hand, and in the other, held up higher, books.

Worth note also is the fact that in the end, Arthur Ashe did come back to Richmond . . . permanently. As he had wished, he is buried today in the city's northside Woodlawn Cemetery next to his mother, Mattie, who died when he was only six. (His father would be buried years later at Gum Springs.) As Packett also wrote in his tenth-anniversary article: "The graves of Ashe and his mother are located close to Interstate 64, where cars and trucks whiz past without their occupants realizing that one of the world's most beloved athletes is buried nearby."

☆ ☆ ☆

Additional note: Sometimes forgotten in the once-hot debate over the Monument Avenue statue or discussions over the degree of Ashe's contributions to his hometown is the fact that for several years he often returned and played in Richmond as an established star on the professional circuit. The venue was an annual indoor pro tournament, in which he won three times and finished as runner-up another three times, Packett noted.

"He did everything he possibly could for Richmond," Lou Einwick, a retired investment banker who ran the tournament, told Packett. "He certainly bent over backwards to do anything I ever asked him. Certainly, whenever you asked Arthur to come here and do a clinic, he always did that."

Tennis "wasn't his single interest," added Einwick. "That's why you remember him more for his trips to South Africa. That's why you have a monument that has a tennis racket in one hand and books in the other hand. That's always going to be Arthur's legacy."

⭐ Part 5 ⭐

Twenty-First Century

Father on Lee's Staff

"The single most amazing thing to me about the General Assembly," said a freshman legislator from northern Virginia in 1978, "is the fact that the [House] Speaker's father was a member of Robert E. Lee's staff."

Amazing but true, House Speaker John Warren Cooke's father did indeed serve as a staff officer for General Lee in the Civil War.

Even more amazing, the same facts still were true twenty-two years later as Virginia slid into the twenty-first century, except that Cooke, age eighty-four, a weekly newspaper publisher from Mathews, had retired from politics and no longer was a House member. But the change in centuries meant that a man of the twenty-first century could hearken back to a father who served in a war from, numerically, two centuries before. That is, the year 2000 versus the span of 1861 to 1865.

To explain: Cooke's father, Giles Buckner Cooke, a graduate of Virginia Military Institute (VMI), served at Shiloh as a young Confederate officer. He was at the siege of Petersburg. He was on hand for the surrender at Appomattox. Earlier, he had a reconciliation with Stonewall Jackson in the latter's field tent at the battle of First Manassas (Bull Run). "Just before graduating [from VMI, where Jackson was a professor]," said the younger Cooke one time in the last century, "he had a violent argument with Jackson over a grade, and he left the school with a bitter feeling."

The reconciliation was the last time that Giles Cooke saw the famous Stonewall, who picked up his famous nickname at the battle of First Manassas (Bull Run). Two years later, Jackson would be fatally wounded by friendly fire at Chancellorsville.

Giles Cooke graduated from VMI in 1859, settled in Petersburg, "read the law," and opened a law practice just before the war erupted. Unaware of the horrors yet to unfold, he joined the Confederate army as a lieutenant. He then was assigned as a staff aide to several generals, usually as an assistant adjutant or inspector general. His longest service was with Pierre Gustave Toutant Beauregard of Louisiana, who took young Cooke with him on campaigns throughout the South. Finally, in October 1864, by then twenty-six and a major in rank, Cooke was transferred to Lee's staff as Beauregard turned southward again.

As a result, Giles Cooke was destined many years later to become the longest-living survivor of Lee's small staffs, a number that came to no more than two dozen or so officers in all.

With the Civil War over, Cooke returned to Petersburg, joined a friend in opening a boys school, and began "reading" for the ministry. After five years, during which he also was active in a religious education program for the city's newly freed blacks, Giles Cooke was ordained and began a career as an Episcopal minister that lasted until his retirement in 1917. He chose his religious vocation as a direct result of the horrors of war he had witnessed, added his son.

As the nineteenth century slipped into the twentieth, meanwhile, the elder Cooke became quite a celebrity among Civil War scholars as a rare, still-living witness to the events and personalities they studied. He himself had accumulated eight or more volumes of a daily diary.

According to his son, the Civil War veteran remained active, alert, and in good health until he died a few months short of turning ninety-nine. "He just died in his sleep one night of old age," said his son.

In the meantime, the younger Cooke, age eighty-eight at this writing in 2003, had been born in his minister-father's rectory at Mathews in 1915. His father then was seventy-six and his mother, Katherine Grosh Cooke, about forty-two. The older Cooke had been married before but became a widower in the late nineteenth century.

★

2 0 0 3
A Paean to Little Route 5

★

Goodbye, Richmond; hello, Williamsburg, or vice versa . . . and either way, let's take Virginia Route 5, the slightly meandering plantation alley running alongside the northern shores of the James River between the capital city of Colonial times and the present-day capital of Virginia at the falls of the James.

Virginia has its old but now-paved wagon trails, its interstates and other highways that extend up and down and across the commonwealth. It has its Pocahontas and Seminole trails, its Constitutional, Blue Star Memorial, and Jeb Stuart Highways, its Jefferson Davis and Lee Highways as well. Old U.S. Route 1, an outgrowth of the original Boston Post Road, carries on to Florida, or uppermost New England, after leaving Virginia. Two routes, U.S. 50 and U.S. 60, stretch all the way to the West Coast.

But let's instead tool eastward today along Virginia's completely self-contained Route 5, which can be picked up at Twenty-fifth and Main Streets in Richmond. Thus, we're now on the John Tyler Memorial Highway, as the roadside shields will soon proclaim.

Happy surprises ahead, too.

Aiming for final landing at Williamsburg or even Norfolk farther east? The wide, high-speed, heavily traveled Interstate 64 may appeal to some, but if speed is no object, that river of concrete pales on a pleasant fall or spring day by comparison with the occasional gentle curve and legendary way stops of Route 5.

What we're entering just beyond Richmond is an old Indian trail that nearly four centuries ago became the English settler's first east-west route of travel, other than his real highway, the James River itself.

Emerging from Richmond's most ancient dock and warehouse area, with its aroma of stored tobacco a lingering memory, the traveler shoots quite suddenly into the sunlit farmlands of Henrico County, usually known as a densely packed bedroom community for the capital city. Open fields and a sign advertising plowing services announce that this part of Henrico hardly is to be regarded as suburbia.

Bolt on through Varina, if we must . . . but keep in mind that John Rolfe and Pocahontas once lived here as man and wife, that Civil War prisoners were exchanged here, and that adjacent Fort Harrison was fought over as a link in Richmond's chain of Civil War defenses.

Route 5, it becomes evident, is as layered with history as any road its length—all of fifty-four miles—in the country, if not more so.

In minutes, we pass on by Curles Neck, home of a twentieth-century dairy that once was the homestead of the seventeenth-century, anti-British rebel Nathaniel Bacon Jr., who for a few historical moments took control of mainland Virginia, the largest, most populous colony at the time. Keep in mind that the *real* American Revolution came in the eighteenth century, a full hundred years later.

Soon Route 5 has arrived at historic Shirley Plantation off to our right, its entrance a long avenue flanked by tall trees and leading to a magnificent mansion and outbuildings of dark brick. In this great home for generation after generation of the Carter family, its centerpiece structure built in 1723, Robert E. Lee's mother was born. Here, too, she was married to Henry "Lighthorse Harry" Lee. And here as well their famous son Robert E. sometimes was schooled.

Also noted for its still-existing, villagelike cluster of dependencies around the manor house, an aspect typical of Virginia's eighteenth-century plantations, Shirley was built by Edward Hill III on a 1,660-acre plantation site for his daughter Elizabeth, who that same year of 1723 married John Carter, eldest son of Robert "King" Carter. It was the couple's granddaughter, Anne Hill Carter, who became Robert E. Lee's mother. Unfortunately, Robert "King" Carter's grand and reputedly even more fabulous Northern Neck mansion, Corotoman, cannot be seen or visited today since it long ago was destroyed by fire.

Meanwhile, detail for the trivia-minded: The Shirley manor house boasts the only curving, apparently unsupported three-story staircase of its kind in America.

Next down Route 5, as we travel east and look to the right, looms Berkeley, home in 1619 of what Virginians consider the first Thanksgiving in America; home also to Benjamin Harrison, three-time governor of Virginia and a signer of the Declaration of Independence; early home and, in fact, birthplace of his son, William Henry "Old Tippecanoe" Harrison, who wrote his inaugural address here before assuming office as ninth president of the United States. Unfortunately for the aging Indian fighter, it was a lengthy oration, given outdoors in foul weather—he caught cold, and in a month he was the first president to die in office, in his case probably of pneumonia. Many years down the road—of time, that is—his grandson, another Benjamin Harrison, also would become president, the nation's twenty-third chief executive. Thus, it seems that Berkeley joins the Adams House of Massachusetts as the only ancestral homes of two presidents.

But Berkeley alone can claim the distinction of witnessing the composition of "Taps" by Union Maj. Gen. Daniel Butterfield, who briefly was quartered at Berkeley during the Civil War (and who earned a belatedly bestowed Medal of Honor for his heroics in the battle of Gaines's Mill during George B. McClellan's Peninsula campaign of 1862).

As for the early, early Thanksgiving, it seems that on December 4, 1619, a year before the Pilgrims landed at Plymouth, the English Berkeley Company founded the Berkeley Hundred and Plantation at this site on the James River, then proclaimed, "The day of our ships' arrival . . . shall be yearly and perpetually kept as a day of Thanksgiving." This was the same year, by the way, that the first Virginia legislative body was created, and the year the first African Americans were taken into the Virginia Colony, initially as indentured servants, both events taking place at Jamestown downriver from Berkeley.

Just a few years later, in 1622, Berkeley produced the first bourbon whiskey distilled in America . . . but it also shared in the 1622 massacre of English settlers up and down the James by Indians.

The Harrison family purchased the plantation in 1691 and opened the first commercial shipyard in America here just four years later. The present manor house was built by Benjamin Harrison IV in 1726, father of the three-time Virginia Governor Benjamin Harrison V.

During the American Revolution, the turncoat Benedict Arnold plundered the place as part of his punishing forays up and down the James River. In 1862, not only did General Butterfield stay here, so did his commanding general, George B. McClellan.

A long drive leads to the manor house and outbuildings. And if it seems a bit slow and bumpy, it was, after all, originally designed for the horse carriages of another day, reminds a sign at the entrance.

The two-lane macadam road linking these great plantations, along with other historic stops still to go, winds right or left, then straightens out for a spell. Except for a gentle swell here and there, it and the surrounding terrain are almost always flat. Yet the road is shrouded by banks of trees, some of them flowering dogwood, and it is broken by bursts of sunlight and pools of shadows.

The James, glimpsed only from the plantation lawns, is an entirely different creature from the bubbling, narrow, and rocky stream seen at Richmond and above. All along here, below the fall line at Richmond, this now is an inland sea, wide and complacent, speckled with islands, boats, and barges. No rushing waters here.

Hard by Berkeley is Westover, another classic brick structure overlooking the water . . . and considered "one of the most beautiful houses in the United States," noted David King Gleason in his book of stunning photographs, *Virginia Plantation Houses.* Busy Benedict Arnold stopped here, too. The Indians massacred here as well. And poor old Lord Cornwallis crossed the river here in pursuit of Lafayette, only to fetch up at Yorktown and confront a nemesis named George Washington some weeks later.

A good bit later still, Union troops not only occupied the manor house, they resorted to the roof for a signals platform.

This magnificent old place, built about 1730, was the creation of William Evelyn Byrd II, the founder of Richmond itself. The twelve-hundred-acre plantation had been purchased by his father. On the river side of the old home, tall tulip poplars—going on two centuries in age—form a silent but ever-so-grand parade.

Not far away, facing Herring Creek but also entered from Route 5, is sad Evelynton, so named for Byrd's daughter Evelyn and occupying a 860-acre piece of the original Westover plantation. "Denied permission to marry her English suitor, Evelyn is said to have died of a broken heart," wrote Gleason, "and according to legend her ghost is still seen at Westover and Evelynton."

The wonder is that it hasn't been haunted by a later owner, Edmund Ruffin, the agronomist and Secessionist fire-eater who helped bombard Fort Sumter in Charleston Harbor to begin the Civil War and, again as a gray-headed volunteer, joined the Confederate troops in battle elsewhere as well. The Union troops visiting the James River plantations during the Civil War didn't react kindly—they burned down the plantation buildings, cut rings around his trees, and salted the fields. After the war, the embittered Ruffin shot himself—while wrapped in a Confederate flag, legend has it.

Turning up next on the eastward sojourn is Sherwood Forest, a wooden structure of clapboard and, at three hundred feet in length, allegedly the longest antebellum frame house in Virginia . . . if not the entire country. Here, in 1845, came President John Tyler, born a few miles away at Greenway, after his tour in the White House as sudden successor to the ill-fated William Henry Harrison, himself of course born a Route 5 neighbor. Coming with Tyler was his recent bride and second wife, Julia Gardiner of Long Island.

Sherwood Forest dates back to 1730, actually—Tyler bought the sixteen-hundred-acre property while in the White House, then added wings and a sixty-eight-foot ballroom to the existing eighteenth-century house on the property. Retiring here after his presidential stint, Tyler later would serve as convenor of the 1861 peace conference in Washington that tried, but failed, to head off the Civil War. He then was elected to the Confederate Congress, but before he could take his seat he died—in a Richmond hotel. During the hostilities, ironically, Northern-born Julia Tyler felt constrained to flee her Sherwood Forest home with her children before the advance of Union troops.

In the meantime, it must also be noted, Route 5 already has coursed on by the site where Thomas Jefferson was married, the early Turkey Island homestead of the Virginia Randolphs, a scene also of Revolutionary War and Civil War battles, pursuits, encampments, and river crossings, one of them by pontoon bridge.

Beyond Sherwood Forest, as we wonder where our journey may end, the road turns suddenly left, to cross the Chickahominy River, itself associated with Virginia history dating back to the days of the Jamestown settlement. Soon we are at the outskirts of Williamsburg, the second Colonial capital (after Jamestown). The roadside shields lead us into Colonial Williamsburg itself. Right, left, left, and right . . . we take a tortuous path through the restored Colonial section of town before we again approach our first Williamsburg turn and realize Route 5 has doubled back to meet itself.

The journey is over. We have reached the end of Route 5—which, in reality, as the path now turns westward toward Richmond to follow the outward flight of the early settlers from nearby Jamestown—is only the beginning.

The Women
Who Counted

By Ingrid Smyer

IF VIRGINIANS REALLY WANT to understand themselves and their values, Virginia biographer Douglas Southall Freeman once said, they should pay attention to the history of their women. But who was listening? As well-known women's historian Anne Firor Scott later noted, "Few people were prepared to hear what he said, and historians went their accustomed way, writing about men and the things men do, and calling their work 'history.'"

Then, in the 1960s, "things began to change." Historians began to look beyond their traditional, often male-oriented interests. Spurred by a resurgence of feminism, many women began to examine their own lives. Just as important, they began to address mothers and grandmothers with a key question: What was it like back then?

New methods of research made it possible "to ask and answer questions about large numbers of hitherto unexamined groups," added Scott in an introduction for Suzanne Lebsock's book *Virginia Women, 1600–1945: "A Share of Honour."* New technology gave added incentive to researchers and attracted young women who were entering colleges and universities in great numbers. So began "an explosion of studies about women and families that are remaking the historical landscape." Studies that of course included Virginia, where the history of English America had its start . . . where scholars and many others have begun to ponder the lives, the dreams, and the aspirations of the Other Half who were here almost from the very beginning of the first English settlement in the Old Dominion.

Nor have such studies by any means been limited to the European-born Other Half. Not at all. Our attention these days also is focused upon the women who were here before Jamestown. And no, not simply upon the romantic story of Pocahontas that every American schoolchild knows so well. No, it's been important to realize, if proper history is to be written, that Chief Powhatan's daughter did have her sister Native Americans, not all of whom could aspire to visit the royal court of England. Or even to have a chief for a father.

Another group of sisters under study these days are the first black women to land on Virginia shores, not all of them directly from Africa, not slaves exactly, but perhaps not brought to Virginia entirely of their own free will, either.

☆ ☆ ☆

From the beginning, Virginia owed a debt to a woman—Virginia's very name came from a queen, the great virgin queen of England, Elizabeth I, thanks to seafaring explorer Walter Raleigh's expeditions of the 1580s that penetrated the Outer Banks of today's North Carolina.

The first time Raleigh's sailors enthusiastically set foot on North American soil, they affixed their monarch's seal to an upright post and claimed the "sweete, fruitfull, and wholsome" land for their queen. Returning to England, Raleigh was knighted by Queen Elizabeth as reward for his adventure, which potentially added vast new territories to her kingdom.

Appointed as the lord and governor of all Virginia, Sir Walter wasted no time in preparing to colonize the new land he had named for his virgin queen. When his second expedition didn't work out after briefly landing on Roanoke Island just past the beaches of the Outer Banks, Raleigh gathered personnel in May 1587 for yet another attempt at a lasting settlement in the new land. He appointed "Gentleman" John White of London to be the settlement's governor.

Little is known of John White's background except that he was an artist whose intricate drawings of Indians, their villages, and the surrounding terrain and environment have been of lasting value. As a veteran of Raleigh's previous Roanoke expeditions, he was well aware of the dangers that lay ahead. Still, he persuaded his daughter **Eleanor** and her husband, Ananias Dare, to make the voyage across the Atlantic, even though Eleanor was pregnant.

Once again, Roanoke Island was the destination, this time for more than a hundred newly landed colonists who faced problems right from the beginning, with unfriendly Indians at the top of the list. One happy event did brighten life in the troubled settlement. On August 18, 1587, Eleanor gave birth to a baby girl who was christened Virginia. Little **Virginia Dare** thus became the first English child born in North America. And yes, a girl was the first, even if joined just days later by a boy delivered to Dyonis and Margery Harvie.

But now, John White, both a new grandfather and governor of the struggling colony, made ready to sail back to England for badly needed supplies. He and the settlers agreed they would move to the mainland and leave him a message carved into a tree or post to indicate their new location. If in distress, they also would use a cross-mark. White, for his part, promised to return in three months.

Unfortunately, this was a vow that could not be kept. After three *years* of delay and plans gone awry back in England, largely to be blamed on war with Spain, John White finally returned to Roanoke Island . . . and found no one there. As agreed earlier, the troubled colonists had carved a message on a tree: the single word "CROATOAN," the Indian name for Ocracoke Island. That was the only clue to the disappearance of the entire colony he had left behind three years before.

Unable to find a trace of the colonists—his own daughter and granddaughter among them—the dispirited White returned to England, never to learn what became of them. Even today, the fate of the "Lost Colony" remains unknown (although Lee Miller's recent book *Roanoke: Solving the Mystery of the Lost Colony* offers interesting facts and theories).

The unsettling disappearance of the Roanoke Island settlers was not an ending, but rather a beginning—in 1607, thirteen years ahead of the Pilgrims' arrival in future Massachusetts, an English settlement, this time a permanent colony, was established within the boundaries of Virginia as we know it today. The course of American history had made a sharp turn and was back on track.

The London-based Virginia Company, chartered in 1606 to organize, oversee, and finance such a colony, sent three wooden sailing ships, the *Susan Constant,* the *Discovery,* and *Godspeed,* across the Atlantic under the command of seasoned voyager Christopher Newport. With a combined manifest of 104 men and boys (no women!), the flotilla made its first Virginia landfall in 1607 at what is today Cape Henry, at the entrance to Chesapeake Bay. Here the Englishmen came ashore, erected a wooden cross, and knelt in thanksgiving for a safe end to their long journey. Standing on solid ground again after weeks aboard ship (except for a brief stay in the West Indies), many of the men must have doubted their wisdom in joining this band of adventurers—and many surely were missing wives or girlfriends.

As the ships then moved up a broad river and were tied to trees on an islandlike peninsula, both Captain Newport and the widely traveled soldier of fortune Capt. John Smith understood the potential challenges of colonial life without illusion. But Newport, an officer in the Virginia Company, was anxious to make a success of this new settlement on the sliver of land they named James Towne (or Jamestown) in honor of King James I. Even though the struggle merely to survive soon would be an overriding concern for the settlement, Newport stressed money-making enterprises, such as felling trees for making ship masts and clapboard that could be sold in England. Hampering all such aspirations (and the struggle to survive, for that matter) was the fact that most of the first Jamestown settlers hardly were accustomed to hard labor, as Martha W. McCartney pointed out in her book *Jamestown: An American Legacy.* "Nearly half of Virginia's first settlers were gentlemen, scholars, artisans, and tradesmen, not laborers or sturdy yeoman farmers whose basic skills and physical conditioning might prove invaluable in a wilderness environment," she noted.

Nor were there any women on hand . . . yet.

They—their first advance scouts in any case—would make their first appearance in October 1608 as the Second Supply of pioneers landed at Jamestown, among them exactly twenty-eight more gentlemen, fourteen tradesmen, eight Germans and Poles—and Mrs. Thomas Forrest, together with her fourteen-year-old maid, **Ann Burras.** Historic figures to be sure, but take pity on them for what they now faced—as James M. Wamsley and Anne M. Cooper so aptly summed up in *Idols, Victims, Pioneers: Virginia Women from 1607,* their future would be "a new life of Indians and disease, tobacco and corn, un-English weather, discomfort, and privation."

Mrs. Forrest, seemingly unable to face the trials of primitive life in the colony, sailed back to England. But young Ann stayed, despite the tribulations, because for a woman of such lowly station as hers, the New World offered open-ended possibilities.

No surprise considering the overwhelming ratio of men to women, Miss Burras almost immediately was betrothed to Jamestown carpenter John Laydon; the wedding that soon followed would be the first such ceremony to take place in Jamestown (or in Virginia as we know it today). By late 1609, they had become the proud parents of a baby girl—named **Virginia,** appropriately enough.

By 1619, with women only occasionally filling out the ranks, it was obvious the settlement in Virginia suffered from "solitary uncouthness," in the words of Sir Francis Bacon, and was not going anywhere unless it included more women. Sir Edwin Sandys, the Virginia Company's treasurer, had the fine idea that one hundred "maids young and uncorrupt" should be sent to Virginia as wives. If they married tenants on any of the company's four tracts of public land—named Charles, James, and Elizabeth and Henrico—their transport would be at company expense.

On the other hand, if a maid was fortunate enough to marry an independent landowner of her own choosing, he would be held responsible for her transportation cost, to be satisfied in most cases by payment in the form of 120 pounds of the "best leafe Tobacco."

Few if any of the young women responding to the offer were aware that in 1618 Chief Powhatan had died, soon to be succeeded as ruler of the powerful Indian confederation occupying Tidewater Virginia by his cruel and merciless brother Opechancanough. And it wouldn't be long before Opechancanough meticulously planned a devastating response to the growing English intrusion upon his people's land—more than twelve hundred new settlers had arrived in 1619 alone, a number doubling the white population of Virginia in a single stroke. On Good Friday, March 22, 1622, the Indians staged a simultaneous attack on homes and plantations stretching for 140 miles up and down the James River, from Hampton Roads to the falls of the James, future site of Richmond. More than 350 men, women, and children were killed, many of them in farm fields, gardens, or homes before they could even reach for their guns. Both surviving or dying horribly in the massacre were the same women who had so recently arrived—the innocent maidens who had come with expectations of a better life.

The survivors now huddled together wherever they could find shelter. Unable to plant their crops safely, they faced famine as well as the ever-present fevers. Some of the women were pregnant, and at the time of delivery lacked the help of a midwife. In those days, incidentally, a surprising number of the married women had no children. Wamsley and Cooper suggested the small numbers of children may have resulted from high infant mortality, low fertility, or deliberate birth control. And, yes, methods of birth control ranged in those times from the effective to the ridiculous. The word *condom* first appeared in print in England in 1706, but such devices, made of animal membrane, apparently were in use earlier.

These trying times were doubly hard on the women who worked alongside their husbands in rebuilding burned-out buildings and in clearing new fields. No wonder, too, that the pace of immigration to Virginia came to a standstill after the news of the massacre reached London, not to pick up again until the 1630s.

Aside from the human cost, the massacre also was the undoing of the Virginia Company of London, which bore much of the blame for the disaster. Still, the London managers were able to keep the colony going for better than a year, until the Crown itself took over in 1624. Shortly thereafter, newly seated King Charles I sent a group of census takers to list the assets of the colony. The same census today is considered a most valuable font of information about Virginia's early women.

☆ ☆ ☆

Early *white* women, that is. As we already know, they weren't alone; they had their non-white sisters, and one who really counted in the history of Virginia was a stately young woman whose arrival in London four centuries ago caused quite a stir. It was a first—the very first time that an Indian princess known as **Pocahontas** would set foot in the homeland of her husband, John Rolfe. It also was the very first time any Native American had been seen by these stay-at-home English.

The young couple's journey to England had been arranged by the same Virginia Company that sponsored the Jamestown settlement . . . arranged with purpose. Although the organizers had some genuine interest in seeing Virginia's Indians Christianized, the company constantly was in need of investors and was eager for the financial rewards that colonization would bring. And, with the visit of Pocahontas, here, for all to see, was evidence that the Jamestown venture was a success, a venture quite worthy of support.

Here, too, was an Indian who had become a Christian convert, who was dressed in the proper fashion of the day, who in every way displayed the demeanor of a civilized matron. And, yes, she was the mother of an infant son who had made the arduous journey across the Atlantic with his mother and father.

Pocahontas, John Rolfe, and their son, Thomas, left Virginia in the spring of 1616, with up to a dozen other Virginia Indians, among them Chief Powhatan's trusted priest and adviser, Uttamatomakkin, who was to report his impressions of the English homeland. As matters turned out, he apparently was not overly impressed by his presentation at the royal court since he complained later that the king "gave me nothing," according to William R. S. Rasmussen and Robert S. Tilton in their book *Pocahontas: Her Life & Legend*.

Meanwhile, the Virginia Company saw to it that the stately Pocahontas was presented to English society, as well as to the royalty. The former governor of the Virginia Colony, Thomas West (Lord De la

Ware), and his wife were a natural choice to do the honors. And it seems that Powhatan's daughter, John Rolfe's Indian wife, in turn was received most graciously by the same London society, not only because she was sponsored by the powerful Virginia Company—which also provided for her and her son's living expenses—but also because "she carried her selfe as the Daughter of a King," wrote the English minister Samuel Purchas. Said he also: "I was present, when my Honorable & Revered Patron, the . . . [Lord] Bishop of London, Doctor King, entertained her with festivall state and pompe, beyond what I have seene in his great hospitalitie afforded to other Ladies."

The visiting Virginians were also introduced to the literature and theater of the day, as also noted by Rasmussen and Tilton, who cited this comment by Londoner John Chamberlain: "The Virginian woman Poca-huntas, with her father counsaillor hath ben with the King, and graciously used, and both she and her assistant well placed at the maske." The "maske" he referred to was "The Vision of Delight" a Twelfth Night masque staged by Ben Jonson in January 1617.

The couple and their baby remained in London for ten months, with Pocahontas continuing to charm and delight the English around her. Today, we can only wonder at the adaptability of this New World *primitive,* so quickly dubbed a "princess" by the Jamestown settlers, so willingly converted to Christianity, and so easily married to an Englishman . . . a young woman born to total ignorance of the Old World and in the next moment to be bearing an Old World visitor's child, then to be captivating the sophisticated Old World retinue of King James I.

Back in Virginia, she had grown to maturity as the daughter of Chief Powhatan, ruler of the Powhatan Indians, part of the Algonquian-speaking tribe living in the land that is today Virginia and North Carolina. When the first English arrived at Jamestown in 1607 she was a mere girl of about twelve, a precocious and curious young woman, named Matoaka, but well known among her people as Pocahontas ("little wanton" or "little plaything"). Later, when baptized in the Christian faith, she would take the given name Rebecca. As Thomas L. McKenney and James Hall recalled this important moment in their classic nineteenth-century treatise *History of the Indian Tribes of North America,* she was "the first fruits of the western wilderness—a precious exotic, transplanted from the wilds of America to the garden of the Lord."

Legend and myth prevail about this lovely "exotic," who not only took on the religion of the strangers from across the sea, but accepted their culture as her own. In the early days of the Jamestown settlement, she would become the savior not only of Capt. John Smith but also of the English band of settlers altogether by daring to traverse the deep woods bearing corn and other foods to the floundering community on the shores of the James.

"Pocahontas has been called America's Joan of Arc, because of her saintlike virtue and her courage to risk death for a noble cause," aptly noted Rasmussen and Tilton in their treatment of America's earliest heroine. As is well known, perhaps with some embellishment here and there, the Indian maiden's major historical appearance came in her heroic act of saving John Smith's life.

Captured by her father, Powhatan's, warriors, Smith had been paraded from village to village for several weeks, with the specter of death hanging over him at every stop, Smith himself later wrote. Perhaps the Indians merely wished to size him up, to decide if he meant them ill or not, Smith surmised. In any case, Powhatan's brother Opechancanough at last escorted Smith to Powhatan's village of Werowocomoco, where Smith was presented to the fabled Indian chief himself. History is silent on what Powhatan thought of the usually brash Englishman before him, but we do know that Powhatan made a lasting impression on the captive for his "grave and majesticall countenance."

Regal or not, the king of the Powhatans gave his signal and, wrote Smith in his customary third-person: "Two great stones were brought before Powhatan: then as many as could layd hands on him [Smith], dragged him to them and thereon laid his head, and being ready with their clubs, to beate out his braines."

Just then, continued John Smith, "Pocahontas the Kings dearest daughter, when no intreaty could prevaile, got his head in her armes, and laid her owne upon his to save him from death." That did it— Powhatan signaled his change of heart. Smith could live after all.

Perhaps to save face, Powhatan explained he was sparing Smith so he could "make him hatchets" and make Pocahontas "bells, beads, and copper." Such an explanation may sound simplistic, even condescending, to modern ears, but that's the way Smith explained the great chief's change of heart . . . or had it been merely a test of Smith's courage from the start? Experience as a soldier had taught Smith to be stoic in the face of danger, and this reaction certainly would have served him well with his Indian captors, whose "courages," he wrote, "proceede from others feare."

While delightful, the story always has piqued scholars and ethnologists seeking confirmation and plausibility. After all, John Smith himself, widely known as an unabashed self-promoter, was the basic source. New England historians in particular seemed to have their doubts, their cadre led by a highly skeptical Henry Adams, who gave the impression that he was somewhat loath to grant the South, especially the Virginia aristocracy, any extra edge in claims to the formation of early America.

Aside from a detail here or there, perhaps the plausibility of Smith's tale lies in the very fact that he willingly credited his salvation to the timely intercession of a mere slip of a girl rather than to any startling bravado or swashbuckling act of his own. Then, too, as Rasmussen and Tilton pointed out, "Smith's account of the rescue was apparently accepted by his contemporaries, such as Samuel Purchas, who published accounts about Virginia and who interviewed in London principal figures involved in the Virginia settlement (including Pocahontas and John Rolfe), as well as other individuals who had played a part in Virginia history."

Whatever the detail, Smith's return, unharmed, to his fellow Jamestown settlers heralded a period of peace between the white interlopers and their Indian neighbors, but it was a peace that would not last. The days, plural, would come when Powhatan himself would order Smith captured again, a plot foiled by a warning from none other than Pocahontas, and when the chief would decree the "utter extermination of the intruding race," as McKenney and Hall described the chief's order.

Once again, Pocahontas was at the center of the situation—more complex than her meeting with John Smith, the story this time begins with her being seized as a hostage for the release of two Englishmen held captive by the Indians. Detained at Jamestown under the supervision of the tough Governor Thomas Dale, she then was placed in the care of the Reverend Alexander Whitaker at Henrico on the James, a settlement founded by Dale in 1611. Here she began instruction in the English language and customs . . . and Christianity. Here, too, she soon met John Rolfe.

Thus, all the ingredients for a storybook romance were in place— the heroic Indian maiden now was courted by the worthy English suitor whose experiments with tobacco would provide the economic lifeblood of the colony—a suitor whose intentions were strictly honorable from the start, it also seems. Addressing Governor Dale, he wrote for permission to marry the Indian princess, "for the good of this plantation, for

the honour of our countrie, for the glory of God, for my owne salvation, and for the converting [of] . . . an unbeleeving creature." Moreover, he promised, "carnall affections" were *not* his objective.

Whatever his motives, the couple seemed happy and in love. With
Pocahontas first becoming baptized, John and *Rebecca* were married on
April 5, 1614, with the blessing of the governor. All the better, old
Chief Powhatan also seemed to welcome the union of his favorite
daughter and the Englishman. As a wedding present he granted them a
tract of land . . . then, too, as a present for the English in general, he
was willing to grant a period of peaceful relations.

Imagine, now, this same Indian woman's excitement over the next
unprecedented step in her young life—the voyage across the vast
Atlantic Ocean to England, her husband's distant homeland, for their
months-long visit. And naturally she would want to see the man who,
more than Rolfe, had made her such a historic figure—John Smith.
Whatever the lingering doubts about his account of their dramatic
meeting, by the way, all the evidence certainly points to a special relationship between Smith and the young Indian princess from Virginia.
Not only did she want to see him, he wanted to see her.

Hearing of her pending visit, Smith had written to Queen Anne,
wife of King James I, praising the young princess and retelling his story
of rescue at her hands. Pocahontas, he said, just moments before his execution, "hazarded the beating out of her own brains to save mine, and
not only that, but prevailed with her father, that I was safely conducted
to Jamestowne." He also noted that had she and her people not provided the settlers food, the precarious settlement might not have lasted.

They had not seen each other since Smith left the colony in 1609
for treatment of gunpowder burns, and now, nearly ten years later, they
would meet again . . . but with Smith uncharacteristically subdued. In
fact, he greeted Pocahontas with such decorum that she complained of
his apparent coolness toward her. He explained that she was a king's
daughter and that his king would expect him to treat her with the
respect due to her own high station. Her gracious reply, according to
McKenney and Hall: "You did promise Powhatan that what was yours
should be his, and he made a like promise to you. You being in his land
a stranger called him father, and by the same right, I will call you so."

And so, it was the Indian visitor to a strange land who was able to
put the native-born soldier-explorer at ease. From this moment forward, their meetings were warm, and she did call him father.

In time, though, John Rolfe felt he had been away from his tobacco fields and experiments with the moneymaking crop long enough. They had been in England for almost a year . . . it was time to go home, he decided. Over his wife's protests, he made arrangements for their journey back to Virginia—on a ship commanded by Capt. Samuel Argall, the same one who had seized Pocahontas as a hostage not so many months before.

However she may have felt about that unhappy interlude would be altogether a moot point. The voyage home for Pocahontas was not to be. Before the ship could go to sea, she suddenly fell ill—of smallpox, apparently—and, almost as quickly, died. She was buried at St. George's Church at Gravesend on March 21, 1617.

☆ ☆ ☆

Thus, too, Pocahontas missed an event of great historical importance to Virginia and America: the start, in 1619, of America's black heritage.

The first blacks to arrive in Virginia came in 1619 by way of an English-owned or controlled ship incorrectly described by the widowed John Rolfe as a Dutch man-of-war. He was more correct in informing Sir Edwin Sandys that it "sold us 20, and odd Negars." These new arrivals came not from Africa but from Spanish territories in the Caribbean, and probably were born in the Western Hemisphere. Indeed, most of the blacks brought to Virginia from 1635 to 1699 came from the Caribbean, some baptized in the Christian faith, some not.

Also important, the first blacks to reach Virginia were indentured servants who could work their way to freedom after a fixed period of time. For the historical moment, Virginia's blacks were not slaves in the traditional sense . . . not quite yet, anyway. As Virginius Dabney commented in his *Virginia: The New Dominion: A History from 1607 to the Present:* "It would be several decades before Virginia law formally recognized slavery. But the disastrous trend was under way."

With slightly more than four thousand black immigrants to Virginia recorded from 1635 to 1699, their chief importers were the plantation owners. The gender ratio among the black newcomers apparently was about two men for every woman. Whatever the gender, however, these first black Virginians could gain freedom only by working out their indentures or by being born of free parents. And sometimes not all was quite so cut and dried—there could be the occasional legal dispute. Take the case of the twenty-five-year-old mulatto **Elizabeth Key,** who, in 1656, convinced the authorities that she should be free. Using various documents and the favorable testimony of five witnesses, she told the convincing story that she had worked beyond her indenture period for plantation owner Thomas Key, and, further, she bore him a child. He, in fact, had been "fined for getting his Negro woman with Childe." Thus, she argued, both she and her child ought to be freed.

Not only was her demand granted, but Elizabeth Key married and lived out her life free. Ironically, such a happy ending wouldn't have been allowed just a few years later, since her own case raised doubts in the predominantly white colony about the status of mulattos born of black mothers and English fathers. Their doorway to freedom would be considerably narrowed, wrote Wamsley and Cooper in *Idols, Victims, Pioneers,* with enactment of a new law holding that such children "shall be held bond or free only according to the condition of the mother." Ten years later, "'Negro and mulatto' children were declared tithable by age sixteen, indicating that the two racial types had become equated."

☆ ☆ ☆

By the eighteenth century, systematic slavery had taken hold in eastern Virginia. Blacks, most of them seized in Africa, were being exported to Virginia in huge numbers. Added to the blacks already on hand, the effect on Virginia's overall black population was astounding. In 1690, about 15 percent of Virginians were black. By 1775, blacks were the majority in most Tidewater counties, and they made up from 40 to 50 percent of the population of the Northern Neck. By 1750, added historian Suzanne Lebsock in her book *Virginia Women, 1600–1945,* "almost half of Virginia slaves lived on plantations of twenty slaves or more, and networks of well-worn paths connected slaves of neighboring plantations to one another."

Such conditions afforded the Virginia slaves opportunity to form community life and to develop their distinctive Afro-American culture. And now came the formation of black families, especially in the latter part of the eighteenth century, when the number of slave women began to equal the male population. "While we know very little about the family lives that slaves were able to fashion," wrote Lebsock, "we have reason to believe that family ties shaped the ways in which slave men and women resisted the slave system: Men might run away; women more often resisted close to home."

As Lebsock's comment would indicate, we know very little about the day-to-day lives of the women, since most were illiterate and left no diaries, letters, or like record for posterity. The few we do know about are those who were house servants, who were chosen for their loyalty, trustworthiness, skill, and appearance. "They were treated with kindness and respect in the family circle," wrote Wamsley and Cooper, "and they returned it amply." These black women often were the lovable "mammies" of Southern lore. Who can forget Hattie McDaniel's Oscar-winning portrayal of such a mammy in *Gone with the Wind*?

The mammy seems to have evolved along with the great plantations. She was generally a personal servant to a young mistress, relieving the mother of child care as more and more children were born. Keeping close, if often indulgent, eye on their charges, the mammies became surrogate mothers who won the respect and hearts of the children in their care.

Those children, in turn, often did provide a substitute record for the missing memoirs of the slave women—diaries, letters, and memoirs of their own, albeit much more from the white view of their shared world than from the black perspective. Mary Kelly Watson, who spent her childhood in antebellum Charlottesville, would remember her mammy, **Bibby Mosby,** in glowing terms. Watson wrote that she was bright, active, and, more important, notable for her "high-toned character and inflexible principle."

The well-known, Virginia-born author Ellen Glasgow, writing in the twentieth century, remembered her beloved mammy, **Lizzie Jones,** as a woman "endowed with an unusual intelligence, a high temper, and a sprightly sense of humor." In sadder vein, Glasgow added, "If fate had yielded her even the slightest advantages of education and opportunity, she might have made a place for herself in the world." But mammies did make an important place for themselves—in the homes they served at a time when so little else was open to them. The mammy tradition, in fact, survived both slavery and the Civil War, continuing on in the South for many generations.

☆ ☆ ☆

One Virginia-born black woman who found a way to freedom, even to a life in high places, long before the Civil War would set her people free, was **Elizabeth Keckley** . . . no ordinary dressmaker. Born in 1818 on the Burwell plantation at Dinwiddie, she was taken to St. Louis by a married daughter of the family. While in Missouri, she learned to sew and became such a skilled dress designer and seamstress that, by some accounts, she may even have helped support her white family with her sewing. During this time, too, she had a son, George, by a white father.

Determined to gain freedom for her son and herself, she borrowed twelve hundred dollars from her dressmaking customers in 1855, bought freedom for them both, and later repaid the loan in full.

In 1860, she and her son moved to Washington, D.C., where she quickly established herself as a dressmaker to high society. Among her many customers was Varina Davis, wife of the senator from Mississippi, Jefferson Davis. In just a year's time, Mrs. Davis would become the first lady of the Confederate States of America, but Elizabeth Keckley would get along in her absence very nicely, thank you. When newly inaugurated President Abraham Lincoln and his wife moved into the White House, Keckley was quick to ingratiate herself to the new first lady of the Union—and she soon became much more than just a dressmaker to the emotionally unstable Mary Todd Lincoln. For here, in the personage of Keckley, Mary Todd found a calm, efficient, and unruffled companion whom she came to rely upon more and more. When the Lincolns lost their young son Willie to a fever, it was to Keckley whom Mary Todd Lincoln turned for solace.

Soon Mrs. Lincoln's companion could share the grief even more personally—George died in combat as a Union soldier.

As the first lady found ever-increasing comfort in her companion, she poured out her thoughts, even venting her opinions about the men who were in the Lincoln cabinet or others who were close to the president and the Union cause. Mary Todd could be jealous of anyone who seemed to keep the president away from her. Considered suspect by many Washington figures for her Southern birth and slaveholding Kentucky family, the first lady found few friends in Washington society. But the gossips around town credited Keckley with "liberalizing" Mrs. Lincoln's views on race, and it was generally known that the first lady supported an organization of black women founded by Keckley—the Contraband Relief Association, formed to help former slaves who had run away to Washington.

After the Civil War, after the Lincoln assassination as well, Keckley wrote what may have been the first bestseller by a black American— her book, *Behind the Scenes,* was a devastating exposé of life inside the Lincoln White House. Mary Todd Lincoln felt she had been betrayed and permanently broke all ties to her former friend and confidante. The black community, so recently freed by Lincoln, called Keckley a traitor to the Great Emancipator.

Her moment in the sun essentially over, Keckley lived on for forty more years in virtual obscurity, "clinging pathetically to some bits of Lincoln's hair," according to Wamsley and Cooper.

☆ ☆ ☆

With freedom at last gained, many black women who looked to the future began to work for the betterment of their race. One such woman was **Jane "Janie" Porter Barrett,** who was born on the eve of the war's end in 1865 to a mother who was a housekeeper in a well-established Georgia home. She grew up in Georgia during the Reconstruction era, but she would find her calling in Virginia. At age fifteen, the ambitious young Georgian entered Hampton Institute, from which she was graduated in 1884 with a burning desire to help her fellow blacks. After a period spent teaching back in her home state, she returned to Virginia to teach at her alma mater, Hampton Institute. Here she met a fellow faculty member, Harris Barrett, and they were soon married.

The energetic young woman saw needs in their community and founded the Locust Street Social Settlement, a new approach to helping those who could not help themselves. Partly financed by the Barretts and partly by Northern philanthropists, the settlement offered practical instruction courses in child care, cooking, sewing, and vegetable gardening.

By 1908, Jane Barrett was the first president of the Virginia State Federation of Colored Women's Clubs. Not one to rest on any laurels, she moved into areas of greater needs. Her era was a time when no adequate provisions were made for delinquent black girls. To correct this oversight, she set out to raise the funds allowing her federation to buy a farm north of Richmond and establish the Virginia Industrial School for Colored Girls on the farmland. She served as board secretary and soon realized that the school needed her full-time involvement.

By this time, she was widowed and had been offered the job of dean of women at Tuskegee Institute in Alabama. But her life's work still lay in Virginia, so she moved to the new school as resident superintendent. In a short time, in the 1920s, her institution had achieved national recognition for its highly successful techniques—"social scientists heaped honors on Mrs. Barrett," noted Wamsley and Cooper. She served on the executive boards of the National Association of Colored Women and the Richmond Urban League and on the Southern Commission on Interracial Cooperation—all this before the civil rights movement of the twentieth century even got rolling!

She retired in 1940, and two years after her death in 1948, the state of Virginia honored the memory of this outstanding woman by renaming her institution the Jane Porter Barrett School for Girls.

☆ ☆ ☆

For **Maggie Lena Walker,** "a pivotal leader in the Richmond black community," the path to achievement would begin in 1867 with her birth to a mother who had been a cook in the Richmond home of the socially connected but controversial Yankee spy Elizabeth Van Lew. Maggie helped to care for her younger brother and delivered the clothes her mother had taken in to wash as a means of supporting the family. Maggie still attended city schools and kept up her studies, and after graduating she became a teacher, married, and had three children.

All the while, but not yet evident, Maggie had a "knack for business," wrote Suzanne Lebsock in her *Virginia Women, 1600–1945*. At a time when leaders such as Booker T. Washington were urging blacks to improve themselves, leading blacks indeed were forming fraternal and cooperative insurance organizations to provide health care and burial money. One such organization was the Independent Order of St. Luke, to which Maggie Walker belonged, serving as secretary-treasurer of the Richmond-based venture with the grand-sounding title, "Right Worthy Grand Secretary-Treasurer." "Right worthy" was the operative term, however, since it was business-savvy Maggie Walker who would lead the organization from near bankruptcy to a doubling of its membership.

Her various interests also led her into the newspaper business, as founder of the *St. Luke Herald.* Next, seeing a growing need in the black community, Maggie branched into banking in 1903 by starting the St.

Luke Penny Savings Bank. She served as its president until 1929—apparently the first black woman bank president in the United States.

A woman of integrity with a strong sense of social consciousness, she always began the day's work in her offices with devotions. Understandably, people of all kinds, the white business community included, trusted her honesty and her business acumen, and always with good cause. After the horrendous Crash of 1929, her bank was able to absorb less-stable black banks in the Richmond area then become the Consolidated Bank and Trust Company. Maggie Walker remained as chairman of the board until 1934, when she died as one of the most beloved and respected figures in Richmond's history.

☆ ☆ ☆

Virginia saw many of its talented black women leave the Commonwealth to find national fame. Start with **Adah B. Samuels Thoms,** born in the tumultuous year of 1863 in Richmond, capital of the Confederacy. Obtaining a good basic education in the city's postbellum schools, she left Virginia for her training as a nurse. Soon gaining recognition for her nursing skills, she was appointed to supervisory positions, her life's calling to be the betterment of nursing. She helped organize the National Association of Colored Graduate Nurses, and, in 1912, she was one of three black delegates to the International Council of Nurses meeting in Cologne, Germany.

Lucy Diggs Slowe was born in Berryville in 1885 and grew up in Lexington. She left Virginia to study in Baltimore and at Howard University in Washington, D.C. After teaching in the public schools, she became dean of women at Howard in 1922. She was a founding member of the National Council of Negro Women and other national organizations. And still she found time to become a skilled tennis player, as well as a concert contralto. She died at age fifty-three in 1937.

The Tidewater area has produced many black women of great musical talent, starting with singer **Matilda Sissieretta Joyner,** once a great star. Born in 1869, she left Virginia in a family move, studied in Providence, Rhode Island, and Boston, then made her debut in New York in 1888. From 1896 to 1916, she led the Black Patti Troubadours, a popular entertainment company playing to largely white audiences. She died in 1933.

Dorothy Maynor was a black soprano who was born in Norfolk in 1910 and began singing in the choir of the Methodist church her father served as pastor. She studied at Hampton Institute and left Virginia for further vocal studies in New York before making her debut in Town Hall in 1939 to critical acclaim. She also sang at Carnegie Hall. She added to the understanding of black spiritual music by writing a history of black music. She and her husband made their main residence in New York City but also kept a country home on Virginia's York River.

Remarkably, Virginia's two best-known black singers, both truly great, were born in Newport News in the same year, 1918. Both left Virginia at an early age. **Ella Fitzgerald** then was raised in a Yonkers, New York, orphanage and began singing professionally in 1934. **Pearl Bailey** was raised in Philadelphia and began her professional career just a year later, in 1935.

☆ ☆ ☆

Meanwhile, greater in number and granted far greater opportunity all along were the white women of Virginia, among them the *ladies* who began life with the greatest opportunities of all . . . and *ladies* is precisely what the well-born female half of the white southern population called themselves until the mid-twentieth century, Virginia very much included. Consider the term overblown, snooty, or derisive, the middle-ground fact is that they formed a hardy, industrious, intelligent, innovative, compassionate, nurturing, and accomplished historical stream of *women* who were right there alongside the men in the entire evolution of modern Virginia, albeit not quite from day one. Unfortunately, the historical record often fails to mention this interesting and essential fact, since it so often was written by the men (or in some cases by women all too accustomed to seeing their own fair sex left out of such things). Thus, histories of early Virginia tend to leave the impression that half the white population made only a negligible contribution.

Even when the historical camera began to focus on society at large—to include the role of women specifically—the primary data wasn't always complete in regard to women and their activities. Still, with the widened interest in women's history these days, a wealth of information has surfaced as to the lives and works, the public activities, the leadership roles, the voluntary associations, and the cultural values of Virginia's white women.

Their historical stream of course goes back almost to 1607, when the first permanent European settlement in Virginia brought two distinct cultures together. Within two years, English women had joined the men in meeting the Native American peoples. And in the year 1619, with the advent of the first blacks in Virginia, a third culture would rub shoulders with the first two.

By this time, the English women making the long sea voyage to Virginia had taken note that the Native American women did most of their society's work. They were responsible for planting, growing, harvesting, preserving, and storing food crops. They gathered berries, plums, persimmons, acorns, nuts, roots, and firewood. They made fires for cooking, prepared meals, made the clay pots, and hardened them in the fire. They made clothes and accessories from deerskins, decorated them with beads, designed and wove baskets, and repaired clothing. To the English women, these chores seemed reasonable enough, but they were astounded when they learned that the Indian women also were in charge of homebuilding.

Astonishing, too, was the fact that Indian women decorated their bodies. "Some of them have their legs, hands, brests and face cunningly imbrodered, with diverse workes, as beasts, serpents artificially wrought into their flesh with black spots," wrote John Smith. As the real shock for the English newcomers, male or female, they soon would learn the Indian women also were quite capable of torturing their tribe's English captives to the death.

At more peaceable moments, naturally, the English women would have been grateful for the bounty that Indian women occasionally gave the struggling new Jamestown settlement in the way of corn and other food. Also tutored by the Indian women on how to plant, tend, and harvest corn, the English women were learning many new ways to cope in a rugged environment.

Since it was so rugged, however, the news reaching London was no great incentive for young women to rush across the Atlantic to join the new colony. The better news, on the other hand, was that John Rolfe had made his first sale of tobacco, thus proving that the "vile weed" was profitable, and that the Virginia Company's venture indeed would offer both its investors and the settlers profit. In 1618, in order to induce indentured servants to stay and to encourage new settlers, the

Virginia Company offered free land . . . to men in those categories—no mention of such grants to women.

Even so, the new land policies did attract an increasing number of married women settling in Virginia with their husbands. One such couple, Christopher Branch and **Mary Addie,** married in London in September 1618 and set sail for Virginia in March of the next year. Here, they produced three sons—in time their descendants would include the writer James Branch Cabell and Founding Father Thomas Jefferson. For that matter, **Mary Isham** and her husband, William Randolph, who married in the 1670s, established a lineage that included Jefferson, John Marshall, Henry "Lighthorse Harry" Lee, and Robert E. Lee, to say nothing of a string of historically influential Randolphs. No wonder they have been called the Adam and Eve of Virginia.

As thriving communities sprang up in Virginia (and elsewhere in the British colonies up and down the East Coast) there were as yet no institutions to care for the needy, such as orphans, the sick, or the elderly. Since local authorities considered their care a community responsibility, women and their families took in the needy and were compensated by the taxpayers. Meanwhile, court records have proved a good (if often negative) source on how the newly formed communities maintained order at a time when there were few jails and no police. Instead, society relied upon the public stock, whipping post, and ducking stool. Through pain and humiliation, transgressors were expected to beg forgiveness. Records show that the offenses most often charged against women involved allegations of fornication and adultery. Premarital sex was less likely to result in charges, since possibly a third of Virginia brides were already pregnant at the time of their weddings, according to some historical estimates.

In other veins, the seventeenth-century women of Virginia did enter into political battle, even real physical battle on occasion. In 1676, one hundred years before the American Revolution, Nathaniel Bacon and his followers rebelled against Royal Governor William Berkeley, burning down Jamestown and pillaging the governor's own Green Spring plantation in the process (see pages 33–39). Alongside the fighting Bacon and his men were several fiery women. One, **Sarah Drummond,** whose husband, William, would be executed for his role in the rebellion, was said to be "a notorious and wicked rebel" who encouraged Bacon's followers to persist in the cause. **Lydia Chisman,** another whose husband would be executed for his part in the rebellion, threw herself at the feet of Governor Berkeley and offered herself in her husband's stead, since she had incited him to rebel in the first place.

Then, too, there was the rebellion's articulate witness **Anne Cotton,** wife of John Cotton and mother of two. They had settled at Queen's Creek, near today's Williamsburg. John, the son of the Reverend William Cotton, was a planter and a merchant who, along with many of his neighbors, viewed Bacon as a genuine reformer. More to the point here, his wife, Anne, wrote a narrative of the upheaval titled *An Account of Our Late Troubles in Virginia.* According to modern-day historian Lebsock, Anne Cotton's work was "an eloquent summary—and it earned her the distinction of having been Virginia's first historian."

With the sudden death of Bacon in the fall of 1676, the aftermath of the rebellion for Governor Berkeley was a return to England, where he died before he could face King Charles II and defend his actions. Meanwhile, his young widow, **Lady Frances Berkeley,** while maintaining her connections at court, remained in Virginia restoring her severely damaged Green Spring.

In 1680 she married Phillip Ludwell, a leader in a pro-Berkeley group called the "Green Spring faction," but she refused to adopt her new husband's name. Probably the first woman in Virginia to take such a stance, Lady Frances had no children by any of her three husbands—she apparently devoted her time to political and social activity.

Childless she may have been, but with her—in an indirect way—began another significant and historical line of Virginians. Her stepdaughter, **Lucy Ludwell,** married seventeen-year-old Daniel Parke Jr., and bore him two daughters. By age twenty-one, the handsome Parke was off to England, where he acquired a mistress whom he called "Cousin Brown." He then returned to Virginia together with the woman, to the great embarrassment of poor Lucy. More happily, it first appeared, her two spirited daughters grew up to marry very well—daughter **Lucy** to William Byrd II, founder of Richmond, and **Frances** to John Custis of the Eastern Shore.

The two daughters had not inherited their mother's meek disposition, a factor that now stood them well in their notoriously difficult marriages. Divorce in those days was not an option since the Virginia Colony lacked an ecclesiastical court, and the civil courts generally would approve separation for a woman only if her life was in danger. (In 1700, an **Elizabeth Wildy** did prove her husband had beaten her and thrown her into a fire—she was granted separation.)

Feisty Frances Custis and her husband, "Colonel John," came to a brilliant solution to settle their differences. They agreed to a husband-wife contract. "Colonel John promised to give Frances adequate supplies, such as wheat, meat, and brandy, and in general keep out of her household affairs; she in turn promised to live within her budget and not meddle in his business," noted Wamsley and Cooper. Unfortunately, Frances died before they could execute this innovative agreement.

Custis became ever more irascible in his old age, and with daughter Fanny married, he seemed intent on running the life of his son, Daniel. His goal for Daniel: finding a suitable wife. Enter now, **Martha Dandridge.**

At age eighteen, Martha was used to the easy life of a childhood spent on her family's extensive plantation in New Kent County. Her spunky personality attracted the son, and she soon won over the crotchety old patriarch as well. Daniel and Martha were married in 1749, and in the same year, old John Custis died.

After eight years of marriage, the now middle-aged Daniel Custis also died, leaving a still young Martha Custis, mother of two children (Jackie and Martha, called Patsy), the richest widow in Virginia. And who should come a-calling at a mutual friend's home not long after but . . . George Washington.

☆ ☆ ☆

No one who knew the widow Martha Dandridge Custis really expected her to sit around bemoaning the fact that she had been left to raise children and manage a plantation by herself. Not with *her* ingrained, can-do philosophy. As she herself would tell a timid and similarly widowed niece many years later, "If you doe not, no one else will."

It should be no surprise, then, that she was out and about the day she found herself at the same place and same time as the young, home-grown militia leader George Washington from Fredericksburg. We don't really know today who saw a bright future with the other first, but legend has it that Washington, supposedly in a hurry to reach Williamsburg, now stayed with their mutual friend an extra day instead of traveling on.

As *is* well known, Martha's charming and sensible personality did indeed capture the imagination of the ambitious young leader, while his winning ways captured her heart. Soon they were betrothed, and on the twelfth night after Christmas, on January 6, 1759, George and Martha were wed at White House, her plantation on the Pamunkey River.

As the young bride knew, she would be moving to a new home on another river, Mount Vernon on the Potomac. But Martha could not in her wildest dreams have guessed that just upriver one day would appear a vast, almost magical city and national capital named for her new husband. And she may never have quite realized how right she was for her very special role in American history, how much she personified the dignified, gracious, and efficient helpmate to a distinguished husband.

The fact is, she had very little formal education, but she was well trained in domestic and social skills. Thus, when George Washington was appointed commander in chief of the Continental army, Martha knew exactly what she had to do. Both here and in her later role as wife of the first president, her moral and courageous example set the tone for a long line of successors in similar leadership roles.

Certainly the soldiers suffered from the harsh winters spent at Valley Forge in Pennsylvania and Morristown in New Jersey, but each time, there was Martha, too. There she was, knitting socks for her "General," as she called him—and for his soldiers as well. Or mending tattered uniforms. Or playing hostess when the visiting dignitaries came a-calling. Her practical contributions, as needed and helpful as they were, however, could not rival the morale-boosting psychological benefits she provided the troops as she walked among them, encouraging the disheartened and urging on the more cheerful.

During the summers, she was back at Mount Vernon supervising and coordinating the work of a major plantation in the six years of her husband's total absence from Virginia.

Martha and George much preferred life at Mount Vernon, surrounded by family and friends, to the whirlwind of the public life that came in the wake of the successful Revolutionary War. Even so, as George Washington took the oath of office in New York City on April 30, 1789, as the nation's first president, she again brought her good graces into play.

If truth be known, she was not particularly happy in this new role as the president's lady—she confessed to her niece in a letter that she felt "more like a prisoner than anything else." Despite such feelings, Martha's fifty-eight years in Virginia society had prepared her well for her historic role as the nation's initial first lady.

Both she and her president-husband realized the importance of social events to the new federal government, to the brand-new presidency itself. But the tone had to be just right. It shouldn't cater exclusively to the lingering aristocratic and monarchal strain in the American psyche, nor go overboard in the direction of the masses. As the true pioneer in the area of presidential soirees, Martha managed to accommodate both elements—a combination of courtly, gracious dignity and the high ideals of republican simplicity, a combination that came to be called the "Republican Court" . . . that also was among her most outstanding achievements.

☆ ☆ ☆

If Martha Washington and, subsequently, Abigail Adams set the stage for future first ladies in a traditional, perhaps even somewhat staid manner, **Dolley Madison,** following the widowed Thomas Jefferson in the President's House, certainly set the style.

Truly an innovator, as Catherine Allgor suggests in her book, *Parlor Politics,* Dolley "built successfully on the work of her predecessors." She and husband James Madison called their entertainments "drawing rooms," instead of the usual "levees" or "soirees," but the purpose was the same as before—accessibility to the president.

Dolley saw to it that Americans of all classes were represented at her "Wednesday Night" or "Mrs. Madison's crush."

And did they say "*Mrs.* Madison's"? Yes, in a patriarchal age, Dolley's soirees were thus dubbed by an adoring public.

Not everyone held a positive view of her "drawing rooms," however. Some guests hated the crush or "squeeze," the noise, the refreshments, and the odd assortment of people one might meet. Even the critics had to admit, however, that Dolley did create a social and political milieu in which many things were possible. Using three public rooms at the White House, she was able to combine "the most formal of settings with extensive freedom of movement," Allgor also wrote.

At the time the Madisons came to the White House, just before the War of 1812 broke out, Washington City was in a period of urban growth and political realignment—Dolley used her drawing-room soirees as a means of bringing together the social elite and the federal government elite, to the benefit of her own family and the family of an increasing governmental structure. So skilled was she at masking her own political feelings that even the opposition party members were complimentary of the charismatic Dolley and gladly attended her gatherings. Allgor cited the comment of Pennsylvania Representative Jonathan Roberts that "by her [Dolley's] deportment in her own house, you cannot discover who is her husband's friend or foe."

Dorothea Payne Todd Madison was born in the Piedmont of North Carolina to John and Mary Coles Payne, settlers from Virginia. Always called Dolley, she moved with her family, in 1783, to Philadelphia. Despite a strict Quaker upbringing, Dolley had a sparkling personality and was known for her warm heart. She married John Todd Jr., a lawyer, in 1790, but three years later she was left a widow with a young son.

By this time Philadelphia was the capital city of the new republic, and soon the charming Dolley was attracting the interest of a distinguished Virginian often in town as a U.S. House member. All of Dolley's friends were happy that she was being courted again, and it was whispered about that she was soon to wed Mr. James Madison.

When the rumors reached Mrs. Washington, she invited Dolley to the presidential mansion, perhaps to satisfy herself that the young widow was in earnest. Greeting Dolley, Martha took both of her hands, looked straight into Dolley's eyes, and asked if she really was engaged to the Washingtons' good friend Madison. The blushing visitor, so the story goes, lowered her eyes and replied falteringly, "I— think—not." In spite of this answer, as Peter Hay tells the anecdote in his book *All the President's Ladies,* "Mrs. Washington seemed satisfied. The young widow's manner told her more than the words."

The wise Martha then affectionately said, "Mr. Madison will make you a good husband. The president and I are much pleased with your choice."

Thus armed with the blessing of the beloved Virginian couple— more like a "royal sanction" from the first family, if you will—Dolley allowed her engagement to be announced. She and James Madison were married late in 1794.

The Madisons moved into his family home, Montpelier, outside Orange in the Virginia Piedmont, a mansion built by Madison's father, who had died earlier. Dolley's new mother-in-law still lived in the grand house but gladly turned over its management to her son and his new wife. Here Dolley honed her social skills among the Virginia gentry . . . and here, after their storied life in nearby Washington as

BEST LITTLE STORIES FROM VIRGINIA

President and Mrs. James Madison, she and her husband would find pleasant retirement.

Part of that storied life in Washington of course was the drama of war and their forced flight from the capital—and the White House—when the British swept in and burned down the presidential home. Earlier, Dolley had orchestrated the nation's first inaugural ball as her diminutive and frail-looking husband took office as president in 1809. Nor were first lady duties totally new to Dolley . . . she had played presidential hostess many a time for the widowed Jefferson while he occupied the executive mansion just ahead of the Madisons.

After Dolley's husband died in 1836, she returned to Washington from Virginia, took up residence on Lafayette Square within view of the newly rebuilt White House, and continued as a revered and stylish hostess despite her increasingly difficult financial circumstances. When she died in 1849, President Zachary Taylor said she would never be forgotten "because she was truly our First Lady for a half century."

☆ ☆ ☆

Two women who were not Virginians by birth should be in the hearts of every Virginian anyway—for saving the most visited historical shrine in America, Virginia's own Mount Vernon.

Their story begins with a South Carolina matron, **Louise Cunningham,** who *was* born and raised in Virginia. Visiting her hometown of Alexandria in the winter of 1853, she took an evening riverboat ride, and as her vessel steamed past an old mansion on the Potomac River shoreline, the captain rang the ship's bell. Tradition, he explained, in honor of George and Martha Washington's beloved Mount Vernon.

What Mrs. Cunningham saw in the bright winter moonlight, though, was a shabby, run-down old house obviously fallen on hard times. That was Mount Vernon? She could hardly believe it.

Making inquiries, she discovered the historic plantation and home were owned by John Augustine Washington Jr., great-great-nephew of George Washington, and he was trying to sell it to the federal or the Virginia state government for $200,000.

Unbelieving, even outraged, Mrs. Cunningham wrote to her daughter back in South Carolina to ask, a bit rhetorically to be sure, why the women of the country didn't step forward to keep this national treasure in good repair if the men were not willing or able. "It does seem such a blot on our country," Mrs. Cunningham declared.

As events soon turned out, the happy result of Louise Cunningham's concern would be a campaign mounted by her own spinster daughter, **Ann Pamela Cunningham,** a semi-invalid who not only would take up her mother's challenge but would devote the rest of her life to the preservation of Mount Vernon.

Naturally, she would need allies. She wrote a letter to the *Charleston (S.C.) Mercury* addressed to "Ladies of the South" and challenging them to join in the crusade to rescue Mount Vernon. By 1854, her efforts had begun to make tangible gains, and she traveled to Richmond with intentions of forming a coordinating committee. There, she met the woman destined to become her chief ally, **Anna Cora Mowatt Ritchie,** a New York actress and author now married to the editor and publisher of the *Richmond Enquirer,* William Foushee Ritchie.

A stranger team one cannot conjure up, wrote Wamsley and Cooper in their book, than the "pain-wracked, drab little spinster" and "the glamorous woman of the world who was now one of the social lionesses (albeit a moderately controversial one) of Richmond." Although Mrs. Ritchie was a bit suspect as an actress, her credentials otherwise were impeccable, thanks to her husband, whose father had been a friend and supporter of Thomas Jefferson, whose sister, Mrs. George Harrison, was mistress of historic Brandon Plantation on the south side of the James. In addition, Mrs. Ritchie's charming ways had won over most in the capital city's high society.

Disparate as they appeared, these two women, an Ann and an Anna, would become fast friends in a great cause. Overnight, the Ritchie home on Ninth Street became a meeting place for their lobbying effort to obtain the special act from the General Assembly that would incorporate the Mount Vernon Association. The former actress gave parties toward this end, inviting influential figures such as former Governor John Wise, editor J. R. Thompson of the *Southern Literary Messenger,* and sculptor Edward Valentine. "She pressed for the cause's advantage on every front," wrote Wamsley and Cooper. She kept busy "wining, dining, and lobbying."

And glory be! The bill passed both the House of Delegates and the state senate in March 1856. And with that action, history had been served in more ways than one. For this was the first time that women in this country had lawfully organized to accomplish a goal of this kind. Further, Ann Cunningham's crusade "came to be regarded as the birth of the historic preservation movement in America," notes the National Building Museum in Washington, D.C. Her Ladies Association, the first national women's organization in the country, "became a model" for others to follow in restoration and preservation efforts all over the country.

"Victory victory!" flashed Mrs. Ritchie to Miss Cunningham, who was in Philadelphia under a doctor's care. As Wamsley and Cooper also noted, Mrs. Ritchie added, "Heaven smiles upon our efforts."

Still, it would take more time, and a revised charter, before the Mount Vernon Ladies Association would be in business. Finally, on April 6, 1858, John Washington accepted a down payment of $18,000 for Mount Vernon, with the remaining $182,000 to be spread over the next four years. To his credit, he many times had turned down offers from private, developer interests over the years in hopes of placing his family's historic home in caring hands.

With the advent of the Civil War in 1861, however, all progress on preserving the old home came to a screeching halt. It was with the greatest of difficulty that the Mount Vernon Ladies Association managed to keep the old place together. Fortunately, it did become a no man's land, a buffer between North and South, off-limits to the fighting forces . . . and a home to Ann Cunningham.

Sadly, though, John Augustine Washington was killed in action while serving under Robert E. Lee in battle in the Virginia mountains. Mrs. Ritchie died in London in 1870.

The frail Miss Cunningham stayed on as regent of Mount Vernon until she retired to her home in South Carolina in 1874. She died a year later, but her Mount Vernon Ladies Association lived on . . . and on. And today, the fully restored Mount Vernon is the most visited historic site in the nation.

Adds the National Building Museum: "Over the past quarter century, the Mount Vernon Ladies Association has made great strides in restoring Washington's home to its actual appearance in 1799." Special new paint-analysis techniques led to use of interior colors "similar to the original hues chosen by Washington." Further, "New draperies and carpets have been reproduced based on descriptions and eighteenth-century fragments. Gradually, original pieces of furniture have been obtained and returned to their original rooms as indicated by historical documents." In sum: "Through the use of new restoration techniques and careful historical research, Mount Vernon has been authentically restored to appear much as it did more than two hundred years ago."

☆ ☆ ☆

Not only Mount Vernon, but the Commonwealth had fallen into difficult times by the mid-nineteenth century. No longer the most populous state, Virginia had slipped to number five by 1860; the state had lost nearly four hundred thousand citizens to the West and less-populated areas of the South. Once a star among the former colonies, Virginia had become far less influential in the councils of the South and the nation.

Blame, in large part, tobacco, which had exhausted much of Virginia's farmland, and slavery, which wasn't all that economically efficient as a labor system and had placed Virginia on the defensive in the face of mounting abolitionist criticism.

Among other reasons for Virginia's decline, the Revolutionary War and the post-Revolutionary period had subjected many of Virginia's grand plantations to ruinous damage and neglect. Further, suggested Virginius Dabney in his *Virginia: The New Dominion,* the "disestablishment of the Anglican Church added to the general disorganization." He also placed some of the blame on Virginia's usually sacrosanct Founding Fathers—Jefferson, Madison, and Monroe, and others like them—for a lavish and "wasteful mode of living" that contributed to their own straitened financial circumstances.

The real undermining factor as the century wore on, though, was the practice of slavery, which subjected Virginians to constant criticism from the North. New England, observed Dabney, was being swept by new idealism while "Virginia's thinking was largely static." The undermining result: "Defense of the status quo against the assaults of outsiders became the chief concern of nearly all the [Virginia] leaders."

Women, too, found themselves defending the "peculiar institution" of slavery in the South. Then, in 1852, came Harriet Beecher Stowe's stinging novel *Uncle Tom's Cabin,* which "irrevocably transformed the literary debate over sectionalism," noted Elizabeth R. Varon in her book *We Mean to Be Counted.* Stowe did "what no other female novelist had done—she declared slavery a sin."

Uncle Tom provoked an uproar in the South, but some Southern women, two Virginia women among them, immediately rallied in defense of their way of life with books purporting to show the truthful picture. "The first—and generally considered the best—fictional proslavery response to *Uncle Tom's Cabin*," wrote Varon, was **Mary Eastman**'s *Aunt Phillis's Cabin: Or Southern Life As It Is.* The story line depicts Aunt Phillis, a mulatto house servant, as the archetypal contented slave, a pious woman who is loyal and true to her white "family," and whose household is the very picture of good order. At the same time, the novel explored the tension between the "positive good" and the "necessary evil" of slavery. The only remedy for the evil of the institution, suggested Eastman, would be colonization of Liberia by freed American slaves.

Stowe also advocated colonization in her *Uncle Tom's Cabin,* but Eastman and Stowe offered different interpretations of the concept—for Eastman it was not a means to end slavery, but only an alternative to it. Meanwhile, **Mary Berkeley Minor Blackford** of Fredericksburg, well known for her antislavery views, decried the fact that both the law and her society stood in the way of teaching blacks to read and write. Like Harriett Beecher Stowe, Blackford viewed slavery as inherently sinful and favored colonization as a means to dismantle the slavery system.

The other Virginia woman writer who entered the fray as a critic of Stowe's abolitionist views was **Martha Haines Butt,** whose book *Antifanaticism: A Tale of the South* repeated Eastman's message but less skillfully. A Norfolk native, Butt felt it was her duty to stand up for her native land. Her thesis was a comparative study of the Southern slave system versus Northern capitalism, noted Varon, with the novel's fictional characters "endlessly" asserting that slaves were better treated than the wage earners of the North.

Yet another defender of slavery, a Northerner at that, was **Julia Gardiner Tyler,** known as the "Rose of Long Island." At age twenty-four, after a grand tour of Europe, she came south for the social season of 1843–44 in Washington. There she met the recently widowed President John Tyler, thirty years her senior. After a whirlwind courtship, they were married in 1844, with Tyler's five living children shocked that he would marry so soon after their mother, Letitia's, death.

During the second Mrs. Tyler's short "reign" as first lady, her detractors criticized her for putting on airs and greeting guests while seated on a platform in queenly fashion. But admirers sometimes addressed her as "Lady Presidentress."

The Tylers retired to his Sherwood Forest plantation in Charles City County, Virginia, and Julia readily adapted to her new home and life as a plantation mistress. In 1853, she wrote an essay in defense of slavery for the *Southern Literary Messenger*. It was addressed, "To the Duchess of Sutherland and Ladies of England," since the duchess and her circle had accepted Stowe's *Uncle Tom* book as an accurate picture of slavery. They had held a convention that condemned slavery and circulated an address urging the women of America to support abolition. Tyler countered with the argument that Southerners were trying to do right by their slaves. She asserted that the plantation was a civilizing influence upon its black slaves. She further contended that England was to blame for slavery in the first place, since the English had introduced slavery in the Southern colonies.

With a touch of asperity, Julia Tyler reminded the duchess that the British had their own poor whites to care for, so, "Leave it to the women of the South to alleviate the sufferings of their own dependents."

☆ ☆ ☆

While none of these slavery defenders called for secession over the troublesome issue, the Southern states eventually did secede—North and South went to war in April 1861. Virginians, man or woman, suddenly were living in momentous times, were surrounded on all sides by dramatic events. For the first time, many women began keeping diaries, making entries of events of the day, often describing their anxiety but also reflecting the heightened purpose of their daily lives. **Mary Boykin Chesnut,** a South Carolinian who spent much of the war in Richmond, capital of the new Confederacy, wrote her observations with a clear eye and penned probably the most comprehensive, nonmilitary document of the war. In one entry, she wrote: "I say we are no better than our judges in the North, and no worse. We are human beings of the nineteenth century and slavery has to go, of course."

Typical of the ambivalence of many Southerners during this period, she and her husband, Gen. James Chesnut, owned slaves themselves.

The Civil War made Virginia women more cognizant of their constraints as women. Some bewailed the fact they could not be fighting alongside their menfolk. **Lucy Gilmer Breckinridge,** a young diarist from Botetourt County, reacted to the simultaneous Southern defeats at Gettysburg and Vicksburg by writing: "I wish the women could fight, and I do think they might be allowed to do so in the mountains and in the fortified cities. . . . I would gladly shoulder my pistol and shoot some Yankees if it were allowable." Actually, so strong and well known were the partisan emotions of Southern women that some Union soldiers honestly believed the women were pressuring their men to fight on. Commented one male onlooker years later: "All through the war the cowards were between two fires, that of the Federals in front and that of the women in the rear."

If the women couldn't exactly shoulder a gun themselves, meanwhile, they nonetheless stretched their traditional roles to the limit and took on many a job left behind as the men marched off to war. Thus, the women became plantation and finance managers, hospital workers, field hands . . . even message-bearers, smugglers, and spies. After all, those flaring hoop skirts down to the ankles could hide a passel of messages, medicines, or smallish weapons.

Among the female spies of Virginia, probably the best known was the tall, stately looking alleged blond from Martinsburg (now a part of West Virginia), **Belle Boyd,** and here was a woman—a very young woman of just seventeen when she began her career—who had real style! "She was a supreme example of the mid-Victorian woman who, while paying lip service to all the windy cant of the day, lived her own life with independent verve," wrote Wamsley and Cooper in their book *Idols, Victims, Pioneers.*

Accused of shooting a Union soldier in defense of her mother, she made good use of her natural assets to flirt with the troops occupying her hometown, gather snippets of information, and pass them along to Confederate contacts. Arrested early in the game and sent to live with an aunt in Front Royal, she now became a courier for the Confederate intelligence service—and allegedly a top-notch professional as a spy. Arrested two or three more times, she confounded her enemies in true storybook fashion by marrying a Union officer infatuated with her.

Becoming a household name before the war was over, she capitalized on her fame in the postwar years, packing theaters in North and South with audiences come to see her performances. Belle Boyd the Rebel Spy married several times and raised five children before she died in 1900—supposedly with a pistol under her pillow.

Maryland-born **Rose O'Neal Greenhow**'s Virginia "connection" was her husband, Robert, a native of Richmond, although she was good friends in the antebellum years with Dolley Madison. She once counted Lexington native **Jessie Benton Frémont,** wife of the western explorer John C. Frémont, as a friend also, but they had a falling-out when Jessie accused Rose of betraying secrets to the British in a territorial dispute in Oregon . . . and this before the Civil War.

Meanwhile, Rose's husband had died after they moved to Washington, and Rose became quite the gay widow in town. She had a close relationship with President James Buchanan . . . who in 1856 had defeated Frémont, the first Republican nominee ever, to become president. The gossips also were all atwitter over the rumor that Senator Henry Wilson of Massachusetts was wooing her.

Once the Civil War erupted, Rose Greenhow's Washington connections served her so well as a Confederate spy "embedded" in the Union capital, Union Gen. George B. McClellan reportedly complained, "She knows my plans better than Lincoln or the cabinet."

Finally caught and jailed for a time, she was banished to Richmond . . . where she was able to catch up with old Washington friends Jefferson Davis and his wife, Varina, the first couple of the Confederacy. In 1863, she was sent to England and France carrying messages from President Davis. While abroad, she published a pro-Confederate book that sold well. Returning home to the South, and weighed down by gold coins, however, she drowned trying to come ashore from a blockade-running ship off the Carolina coast.

Perhaps the most effective female spy of the Civil War was a wealthy Virginia woman from a top family who had a "mole" emplaced in the president's own house and a systematic message-relay system carrying her information straight to the top generals of the other side. Suspected of being a spy and kept under surveillance, she threw off the watchers by walking around town talking to herself—indeed, people called her "Crazy Bet." She was ostracized for life when the truth of her activities came out after the war . . . especially when President Ulysses S. Grant appointed **Elizabeth Van Lew** postmistress of Richmond as reward for her wartime services as a faithful spy for the Union. Her helper working as a servant in the Confederate White House was Van Lew's own one-time slave **Mary Elizabeth Bowser,** actually freed since 1850.

Richmond and the Confederacy's top brass obviously were much fonder of **Sally Tompkins,** who opened a small private hospital in Richmond that eventually took care of 1,333 Confederate soldiers while losing only 73 of them. Appointed a captain in the cavalry to keep her hospital going as a military operation, she thus became "the

first American woman to be commissioned as a regular military officer," noted historian Lebsock in her *Virginia Women.*

More generally during this absolutely ruinous war, Virginia
women facing shortages of all kinds had to become unusually resource-
ful. They pulled out old spinning wheels and looms, rediscovered
Grandmother's medicinal recipes, and invented substitutes for coffee,
tea, wheat, and like staples. They also worked to keep their churches
and Sunday schools going. Dedicated churchgoer **Hanora Flynn
Kelly** late in the war managed to slip through the lines at Union-held
Harrisonburg, travel to Richmond, and exchange a wad of soon-to-be-
worthless Confederate paper money for real gold—as a result, wrote
Lebsock, "Harrisonburg Catholics acquired their first church."

☆　☆　☆

Opinions vary as to how much or how little the Civil War contributed
to female liberation in Virginia and the South generally, but one thing
is for sure: Suddenly, quite a few women in the postwar years were
becoming published writers . . . and on subjects beyond a defense of
the South against abolitionist attack.

Now, true, the humiliation of the South did stop the work of many
a wartime diarist. Typical of the shock and depression many of them
felt, **Emma Mordecai** "told" her diary, "I feel as if there is nothing
more to live for in this world." Still, there were many other women
who couldn't wait to take up the pen. Those writing novels, interestingly enough, often depicted romance blossoming between Southern
women and Northern men. **"Winnie" Davis,** born into the Confederate White House in the last months of the Civil War to Jefferson Davis
and his wife, Varina, nearly lived out that very plot, becoming engaged,
but then unengaged, to an upstate New York man. After her real-life
story ended sadly, the one-time "Daughter of the Confederacy" wound
up a young spinster writing syrupy romance novels herself.

In line with the sectional theme of romantic encounters, Virginia
novelists such as **Julia Magruder** and **Mary Greenway McClelland**
had begun to examine the gender conventions of the South by the
1880s; they were comparing Southern men unfavorably with their
Northern counterparts. Meanwhile, the state's most celebrated writer
of the period was **Mary Virginia Terhune,** who published novels,

biographies, domestic manuals, travel books, and magazine and news-paper articles under the pen name **Marion Harland.**

All, of course, now lived in a land devastated by the recent war. Winchester had changed hands so often—at least seventy times—the final count was anybody's guess. By war's end, railroads and bridges were destroyed, a large part of Richmond, once the beauteous capital of the Confederacy, was in ashes. Rich families now were poor, slaves were free, and some blacks—men only—were voting and even holding public office. For Virginia's white women, it was a grim new world turned upside down from the old. And if it was a setback for the whites, it also presented a real uphill battle for black women.

But old attitudes toward women's participation in political matters were changing. The burgeoning number of women's organizations and associations, particularly those devoted to missionary work, temper-ance, and historical preservation, suggested that Virginia women were turning their wartime energies into peacetime activities that "strength-ened their claim to a role in politics," noted historian Lebsock.

With the tired old 1800s fast waning, women wanted to know just what roles they would be allowed to play. As one organization after another defined its goals and went to work, the answers began to unfold. It was known as the Progressive Era—the period from the late 1880s to the First World War. By 1915, opined Lebsock, women "had achieved nothing less than an organizational revolution in Virginia."

One of the first causes Virginia women espoused was preserva-tion—not only of Mount Vernon, but of Virginia's many other histori-cal treasures in various states of disrepair. In 1889, a group of Williamsburg women got busy and formed the now-powerful Associa-tion for the Preservation of Virginia Antiquities. And they meant busi-ness—they worked, they raked, they weeded, and they even hauled brick to spruce up their town, now the home of the fabulous Rockefeller-funded restoration known worldwide as Colonial Williams-burg. Soon to come along, too, were the Daughters of the American Revolution (DAR), the Virginia Society of Colonial Dames, and the United Daughters of the Confederacy (UDC), all founded in the 1890s.

Then, too, for many women there was the burning issue of suf-frage—the right to vote.

One such was **Orra Langhorne,** a Hollins Institute graduate who in 1880 began to write for publications such as the *Southern Work-man* and petitioned the General Assembly to allow women a vote in presidential elections (with no result). By 1893, she had organized and become president of a small suffrage-minded group of women, but nothing was to come of her efforts for another sixteen years, noted Wamsley and Cooper in their history of Virginia women. "When she died at 63 in 1904, suffrage was many years away," they added; "new, strict 'Jim Crow' laws were setting back the racial progress she had reported in the '80s and '90s." With her death, the baton would pass to others, with the race not to be won until 1920.

Toward the end of the nineteenth century, Virginia women were in the vanguard of another national trend—women's clubs devoted to cultural pursuits such as literature. The Progressive Literary Association, organized by Jewish women in Richmond, was the first of dozens of similar book clubs springing up in communities across the state.

In the decade before and during the Civil War, it had become acceptable for women to become publicly known for their literary works. Authors such as **Margaret Junkin Preston** of Virginia and Augusta Evans of Alabama were well known. The postwar period and the Progressive Era would see that trend greatly accelerated, with one Virginia woman in particular reaping national acclaim and honor.

At first a "closet" writer unsuspected even by her own family, she was born and raised in Richmond. "Delicate" as a child, she had little schooling but spent hours with the books in her well-to-do father's extensive library. As she reached maturity, her love of books would become a love of writing, but at first in secret. Her family was so unaware of her literary aspirations, they were greatly surprised when she announced that the anonymous author of the 1897 novel *The Descendant* was herself. Even so, they hardly could have guessed their young Ellen—**Ellen Glasgow**—one day (in 1941) would win a Pulitzer Prize for her writing, in that case for her novel *In This Our Life*. In the meantime, Ellen Glasgow, never married, had become widely known for her novels of manners—of her own cultivated, upper-class Southern (that is, Virginia) society. She fit that category so well, in the best possible sense, that her fellow Richmond writer James Branch Cabell once called her "a grande dame of a rare and almost extinct type."

The story of women's suffrage in Virginia picks up again with Ellen Glasgow and a formative tea held at her home in Richmond for the newly constituted Virginia Equal Suffrage League, formally founded in 1909, with **Lila Valentine** named its president, her cause so controversial at the time that "old friends would turn away from her on the streets without speaking," reported Wamsley and Cooper. But she (with support from others, such as the writer **Mary Johnston**) persisted to the very day in 1920 that the General Assembly refused to become the thirty-sixth and final state needed to ratify the Nineteenth Amendment to the U.S. Constitution at last giving women the right to vote. Tennessee then took credit for the final ratification vote instead of Virginia.

☆ ☆ ☆

While these dramatic events were unfolding in the Old Dominion, another Virginia woman had completed a historical circle of sorts by crossing the Atlantic to live in England as the wife of an immensely wealthy Englishman, and then take his place in the British Parliament as the first woman to serve in that historic legislative body.

Born at Danville in 1879 as one of the five Langhorne sisters of Virginia, **Nancy Astor** became *Lady* Astor after her husband, Waldorf, a descendant of the original John Jacob Astor, became the Viscount Astor of Hever Castle in 1919 and left his seat in the House of Commons open. She then quickly won election to succeed him and remained an outspoken and colorful member of Parliament for more than twenty-five years thereafter—so colorful, she once insisted that leftist British playwright George Bernard Shaw travel to Moscow with her and see the Communist "paradise" for himself. James Fox, in his multiple biography *Five Sisters: The Langhornes of Virginia,* evoked this picture of their trip: "The archcapitalist Nancy and the archsocialist Shaw hand in hand, touring the country as semiofficial guests, the one loudly eulogizing the Soviet system, the other telling the Communists that they had taken the wrong path, the path of the Anti-Christ: 'I am a conservative. I am a Capitalist. I am opposed to Communism. I think you are all terrible,' Shaw recorded Nancy saying at one point."

She, in fact, treated the bloody Soviet dictator Stalin to a pugnacious lecture of more than two hours, "going at him, according to Shaw, 'like a steamroller.'"

That was in the 1930s, and Nancy Astor remained in Parliament until her retirement in 1945. She was noted for her support of temperance efforts and the rights of women and children.

Less well known publicly, but a woman with quiet national and even international impact of her own, was Lady Astor's sister **Irene**

Langhorne, who married the illustrator Charles Dana Gibson and became the model for his popular Gibson Girl image of a poised society woman, always attractive, youthful, and athletic-looking in long flowing skirt, tightly cinched belt, and long-sleeved blouse topped by a cufflike high collar.

With the achievement of the women's vote, the passage of two world wars, a population explosion, the advent of television and then computers, the entertainment explosion, all coming during the recent twentieth century, whole new worlds of opportunity were open to women in Virginia and elsewhere. Suddenly, they were political activists and even public officeholders; they were in the workplace, sometimes even as the boss; some, like Richmond-born actress **Shirley MacLaine** (along with her brother Warren Beatty), or Arlington's own **Katie Couric** of NBC Television's *Today Show,* became national figures through the media of film and television.

Country music, on the other hand, was the hallmark of **June Carter Cash,** wife of Johnny Cash and a singer/songwriter in her own right. Born in Maces Spring, in Virginia's Scott County in 1929, a very young June Carter began singing professionally in the mid-1930s with her mother, Maybelle, and her sisters. The Carter Family singers were "considered by many," says the Virginia Historical Society, "to be the founding clan of country music." June provided Johnny Cash the hit song "Ring of Fire" in 1963 then married him in 1968. Both died in 2003.

Perhaps typical of the difference between the worlds of recent days and the more distant past is the fact that a woman, **Mary Sue Terry,** a Democrat, was elected attorney general of Virginia late in the twentieth century, but then lost a race for governor. In addition, Katie Couric's sister, the late **Emily Couric,** was a popular state senator from the Charlottesville–Albemarle County area when she died of pancreatic cancer in 2002. More pointedly here, before her illness became known, Emily Couric, the wife of a cardiologist, was being touted as the Democratic Party's likely nominee for lieutenant governor of Virginia and thus also might have aspired to become the Old Dominion's first female governor just a few years down the road.

She still is missed by those who knew and loved her, but someday it likely will come about anyway . . . Someday, some other woman will become governor of Virginia, the same Virginia that began with a group of settlers landing at Jamestown four centuries ago, with not a woman among them.

Epilogue: Past, Present, and Future
1607–2003: Missing Persons
A Short Chronology of Virginia History
Selected Bibliography
Index

✦

EPILOGUE
Past, Present, and Future
✦

In the early months of 2003, the deaths of three Virginians came together as poignant reminders of past, present, and possible future. Their commonplace surnames—Brown, Cook, May—don't reveal their historical significance in the slightest, but historical significance there is.

Try, please, David Brown, *astronaut;* Tecumseh Deerfoot Cook, *Pamunkey Indian chief;* and Donald C. May Jr., *staff sergeant, U.S. Marine Corps,* and the picture, the historical context, begins to emerge.

☆ ☆ ☆

In the great tradition of his fellow Virginians Meriwether Lewis and partner William Clark, or Thomas Jefferson Page (see pages 170–79), and Adm. Richard Evelyn Byrd (see pages 290–94), **David M. Brown, captain, U.S. Navy,** first and foremost was an explorer . . . but his realm would be outer space rather than the land, sea, or icepacks of Mother Earth.

Born in Arlington, Virginia, he always wanted to fly. He experienced his first flight, in a family friend's private aircraft, before he finished high school at Arlington's Yorktown High, previously famous for its graduates Katie Couric of NBC television's *Today Show* and the late U.S. Senator Paul Wellstone, Democrat of Minnesota, killed in an airplane crash in late 2002.

Young David Brown did his first "solo flying" as a high-school and college gymnast briefly flying through the air off the gymnastic apparatus. While attending the College of William and Mary, he not only spent four years as a varsity gymnast, he opted to spend a summer performing as an acrobat, seven-foot unicyclist, and stilt walker.

But he had more horizons, so many more horizons, to conquer. After graduation from William and Mary in 1978, he obtained a medical degree from Eastern Virginia Medical School then moved on to the U.S. Navy as a naval flight surgeon. But all that still wasn't enough for David Brown's restless, inquiring mind. A doctor could fly, couldn't he? In David Brown's case, he certainly could. Accepted for naval pilot training as the first flight surgeon so chosen in ten years, he graduated from naval flight training ranked first in his class and in time was serving aboard the carrier *Independence* out of Japan. Qualified to fly the F-18 Hornet and the A-6E Intruder, he accumulated more than twenty-seven hundred hours of flight time overall, including seventeen hundred hours in high-performance military jets.

It seemed only natural to family and friends that his next step would be astronaut training with the National Aeronautics and Space Administration (NASA), a step he took in 1996. "He was a man who always pushed the envelope, the envelope of positive human evolution," said long-time friend Cliff Gauthier, once upon a time Brown's college gymnastics coach.

Designated a mission specialist by NASA, Astronaut Brown was returning to earth from his first trip into space on the morning of Saturday, February 1, 2003. He was one of seven astronauts aboard the space shuttle officially designated the STS-107 . . . but more familiar to the public at large as *Columbia,* the space shuttle that broke apart during reentry that fateful morning, with all seven crew members lost, among them Virginia's own David M. Brown, forty-six.

☆ ☆ ☆

Born in November 1899, this Virginian had a foot in each of the last three centuries—the nineteenth, the twentieth, and the twenty-first. He saw eighteen U.S. presidents come and go and yet another one take office just in time to lead the worldwide war on terrorism. It was a war waged, in part, by use of wiretaps, airplanes, even pilotless aircraft, none of which existed at the time of his birth.

Chief Tecumseh Deerfoot Cook was Pamunkey through and through—he was the historic tribe's unpaid chief for forty-two years, from 1942 to 1984. For most of his life, he lived on Pamunkey land, the tribe's twelve-hundred-acre reservation in King William County—

and he hunted and fished and trapped like the Indians of old. Indeed, at the time of the Jamestown landing four centuries ago, his Pamunkey tribe, about a thousand strong, probably was the largest in the Powhatan Confederacy headed by the chief the English called by the same name, Powhatan. It is said that Powhatan himself may be buried in the large mound at one end of the Pamunkey reservation.

This last tribal home of the Pamunkey is a flat peninsula on the Pamunkey River, north of West Point. The Pamunkey converges with the Mattaponi River at West Point itself to form the York River. Chief Powhatan's home village of Werowocomoco apparently was located downstream on the north banks of the York in today's Gloucester County. This presumably would have been the site of Capt. John Smith's rescue by Powhatan's daughter Pocahontas.

While war and peace waxed and waned between the early English settlers of Virginia and Powhatan's Tidewater Indians, the ever-replenished white settlers eventually came to dominate. But first came the massacre of more than 350 English, men, women, and children in 1622 in a coordinated attack raging for 140 miles up and down the James River and engineered by the deceased Powhatan's brother, Opechancanough. In response, the outraged English mounted a years-long punitive campaign against the Powhatans that nearly eliminated them from the lower James and York Rivers altogether. For three years running, the English attacked their villages and kept them from planting their crops or rebuilding their homes. And this was only the start of sporadic hostilities lasting fourteen years and costing the lives of many Indian men, women, and children. In one major battle, the greatest English victory of all, the settlers defeated an estimated one thousand Pamunkey in the year 1625 and burned down the central Pamunkey town.

Somehow, Opechancanough found the resources to strike back in 1644, this time organizing a massacre of up to five hundred of the white settlers in their Tidewater homes and plantations. Taken into custody, the elderly Indian chief was shot and killed before he could be tried for his leadership role in the latest massacre.

Nearly four decades later, after a long period of peace with the English, the now-friendly Pamunkey briefly found themselves a target of the rebel Nathaniel Bacon's wrath against Indians in general . . . but only briefly, since Bacon died of a fever at the height of his rebellion in 1676 (see pages 33–39).

Bacon, in fact, was such a small item in the centuries-old history of the Pamunkey both before and after the advent of the English, that Chief Cook, a hunting guide by trade, said in the 1970s that he was unaware of Bacon's alleged battle with a party of Pamunkey in 1676 in nearby Dragon Swamp, a clash that some historians consider the end of early Virginia's "Indian troubles" altogether.

Cook was far more familiar with the Pamunkey of his own day, saying that most of those still living on the Pamunkey reservation were older, retired persons. "We don't have any young ones," he said. "There's nothing for them to do here to make a living, so they leave." He himself had gone off to live and work for a time in Philadelphia as a young man.

His reign as chief was marked by several crucial improvements for the Pamunkey and their reservation. The tribe's shad hatchery was expanded, and he was credited with lining up federal grants needed to build the Pamunkey Indian Museum and Community Center on the reservation. He also helped to negotiate compensation for a railroad's use of track running through a part of the reservation. "People who don't know us think there is nothing to being a chief," he said back in 1984, the year he stepped down as chief. "There have been many nights when I have gone to bed and woken up with my pillow wet. You are always fighting to get something done."

Which is not to say he and others were neglectful of their heritage in any way. For many years as tribal chief, by terms of a 1646 treaty, Cook delivered the freshly slain game—often a deer—that the Pamunkey (and their neighbors the Mattaponi) still present as "tribute" to the governor of Virginia, in lieu of paying taxes on their land. Chief Cook paid the tribal tribute in person sixty or more times, the last time in the year 2000.

At the time of his one-hundredth birthday, in 1999, Chief Cook, very much aware of his Native American heritage, danced the dance of celebration and wore his turkey-feather headdress.

How had he lived so long? "Eat plenty of raccoons and muskrats," he said, "and drink Pamunkey River water. But lay off the possum."

When he died in April 2003 at the age of 103, he arguably, by reason of his advanced age alone, was Virginia's closest connection with both its Indian and English heritage.

He also personified the fact that times change, and the result can be a combination of historical streams. For years the old Indian chief attended the Pamunkey Baptist Church and sat in the same pew every week. His funeral took place there, with the former pastor, the Reverend Michael Gregory, telling the overflow crowd that the chief loved the hymn "Amazing Grace" and asked to hear it sung every Sunday.

"Tecumseh was very outgoing, was very patient with visitors, and loved to have his picture taken," said Gregory. "He never turned down ice cream. He was a family man."

The chief's son Warren said, "He loved the outdoors."

But it was Warren's wife, Susan, who may have articulated the most fitting epitaph when she said, "He was the last of the old-time Indian chiefs."

What would Chief Cook himself have said? What he did say, when stepping down as chief in 1984, was: "I served because I was asked to serve."

☆ ☆ ☆

French and Indian War, Revolutionary War, War of 1812, Civil War, the world wars of the twentieth century, Korea, Vietnam, Persian Gulf . . . whatever the war, Virginians have served, and many have not come back home. Count among those now **U.S. Marine Corps S.Sgt. Donald C. "D. J." May Jr.**, thirty-one, father of two, tank commander, First Marine Division, and Iraq War casualty, the first Virginian to be lost in the nation's first foreign war of the twenty-first century (other than the less well-defined but equally important war without borders against terrorism).

He died in March 2003 when his tank vaulted from a bridge over the Euphrates River in Iraq and sank, upside down, in the water. At his funeral in Chesterfield County's St. Augustine Roman Catholic Church, his pregnant wife, Deborah, and other family and friends grieved over this latest of a long line of fallen Virginia warriors. "As sad as this is," said good friend Shannon Bannister, "we can't forget that D. J. was living his dream. He made it to the frontlines. We lost a devoted soldier, a hero, an icon, and a friend."

Father Michael S. C. Schmied, pastor at St. Augustine, where May had been baptized, taken First Communion, and been confirmed, said, "He symbolized '*Semper Fi*' indeed. He was always faithful. He was always faithful to God. While it is not an easy task, we must let go."

☆ ☆ ☆

Brown, Cook, and May, commonplace names in the Virginia of today but far from commonplace men . . . and, more pointedly, symbols of the Commonwealth's past, present, and possible future. Astronaut Brown, the explorer of outer space and link to man's future endeavors in that direction; Chief Cook, the reminder of the state's earliest heritage . . . a rare link to the past; and marine Sergeant May, casualty of our first foreign war of the twentieth-first century, symbol of our present, and a possible link to whatever the future may hold. More wars? No wars? We can hope, we can pray, but we just don't know . . .

1607–2003: Missing Persons

Thousands more persons than the mere dozens mentioned herein made Virginia history, and among those persons "missing" are a few in particular whose names and deeds should be noted or amplified:

• **Peter Francisco,** "Boy Hercules of the American Revolution," possibly was of Portuguese origin, via the Azores, but he first came to history's view as a small boy left behind by a ship sailing from the Hopewell of today, then known as City Point. Taken in and raised by Judge Anthony Winston of Buckingham County, he was present when Winston's nephew Patrick Henry gave the fiery "Give me liberty or give me death!" speech at St. John's Church in Richmond. An enthused and giant-sized young soldier in the Revolutionary War that followed, Francisco gained fame for his strength and bravery in battles from Pennsylvania to North Carolina and back. Married after the war, he tried blacksmithing and farming, once allegedly pulling a cow out of a mudhole by hand. He later became sergeant-at-arms for the Virginia House of Delegates.

• Two political giants of the Revolutionary and post-Revolutionary era deserving more attention herein were **James Madison** and **James Monroe,** the fourth and fifth presidents, respectively, of the nation and the last two of the first four Virginians to serve as president. Madison, called the "Father of the Constitution" for his leadership during the Constitutional Convention of 1787, remains best known for his contributions to political theory and his legislative abilities, but he also served Thomas Jefferson, the nation's third president, as secretary of state. Then, as president himself, he presided over much of the War of 1812. Monroe, once a young Revolutionary War soldier and later Madison's secretary of state and secretary of war, played a negotiating role in the Louisiana Purchase. Like Jefferson and Madison, he also was a two-term president and is best known for the Monroe Doctrine, which warned all nations against interfering in the affairs of South America.

• Also a Revolutionary War soldier but better known for his career afterward was the jurist **John Marshall,** who served John Adams as secretary of state then was appointed chief justice of the Supreme Court in the closing days of the Adams administration. Considered no great friend of his cousin Thomas Jefferson (who succeeded Adams in the presidency), Marshall presided over decisions establishing the bedrock of American constitutional law. Cases such as *Marbury v. Madison* and *McCulloch v. Maryland* helped to create his enduring reputation as probably the greatest of the Court's chief justices.

• **Cyrus Griffin,** also a Virginia-born (1748) jurist but hardly remembered today, once was the young American nation's chief executive . . . *before* George Washington. Studying law at the University of Edinburgh and the prestigious Inner Temple in London, he returned to Virginia in time to serve in the Revolutionary House of Delegates and the Continental Congress. It was as president of the Congress the year *after* it adopted the U.S. Constitution and sent it to the states for ratification and the year or so *before* George Washington became president under terms of the basic charter that Griffin, in effect, was the nation's chief executive. His term ran from January 1788 to April 30, 1789, when he was "succeeded" by fellow Virginian Washington. Griffin then became judge of the U.S. District Court of Virginia until his death at Yorktown in 1810.

• The state of Texas owes Virginia big time for the two Virginia-born "fathers" of the Lone Star State, **Stephen F. Austin** and **Sam Houston.** Of the two, Austin was the first to find his way to Texas (1822), as founder—in place of his deceased father, Moses—of the future state's first American settlement. While born in Virginia, the younger Austin was raised in Missouri, where he served in the territorial legislature. Just eleven years after his arrival in Texas, more than a thousand families had joined his Texas colony. But newly independent Mexico was becoming nervous over the influx of Americans to Texas . . . and over the growing pressure for Texas independence from Mexico. Austin was imprisoned for months while other Texas leaders girded for the struggle ahead, Sam Houston among them. Known as a hero of the battle of Horseshoe Bend, a former congressman, and a former governor of Tennessee, Houston arrived in Texas in 1833 just in time to take charge of the Texas forces that won independence in 1836 with the defeat of Mexican strongman Santa Anna at San Jacinto in 1836. Houston then defeated Austin in their joint bid to become first president of the newly formed Texas Republic. Houston later served as an early U.S. Senator from the new state of Texas, but he would be deposed as governor because he would not accede to his state's secession at the time of the Civil War. Austin, the capital of Texas, and Houston, the state's largest city, are named for these two Texas pioneers.

• It also was in the 1830s that the Virginian **Cyrus McCormick,** "Father of Modern Agriculture," made his significant mark upon the world, as inventor of a horse-drawn reaping machine that would become the basic model for all labor-saving grain reapers to follow. In 1831, adding his own improvements to a reaping machine his father, Robert, had put aside as a failure, Cyrus produced a working model in just six weeks, with the aid of a black helper, Jo Anderson. After obtaining his patent in 1834, McCormick built a reaper factory in Chicago in the 1840s to begin producing large numbers of his harvesting machines, but this faltered after a lean decade of few sales to wary farmers. He then had to begin all over again as a manufacturer when the Chicago fire burned down his first plant. A business pioneer as well as inventor, McCormick built his ultimate success on easy credit for his customers, along with guarantees that his product would work as advertised. The McCormick Harvesting Machine Company that he and two brothers founded became the genesis of the International Harvester Corporation, a towering giant of the agricultural industry. Freeing farmers from hours of back-breaking harvest work by hand, McCormick had such a worldwide impact that Governor E. Lee Trinkle once said, "In all the long list of men preeminent in statesmanship or in arms in Virginia, I doubt if the name and fame of any will live longer with the people than that of Cyrus Hall McCormick, youthful inventor of the harvesting machine."

• As mentioned earlier, a double presidency of Virginia origin came in the 1840s, but not by anyone's plan or design, when Vice President **John Tyler** succeeded **William Henry Harrison,** son of Benjamin Harrison, a signer of the Declaration of Independence. The "old hero," as William Henry Harrison sometimes was called, had achieved fame as an Indian fighter in the Northwest Territory (Indiana, Michigan, and Illinois) and for his defeat of the British on the Thames River in Canada during the War of 1812. He caught cold at his inauguration in 1841 and died a month later. As first-president George Washington had done for the American presidency, Tyler established precedent for future vice presidents by eschewing any mere caretaker's role as the first vice president to succeed a deceased president. Often called "his accidency," Tyler stubbornly pursued his own agenda but encountered such strong political opposition that he had to give up any thought of seeking election in 1844. Tyler later would seek to avert the Civil War by calling a peace convention in Washington while Harrison's grandson, Benjamin Harrison, would become one of the seven presidents from Ohio in 1889.

• **Zachary Taylor's** Virginia tie was nearly accidental and fleeting at best . . . still, he was born in Virginia and would take his place in her pantheon of eight U.S. presidents. While his birthplace was Orange, he did his growing up near Louisville, Kentucky. He achieved national fame and became a presidential candidate in 1848 strictly for his military successes in the Mexican War, but he had no previous political experience when he took office the next year. Known as "Old Rough and Ready," he became great friends with his one-time son-in-law Jefferson Davis, future president of the Confederacy who briefly had been married to Taylor's daughter, Knox, before her sudden death from a fever. While in office, Taylor himself took ill on July 4, 1850, and died on July 9, apparently from cholera.

• Born a slave in 1856 even though his father may have been white, **Booker T. Washington** rose from the humblest of beginnings—as a slave child in Franklin County he slept in rags on the floor—to the presidency of Tuskegee Institute in Alabama, which he himself organized. He achieved his own education at Virginia's Hampton Institute, where he both studied and worked as a janitor after walking five hundred miles to reach the school. Book author, lecturer, educator, he remains one of the leading black figures in the nation's history.

• No Virginian by birth, a New Yorker and murder victim, architect Stanford White yet left his permanent stamp in a venue that once was all Thomas Jefferson's—the University of Virginia. When a fire in 1895 destroyed much of Jefferson's widely esteemed Rotunda at the top of the university's Lawn—capstone of his beloved "academical village"—White was called in for the reconstruction job. The result, explains the university nowadays, was "an elaborate Beaux Arts interpretation of Jefferson's Roman classicism [based on the second-century Pantheon in Rome]." Undoing many of White's changes (but not all), a further restoration job completed in the U.S. bicentennial year of 1976 left the Rotunda appearing "essentially as it did when it was built." Still, at bottom of the vaunted Lawn, or to the south, Stanford White's further imprint on the "academical village" today remains in the form of Cabell Hall as a staunch anchor and two adjoining classroom buildings, Rouss and Cocke Halls. White, in his early fifties, was murdered just a few years later (in 1906) by millionaire playboy Harry K. Thaw, a jealous rival for the affections of White's mistress, showgirl Evelyn Nesbit.

• Few presidents left a more dramatic legacy than the bookish, Virginia-born **Woodrow Wilson,** minister's son, college professor, and college president until lured into politics as governor of New Jersey. Here was a man who overcame several strokelike episodes to serve as president of Princeton, governor, and then president of the United States. As president he lost one wife, courted and married a second; resisted entering World War I, then reluctantly led the nation into the largely European war; spent half a year out of the country while personally negotiating the peace at Versailles; became chief "father" of the League of Nations but failed to win endorsement of the international compact by the U.S. Senate; suffered a major stroke while in office and, with the help of his second wife, Edith Galt, his staff, and his cabinet, continued in office to the end of his second term even though significantly (and secretly) impaired.

• Should a novelist and television writer appear on a short list of influential Virginians down through the centuries? If he is **Earl Hamner,** creator of the television series *The Waltons,* absolutely. No statesman, battle hero, explorer, inventor, or thundering orator, Hamner nonetheless transformed his Depression-era childhood at the foot of the Blue Ridge into a warm, homespun television series that captured a worldwide audience with stories exuding the virtues of honesty, kindness, the work ethic, responsibility, and respect for others. The series, in turn, sprang from his two largely autobiographical novels *Spencer's Mountain* and *The Homecoming.* The eldest of eight children, Hamner wrote with loving nostalgia about his grandparents, mother and father, brothers and sisters. "We were eight," he once noted. "Standing together we made stair steps, a row of lean small-boned children who were living through a Depression but rarely knew what it was to be depressed. We knew we were loved because our mother and father loved each other and passed that love on to each of us."

A Short Chronology of Virginia History

SIXTEENTH CENTURY

1526–27: First would-be Spanish settlers come and go at or near future Jamestown.

1561: Spanish visitors take teenaged Virginia Indian "Don Luis" to Spain, not to return him for almost a decade.

1570: Don Luis returns to Virginia with a Jesuit missionary party headed by Father Juan Bautistia de Segura . . . but the Spaniards soon are killed by local Indians, allegedly led by Don Luis. Only a boy named Alonso is spared.

1572: The Spanish mount a punitive return visit, killing more than twenty of Don Luis's fellow tribesmen and rescuing Alonso.

SEVENTEENTH CENTURY

1607: The English arrive at Jamestown to establish the first permanent English settlement in North America.

1609–10: The winter known as the "starving time," during which the English settlement almost fails to survive.

1614: Tobacco pioneer John Rolfe marries Chief Powhatan's daughter Pocahontas, who earlier had dissuaded Powhatan from ordering the execution of Capt. John Smith.

1617: Pocahontas dies in England just before returning from a visit of ten months with her husband, John Rolfe, and their son, Thomas.

1619: Genesis of the Virginia General Assembly as the first legislative body in North America; genesis also of the American slavery system with the arrival at Jamestown of about twenty blacks as indentured servants.

1622: New Indian chief Opechancanough, the late Chief Powhatan's brother— and possibly the same Don Luis known to the Spanish—leads a massacre of more than 350 settlers up and down the James River corridor.

1644: Now frail and elderly, Opechancanough instigates a second great massacre of the white settlers; four hundred to five hundred men, women, and children killed this time. Soon captured, the old Indian chief is shot and killed by a guard.

1676: Recently arrived English squire's son Nathaniel Bacon Jr. leads an uprising against Royal Governor Sir William Berkeley, burns Jamestown to the ground, seizes the mainland while driving Berkeley across the Chesapeake Bay to the Eastern Shore, but then dies of fever at the height of his rebellion.

1698:   Capital of Colonial Virginia moves from Jamestown to Williamsburg.

EIGHTEENTH CENTURY

1732:   Birth of George Washington, future commander in chief of the Continental army, future first president, future father of his country.

1755:   British Gen. Edward Braddock's defeat by the French and their Indian allies near future Pittsburgh, with Washington emerging as hero of the day.

1763:   French and Indian War in North America (same worldwide as the Seven Years' War) ended by treaty.

1775:   Patrick Henry's "Give me liberty or give me death!" speech at St. John's Church.

1775:   Start of the Revolutionary War at Lexington and Concord, Massachusetts; George Washington named commander in chief of the Continental army.

1776:   Virginian Thomas Jefferson drafts the Declaration of Independence, which is then adopted by the Continental Congress in Philadelphia on July 4, celebrated ever since as Independence Day.

1779:   Richmond becomes capital of Virginia.

1781:   The surrender of British General Cornwallis at Yorktown signals an inevitable and victorious end to the American Revolution.

1783:   Treaty of Paris ends the Revolutionary War and confirms America's independence.

1787:   The U.S. Constitution is adopted and sent to the states for ratification, with key leadership from Virginians James Madison, George Mason, Edmund Randolph, and others.

1789:   Washington becomes the new nation's first president; New York City briefly will be his capital, followed by Philadelphia.

1790:   At tiny Edom, first Caesarean in North America; mother and baby will survive and grow to old age.

1792:   Formation of Kentucky from Virginia's three western counties. Construction underway of a "President's House" built of Virginia sandstone blocks in the future federal city named for Washington.

1799:   George Washington dies in his bed at Mount Vernon after catching cold while horseback riding at his beloved plantation on the Potomac on a nasty winter's day in December.

NINETEENTH CENTURY

1800:   "Gabriel's Insurrection," potentially widespread slave revolt, stymied at the outset by bad weather and warnings from other slaves.

1801:   Thomas Jefferson elected third U.S. president by a previously deadlocked U.S. House, will serve two terms, 1801–9.

1803:   Louisiana Purchase negotiated by Jefferson protégé James Monroe of Virginia, acting as U.S. Minister Plenipotentiary to France, and fellow envoy Robert Livingston.

1804:   Virginians Meriwether Lewis and William Clark set out from the St. Louis area on their great journey to the West Coast and back.

1805: Thirty-three strong, including the Indian woman Sacagawea and her infant son, the Corps of Discovery headed by Lewis and Clark reaches the Pacific Ocean at site of future Astoria, Oregon.

1806: Lewis and Clark expedition returns home in triumph. Also, death of George Wythe, legal scholar known as the "Virginia Socrates," allegedly poisoned by his nephew.

1807: Aaron Burr indicted for treason, tried in Richmond under Chief Justice John Marshall, and acquitted.

1808: Thomas Jefferson's secretary of state and fellow Virginian James Madison elected fourth U.S. president.

1809: Jefferson leaves the presidency to end forty-four years of public service; Meriwether Lewis dies on the Natchez Trace of gunshot wounds, widely thought to have been self-inflicted.

1812: President James Madison presides over the War of 1812 . . . soon to be marked by the burning of the White House (1814) by invading British.

1817: James Monroe, secretary of state under Madison, now succeeds Madison in the presidency. This means four of the first five U.S. presidents came from Virginia. Only John Adams of Massachusetts, number two in the office, has interrupted the sequence.

1826: Fifty years to the day after adoption of the Declaration of Independence, both Thomas Jefferson and John Adams, his old colleague from the Continental Congress, die on July Fourth, Jefferson first.

1834: Virginia-born Cyrus McCormick obtains first patent on his grain-reaping machine, a labor-saving invention that will revolutionize the harvesting of grain throughout the world.

1836: Virginia-born Sam Houston salvages the Texas Revolution by defeating Santa Anna's Mexican army at San Jacinto.

1841: Two more Virginia-born aristocrats become presidents as William Henry Harrison takes office then dies a month later; he is immediately succeeded by his vice president, John Tyler.

1848: Election of Mexican War hero Gen. Zachary Taylor as the seventh president born in Virginia, but "Old Rough and Ready" will die in office two years later, possibly from cholera.

1849: Early (and mysterious) death of Virginia's best-known literary light, Edgar Allan Poe.

1855: Yellow fever sweeps through Norfolk, killing one-third of the population.

1856: Completion of the Crozet railroad tunnel piercing the Blue Ridge and allowing rail traffic into the Ohio Valley. Also, birth of Woodrow Wilson at nearby Staunton.

1858: Newly formed Mount Vernon Ladies Association rescues George Washington's beloved Mount Vernon from disrepair and possible oblivion.

1861–65: Civil War years—Richmond serves as capital of the Confederacy; more battles (two thousand–plus, counting minor skirmishes) fought in Virginia than in any other state. Largely pro-Union western Virginia (fifty counties) splits off to form a new state in 1863.

1865: Lee surrenders to Grant at Appomattox Court House; Lincoln assassination and the mortal wounding of his assassin, John Wilkes Booth, at a farm outside Bowling Green, Virginia.

1870: In January, Secessionist Virginia readmitted to the Union. In October, death of the venerated Robert E. Lee.

TWENTIETH CENTURY

1900: Virginia-born Dr. Walter Reed ascertains that the yellow fever virus is carried by mosquitoes.

1907: Exposition in Norfolk celebrating the three hundredth anniversary of the founding of Jamestown. The site to become home of the Norfolk naval base, eventually the largest naval facility in the world.

1912: Virginia-born Woodrow Wilson elected president, will serve two terms and win the Nobel Peace Prize but be left partially incapacitated by a stroke toward the end of his second term.

1927: Democrat Harry F. Byrd leads a reorganization of state government as governor; he later will serve more than three decades in the U.S. Senate, followed by his son, Harry F. Byrd Jr. Also, the Rev. W. A. R. Goodwin's suggestion to John D. Rockefeller Jr. leads to his funding for restoration of historic structures as the start of Colonial Williamsburg.

1943: A product of World War II, the Pentagon rises in Arlington—as the world's largest office building, it will house the War and Navy Departments under one roof.

1944: D-day toll for Bedford, Virginia, is the highest per capita of any town in America.

1956: Virginia's response to the Supreme Court's 1954 school integration decision is a policy of "massive resistance," or closure of public schools rather than allow their racial integration. The policy is struck down by the federal courts in 1959, and in that same year black students attend integrated public schools in Norfolk and Arlington for the first time.

1969: A. Linwood Holton elected as the first Republican governor of Virginia since the end of the Civil War a century before. Also, Nelson County in particular is devastated by remnants of Hurricane Camille.

1975: Widespread air, water, and soil contamination by the pesticide Kepone discovered at Hopewell, with the James River soon closed to all forms of fishing.

1990: On January 13, former state senator and lieutenant governor L. Douglas Wilder, the grandson of slaves, is sworn in as Virginia's sixty-sixth governor—and as the first African American ever elected governor of an American state.

TWENTY-FIRST CENTURY

2001 On September 11, the Pentagon in Arlington joins the World Trade Center in New York City as a target of Middle Eastern terrorists using hijacked airliners as flying "bombs." At the Pentagon, 189 persons killed.

Selected Bibliography

Alexander, James. *Early Charlottesville: Recollections of James Alexander, 1828–1874.* Edited by Mary Rawlings. Charlottesville: Albemarle County Historical Society, 1942..

Allgor, Catherine. *Parlor Politics, In Which the Ladies of Washington Help Build a City and a Government.* Charlottesville: University Press of Virginia, 2000.

Ambrose, Stephen. *Undaunted Courage: Meriwether Lewis, Thomas Jefferson and the Opening of the American West.* New York: Simon & Schuster, 1996.

Barnes, Brooks Miles, and Barry R. Truitt. *Seashore Chronicles: Three Centuries of the Virginia Barrier Islands.* Charlottesville: University Press of Virginia, 1997.

Breckinridge, Lucy. *Lucy Breckinridge of Grove Hill: The Journal of a Virginia Girl, 1862–1864.* Edited by Mary D. Robertson. Columbia: University of South Carolina Press, 1994.

Bridenbaugh, Carl. *Jamestown, 1544–1699.* New York: Oxford University Press, 1980.

———. *Early Americans.* New York: Oxford University Press, 1981.

Brown, Kathleen M. *Good Wives, Nasty Wenches and Anxious Patriarchs: Gender, Race, and Power in Colonial Virginia.* Chapel Hill: University of North Carolina Press, 1996.

Burton, H. W. ("Harry Scratch"). *The History of Norfolk, Virginia: A Review of Important Events and Incidents Which Occurred from 1736 to 1877; Also a Record of Personal Reminiscences and Political, Commercial, and Curious Facts.* Norfolk: Norfolk Virginian, 1877.

Byrd, Richard E. *Alone.* New York: Putnam, 1938.

Chesnut, Mary Boykin. *Mary Chesnut's Civil War.* Edited by C. Vann Woodward. New Haven: Yale University Press, 1981.

Commager, Henry Steele, ed. *The Blue and the Gray: The Story of the Civil War As Told by Participants.* New York: Dobbs-Merrill, 1950.

Crotty, Gene. *The Visits of Lewis & Clark to Fincastle, Virginia.* Np: History Museum and Historical Society of Western Virginia, 2003.

Cunliffe, Marcus. *George Washington: Man and Monument.* 1958. Reprint, New York: Mentor Books, 1963.

Dabney, Virginius. *Virginia: The New Dominion.* 1971. Reprint, Charlottesville: University Press of Virginia, 1983.

————. *The Last Review: The Confederate Reunion, Richmond, 1932.* (Includes "The Last Parade," by Douglas Southall Freeman.) Chapel Hill, N.C.: Algonquin Books, 1984.

Davis, Julia. *The Shenandoah.* New York: Farrar & Rinehart, 1945.

Donald, Herbert David. *Lincoln.* New York: Simon & Schuster, 1995.

Dowdey, Clifford. *The Great Plantation: A Profile of Berkeley Hundred and Plantation Virginia from Jamestown to Appomattox.* Charles City, Va.: Berkeley Plantation, 1988.

————. *The Virginia Dynasties: The Emergence of "King" Carter and the Golden Age.* New York: Bonanza Books, 1969.

Evans, Sara M. *Born for Liberty: A History of Women in America.* New York: Free Press, 1989.

Farnham, Christie Anne, ed. *Women of the American South.* New York: New York University Press, 1997.

Fox, James. *Five Sisters: The Langhornes of Virginia.* New York: Simon & Schuster, 2000.

Freeman, Douglas Southall. *George Washington.* Seven volumes abstracted in one volume, by Richard Harwell. New York: Scribner's, 1968.

Gleason, David King. *Virginia Plantation Homes.* Baton Rouge: Louisiana State University Press, 1989.

Hale, John P. *Trans-Allegheny Pioneers: Historical Sketches of the First White Settlements West of the Alleghenies, 1748 and After.* Edited by Harold J. Dudley. 3d ed. Radford, Va.: Roberta Ingles Steele, 1971.

Hay, Peter. *All the President's Ladies: Anecdotes of the Women Behind the Men in the White House.* New York: Penguin, 1989.

Herzog, Brad. *The Sports 100: The One Hundred Most Important People in American Sports History.* Np: Hungry Mind, 1990.

Hoffman, Ronald, and Peter J. Albert, eds. *Women of the Age of the American Revolution.* Charlottesville: University Press of Virginia, 1989.

Kelly, C. Brian, and Ingrid Smyer-Kelly. *Best Little Ironies, Oddities & Mysteries of the Civil War.* Nashville, Tenn.: Cumberland House, 2001.

————. *Best Little Stories from the American Revolution.* Nashville, Tenn.: Cumberland House, 1999.

————. *Best Little Stories from the Civil War.* Nashville, Tenn.: Cumberland House, 1997.

————. *Best Little Stories from the White House.* Nashville, Tenn.: Cumberland House, 1999.

Kerber, Linda K. *Women of the Republic: Intellect & Ideology in Revolutionary America.* 1980. Reprint, New York: Norton, 1986.

Lebsock, Suzanne. *"A Share of Honour": Virginia Women, 1600–1945.* Richmond: Virginia State Library, 1987.

Leon, Vicki. *Uppity Women of the New World.* Berkeley, Calif.: Conari Press, 2001.

McCartney, Martha W. *Jamestown: An American Legacy.* Np: Eastern National, 2001.

McCullough, David. *John Adams.* New York: Simon & Schuster, 2001.

McKenney, Thomas L., and James Hall. *History of the Indian Tribes of North America.* Vol. 2. Reprint, Kent, Ohio: Volair, 1978.

McPhee, John. "Centre Court," in *The Best American Sports Writing of the Century.* Edited by David Halberstam. Boston: Houghton Mifflin, 1999.

Malone, Dumas. *The Sage of Monticello.* Volume 6: *Jefferson and His Times.* Boston: Little Brown and Co., 1981.

Miller, Lee. *Roanoke: Solving the Mystery of the Lost Colony.* New York: Arcade, 2000.

Morgan, Edmund S. *American Slavery, American Freedom: The Ordeal of Colonial Virginia.* New York: Norton, 1975.

————. *Virginians at Home: Family Life in the Eighteenth Century.* Williamsburg: Colonial Williamsburg Foundation, 2002.

Munford, Robert Beverly, Jr. *Richmond Homes and Memories.* Richmond: Garrett and Massie, 1936.

Padover, Saul K. *Jefferson: A Great American's Life and Ideas* 1942. Abridged, New York: Mentor and New American Library, 1970.

Rasmussen, William M. S., and Robert S. Tilton. *Pocahontas: Her Life & Legend.* Richmond: Virginia Historical Society, 1994.

Scheer, George F., and Hugh F. Rankin, eds. *Rebels & Redcoats: The American Revolution Through the Eyes of Those Who Fought and Lived It.* 1957. Reprint, New York: Da Capo, 1987.

Scott, Anne Firor. Introduction in Julia Cherry Spruill, *Women's Life and Work in the Southern Colonies.* New York: Norton, 1972.

Smith, Richard Norton. *Patriarch: George Washington and the New American Nation.* Boston: Houghton Mifflin, 1993.

Spruill, Julia Cherry. *Women's Life and Work in the Southern Colonies.* 1938. Reprint, New York: Norton, 1972.

Squires, W. H. T. *Through the Years in Norfolk.* Portsmouth, Va.: Printcraft Press, 1936.

Stanard, Mary Newton. *Colonial Virginia: Its People and Customs.* Philadelphia: Lippincott, 1917.

Tombes. Robert M., ed. *When the Peaches Get Ripe, Tell the Children I'll Be Home: Letters Home from Lt. Robert Gaines Haile, Jr., Essex Sharpshooters, 55th Va., 1862.* Richmond: Tizwin, 1999.

Varon, Elizabeth R. *We Mean to Be Counted: White Women & Politics in Antebellum Virginia.* Chapel Hill: University of North Carolina Press, 1998.

Wamsley, James S., with Anne M. Cooper. *Idols, Victims, Pioneers: Virginia's Women from 1607.* Richmond: Virginia State Chamber of Commerce, 1976.

Warner, Ezra J. *Generals in Blue: Lives of the Union Commanders.* Baton Rouge: Louisiana State University Press, 1964.

———. *Generals in Gray: Lives of the Confederate Commanders.* Baton Rouge: Louisiana State University Press, 1959.

Washburn, Wilcomb E. *The Governor and the Rebel: A History of Bacon's Rebellion in Virginia.* New York: Norton, 1972.

Watterson, John Sayle. *College Football: History, Spectacle, Controversy.* Baltimore: Johns Hopkins Press, 2000.

———. *The Games Presidents Play.* Forthcoming.

Wertenbaker, Thomas J. *Norfolk: Historic Southern Port.* Durham, N.C.: Duke University Press, 1931.

———. *Torchbearer of the Revolution: The Story of Bacon's Rebellion and Its Leader.* Princeton, N.J.: Princeton University Press, 1940.

Index

C. Brian Kelly has written for the *Richmond Times-Dispatch,* the *Richmond News Leader,* the *Harrisonburg Daily News-Record,* and the *Washington Star.* He went on to teach journalism at the University of Virginia and to help inaugurate *Military History* magazine, for which he also served as editor for eleven years. He was also editor of *World War II* magazine and helped in the startup of *America's Civil War, Vietnam, Wild West,* and other historical magazines. He still writes a bimonthly Best Little Stories column for *Military History.*

Ingrid Smyer serves on the Charlottesville Historic Resources Task Force and the board of directors for the future Lewis and Clark Exploratory Center of Virginia, an interactive museum to be situated on the Albemarle County property where George Rogers Clark was born. Both authors are members of the Lewis and Clark Trail Heritage Foundation as well.

They have previously collaborated on six Best Little titles: *Best Little Stories from World War II, Best Little Stories from the White House, Best Little Stories from the Civil War, Best Little Stories from the American Revolution, Best Little Stories from the Wild West,* and *Best Little Ironies, Oddities, and Mysteries of the Civil War.*